THE PASSIONATE SOCIETY

ARCHIVES INTERNATIONALES D'HISTOIRE DES IDÉES

INTERNATIONAL ARCHIVES OF THE HISTORY OF IDEAS

191

THE PASSIONATE SOCIETY

The Social, Political and Moral Thought of Adam Ferguson

By

Lisa Hill

The Passionate Society

The Social, Political and Moral Thought
of Adam Ferguson

By

Lisa Hill
University of Adelaide, Australia

 Springer

A C.I.P. Catalogue record for this book is available from the Library of Congress.

ISBN-10 1-4020-3889-5 (HB)
ISBN-13 978-1-4020-3889-1 (HB)
ISBN-10 1-4020-3890-9 (e-book)
ISBN-13 978-1-4020-3890-7 (e-book)

Published by Springer,
P.O. Box 17, 3300 AA Dordrecht, The Netherlands.

www.springer.com

Printed on acid-free paper

CONTENTS

LEGEND

Essay: *An Essay on the History of Civil Society.*
P.I. and P.II.: *Principles of Moral and Political Science.*
Institutes: *Institutes of Moral Philosophy.*
Analysis: *Analysis of Pneumatics and Moral Philosophy.*
History: *History of the Progress and Termination of the Roman Republic.*
Correspondence: *The Correspondence of Adam Ferguson.*
'Sermon Preached in the Ersh Language': 'A Sermon Preached in the Ersh Language to His Majesty's Highland Regiment of Foot'.
Stage Plays: *The Morality of Stage Plays Seriously Considered.*
Reflections: *Reflections Previous to the Establishment of a Militia.*
Remarks: *Remarks on a Pamphlet lately Published by Dr. Price, intitled 'Observations on the Nature of Civil Liberty...', in a Letter from a Gentleman in the Country to a Member of Parliament.*
'Biographical Sketch': 'Biographical Sketch or Memoir of Lieutenant-Colonel Patrick Ferguson'.
Sister Peg: *History of the Proceedings in the Case of Margaret Commonly called Peg, only Lawful Sister to John Bull, Esq.*
'Joseph Black': 'Minutes of the Life and Character of Joseph Black M.D', Addressed to the Royal Society of Edinburgh.

ACKNOWLEDGEMENTS

I would like to thank the following people for their support in writing this book: The Australian Research Council for the generous funding that made its completion possible; Jonathan Louth, Luke Trenwith and Nicole Vincent for their able and untiring research assistance; Pauline Gerrans for carefully proofing an earlier draft; four anonymous readers commissioned by Springer for their learned and detailed recommendations; and my spouse, Philip Gerrans, for his loving friendship and support.

I also thank the respective journals for their kind permission to reprint substantial portions of the following articles: 'Anticipations of Nineteenth and Twentieth Century Social Thought in the Work of Adam Ferguson', *European Journal of Sociology,* 37 (1), 1996, pp. 203-228; 'Adam Ferguson and the Paradox of Progress and Decline', *History of Political Thought,* 18, (4), 1997, pp. 677-706; 'Ferguson and Smith on 'Human Nature', 'Interest' and the Role of Beneficence in Market Society', *Journal of the History of Economic Ideas,* 4 (1-2) 1996, pp. 353-399; 'The Invisible Hand of Adam Ferguson', *The European Legacy,* 3 (6), 1998 pp 42-65, http://www.tandf.co.uk and 'Eighteenth Century Anticipations of a Sociology of Conflict', *Journal of the History of Ideas*, 62 (2) April, 2001, pp. 281-299, The Johns Hopkins University Press.

DEDICATION

To my parents, Ben and Charmaine Hill.

CHAPTER 1

INTRODUCTION: THE PASSIONATE SOCIETY

The Social, Political and Moral Thought of Adam Ferguson

Adam Ferguson (1723-1816) lived and wrote during the period of intense intellectual activity commonly referred to as the Scottish Enlightenment, a time that has been described as 'one of the greatest...in the history of European culture'.[1] A famous and highly esteemed figure in his day, Ferguson's thought was original and distinctive. He held the prestigious and coveted Chair in Moral Philosophy at the University of Edinburgh (1764-1785) and exerted considerable intellectual influence, not only in Britain and Europe,[2] where his publications were translated into all the principal languages, but also in America. Nevertheless his reputation has long been overshadowed by those of his more luminous contemporaries, David Hume and Adam Smith.[3] Further, despite his disagreements with both of them, it is common to encounter readings in which his ideas and orientations are automatically conflated with theirs as well as with those of other members of the Scottish Enlightenment.[4]

Ferguson's virtual disappearance from view in the nineteenth century has been attributed to his sustained attack on the 'selfish system' just as it had achieved a kind of muted respectability. As Duncan Forbes suggests, Ferguson's sin consisted in his oracular 'unmasking' of a 'second-rate sort of society, full of second rate citizens,

---

[1] Alexander Broadie, *The Scottish Enlightenment*, Edinburgh: Birlinn Ltd.; 2001, p. 5.

[2] 'Ferguson's admirers in France included D'Holbach and Voltaire in his time, and later Comte; in Germany, Herder and such literary figures as Schiller and Jacobi, along with nineteenth century German social thought in general; and in his lifetime he was elected an honorary member of the Academy of Social Sciences in Berlin'. A.G. Smith, *The Political Philosophy of Adam Ferguson Considered as a Response to Rousseau: Political Development and Progressive Development*, Unpublished Doctoral Thesis, Yale University, p. 9. Along with the rest of the 'Scottish School' John Stuart Mill esteemed Ferguson highly, naming his father, James Mill, as the last in the line of succession of 'this great school' of Hume, Kames, Smith and Ferguson. Letter to A. Comte, January 28, 1843 in J.S. Mill, *Collected Works of John Stuart Mill*, J. Robson, F. Mineka, N. Dwight, J. Stillinger, and A. Robson, (eds), Toronto: University of Toronto Press, 1963, Vol. 13, p. 566.

[3] As was 'the fate of most Scots' after 1800. Fania Oz-Salzberger, *Translating the Enlightenment: Scottish Civic Discourse in Eighteenth Century Germany*, Oxford: University Press, 1995, p. 130. Even closer to his own time Ferguson's 'popular success was greatly overshadowed by that of his successor to the Edinburgh Moral Philosophy chair, Dugald Stewart'. N. Phillipson, 'The Scottish Enlightenment', in Porter, R and Teich, M. (eds), *The Enlightenment in National Context*, Cambridge: Cambridge University Press, 1981, p. 37.

[4] John Robertson has recently urged a greater awareness of 'potential fault lines within Scottish moral philosophy', drawing special attention to the eccentricity of Ferguson's work. 'The Scottish Contribution to the Enlightenment', in *The Scottish Enlightenment, Essays in Reinterpretation*, Paul Wood (ed), Rochester: University of Rochester Press, 2000, pp. 47-8.

pursuing comparatively worthless objects'.[5] For Ferguson, civil society could not be reduced to market society. Worse than that, the market may itself contain the seeds of despotism.[6]

Whereas the Scottish Enlightenment has been characterised (principally in the figure of Smith) as an attempt 'to legitimise bourgeois civilisation at an early stage of its growth',[7] Ferguson stood apart as a figure that frequently acted to subvert and *de*-legitimise it. He was rescued from obscurity in the first part of the twentieth century by those interested in the origins of sociology and early critiques of modernity. He continues to be rediscovered, more recently by scholars looking for early sources on the nature and preservation of civil society.[8]

Like other members of the Scottish Enlightenment (among them David Hume, Adam Smith, William Robertson, John Millar, Dugald Stewart and Lord Kames) Ferguson was motivated to apply himself to the study of society by the intense social and material changes he saw around him. The purpose of the exercise was not simply to describe and enumerate laws (to develop a kind of science of morals). His social science was inextricably linked to a normative critique of these changes, particularly in their effects upon virtue, community and the affective content of social life.

It is sometimes suggested that Ferguson's concern with political corruption led him to anticipate much of nineteenth-century sociology in disclosing the causal status of such social structural variables as mechanisation, the division of labour, bureaucratisation, commercialisation, apathy and over-extension. There is much truth to this claim though he finds his initial inspiration in the civic humanist concerns of citizenship and virtue.[9] It should also be remembered that he did not work alone but developed his ideas alongside and together with other Scots like

---

[5] Duncan Forbes, 'Introduction' to Ferguson, A, *An Essay on the History of Civil Society*, Edited and With an Introduction by Duncan Forbes, Edinburgh: Edinburgh University Press, 1967, p. xiii-iv. Here was a culture 'in search of perfection, to place every branch of administration behind the counter, and come to employ, instead of the statesman and the warrior, the mere clerk and accountant'. Adam Ferguson, *An Essay on the History of Civil Society* (hereafter cited as *Essay*), Edited by Fania Oz-Salzberger, Cambridge: Cambridge University Press, 1996, pp. 214-16. Please note: The latter edition is used throughout this work.

[6] To be explored in further chapters. See also John Varty, 'Civil or Commercial?: Adam Ferguson's Concept of Civil Society', *Democratisation,* Vol. 4, 1997, pp. 29-48.

[7] Hiroshi Mizuta, 'Towards a Definition of the Scottish Enlightenment', *Studies in Voltaire*, Vol. 154, 1976, pp. 1459-64, p. 1459.

[8] For example, Ernest Gellner, 'Adam Ferguson and the Surprising Robustness of Civil Society', in *Liberalism in Modern Times: Essays in Honour of Jose G. Merquior,* Ernest Gellner and Cesar Cansino (eds), London: CEU Press, 1996 and, by the same author, 'Adam Ferguson', in *Conditions of Liberty: Civil Society and Its Rivals*, London: Penguin Books, 1994; M. Foley, and R. Edwards, 'The Paradox of Civil Society', *Journal of Democracy*, Vol, 7 (3) 1996, pp. 38-52 and Varty, 'Civil or Commercial? Adam Ferguson's Concept of Civil Society'.

[9] As also noticed by John Brewer in his insightful work on Ferguson. J.D. Brewer, 'Conjectural History, Sociology and Social Change in Eighteenth Century Scotland: Adam Ferguson and the Division of Labour', in *The Making of Scotland: Nation, Culture and Social Change*, D. McCrone, S. Kendrick and P. Straw (eds), Edinburgh: Edinburgh University Press, 1989 and, by the same author, 'Adam Ferguson and the Theme of Exploitation', *The British Journal of Sociology*, 37, 1986, pp.461-78.

Smith, Hume, Robertson and Millar and they are certain to have influenced and aided one another.

Ferguson was well placed to notice the full force of social change brought on by modernisation. As Bjorn Eriksson has noted, in Ferguson's time Scotland was 'a living sociological museum of stages or modes of existence'.

> [T]he highland clans could without much ado be characterised as belonging to the shepherd stage. The stage of agriculture was still vivid in mind even if farming was in a process of transformation into a capitalistic, market-oriented production; and the stage of commerce was rapidly gaining in the second half of the eighteenth century when the Scottish lowlands were the economic wonder region of Europe.[10]

It was hardly surprising that the Scots were the first to articulate an early form of sociology.[11] Ferguson was particularly sensitive to this singular set of circumstances. As a highlander and a speaker of Gaelic he was unique among his contemporaries within the Scottish Enlightenment.[12] Part of this uniqueness lay in his agreement with Rousseau that modernity had disagreeable social, moral and emotional costs, costs that many his contemporaries seemed less willing to acknowledge. Although there are many points of disagreement,[13] Ferguson could not help but wonder if Rousseau had been right when he declared that 'our minds have been corrupted in proportion as the arts and sciences have improved.'[14] Against the rationalisation, individualism, hedonism and self-interestedness which he perceived as increasingly dominating social and commercial life, Ferguson wanted to rediscover community and the animating principles that governed it, namely the passions, and therefore, by implication *not* reason, or at least, not reason exclusively. He endorses Rousseau's suspicion of those who 'smile contemptuously at such old names as patriotism and religion'[15] by lauding the 'simple passions' of 'friendship, resentment, and love'.[16]

---

[10] Bjorn Eriksson, 'The First Formulation of Sociology: A Discursive Innovation of the Eighteenth Century', *Archives-Europeennes-de-Sociologie*; Vol. 34 (2), 1993, pp. 251-76, p. 272. David Hume wrote to Edward Gibbon that Scotland had arguably been 'the rudest...of all European nations; the most necessitous, the most turbulent and the most unsettled'. Letter to Edward Gibbon, March 18 1776, David Hume, *The Letters of David Hume*, edited by J.Y.T. Greig, in Two Volumes, Oxford: Clarendon Press, 1932, Vol. 2, p. 310.

[11] Eriksson, 'First Formulation of Sociology', pp. 251-76; Phillipson, 'The Scottish Enlightenment', p. 21.

[12] As Forbes puts it: 'The *Essay* was the work of a man who knew intimately, and from the inside, the two civilisations...which divided eighteenth century Scotland: the *Gemeinschaft* of the clan, belonging to the past, the *Gesellschaft* of the "progressive", commercial Lowlands'. Forbes, 'Introduction' to *Essay,* pp. xxxviii-ix.

[13] Such as, for example, Rousseau's belief in a state of nature, his attitude to great legislators and social contracts and also his perceived primitivism. Although Rousseau was not a strict primitivist, in Britain 'he was continuously and usually unfavourably associated' with it. James H. Warner, 'The Reaction in Eighteenth-Century England to Rousseau's Two Discourses', *Publications of the Modern Language Association of America,* Vol. 48 (2) June, 1933, pp. 471-87, p. 480.

[14] Jean Jacques Rousseau, 'A Discourse on the Moral Effects of the Arts and Sciences', in J. J. Rousseau, *The Social Contract and Discourses*, Translation and Introduction by G.D.H. Cole, London: Everyman Library, p. 8.

[15] Rousseau, 'A Discourse on the Moral Effects of the Arts and Sciences', *Social Contract and Discourses*, p. 17.

[16] *Essay*, p. 166.

The result is a defence of non-cognitive processes mounted on two fronts. The first is moral and emotional, couched within the framework of a civic humanist interest in corruption and the solidary virtues and focused on the importance of spontaneous affection. The second is social scientific. In the course of defending the passions as the source of social order, Ferguson devises an extremely well developed theory of spontaneous order, thereby signposting and aiding the emergence of social science proper. Here his main target is the type of *a priori* reasoning associated with rational constructivism and contractarianism, including any over-reliance on the principle of instrumental rationality to explain the maintenance of social life. Ferguson's alternative is a non-cognitive, irrationalist theory of history and society, one that presages structural-functionalist explanations of the development and maintenance of social patterns, institutions and mores. Rationality, explicit contract and long term planning are given second place to passions and sub-rational drives as the real generators, not only of our complex social structures, but also of historical progress and the general equilibrium of society.

1. THE FIRST SOCIOLOGIST?

Though it is generally the case that sociologists place the birth of their discipline 'in the first half of the nineteenth century'[17] Ferguson is sometimes identified as 'the first sociologist' or 'Father of Modern Sociology'. He influenced or anticipated, among others, Durkheim, Tönnies, Weber, Elias, and Hayek.[18] Comte recognised his contribution to the development of positivism[19] while Spencer read him and may well have been influenced by his work in the development of his own ideas on the 'division of labour...social differentiation and individuation and integration'.[20] Ferguson's work was well known in Germany where it exerted some influence.[21]

---

[17] H. Strasser, *The Normative Structure of Sociology: Conservative and Emancipatory Themes in Social Thought*, London: Routledge and Kegan Paul, 1976, p. 225.

[18] For example, Frederick Von Hayek explicitly cited his debt to Ferguson in expounding his theory of spontaneous order. F.A. Hayek, 'The Results of Human Actions But Not of Human Design', *Studies in Philosophy, Politics and Economics*, London: Routledge and Kegan Paul, 1967, p. 97. The title of this essay is a direct quote from Ferguson and indicates how struck was Hayek by the former's theory.

[19] Nevertheless Comte described Condorcet, not Ferguson, as his 'spiritual father' and regarded the former as second only to Montesquieu as a founder of sociology. Robert Bierstedt, 'Sociological Thought in the Eighteenth Century', in T. Bottomore and R. Nisbet (eds), *A History of Sociological Analysis*, London: Heinemann, 1979, p. 22.

[20] W.C. Lehmann, *Adam Ferguson and the Beginnings of Modern Sociology*, New York: Columbia University Press, 1930, p. 240. Lehmann's book represents the first systematic attempt to establish Ferguson as a founder of sociology.

[21] On, among others, Herder, Lessing, Schiller, Hegel, Marx, Isaak Iselin, Friedrich Heinrich Jacobi and Christian Garve. For a complete discussion of Ferguson's impact in Germany, see Oz-Salzberger, *Translating the Enlightenment*, especially Chapter 5. According to Robert Solomon, Ferguson exerted considerable influence over the work of both Schiller and Hegel. Robert C. Solomon, *In the Spirit of Hegel: A Study of G.W.F. Hegel's Phenomenology of Spirit*, New York: Oxford University Press, 1983. See also Laurence Dickey, *Hegel: Religion, Economics and the Politics of Spirit 1770-1807*, Cambridge: Cambridge University Press, 1987 and Dushan Bresky, 'Schiller's Debt to Montesquieu and Adam Ferguson', *Comparative Literature*, Vol. 13 (3), 1961, pp. 239-53.

He influenced Marx[22] and seems sure to have informed Hegel's views on needs, civil society and the effects of the division of labour.[23] Ludwig Gumplowicz and Werner Sombart have both traced the origins of sociology back to him[24] while Harry Barnes once claimed that '[i]f anyone before Saint-Simon and Comte has the right to be designated as the "father of sociology" it is...Ferguson'. [25] In the first half of the twentieth century it was commonplace to encounter identical claims.[26] Though such claims are sometimes either exaggerated or taken out of context, nevertheless they should be taken seriously.

There have been many allusions to Ferguson's contribution to modern social science[27] including suggestions that his work represents the first sustained critique of

---

[22] Karl Marx, *The Poverty of Philosophy*, With an Introduction by Frederick Engels, International Publishers: New York, 1969, pp. 129-30. According to Ronald Hamowy, Ferguson 'can claim priority over Smith in offering, not an economic analysis of the question which was original with neither writer, but rather, the first methodological and penetrating sociological analysis, an analysis which was to have far-reaching consequences in intellectual history by contributing substantially to the sociological groundwork of Marxism'. R. Hamowy, 'Adam Smith, Adam Ferguson and the Division of Labour', *Economica*, Vol.35 (139), August, 1968, pp. 244-59, p. 259. Jack Barbalet identifies Ferguson as perhaps the most important precursor of 'modern sociology in his explicit understanding of the social as distinct from the economic consequences of the division of labour and for his account of historic development'. J. M. Barbalet, *Emotion, Social Theory and Social Structure,* Cambridge: Cambridge University Press, 1998, pp.11-12. Though Rousseau had pre-empted Ferguson by canvassing the theme of alienation in his *Discourse on the Origin of Inequality*, the division of labour does not play as central a role in his account. Forbes, Introduction to *Essay*, p. xxxi.

[23] Norbert Waszek, The Scottish Enlightenment and Hegel's Account of Civil Society, Boston: M. Nijhoff, 1988, pp, 137-41, 225-7.

[24] Gumplowicz rated the *Essay* 'the first natural history of society'. Strasser, *Normative Structure of Sociology*, p. 52. According to Ronald Meek 'Adam Ferguson's *Essay*....is undoubtedly one of the most notable works of the epoch. Original, subtle and provocatively complex, it is nowadays rightly regarded as one of the first important exercises in the field which modern sociologists have marked out as their own'. R. Meek, *Social Science and the Ignoble Savage*, Cambridge: Cambridge University Press, 1976, p. 150. Similarly, Robert Bierstedt has described Ferguson's sociological insights as a triumph 'of major proportions'. Bierstedt, 'Sociological Thought in the Eighteenth Century', p. 29.

[25] H. Barnes, 'Sociology Before Comte: A Summary of Doctrines and an Introduction to the Literature', *American Journal of Sociology*, Vol. 23, July 1917, pp. 174-247, p. 234.

[26] Barnes, 'Sociology before Comte', p. 235; D. Macrae, 'Adam Ferguson; Sociologist', *New Society,* Vol. 24, 1966, 792-94 and by the same author, 'Adam Ferguson' in T. Raison, (ed.) *The Founding Fathers of Social Science*, London: Penguin Books, 1969, pp. 27-35. See also N. Waszek, *Man's Social Nature: A Topic of the Scottish Enlightenment in its Historical Setting*, Frankfurt: Peter Lang, 1986, 141; Strasser, *The Normative Structure of Sociology*, p.52; A. Swingewood, 'Origins of Sociology: The Case of the Scottish Enlightenment' *The British Journal of Sociology*, Vol. 21, 1970, pp. 164-80; Lehmann, *Adam Ferguson*, passim;

[27] As there have of the Scottish Enlightenment thinkers in general. The 1967 German Edition of John Millar's *Origin of the Distinction of Ranks* asserts on 'its unnumbered terminal page' that Millar, along with Smith and Ferguson, was 'one of the three great Scots of the second half of the eighteenth century who founded sociology'. Louis Schneider, 'Tension in the Thought of John Millar', *The Grammar of Social Relations: The Major Essays of Louis Schneider*, Jay Weinstein (ed) with an Epistolary Foreward by R.K. Merton, New Brunswick: Transaction Books, 1984, p. 109, n.8. For a subtle account of Ferguson's place in the history of sociology see Brewer, 'Adam Ferguson and the Division of Labour'. Herta Jogland has noted that the importance of Ferguson's contribution to modern sociology has been both under- and over-estimated by his various commentators. Herta Helena Jogland, *Ursprunge und Grundlagen der Sociologie bei Adam Ferguson*, Berlin: Dunker and Humbolt, 1959, pp. 18-19. See also: D. Kettler, *The Social and Political Thought of Adam Ferguson*, Indiana: Ohio State University Press, 1965, pp. 8-9; Lehmann, *Adam Ferguson*; *passim;* Fania Oz Salzsberger, *Translating the Enlightenment,*

capitalism and market society based on the detection of nascent alienation and *anomie* effects, the destruction of social intimacy and a theory of class exploitation. His conjectural history and detailed exposition of the social effects of the division of labour have also been hailed as major contributions to modern sociological method and thought.[28]

It is certainly true that Ferguson's work foreshadowed a good deal of nineteenth and twentieth century social thought but the question of whether he merits the title 'Father of Sociology' is a controversial one, not least because he appeared to have been forgotten for the duration of the century in which Anglo-American sociology began to emerge and define itself as a discrete discipline. What the public could not see during this time, though, was the way in which his influence had been funnelled into the discipline via important figures like Karl Marx, G. W. F. Hegel, Herbert Spencer and Ludwig Gumplowicz.

Obviously, the discipline of sociology had not yet separated itself out from moral philosophy[29] but it would be perverse to use this as a reason for disqualifying Ferguson as the *first* sociologist. At the same time, to attach the title 'Father of Sociology' to any one thinker is to deny the polygenesis of the discipline.[30] And if

---

pp. 89-92; L. Hill, 'Anticipations of Nineteenth and Twentieth Century Social Thought in the Work of Adam Ferguson', *European Journal of Sociology*, Vol. 37 (1), 1996, pp. 203-28; Barnes, 'Sociology before Comte', p. 235; F. Ferrarrotti, 'Civil Society and State Structures in Creative Tension', *State, Culture and Society*, Vol. 1, Fall 1984, pp. 3-25; R. Meek, *Economics and Ideology and other Essays*, London: Chapman and Hall Ltd., 1967, pp. 34-50; A. Ryan, 'An *Essay* on the History of Civil Society', *New Society*, Vol. 3, 1966, pp. 63-4. L. Schneider, *The Scottish Moralists on Human Nature and Society*, Chicago: University of Chicago Press, 1967; A. Silver, 'Friendship in Commercial Society: Eighteenth-Century Social Theory and Modern Sociology', *American Journal of Sociology*, Vol. 95 (6), 1990, pp. 1474-1504, p.1479 ; R. L. Emerson, 'Conjectural History and Scottish Philosophers' *Historical Papers*, Vol. 63, 1984, pp. 63-90; R. Pascal, 'Herder and the Scottish Historical School', *Publications of the English Goethe Society*, Vol.14, 1938-9, pp. 23-49 and by the same author, 'Property and Society: The Scottish Historical School of the Eighteenth Century' *Modern Quarterly*, Vol. 1, March,1938, pp. 167-79; Christopher J. Berry, *Social Theory of the Scottish Enlightenment*, Edinburgh: Edinburgh University Press, 1997; D. Forbes, 'Scientific Whiggism: Adam Smith and John Millar' *Cambridge Journal*, Vol. 6, 1954, pp. 643-70; Brewer, 'Adam Ferguson and the Theme of Exploitation'; Swingewood, 'Origins of Sociology'; G. Bryson, 'Some Eighteenth Century Conceptions of Society', *The Sociological Review*, Vol. 31, 1939, pp. 401-21, p. 403; R. Hamowy, *The Scottish Enlightenment and the Theory of Spontaneous Order*, Southern Illinois University Press, 1987; H.M. Hopfl, 'From Savage to Scotsman: Conjectural History in the Scottish Enlightenment', *Journal of British Studies*, 17 (2) 1978, pp. 19-40.

Not all scholars have shown enthusiasm for Ferguson's contribution to social science. For example, Bernard Barber asserts that [t]here is no great, undiscovered or startling new knowledge of society in Ferguson'. B. Barber, 'An Essay on the History of Civil Society', *Contemporary Sociology*, Vol. 9, (2), March, 1980, pp. 258-9, p. 258. According to Ernest Mossner, Ferguson's reputation during his own time as one of Edinburgh's 'most brilliant' minds was 'never fully justified'. He continues: 'there was always something superficial in Ferguson'. Ernest Campbell Mossner, 'Adam Ferguson's "Dialogue on a Highland Jaunt" with Robert Adam, William Cleghorn, David Hume, and William Wilkie', *Restoration and Eighteenth-Century Literature: Essays in Honour of Alan Dugald McKillop*, Chicago: University of Chicago Press, 1963, p. 297. We know that Hume was disappointed in the *Essay*, though for reasons unknown. Mossner suggests one possibility, namely, that Hume objected to Ferguson's insistence that progress was inevitable. E. Mossner, *The Life of David Hume*, London, Thomas Nelson and Sons, 1954, pp. 542-3.

[28] Brewer 'Adam Ferguson and the Division of Labour', passim.

[29] Forbes, Introduction to *Essay*, p.i; Ryan, 'Essay', p. 63.

[30] As noted by John Brewer, 'Adam Ferguson and the Theme of Exploitation', p. 462.

anyone deserves the title it could be argued that either Charles-Louis Montesquieu or Ibn Kaldhoun have prior entitlement. Certainly Ferguson, by his own account, is simply building on and improving the project begun by Montesquieu (the former seems to have been unaware of Kaldhoun). But it should also be noted that in the process he succeeds in creating something far richer and more 'distinctively sociological' than Montesquieu's less systematic and organised attempt.[31] He can thus be rightly identified as *one of* the many parents of sociology and a major one at that.

But it is important not to allow the attachment of the modern label 'sociologist' to obscure the classical tendencies of Ferguson's project. From his own (as opposed to posterity's) point of view, his writings are as much an exercise in moral philosophy and natural theology[32] as they are in history, philosophy and 'sociology'. They are also an attempt to reaffirm the centrality of God's role in understanding the workings of society, a role that had been questioned by the secularist accounts of Mandeville, Hume[33] and much of French eighteenth century-philosophy. And yet Ferguson's vision is little narrowed by this attempt, firstly because the God he refers to acts through secondary laws of nature and hence through impersonal and invariable social laws that can be accounted for within the context of an authentically modern social science,[34] and secondly, because the focus of moral philosophy in the eighteenth century was far broader than a narrowly defined concern with ethics, but rather constituted the discipline from which later developed the various discrete social sciences of the nineteenth century.[35] Ferguson rarely allows his moral prejudices to interfere with the empirical evidence and this is partly related to the fact that his theology is a form of Stoic theodicy. Convinced that society was a system benignly created and therefore governed by social laws that tended towards a positive equilibrium, Ferguson finds in even our apparently vicious

---

[31] S. Mason, 'Ferguson and Montesquieu: Tacit Reproaches?', *British Journal for Eighteenth Century Studies,* Vol. 2 (2), Autumn, 1988, pp. 193-203, pp. 194-5. Montesquieu's insistence on the existence of a pre-social state is an important limit on his attempts at sociology. Charles-Louis Montesquieu, *The Spirit of the Laws*, Translated and Edited by A. M.Cohler B.C. Miller, H.M. Stone, Cambridge: Cambridge University Press, 1990, 1. 1. 2., p. 6.

[32] Specifically in some form of Christian-Stoic theology. To be discussed.

[33] Smith is excepted here for he does not seem to have been an atheist. For a discussion of his belief system see Lisa Hill 'The Hidden Theology of Adam Smith', *European Journal of the History of Economic Thought,* 8 (1), Spring 2001, pp. 1-29.

[34] 'The more we examine the universe, the more we find everything to be governed by general laws...In the case of man, and all the animals, the good of every individual is not separately consulted, but the good of the species of every kind is at the same time provided for; and if it were otherwise, there could be no general laws by which men or beasts could regulate the actions'. Adam Ferguson, *Principles of Moral and Political Science: Being Chiefly a Retrospect of Lectures Delivered in the College of Edinburgh, in Two Volumes,* Edinburgh: Printed for A. Strahan and T. Cadell. London; and W. Creech, Edinburgh, 1792, (hereafter cited as *P.I.* or *P.II.*) p. 338.

[35] Gladys Bryson, 'Some Eighteenth Century Conceptions of Society', pp. 405-6. Ferguson's own definition of moral philosophy is 'the knowledge of what ought to be, or the application of rules that ought to determine the choice of voluntary agents'. Adam Ferguson, *Institutes of Moral Philosophy*, New York: Garland Publishing Company, 1978, (hereafter cited as *Institutes*), p.11. William Lehmann agrees that Ferguson's work is that of a moralist above all else. W.C. Lehmann, 'Review of P. Salvucci's' *Adam Ferguson*: Sociologica e Filosofia Politica', *History and Theory*, Vol. 13 (2), 1974, pp. 163-81, p. 173.

tendencies a positive latent function. The adoption of this metaphysical world-view enables him to approach the empirical world with more scientific curiosity than high handed moralising. Ferguson's attempts to develop a science of society can be partly understood as a continuation of the work of Hugo Grotius who drew upon the pre-Christian natural law tradition of classical antiquity. Natural laws are not found by reference to religious authority or the Scriptures but are perceptible to reasonable persons as being both just (socially beneficial and morally necessary) and natural (universal and unchangeable).[36]

Many of Ferguson's insights *are* groundbreaking and genuinely modern, not least in signposting a crossroads in the history of social science particularly in their anti-rationalist and anti-contractarian tendencies and more specifically, in his observations on the topics of: structural-functionalism; alienation and *anomie* effects; habit; the intersection between environment and society; the sociology of conflict; the sociology of emotion and finally, his insightful exploration of 'proto-liberal' mores and values. Ferguson's macro-sociology of institutions — his theory of spontaneous order — was the most complex and sophisticated to date, while he also contributed significantly to an important strand of classical liberal thinking, namely the anti-constructivist, laissez-faire stream that was developed and popularised by Frederick von Hayek (and who was to cite Ferguson as a direct influence).

Though Ferguson's sociology of emotion builds on Francis Hutcheson's approach (particularly in its emphasis on the utility of the social passions) it is more sophisticated and sociological, indicating an intelligent and subtle mind ahead of its time. By treating our 'passions', 'sentiments', 'desires and aversions' as independent variables he gives us a proper theory of social change and equilibrium that represents a significant break with both traditional historiographies and contractarian myths of the origins of social institutions and order. As one commentator has noted, '[t]here is a contemporary flavour about Ferguson, and we can talk about him in a language that is as appropriate to our own time as to his.'[37]

Finally, Ferguson's objection to the implicit hedonism of early liberalism marks a crucial point in the development of liberal values and sensibilities. Ferguson's was a milieu that celebrated the comforts, political calm and softening of manners that progress brought with it. Ferguson resisted what he perceived to be its torpid, Epicurean tendencies, insisting that no society could prosper without civic virtue; neither could it afford to undervalue benevolence and the solidary virtues. The cool, negative virtues of justice, prudence and propriety, and the secondary virtues of frugality, probity and punctuality (promoted by Smith as the mainstays of modern orders) are certainly useful, but are not enough to sustain a creature as 'passionate' and complicated as 'man'. Nor could they be expected to support society, the matrix of human happiness, safety and virtue and an entity that needs to be understood as something far more complex than a marketplace of prudential interaction. Neither does Ferguson find much solace in Hume's conviction that the age of 'industry and

---

[36] G.H. Sabine, *A History of Political Theory*, Third Edition, London: George Harrop and Co. Ltd., 1964, pp. 422-4.

[37] Bierstedt, 'Sociological Thought in the Eighteenth Century', p. 29.

refinements' is a golden age of unprecedented civility, rationality, refinement and sociability. Though Smith and Hume also proposed well-developed irrationalist theories of social order, they were more complacent about the social effects of this process.

2. SOCIAL CHANGE, VIRTUE AND THE 'REDISCOVERY' OF COMMUNITY

Although it has been pointed out that the discipline of sociology was not yet a discrete one, nevertheless, Ferguson can be rated as a significant figure in its prehistory. The meaning of the term 'sociology' is, of course, contested and 'its boundaries are wide and difficult to draw'.[38] However, if it can be loosely defined as being concerned with the study of society, conflict and change and with establishing knowledge of the laws of the social world, then Ferguson easily qualifies as an early practitioner. And if the proper object for sociology is social structure, (that is, relationship structures which supervene on or are independent of the particular groups or individuals who occupy them at any particular moment in time) then the objects that interest Ferguson may be properly deemed sociological.[39] Ferguson's intentions as an intellectual are also relevant here. Sociology is said to have emerged as an attempt to comprehend the profound upheavals brought on by the transition from traditional to modern societies[40] and this is precisely what motivated Ferguson. He was, as Duncan MacRae puts it so nicely, 'puzzled, justly, to assess what is gained, what [is] lost, in social change'.[41]

Ferguson wanted to understand the processes that underlay the apparent affective and moral decay of his own society. He also hoped to discover what could be done to offset the damage done to a state in which people had become 'incapable of public affections'.[42] He finds particularly provoking the standard argument made by such thinkers as Defoe, Montesquieu and Hume that the ancient concept of virtue was warlike because the societies which entertained it were economically primitive. On this view it followed that modern market economies could manage perfectly well without it.[43] Ferguson counters that no society, however advanced, can survive and prosper without civic virtue and yet this is precisely what is sacrificed in the march towards material progress. Modernity, which brought with it ever increasing levels

---

[38] D. Jary and J. Jary (eds) *Collins Dictionary of Sociology*, Glasgow: Harper Collins, 1991. pp.ix, 603.

[39] As John Brewer has observed 'Ferguson, much more thoroughly than other Scots' discusses 'a range of social structural variables which are given explanatory status, visualising the social structure as an integrated unit with causal relations existing between its parts'. Brewer, 'Adam Ferguson and the Division of Labour', p. 27.

[40] Anthony Giddens, *Sociology: A Brief but Critical Introduction*, 2nd ed., MacMillan Education, London, 1986, p. 9; G. Marshall, (ed) *Oxford Dictionary of Sociology*, Oxford: Oxford University Press, 1998, pp. 629-30.

[41] MacRae, 'Adam Ferguson, Sociologist', p. 793.

[42] *Institutes*, pp. 243-44

[43] J.G.A. Pocock, *Virtue, Commerce and History*, Cambridge: Cambridge University Press, 1985, p. 147.

of specialisation, differentiation, individuation, privatisation, depersonalisation and hedonism, inevitably led to national ruin wherever the signs of moral decay were not detected early enough.

Ferguson's concerns should be appreciated in the context, not only of commercialisation, but also of the specific historical circumstance of the Act of Union (1707). Although the Scottish court and royal family had long since shifted to London as a result of the 1603 Union of Crowns,[44] nevertheless Nicholas Phillipson has described as 'traumatic' the effect of the Act on the Scottish psyche. When the abolition of the Scottish Parliament and Privy Council 'stripped' Scotland of its political institutions and ended any hope of political independence, the Scottish literati were forced to confront the problem of how political virtue could be sustained in the absence of its traditional matrixes.[45] Part of the problem before them was to find 'an alternative language of civic morality' which could help them interpret their unique situation. The early sociology they developed in their efforts to achieve this is, as Phillipson rightly notes, their 'unique contribution' to the Enlightenment project.[46] They wrote from a position of adversity and marginality and yet their achievements were great. Hume captured their spirit of creative resilience well when he observed in private correspondence:

> Is it not strange that, at a time when we have lost our Princes, our Parliaments, our Independent Government, even the Presence of our chief Nobility, are unhappy, in our Accent and Pronunciation, speak a very corrupt Dialect of the Tongue which we make use of; is it not strange…that in these Circumstances, we shou'd really be the People most distinguish'd for Literature in Europe?[47]

But, as was typical of most of his contemporaries in Scottish lowlands, Ferguson never pined for the restoration of Scotland's political independence. It seems he was resigned to the Union on the belief that it would bring to Scotland 'economic prosperity, political liberty, and cultural sophistication'.[48] Scots like Ferguson and William Robertson regarded Andrew Fletcher as a patriot[49] yet at the same time welcomed the civilising and enriching effects of the Union. The Scots, Robertson wrote, have been 'adopted into a constitution' whose laws were superior to and 'more liberal than their own'. As a consequence, they had 'extended their commerce, refined their manners, made improvements in the elegancies of life, and cultivated the arts and sciences'.[50]

---

[44] Oz-Salzberger, Introduction to *Essay*, p. ix. '[W]hen James VI of Scotland became also James I of England'. Broadie, 'The Scottish Enlightenment', p. 7.

[45] Ferguson describes 'political situation' as 'a school of intellectual and moral improvement, in which [people] are destined to advance in knowledge, wisdom, and all the eligible habits of life'. *P.I.*, p. 263.

[46] According to Phillipson, '[w]hat they sought was a language responsive to the economic, social and historical experience of provincial communities and realised that the virtue of a provincial citizen class was more likely to be released by economic and cultural institutions than by a national parliament remote from the provincial citizen's world. And they warned that a polity that did not respect the independence of its provinces could not possibly be said to be free'. Phillipson, 'The Scottish Enlightenment', pp. 21-6.

[47] Hume, *Letters of David Hume*, p. 255.

[48] Oz-Salzberger, Introduction to *Essay*, p. viii; Smith, *The Political Philosophy of Adam Ferguson*, pp. 19-20

[49] Broadie, The Scottish Enlightenment, p.32.

[50] William Robertson, *History of Scotland* in Two Volumes, London: 1759, 2, p. 254.

Yet, unlike most of his contemporaries, Ferguson remained wary of some the long-term effects of the Union and the economic development it brought with it. His fears for the future give rise to a nostalgia for the traditional close-knit warrior cultures of ancient Sparta, Rome, Greece and Highland Scotland. Though in one sense he accepts and embraces progress as natural, he also resists the eclipse of benevolence by self-interested prudence and rails against the decline of community and social solidarity, both of which tendencies are perceived to have been brought on by progress.[51] Nostalgia and fears for community are not Ferguson's only concern either. He also fretted about the increasingly important role of prudential reasoning, bureaucratic rationality and centralised planning in the running of societies and, in particular, their effects upon the moral strength of nations.

But, since progress is natural and must therefore be embraced, something would need to be done about mitigating its worst effects. After suggesting a number of institutional measures Ferguson seeks a more general solution in the idea of developing and cultivating moral character, specifically of the type which seemed to come naturally to 'barbarians'. The loss of national virtue, which is the first casualty of progress, is a product of the 'weakness and effeminacy' of civilised nations. Because this is a mental rather than physical condition Ferguson looks for means by which to psychologically and imaginatively reconstitute such virtue.

This cultural solution involved recovering and even reinventing a tradition that Ferguson recreated from ancient history, a variety of contemporary 'anthropological' sources as well as 'relics of the local past'. Its purpose, it appears, was to somehow repair the social fabric (or 'bands of society') ravaged by progress[52] as well as generate a sense of cultural independence that became more urgent in the aftermath of the Act of Union (1707) and as the homogenising culture of commerce became more firmly entrenched.[53] Ferguson's enthusiasm for these cultural relics, particularly the Highland clans with which he seemed to identify so strongly,[54] reached its high point in his support for (and alleged, but never proven, involvement in the production of) James Macpherson's reproduction of Ossian's (a mythical third

---

[51] *Essay*, p. 215.

[52] Peter Womack, Improvement and Romance: Constructing the Myth of the Highlands, Basingstoke: Macmillan 1989, pp. 43-4.

[53] According to Colin Kidd, Scotland's Celtic identity had already been dealt a number of damaging 'intellectual blows from which it never fully recovered', among them, scholarly discreditations (since the mid sixteenth century) of its 'ancient Dalriadic mythistoire' and challenges to 'the dating and authenticity of the regnal lists upon which the high antiquity of the Fergusian monarchy was based'. Colin Kidd, 'Gaelic Antiquity and National Identity in Enlightenment Ireland and Scotland', *The English Historical Review*, Vol. 109 (434) November 1994, pp. 1197-214, p. 1206.

[54] Though, by Ferguson's own account, he was not a true Highlander since Athole was on the Highland border, 'barely within the limits at which Gaelic begins to be [the] vulgar tongue and where the mythology and tradition of the highlands were likely to be more faint than in the interior parts'. Letter to Henry Mackenzie, March 26, 1798, Adam Ferguson, *The Correspondence of Adam Ferguson*, Edited by V. Merolle with an Introduction by J.B. Fagg, in Three Volumes, London: William Pickering, 1995 (hereafter cited as *Correspondence*), No. 337, II. p. 430. In addition, while still a young boy he had been sent away to school. Jane Fagg, *Biographical Introduction, Correspondence*, I. pp. lxviii, lxxii. For more on Ferguson's provincial identity see: Michael Kugler, 'Provincial Intellectuals: Identity, Patriotism, and Enlightened Peripheries', *The Eighteenth Century: Theory and Interpretation*, Vol. 37, 1996, pp. 156-73.

century bard) epic poems.[55] But, despite initial impressions, Ferguson never resorted to complete atavism. Indeed his own 'complex intellectual fusion of primitivism and progress' has been read back into *Ossian* as 'an abiding presence.'[56] There was to be nothing rough or savage about Ferguson's new moral archetype for 'he' combined the best of the old with the best of the new. Military and civic training also entailed a rounded education for the brave new generation of refined, noble, generous and humane Scotsmen.[57] The new 'man of feeling' was progressive and polite, at once ethical and sentimental, passionate yet civilised and educated.[58] And he is decidedly male. Unlike Hume, Ferguson makes no attempt to appeal to a female readership, nor does he exhibit much interest in the experience of women except where it illustrates an interesting anthropological point. But neither is there any hint of misogyny. It is just that his focus is always upon the public, and therefore by his own definition, the masculine world.

In his attempts to merge the competing high and low cultures of developing Scotland Ferguson sought for (and possibly injected into)[59] *Ossian* precisely what his former pupil Macpherson delivered, not a literal or pragmatic solution, but a figurative one; a kind of reconstructed, affective and moral ideal tailor-made for a Scottish imagination perceived to be impoverished by cultural imperialism, the new

[55] Luke Gibbons, 'Ossian, Celticism and Colonialism' in Terence Brown (ed) *Celticism*, Amsterdam: Rodopi, 1996, p. 284. But as Forbes rightly notes, '[t]here is no direct mention of the Highland clan in the *Essay*...The Highland inspiration is clothed in the fashionable garb; admiration of Sparta, the contrast between classical public spirit and modern selfishness, the appeal to the classics of modern anthropology, the manners of the American Indian, and so on'. Forbes, 'Introduction' to *Essay*, p. xxxix. Ferguson's avoidance of references to Highland culture is likely traceable to a desire to forestall any interpretation of his nostalgia as harbouring Jacobite sympathies. For a general discussion of the historicity of *Ossian* see K.L. Haugan, 'Ossian and the Invention of Textual History', *Journal of the History of Ideas*, Vol. 58 (2) 1998, pp. 309-27. According to Nicholas Phillipson, 'Ossian was the creation of a young, unscrupulous man, James Macpherson, who was sent to the highlanders by Alexander Carlyle, Adam Ferguson and their friends to discover the epic by a Celtic Homer that they were sure must exist. No such epic existed, but Macpherson was perfectly content to construct one out of the fragments of Celtic verse he had been able to find. His patrons provided him with money, a publisher and editorial assistance, and Hugh Blair wrote a brilliant, subtle and influential essay on Ossian which was to present the fictitious bard in the guise in which he was to appear to his readers on the Continent and in the Anglo-Saxon world for the next century'. Phillipson, 'The Scottish Enlightenment', p. 34. For Ferguson's denial of any involvement in a 'cheat' regarding the authorship of the material see Letter to John Douglas July 21, 1781, *Correspondence*, No. 198, II. p. 288.

[56] Gibbons, 'Ossian, Celticism and Colonialism', p. 284

[57] John Dwyer, 'The Melancholy Savage' in Howard Gaskill (ed), *Ossian Revisted*, Edinburgh: Edinburgh University Press 1991, pp. 170-1.

[58] 'The moral sentiments led to goodness as well as civility....though the moral sentiments were thought to be natural to all, Scottish moralists were impressed by the degree to which they would be cultivated through education'. John Dwyer, 'Introduction-A Peculiar Blessing: Social Converse in Scotland from Hutcheson to Burns', in J. Dwyer and R.B. Sher (eds), *Sociability and Society in Eighteenth Century Scotland*, Edinburgh: The Mercat Press, 1993, pp. 6-7.

[59] Fiona Stafford has suggested that Ferguson was not only Macpherson's patron, but may also have exerted a direct influence on him. Fiona Stafford, *The Sublime Savage: A Study of James Macpherson and the Poems of Ossian*, Edinburgh: Edinburgh University Press, 1988, pp. 157-8. On the other hand, according to Jane Fagg, there is no evidence that Ferguson took any part in the alleged cheat over the authenticity of the poems. Fagg, *Biographical Introduction*, lxxi.

ethic of the market and the temperate, dispassionate, strangership which looked set to constitute its primary mode of association.[60] As John Dwyer notes:

> Macpherson's heroes were less ideal types of the primitive past than symbolic models for a sentimental present. The poems of *Ossian* might lament the passing of an ancient Highland society, but they represented much more than a stoic and sentimental seal upon an ideal warrior society which was receding with the tide of commercial and agricultural improvement. Rather, they provided a moral legend or fable for future generations of Scotsmen. [61]

Unlike other Scottish literati of the lowlands, Ferguson did not look upon the rough highlander as 'an embarrassing remnant of a bygone age'[62] but as a type whose characteristics might be admired and, in some respects, even imitated. His 'imaginative reconstruction' of the sentimental at a critical transition point in Scottish social history was intended as an antidote, not only to Scotland's loss of independence but also to the forces of progress; to the affective barrenness, utilitarianism, rationalism and individualism of the market; forces which he was convinced were undermining sociability and thus the whole basis of communal, civic and national life. Nicholas Phillipson suggests that *Ossian* served a further function. For those members of the select society who embraced progress, commerce and the new prosperity of Scotland, *Ossian* enabled them to 'alleviate any guilt they might feel at making a virtue out of adaptability by celebrating the past with nostalgia and sentiment'.[63] With no political institutions to work with, and dwindling hopes for the institution of a Scottish militia, Ferguson may well have sought to replicate the effects in the eighteenth century of a similar 'Celtic antiquarian revival' that took place in the thirteenth century. The latter was believed to have lent a 'sense of collective identity' to an 'ethnically diverse Scottish nation' intent on preserving Scottish independence against the imperialistic Plantaganets.[64] Quite possibly Ferguson believed he could help reconstitute Scottish civic identity in social and cultural, rather than in directly political terms.[65]

---

[60] For a fuller discussion of the idea of commercial 'strangership' see L. Hill and P. McCarthy, 'Hume, Smith and Ferguson: Friendship in Commercial Society', in Preston King and Heather Devere, (eds) *The Challenge to Friendship in Modernity*, London: Frank Cass, 2000.

[61] Dwyer, 'The Melancholy Savage', pp. 170-1

[62] Oz-Salzberger, Introduction to *Essay*, p. x.

[63] Phillipson, 'The Scottish Enlightenment', p. 34.

[64] Kidd, 'Gaelic Antiquity and National Identity', p. 1205.

[65] Many thanks to an anonymous referee for the suggestion of this line of thought.

3. ANTI-RATIONALISM AND AN EARLY SOCIOLOGY OF EMOTION

As a moral philosopher with social scientific ambitions, Ferguson is more than willing to provide a detailed defence of the passions, not only as solidary mediums but just as importantly, as vital engines of social progress and order. This he achieves in grand style, delivering to his reader the most polished, detailed and systematic treatment to date of spontaneous order explanations. Reacting against the kind of rationalist and contractarian views of history which had emerged up to and around his time, Ferguson posits a non-cognitive, irrationalist theory of history and social order, presaging structural functionalist explanations of the development and maintenance of social institutions, patterns and mores. His approach is also anti-individualist. The achievement of order and change are social processes which occur over time, reflecting the unconscious wisdom of generations rather than the conscious intentions of planners, legislators or influential actors. The propagation of the species, the origin and maintenance of the family, the division of labour, language, technological and artistic advances, and the emergence of the modern state are just some of the unintended consequences of actors pursuing their limited goals. Rationality, explicit contract and long term planning are displaced by sub-rational drives as the generators of our complex social structures, historical progress and the general equilibrium of society. The more crucial to the prosperity of our species is the function or institution, the less likely it is to be left to the tenuous will and judgement of individual agents, hence the centrality of drives, passions and emotions to Ferguson's scheme.

3.1   An Early Sociology of Emotion

To the contemporary sociologist of emotion, Ferguson's work seems remarkably prescient. And it is a proper sociology of emotion, not an accidental one, to be read back into an early thinker by over-eager intellectual historians. In his theory of social order and change Ferguson treats emotions, (that is, 'passions', 'sentiments', 'desires and aversions') not as epiphenomena, but as key independent variables.[66] At the same time he is quite careless about making precise lexical distinctions between these various drives, appetites, emotions and passions partly because precision and taxonomy are not his strong suits and partly because his main concern is to contrast this whole range of sub-rational human experience with that of reason. His model is also complicated by the fact that innate impulses are always overlaid with socially acquired meanings. For example, in the normal course of social existence the 'gregarious' or social instinct is far more complex and varied than it could ever be for other species possessing a comparable impulse. Whereas in other animals sociability is usually confined to a herding tendency, in humans it manifests

---

[66] Jack Barbalet has noticed, for example, how important is emotion to 'making sense' of Ferguson's social theory. Ferguson's detailed account of the human constitution 'forms the methodological and theoretical basis of what follows, and is largely concerned with the emotional dispositions associated with social and political relations and organisation'. Barbalet, *Emotion, Social Theory and Social Structure*, p. 12.

variously as 'the mutual disposition of the sexes', the love that exists between 'parent and child', 'the predilection of friends', as well as predispositions like patriotism, 'sympathy', altruism, 'humanity', 'an esteem of merit, and a love of justice'.[67]

Though there are socio-cultural and symbolic interactionist tendencies in Ferguson, by and large he sees emotions, drives and sentiments as innate and hence as causes, rather than symptoms of social structures and relationships.[68] And while he does not use the modern terminology he is nevertheless deeply interested in 'emotional culture', 'emotional socialisation processes' and 'relationships between social structure and emotion norms' in much the same way as are modern sociologists.[69]

Of course, Ferguson does not deny that we have a rational faculty or that it was a faculty worth cultivating. Reason is, after all, what he uses to defend the passions and it is reason that permits us to appreciate Nature's workings and our role in the Creator's scheme.[70] In fact he is careful to correct anyone who has sought to represent 'mankind...as possessed of mere animal sensibility, without any exercise of the faculties' that enable the species to form 'political union', develop exquisite 'moral sentiments' or express itself in complex language.[71] Its just that he saw that there was much more to the human story than either animal drives or conscious intentions. We can understand humanity better if we accept that it is another species of animal, albeit with exceptional powers of consciousness, imagination and artifice. He insisted that we always have power of choice (that is, free will) over the exercise of our natural impulses. Humans possess two sets of faculty powers, those of the understanding and those of the will.[72] On the one hand, we are characterised by the rational, cognitive powers of consciousness, sense and perception, reasoning and foresight, memory, imagination and abstraction but we also have animal or active powers governed by the following laws: the law of self-preservation; the law of society and the law of estimation or progression. But because our 'animal' and 'intellectual nature' is 'joined' so they should be studied co-jointly.[73]

Reacting against rationalistic currents in Enlightenment thinking Ferguson posits a sub-rational account of human life that is both subtle and detailed. Emotion, supported by custom, habit, reason and imagination, is not random or disorganised

---

[67] *P.I.,* p. 125.

[68] 'The explanatory value of emotions categories can also be located in the major sociologists of the nineteenth and early twentieth centuries. Alexis de Tocqueville, Gustave Le Bon, Emile Durkheim, Vilfredo Pareto, Ferdinand Tonnies and Georg Simmel are some of the more notable European sociologists who...regarded emotions categories as important explanatory variables. During this same period American sociology, in the works of such figures as Albion Small, William Graham Sumner, and Lester Frank Ward, as well as Edward Ross and Charles Horton Cooley, found explanatory roles for emotions categories'. Barbalet, *Emotion, Social Theory and Social Structure,* pp. 11-13.

[69] Late modern interests as identified by Peggy Thoits. Peggy A. Thoits, 'The Sociology of Emotions', *Annual Review of Sociology,* Vol. 15, 1989, pp. 317-42, pp. 327, 317.

[70] *P.I.,*p.vii.

[71] *Essay,* p. 8.

[72] *P.I.,* p. 68.

[73] Adam Ferguson, *Analysis of Pneumatics and Moral Philosophy,* For the Use of Students in the College of Edinburgh, Edinburgh, 1766 (hereafter cited as *Analysis), p.*7.

but carefully arranged and calibrated (by a beneficent Creator) to achieve undreamed-of effects. For example, class resentment, covetousness and envy lead to formal government as well as political faction fighting and (therefore, in turn) the preservation of rights and liberties; invidious comparison generates the quest for excellence and the pursuit of wealth and progress; parental affection leads to the formation and maintenance of the family and later the nation-state; shame operates as a powerful means of social control; material and moral progress spring from 'ambition' which is a combination of restlessness, activism and a compulsive desire for improvement; competition, conflict, belligerence and hostility indirectly preserve social cohesion and give rise to such beneficial institutions as an organised state, positive law and advances in defence technology and statecraft; social norms are shaped by and depend upon inter-subjective validation while moral judgements are reinforced by shared or mutual affective responses.

Catharsis is also a major theme for Ferguson. Because emotion is important, powerful and sometimes hazardous, catharsis is both a biological and social necessity. There are some diverting and original excurses on mechanisms for the safe discharge of potentially dangerous emotions, among them, ritual, play, contest, war and even commerce. For example, war provides a socially productive means for the expression of our belligerent tendencies and our inherent need for physical aggression; faction fighting offers an outlet for class resentment while commerce channels our natural restlessness and insatiable 'ambition'. Finally, our love of sport, play and even danger gives rise to organised games which serve to offset the stifling effects of routinised social relations within increasingly ordered societies.

Against, Hobbes, Mandeville, and sometimes even Smith, Ferguson makes much of the sociable passion of 'union'. It is not the interested but the disinterested passions of altruism, friendship, parental affection, national pride, emotional group identification, chivalry and spontaneous trust which make social life both rewarding and possible. People naturally yearn for communion and solidary participation, but it is not for any self-interested motive, but rather to maximise affective arousal, in the short term, and to realise our God-given nature in the long. Ferguson denied that the rational (i.e. utility maximising) self-interest embraced by Smith had more explanatory power than the other-regarding passions. Though the two agreed that the other-regarding passions were highly commendable and therefore worthy of pursuit for their own sakes, they disagreed as to how much social-ordering power they had. For Ferguson, quite a lot of what people do arises from more diffuse, altruistic, and less calculated impulses.

And yet Ferguson by no means discards the self-regarding passions and this is partly what makes him a transitional thinker. Interest, 'self-preservation' and egoism all have vital social functions in his system. They are, after all, natural aspects of our God-given constitutions. In fact, 'self-preservation' is the first task recommended to us by nature. While Ferguson attempts to counter the new politics of interest he does not seek to elide it. He is a kind of liberal-Stoic; at once a civic and commercial humanist (to borrow from John Pocock's taxonomy) alert to the pitfalls of progress yet tolerant of its inevitability, its benefits and even its capacity to generate new virtues. Embracing progress he yet defends the traditional primary virtues and retains his interest in the classical theme of corruption.

Ferguson's attitude should be appreciated within the context of his own version of the civic tradition, which he devised in order to meet the demands of a large scale, commercial polity. It differs from most classical versions (Polybius and Machiavelli notwithstanding) in two important respects: Firstly, strict republics are unsuitable because they only work well in small-scale societies, thus mixed monarchies are endorsed. They are also approved because of Ferguson's commitment to gradualism and spontaneous order. Since mixed monarchy happens to be the existing British constitution (and since Britain is his main concern) it is also likely to be the most appropriate. The second important digression from classical republicanism is that there is to be no strict separation between those members of society whose function it is to act as autonomous citizens and those whose primary function it is to serve the economy.[74] Under commercial conditions, everyone (that is to say, every male of majority age) is self-sufficient and therefore enabled to participate civically. Accordingly, Ferguson is interested in the conditions for economic self-sufficiency and prosperity, not only as ends in themselves, but as indirect means to the preservation of political community.

4. POLITICAL SCIENCE

Ferguson exhibited an unusual willingness to deal with the unavoidable untidiness of life and to explicitly accommodate this fact within his social science. He also thinks that the practical ideal of social harmony cherished by many of his contemporaries is questionable.[75] Life is meant to be conflictual, disharmonious and even confusing at times. The political calm that Hume and Smith both hankered after is especially pernicious, hence Ferguson's approval of factional conflict.

Moral philosophising was, above all, a social act for Ferguson. Philosophy must be of practical service to the community.[76] We must imitate the example of Socrates whose 'first office of moral wisdom' was to 'to recall the attention of mankind from the heavens to the earth, or from the consideration of things remote to the near and immediate concerns of human life'.[77] This probably explains why Ferguson generally avoided metaphysical subjects and fine-grained philosophy in general in favour of more worldly interests such as the writing of political pamphlets on

---

[74] For an indication of Ferguson's awareness of this separation see *P.I.* pp. 252-3. For an excellent discussion of the distinctiveness of the Scottish variant of the civic tradition see John Robertson: 'The Scottish Enlightenment at the Limits of the Civic Tradition' in I. Hont, and M. Ignatieff, and by the same author, 'Scottish Political Economy Beyond the Civic Tradition; Government and Economic Development in the *Wealth of Nations'*, *History of Political Thought*, Vol 4 (3), Winter 1983, pp. 451-82.

[75] Smith disparaged all forms of conflict and social disharmony; in fact '[t]he peace and order of society, is of more importance than even the relief of the miserable'. Adam Smith, *Theory of Moral Sentiments*, Edited and with an Introduction by D.D. Raphael and A. Macfie, Oxford: Clarendon Press, 1976 (hereafter cited as *TMS*), VI. ii.1.20, p. 226. Hume welcomed the fact that people became more temperate and pacific with progress. Hume, 'Of Refinement in the Arts', *Essays*, pp. 273-4. See also Richard Boyd, 'Reappraising the Scottish Moralists and Civil Society', *Polity*, Vol. 33, Fall 2000, pp.101-25, p. 113.

[76] Kettler, *Adam Ferguson*, p.7; *Essay*, pp.169-71.

[77] *P.I.*, p.4.

controversial issues of the day[78] in addition to his various cultural and political involvements.[79]

Political science is central to the maintenance of the good society but such a science must do more than offer practical lessons in statecraft. To this end, Ferguson retains a classical interest in normative moralising. In fact, he divides the *Principles* into two parts. The first deals with the 'facts' of the species' history and constitution while the second is ethical, devoted to 'Principles of Right, or the foundations of judgement and choice, whether in matters of personal quality, law, manners, or political establishments'.[80] But it is not moralising for its own sake. As Ferguson says, the point of all systems and institutions is to make people happy. This is 'the fundamental principle of political science. If the people be happy, we have no title to enquire to what other purpose they serve, for this itself is the purpose of all human establishments.'[81] However Ferguson is no strict utilitarian because happiness consists in the capacity of agents to exercise the beneficent and other-regarding sentiments.[82] Proper and genuinely useful moral philosophising avoids the usual course of analytic hair-splitting ('speculations of little moment') and limits itself to the more practical 'study of what men ought to be, and of what they ought to wish, for themselves and for their country'.[83] Neither is political science reducible to the study of the practical arts of statecraft, political economy and warfare because good governing means more than a utilitarian concern for the expansion of national wealth and might.[84] And it certainly means more than the modest task of constraining and channelling interest, just as liberty means far more than an absence of constraint on private action.[85] Rather, politics is the art of keeping the political realm virtuous, vital and safe from harm, of identifying those 'provisions required for the safety and better government of men in society.'[86]

Further, it should avoid vulgar contractarian assumptions about the origin and nature of the organised state in favour of a deeper apprehension of the social laws that govern it. Ferguson's political science is, in a sense, a continuation of Montesquieu's project. Like the latter, he was interested in far more than providing his readers with detailed taxonomies of constitutional forms, with their usual aetiologies of corruption and pat remedies (though he does, of course, make use of

---

[78] Sir John Dalrymple noted that, whereas other intellectuals had devoted themselves to writing 'great books by which they have gotten wealth and fame, [Ferguson] has often unsolicited and unknown, thrown out pamphlets that have sometimes been of real use to the Government'. Cited in Fagg, *Biographical Introduction*, xlix.

[79] Such as his acting as secretary of the Carlisle Commission, membership of the Poker Club, role in the Douglas affair, interest in parliamentary reform and involvement in Presbytery affairs and election campaigning. Fagg, *Biographical Introduction,* passim.

[80] *P.I.*, p. 9.

[81] *P.II.*, pp. 411-12.

[82] See, for example, *Essay*, p. 244. Happiness is also an effect of acting justly. *Essay*, p. 200.

[83] *Institutes*, p. 80.

[84] After all, participation in civic life is where 'mankind find the exercise of their best talents'. *Essay*, p.149.

[85] For Ferguson's broader definition of liberty see *P.II.*, p. 465.

[86] *P.I.*, p. 206.

these).[87] Like Montesquieu, Ferguson also tried to make his political science more 'broadly cultural and comparative'[88] dealing as it does with the relationship of laws, institutions and practices to a nation's culture and history.[89]

Ferguson's work can be understood in relation to the development of commerce and, in particular, the increasing role attributed to self-interest as a regulating principle in social and economic life. It has been suggested that this latter development shifted the emphasis in political science from 'more cyclical and moralistic conceptions of politics based on the dialectic between virtue and corruption' to a legalistic focus on limited and restrained government. Interestedness was now seen as having both negative and positive functions; there was no point in attempting to counteract its effects by the cultivation of virtue. Rather, the point was to harness and curb it. This new 'politics of interest' was a Realpolitik of modernity, focusing on institutional means for constraining and regulating interestedness in public life. Related to this shift in moral focus was the development of the burgeoning science of political economy and its intrusion into the study of politics. Together, these developments helped to shape a new politics distinct from its 'ancient and Renaissance predecessors'.[90]

Ferguson takes this new perspective on board but without sacrificing his commitment to the theme of civic virtue. Though he welcomed the expansion and diffusion of liberty he was less interested than Smith and Hume in the modern conception of [negative] liberty that underlay the emerging science of political economy.[91] Although he recognised the role of interest in human affairs, and paid considerable attention to how it could be both curbed and channelled productively,[92] he nevertheless insisted that civic virtue was the vital force of political life. The only real liberty worthy of the title came, not from a minimal state, whose main purpose is to secure property and person, but from the preservation of a robust community and a state-led programme of civic revitalisation designed to preserve politics from corruption and eventual despotism. Ferguson attributes a law-like status to the view that, rather than being of peripheral concern, 'political establishments are the most important articles in the external conditions of men'.[93] In an implicit contradiction of Smith's perceived anti-politics, Ferguson tells us that '[n]atural liberty is not impaired...by political institutions' but rather 'owes its existence' to them.[94] And here, again, is where Ferguson displays originality. His was...

---

[87] For a fuller discussion of Ferguson's relationship to Montesquieu see Mason, 'Ferguson and Montesquieu', passim.

[88] S. Collini, D. Winch and J. Burrow, *That Noble Science of Politics,* Cambridge: Cambridge University Press, 1983, p. 17

[89] See, for example, *Institutes*, p. 261.

[90] Collini et al, *That Noble Science of Politics*, p. 29. 'This concern with machinery that would check and balance interests was, of course, to become the keynote of the deliberations of the American founding fathers when they set about the task of constructing a constitution for a federal republic that had to survive in a continent of a "wide extent" and among a people that could no longer be regarded as "virtuous" in either the ancient or the technical sense defined by Montesquieu'. Ibid., p. 19.

[91] Oz-Salzberger, *Translating the Enlightenment*, p.110.

[92] For a fuller discussion of this point see Chapter Five.

[93] Institutes, p. 261

[94] *Institutes*, p. 266.

> ...a polemical message, directed against those friends and colleagues...who were increasingly ready to put their trust in constitutional mechanisms and self-motivated commercial interactions between individuals as sufficient safeguards of political bliss.[95]

Political science is not so much 'the art of the possible', as the art of preserving those virtues and institutional forms congenial to the plans of the Divine Architect. But institutions, while important, are always subordinate to virtues and the characters that embody them. As Ferguson says:

> Liberty is a right which every individual must be ready to vindicate for himself. Even political establishments...cannot be relied on for the preservation for freedom; they may nourish, but should not supersede that firm and resolute spirit, with which the liberal mind is always prepared to resist indignities, and to refer its safety to itself.[96]

The adequacy of the legalist and limited concept of government promulgated by Hume and Smith[97] is thus called into question. Legal restraints on an increasingly professionalised and distant government, while important, are not in themselves adequate to prevent the onset of political corruption. Rather, civic virtue and a vigilant, active populace are its most reliable guards. Of the writ of Habeas Corpus he wrote, '[n]o wiser form was ever opposed to the abuses of power. But it requires a fabric no less than the whole political constitution of Great Britain, a spirit no less than the refractory and turbulent zeal of this fortunate people, to secure its effects'.[98] In a similar vein it is important to be aware of the suffocating effect that laws can have on civil liberties and virtues.

> [I]f a rigorous policy, applied to enslave, not to restrain from crimes, has an actual tendency to corrupt the manners, and to extinguish the spirit of nations; if its severities be applied to terminate the agitations of a free people, not to remedy their corruptions; if forms be often applauded as salutary, because they tend merely to silence the voice of mankind, or be condemned as pernicious, because they allow this voice to he heard; we may expect that many of the boasted improvements of civil society, will be mere devices to lay the political spirit at rest, and will chain up the active virtues more than the restless disorders of men.[99]

In order to accommodate his embrace of progress with his concern for virtue Ferguson looks to a hybrid solution, seeking to blend a classical republican sensibility with the conditions and constraints of commercialism. By his own account he wants to try 'to mix the military spirit with a civil and commercial

---

[95] Oz-Salzberger, *Translating the Enlightenment*, p. 111.

[96] *Essay*, p. 251.

[97] Oz-Salzberger, *Translating the Enlightenment*, pp. 118-9. For example, Ferguson seems to be referring (critically) to Smith's restrained concept of government and his negative and commutative theory of justice when he says: 'If to any people it be the avowed object of policy, in all its internal refinements, to secure the person and the property of the subject, without any regard to his political character, the constitution indeed may be free, but its members may likewise become unworthy of the freedom they possess, and unfit to preserve it. The effects of such a constitution may be to immerse all orders of men in their separate pursuits of pleasure, which they may now enjoy with little disturbance; or of gain, which they may preserve without any attention to the commonwealth.'. *Essay*, p. 210.

[98] *Essay*, p. 160

[99] *Essay*, p. 210.

Policy'[100] One of the tensions between emergent liberalism and republicanism to which he was most sensitive revolved around the relationship between public duty and private autonomy. While he was pleased to note the increasingly high levels of personal liberty that accompanied progress, he remained wary of the effects of progress upon moral character and on the willingness of people to act for the public. The traditional opposition between private wealth and public virtue is a mistaken one for '[h]uman society has great obligations to both'.[101] Accordingly it is important to devise institutional and cultural means for serving both sets of concerns. Unlike his classical mentors, then, Ferguson sought to separate technological and material development from the moral and psychological realms.[102] Community and commerce, wealth and virtue, civic *élan* and private liberty; all could be balanced rather than played off against each other. This at least was Ferguson's hope, though his attempted reconciliation of the two sets of goals was never decisive.[103] Indeed, ambivalence about wealth and progress could be described as the keynote of his *oeuvre*. Much of this apparent indecisiveness flows from a conflict between two key commitments: his classical and atavistic prejudices, on the one hand, and his embrace of progress as an effect of the Providentially inspired laws of spontaneous order, on the other.

Ferguson speaks to us simultaneously in two competing languages of eighteenth-century political discourse: the virtue-focused language of civic humanism and the discourse of rights. It would have been difficult for him to choose between his emotional attachment to a fast-disappearing Scottish identity and Scotland's real and immediate economic problems, brought on by the failure of the Darien scheme coupled with 'a series of disastrous harvests' which took place in the 1690s.[104] Progress (in particular acquiescence to the Union and the economic benefits this might bring to Scotland) was not only natural but appeared to be the only way of feeding hungry Scots. Ferguson finds himself in an awkward position here, one that cost him a good deal of intellectual energy in his attempts to work through it.

---

[100]Adam Ferguson, *Reflections Previous to the Establishment of a Militia*, London; R and J. Dodsley, 1756 (hereafter cited as *Reflections*), p. 3.

[101] *Essay*, p. 141. See also A. Kalyvas, and I. Katznelson, 'Adam Ferguson Returns: Liberalism Through a Glass, Darkly', *Political Theory*, Vol. 26 (2), April, 1998, pp. 173-97, pp. 175-6.

[102] Oz-Salzberger, Translating the Enlightenment, p. 113.

[103] As also noted by Richard Sher, 'From Troglodytes to Americans: Montesquieu and the Scottish Enlightenment on Liberty, Virtue, and Commerce', in *Republicanism, Liberty and Commercial Society 1649-1776*, David Wootton, (ed), Stanford: Stanford University Press, 1994, pp. 394-5. Gellner also notes, rightly I think, that Ferguson never convinces himself completely that the wealth/virtue opposition is, in fact, a mistaken one. Gellner, 'Adam Ferguson', p. 68.

[104] Darien was a 'scheme to establish a Scottish colony in the Isthmus of Panama, a failure that cost Scotland approximately a quarter of the country's liquid capital'. Broadie, 'The Scottish Enlightenment', p. 7. In his recent examination of the Act of Union Paul Henderson Scott has criticised historians for exaggerating the 'impoverishment and political turmoil of pre-Union Scotland', suggesting that it is 'probably deliberately concocted propaganda'. P. H. Scott, *The Boasted Refinements: The Consequences of the Union of 1707*, Edinburgh: The Saltire Society, 1999, p. 1.

4.1   Freedom, Authority and Obligation

In his account of civil liberty Ferguson is relatively silent on traditional questions of authority and obligation, agreeing as he did with Hume that such questions would not be very useful for the practice of politics.[105] Under normal conditions he tends to take for granted the principle of authority[106] because he allows legitimacy to rest on custom, convention and the harm principle rather than on some inviolable or foundationalist principle like divine right.

> When we look back to the origin of government, as there is no where an original right of one person to command another, except so far as is necessary to restrain him from harm, we have recourse to convention as the only principle upon which a right to command can accrue to one, or an obligation to obey can be incurred by another. Prior to such convention, we say, *that sovereignty is lodged in the multitude*; but, when we bring these words to the test of any rational application, they amount to no more than this, that prior to convention, everyone has a right to dispose of himself, so far as is consistent with the safety of others: And that the multitude have this right, because made up of individuals, each of whom is possessed of it; but, in what form the multitude is to exercise it, as a collective body, must depend on agreement to which individuals assent. Prior to convention, the majority has not any right to command the minority, more than any one individual has to command another.[107]

Neither does his insistence on the naturalness of the system of rank distinctions denote any equally natural obligation to obey social superiors.[108] We *are* bound to obey properly constituted authority but only if it is not despotic or arbitrary. But if coercion, tyranny and intimidation is the name of the game then resistance and even revolution may be both an inevitable and natural consequence[109] akin to natural phenomena like 'cataracts' and 'torrents', which, as Kettler rightly notes 'the doctrine of right can neither preclude nor comprehend.'[110]

But this does not mean that the individual's right to resist is supreme since Ferguson regards political society as morally and logically prior to the individual. In the normal course of things, that is to say, under non-despotic rule, conformity is advised and required.

> [E]stablishments are meant for the good of the people, and the people also serve to support their establishment. The greatest measure of happiness bestowed on the people, is that by which they are the means of making a happy community; and if the members of a community accommodate themselves to what is best for the state, this is no more than to be, and to do, what is most for their own preservation and welfare.

---

[105] David Kettler, 'The Political Vision of Adam Ferguson', *Studies in Burke and His Time*, Vol. 9 (1) No. 30, 1967, pp. 763-78, pp. 775-6

[106] For example, *P.II.*, p. 291.

[107] *P.II.*, p. 290. For Hume on authority and custom see David Hume, 'Idea of a Perfect Commonwealth', *Essays Moral Political and Literary* (hereafter cited as *Essays*), Eugene F. Miller (ed), Indiana: Liberty Classics, 1987, p. 512.

[108] *P.I.*, p. 257.

[109] *P.II..*, p. 291.

[110] Kettler, 'Ferguson's Principles', p. 214.

Further, the citizen must 'on occasion...submit to personal hardship for the benefit of his country'.[111] Ferguson's position thus seems to be an adaptation of Hugo Grotius' principle of obedience, namely that citizens are duty bound to obey lawfully constituted government, even when rights are violated but not when they are systematically and persistently so.[112] Though Ferguson does speak at times in terms of individual rights,[113] in general he steers away from any talk of natural rights. In this regard his thinking seems to be a typical of a strand of conservative thought that emerged towards the end of the eighteenth century to oppose 'rights of man' type theories. This strand, which Thomas Schofield has identified as conservative or 'theological utilitarianism' (distinct from a Bentham-like scientific utilitarianism) was best represented in the writings of William Paley. On this view virtue consisted in 'doing good to mankind, in obedience to the will of God, and for the sake of everlasting happiness'. Subjects are bound to obey government according to the following sequence:

> God willed human happiness; civil society was conducive to that end; and so long as the interest of society required it, that is so long as the established government could not be opposed or changed without public inconvenience, it was the will of God that the established government be obeyed.[114]

According to Ferguson, the 'rights of man' approach wrongly tries to cast what are really 'adventitious rights' as natural or 'original'. 'Possession, property and command' (command being 'a right to the services or obediences of other men') are all adventitious and therefore a 'matter of discussion', rather than entitlements to be taken as given. They are worthy of recognition 'only so far as they are proved'. There is no divine right of kings any more than there is any natural right to popular sovereignty. After all, '[n]o-one can have a right to what is not possible, or not real'.[115]

Thus, Ferguson generally tends to avoid hard-and-fast-rules where politics is concerned. The art of governing and of being governed is more of an *ad hoc* and practical exercise in which questions of how rulers and ruled should get along need to be continually worked out. As David Kettler notes correctly, Ferguson is 'among the first and also one of the few serious political thinkers who stress the continuing political effects of actions taken by those who are not themselves rulers.'[116] The duties and activities of the public are of vital interest because history has 'abundantly shown', particularly in republics, that public virtue and political efficacy 'are proportioned to the concern which numbers are permitted to take in the

---

[111] *P.II.*, p. 412.

[112] Two other Scottish thinkers (David Fordyce and Thomas Reid) adopted this same principle. Oz-Salzberger, *Translating the Enlightenment*, p. 104.

[113] These 'original rights' are basically derived from the natural laws of self preservation and society combined and are reducible to the right to self-defence and freedom from harm. *Institutes*, pp.172-4. See also *Institutes*, p. 168. He also alludes to a natural right to dispose of 'natural talents'. *Essay*, p. 63.

[114] T.M. Schofield, 'Conservative Political Thought in Britain in Response to the French Revolution', *The Historical Journal*, Vol. 29 (3), 1986, pp. 601-22, pp. 605-7. There were three strands of conservative thought: 'utilitarianism, contract and natural law' (ibid).

[115] *Institutes*, p. 174.

[116] Kettler, 'The Political Vision of Adam Ferguson', pp. 775-6

affairs of their community...in national councils, in offices of state, or public services of any sort'.[117]

5. CIVIL SOCIETY

What does Ferguson mean when he refers to the central concept of 'civil society'? This is not an easy question to answer because Ferguson himself is not always clear or consistent in his use of the idea, sometimes slipping between his own and the conventional use of the term, namely, as being synonymous with 'polished' or developed society.

The term civil society, which is thought to have originated in ancient jurisprudence, has meant different things at different stages of history. In the middle ages it was a term used to distinguish ecclesiastical institutions from other forms of association. By the seventeenth century it denoted the state of living 'under government' apart from a state of nature. By the eighteenth century it referred to 'a type of society which was larger than and different from a tribe'[118] and which was more advanced and 'civilized' than rude or barbarous types.[119] It wasn't until G.W.F. Hegel that civil society began to be thought of as separate and distinct from the state. But for Ferguson the market, the state and all its legal and political institutions are all generally understood to be part of civil society[120] even though there are times when it is clear that he also perceives the state and the market as threats to non-state and voluntary political activity.[121] Yet, for the most part, he seems to conflate all spheres into the one entity, 'civil society'. The history of civil society is thus a history of progress in political and legal institutions, social structure, arts, sciences, manners, population, literature, production, consumption, wealth and liberty.[122] It is a history of society and the polity broadly understood, referring to a process of development by which people gradually refine political society and 'regulate their relationships' and conflicts legally, where 'civility' and order reign, 'national concert' is achieved and the population is civically active.[123]

---

[117] *P.I.*, p. 266.

[118] Edward Shils, 'The Virtue of Civil Society', *Government and Opposition*, Vol. 26 (1) Winter 1991, pp. 3-20, p. 5.

[119] Varty, 'Civil or Commercial?', pp. 30-1.

[120] 'The fact that Hegel read and used Ferguson's work, and that it was Ferguson's *Essay* in its German translation which helped to make the notion of 'bürgerliche Gesellschaft' fashionable in German scholarly circles, is one of the ironies pervading the history of ideas'. Oz-Salzberger, Introduction to *Essay*, p. xix..

[121] As John Keane has argued in relation to thinkers of the eighteenth century generally. John Keane (ed) *Civil Society and the State: New European Perspectives*, London: Verso, 1988, p. 65.

[122] Varty, 'Civil or Commercial?', pp. 30-1. Pocock, *Virtue, Commerce and History*, p. 194.

[123] Krishan Kumar, 'Civil Society: An Inquiry into the Usefulness of an Historical Term', *The British Journal of Sociology*, Vol. 44 (3) September 1993, pp. 375-95, p. 377. *Essay*, p. 28.

But it is important to appreciate that civil society has no point of inception for Ferguson. [124] Since there never was a state of nature and since humans have always lived in some sort of political order, civil society has always existed. Ferguson's history tracks the progress of a state that is coeval with the species. Civil society is originally characterised by transitory institutions, a diffusion of authority and deployment of organised violence and a more even, that is to say, egalitarian social structure. It proceeds through various stages to more formal, refined, centralised and permanent institutions characterised by structured rank distinctions and hierarchies in which the majority turn away from martial duties towards the concerns of production.[125]

Because he was less triumphalist about progress and less interested in the economy than some of his Scottish contemporaries, Ferguson's stadial history is based on social and political as well as economic/means of subsistence categories[126] in his efforts to track the changes to effective political condition within stages of civil society. Whereas many of his contemporaries saw history as an inexorable march towards better and more refined states of social and political effectiveness, Ferguson is more cautious. Progress brings some gains in effective political condition but it also brings costs. Social cohesion and the solidary passions are damaged on the one hand, but on the other, there is an expansion of freedom and legal rights as well as a diffusion of wealth and therefore economic independence, all of which latter developments have a tendency to *enable* and *enrich* political society.[127] The terms 'civilised' and 'polished' are not, therefore, synonymous for Ferguson. Polished societies are characterised by sophisticated modes of production and consumption, by permanent and formal political and legal institutions and by a refinement in manners. And yet '[c]ivilisation has been conspicuous in nations,[128] who made little progress in commerce, or the arts on which it proceeds.' The Romans, for example, 'had formed a very accomplished republic, and exhibited many an illustrious character; whilst, in respect to family estate and manner of life, they were nearly in the condition of peasants and husbandmen'.[129] 'Polished' society

---

[124] Thus, as Oz-Salzberger notes, 'Ferguson would not subscribe to Rousseau's famous dictum in his *Discours sur l'inegalite* (1755) that the first appropriator of land was "the real founder of civil society"'. Introduction to *Essay*, xviii.

[125] Gellner, 'Adam Ferguson and the Surprising Robustness of Civil Society', p. 121.

[126] His schema is: 'savage', 'barbarous' and 'polished' whereas Smith's, for example, is hunting, pasturage, agricultural and commercial.

[127] Barbarous societies are more virtuous, intimate and cohesive but they are also more prone to 'religious superstition' and its accompanying 'cruelty and malicious effect towards mankind'. *P.I.*, p. 305. Although the 'savage is personally free' and equal with others, s/he lacks the 'liberty' that can only come with 'good policy' and a 'regular administration of justice'. *Essay*, p. 247.

[128] Ferguson seems to hold to a fairly uncontroversial (not to mention vague) definition of 'nation' as denoting a group of people within a given territory. For a discussion of the meaning of the term 'nation' in the eighteenth century see Christopher Berry, 'Nations and Norms', *The Review of Politics*, Vol. 43, 1981, pp. 74-87, p. 77.

[129] *P.I.*, p. 252.

is commercial society,[130] whereas 'civilised' society is something that humans have achieved at every stage of their development.[131]

6. A TRANSITIONAL THINKER

Ferguson's philosophy is complicated by the fact that it reflects a transitional phase in Western political and social thought. It is eccentric because it straddles traditions in two important respects: firstly, it is at once theological and secular, anchored in natural religion yet oriented towards the concerns of modern sociology. Secondly, while it constantly refers to classical antiquity with nostalgic admiration it has many modern, indeed precocious aspects. Though many Ferguson commentators are inclined to group him in either the republican or proto-liberal camp, I hope to show that his entire body of work represents a sustained effort to nudge a space *between* classical civic humanism, on the one hand, and emergent liberalism on the other, in order to create a tradition all its own, a kind of 'liberal-Stoicism'.[132]

While he is not always successful, this attempt yields some remarkable results. It often seems as though Ferguson's world-view is shaped by the abiding issue of how much he is prepared to concede to modernity and proto-liberalism, on the one hand, and the depth of his loyalties to antique sources (mainly in the form of Roman Stoicism). This study aims to locate Ferguson within traditions as closely as is possible given his many divided loyalties. Such conflicts include the following: He simultaneously embraces and regrets progress; he criticises any form of radical reform yet seems to welcome the early stages of the French Revolution; he insists that beneficence and sociability are the perfection of virtue and yet valorises martial vigour, aggression and even violence; he often speaks as a Stoic cosmopolite in an abstract and religious sense, yet was loyal to Britain politically, and equally loyal to Scotland[133] culturally and emotionally. The rationale for Ferguson's appointment to the Black Watch Regiment captures the uniqueness of his position. What made him such an attractive candidate was his possession of a 'very rare combination of

---

[130] See *Essay*, editors note Z, p. 213, where it is indicated that Ferguson uses the terms interchangeably.

[131] Even so, Oz-Salzberger draws our attention to the fact that Ferguson obviously struggled with these categories. In the first edition of the *Essay* he noted: 'The term polished, if we may judge from its etymology, originally referred to the state of nations in respect to their laws and government'. In the 1768 edition he added: 'and men civilised were men practiced in the duty of citizens'. To the sentence which follows there is an addition: 'and men civilised are scholars, men of fashion and traders'. *Essay*, p. 195 and Editor's note.

[132] This attempt was first noticed by John Brewer who wrote: 'Ferguson marks the point where sociological discourse on the structure of society begins to emerge out of the discourse of civic humanism'. Brewer, 'Adam Ferguson and the Division of Labour', p. 26. Brewer also observes the tension between Ferguson's civic humanism on the one hand, and his proto-sociology on the other, in his excellent article 'Adam Ferguson and the Theme of Exploitation', pp. 461-478. John Pocock has described the Scottish fusion in general as 'commercial humanism' (Pocock, *Virtue, Commerce and History*, p. 194) though, in Ferguson's case the fusion is less integrated.

[133] Though he occasionally refers to Scotland as 'North Britain' in private correspondence. This was not uncommon after 1707. Broadie, *The Scottish Enlightenment*, p. 58.

qualifications' namely a 'command of Gaelic', on the one hand, and 'loyalty to Hanover', on the other.[134]

Ferguson's personal political convictions are also difficult to pin down. On the one hand, he appears as a Tory with his intense concern for the maintenance of order but stands with the Whigs in his commitment to the principles of liberty and their opposition to the Jacobites. His use of Roman history to celebrate the Republic is typically Whiggish and yet he opposed all notions of grand reform. Further, his support of Republics is highly qualified.[135]

Because his commitments and orientations often appear to be in conflict, Ferguson is an intriguing, sometimes confounding figure. His system is replete with tensions, paradoxes, even contradictions, many of which are reconcilable but only after some determined textual effort and considerable forbearance on the part of the reader, not only for the lack of systemisation, but for the deep sense of ambivalence to which Ferguson appears content, at times, to consign his reader.

Above all, Ferguson is a practical thinker. He does not moralise for the sake of an abstract idea but in order to find ways of maximising human happiness. Like the pragmatic and influential Roman Stoics he idealised and sought to imitate, Ferguson insisted that philosophy must be of practical use to the community. And it must bear some resemblance to the facts of life. The world is not as simple as some philosophers seem to think, and more often than not it is the unseen, unplanned, sub-rational and seemingly pernicious forces that bring forth order. Accordingly, Ferguson's is a complex, messy and somewhat inelegant system. As David Kettler notes perceptively, Ferguson's thought 'puzzles those who like to classify political thinkers according to so-called 'ideological' patterns'. He 'offers us a vision hard to classify' and yet, at the same time, one that is 'easy to apply to the world that we know' that is to say, one characterised by differentiation, 'conflict and uncertainty' and 'where every political choice exacts costs and poses the next political problem'.[136]

Ferguson does not always exhibit the refinement of a Smith or a Hume, and there are times when his discourse seems banal and pedestrian. But there are also moments of true brilliance, originality and imaginativeness. He was not, as posterity sometimes remembers him, merely an associate of Smith and Hume but rather someone who met them on equal terms, quarrelled with and supported them and sometimes helped to shape not only their ideas,[137] but those of equally impressive, later figures.

Though it would be impossible to appreciate Ferguson's achievement without some attention to history and historicisation, this book is a study of his *ideas*, his

---

[134] Kettler, 'The Political Vision of Adam Ferguson', pp. 777-8.

[135] But to put his situation in context it should be noted that, although these tensions are striking to today's reader, it is doubtful that Ferguson himself would have felt them as acutely since party labels in the eighteenth-century were 'notoriously ambiguous'. Addison Ward, 'The Tory View of Roman History', *Studies in English Literature, 1500-1900*, Vol, 4 (3), 1964, pp. 413-56.

[136] Kettler, 'The Political Vision of Adam Ferguson', pp. 776-7.

[137] As Broadie notes, the Scottish literati treated thinking as a 'social activity'; they were 'writers who committed their writings to the public domain [and who] discussed and disputed with each other in public'. *The Scottish Enlightenment*, p. 20.

moral, social and political thought, rather than his life, his milieu or his specific place in history. To this end, I aim to show where he stands in terms of the prevailing and emerging intellectual traditions of his time. But I'm even more interested in looking at how his thought works as a conceptual *system* and this includes exploring any problems or irregularities within it. And it *is* a system, a coherent, if somewhat tension-ridden one, and not a mish-mash of conflicts and incompatible commitments as it first appears (and as many commentators have concluded). Finally, I'm interested in assessing Ferguson's achievement and the ways in which his ideas might resonate with the contemporary reader.

CHAPTER 2

READING FERGUSON

1. SUBSTANCE AND BACKGROUND OF FERGUSON'S WRITINGS

Ferguson was a somewhat disorderly, prolix scholar but there is an underlying harmony to his body of thought. It has a kind of organic unity that is perceptible once the complex of what might be called 'filiation boundaries' in his work has been mapped out carefully. Ferguson was a literary bowerbird, who, in developing any particular idea, borrowed from a multiplicity of sometimes disparate sources. But he rarely strayed from the set of core beliefs and methodological axioms that he established early in his career. Out of an extensive pool of ideas and influences he constructed his system of thought and the overarching theme of natural and spontaneous order around which it is built. Since moral philosophy was such a broad discipline in Ferguson's time any reader intent on understanding his thought is drawn into a vast range of subjects, among them history, 'pneumatics' or psychology, politics, ethics, theology and anthropology, all of which Ferguson manages to fuse together to create something that is distinctively his.

Ferguson published widely. His first major publication, *An Essay on the History of Civil Society* (1767) had seven editions during his life.[138] It was a resounding success and, along with his third book, *Institutes of Moral Philosophy* (1769), made him famous.[139] The *Analysis of Pneumatics and Moral Philosophy* (a textbook published in 1766), the *Institutes* and *Principles of Moral and Political Science* (1792) were all based on his lecture notes. The *Analysis* had been a prototype for the *Institutes* which was, in turn, a prototype for the *Principles.* They were all fundamentally ethical in nature. Whereas the *Essay* is really *about* history, Ferguson's *History of the Progress and Termination of the Roman Republic* (1783) is a more of a straightforward 'Kings and Queens' history.

Aside from these five major published works, Ferguson produced a large body of published and unpublished essays. His first publication was a pamphlet entitled *A Sermon Preached in the Ersh Language to His Majesty's Highland Regiment of Foot* (1746). In 1756 he published *Reflections Previous to the Establishment of a Militia* followed by *The Morality of Stage Plays Seriously Considered* (1757). Authorship of the 1761 pro-militia pamphlet *History of the Proceedings in the Case of Margaret Commonly called Peg, only Lawful Sister to John Bull, Esq.* (1761) has

---

[138] Fania Oz-Salzberger's edition of the *Essay* (used throughout) is a reproduction of the first (Edinburgh 1767) edition in which all changes to subsequent editions are noted by the editor.

[139] Oz-Salzberger, Introduction to *Essay*, pp. xvi-xvii.

been questioned but it is now generally accepted that Ferguson was its author.[140] Ferguson's pamphlet dealing with his opposition to the American War of Independence came out in 1776. Its short title is *Remarks on a Pamphlet Lately Published by Dr Price*. Ferguson's last published works were biographical in nature. His 'Minutes of the Life and Character of Joseph Black' (1801) was printed in the *Royal Society of Edinburgh Transactions*, while *Biographical Sketch or Memoir of Lieutenant-Colonel Patrick Ferguson* came out in 1816.[141] Most of these publications were well received and Ferguson was a respected, sometimes celebrated, writer in his day.[142] We are also able to enjoy his unpublished philosophical essays, which, presumably he intended to publish but which were not edited and reproduced until late last century.[143] Most are thought to have been written after 1799.[144]

Unfortunately, there is no hidden reserve or *nachlass* of Fergusonia waiting to be discovered. Like Smith before him and equally distrustful of publishers, Ferguson destroyed all his unwanted papers in 1810,[145] but we do have his letters and some important papers which have been recently assembled and edited in a highly accessible form. These provide a privileged insight into areas of Ferguson's thinking previously remote from view.[146]

Despite the relative heterogeneity of Ferguson's writings, the scholar's task is simplified by a general consistency of moral and political viewpoint throughout his corpus. Naturally, as in any large and disparate body of work, there are discrepancies to be found but these are generally of an inconsequential nature.[147] It

---

[140] For a discussion here see Fagg, *Biographical Introduction*, p. cv,, note 116.

[141] Patrick Ferguson was the son of Ann Murray and James Ferguson of Pitfour. Fagg, *Biographical Introduction*, p. xcviii.

[142] For example, there were six editions of the *Essay* and it was translated into French, German, Swedish, Russian and Italian. Fagg, *Biographical Introduction*, p. xl. For a detailed commentary on Ferguson's various publishing successes see ibid, *passim* and also by the same author: *Adam Ferguson: Scottish Cato*, Unpublished Doctoral Dissertation, University of North Carolina at Chapel Hill, 1968.

[143] First by Winifred Philip, *The Unpublished Essays of Adam Ferguson*, in 3 Vols, Edited and Published Privately, Argull: 1986, and more recently by Yasuo Amoh. Adam Ferguson, *Collection of Essays*, Edited and with an Introduction by Yasuo Amoh, Kyoto: Rinsen Book Co., 1996.

[144] The essays lack dates but watermarks from the paper used indicate that they were written between 1799 and 1808. Amoh, 'Introduction' to Adam Ferguson, *Collection of Essays*, p. xviii.

[145] In fact, Ferguson assisted Smith in the task of burning his unpublished manuscripts and papers. V. Merolle, 'Preface' to Adam Ferguson, *Correspondence,* Vol. 1, p. x.

[146] See *Correspondence*, Volumes 1 and 2. Papers not reproduced in this and Amoh's collection of essays are held in the MS collection at the University of Edinburgh library. The most consequential of these are his lecture notes.

[147] Sher suggests that Ferguson's enthusiasm for Reid and common sense philosophy in the *Principles* was not present in his other works. R.B.Sher, *Church and University in the Scottish Enlightenment*, Princeton: Princeton University Press, 1985, p.313. But as early as the *Essay*, Ferguson indicates that his research is being conducted on common sense principles. See, for example, *Essay*, p. 8. Forbes thinks that Ferguson may have re-thought his position on the myth of the Great Legislator in his later work, the *History*. Introduction to *Essay*. p. xxiv. Although it is true that Ferguson refers in this work to particular 'persons on whom the fate of the Roman empire was to depend' this is probably more a by-product of its being a standard 'Kings and Queens' history than anything else. Adam Ferguson, *The History of the Progress and Termination of the Roman Republic*, London: Jones and Company, 1834 edition, (hereafter cited as *History*), p. 110. In any case, there are still signs of Ferguson's continuing commitment to the

has been suggested that Ferguson's *Sermon Preached in the Ersh Language* is his only work Calvinist in nature'.[148] Because the *Analysis* and *Institutes* were explicitly pedagogical in nature, covering 'all the topics which Ferguson deemed appropriate for the edification of young men',[149] some potentially inappropriate topics were excluded, while other conventionally pious ones — omitted from the *Principles* — are included.[150] Nevertheless, both works contain much of interest and are compatible with the rest of Ferguson's thought. It is also worth noting that Ferguson's attempt at conjectural history is mainly limited to the *Essay*,[151] though there is no evidence that he lost faith in the method over time since he employs the insights he gained from it in his later work. A number of scholars have suggested that Ferguson's interest in retrogression and the corrupting effects of commercialisation waned and even disappeared by the time he wrote the *Principles*.[152] In fact, Ferguson maintained an interest in the corruption theme throughout his entire corpus, including the *Principles*.

A number of developments over time in Ferguson's thinking also bear mentioning here. The most conspicuous of these is his attitude to the French Revolution. Like many in Europe and Britain Ferguson initially had a fairly positive attitude to the Revolution.[153] He seems to have perceived it as an instance of vigorous republican activism and egalitarianism,[154] predicting that it would make the French 'better neighbours' in Asia and Europe than they had been previously.[155] Though Ferguson generally decried radical change of any kind he considered 'tumults' to be acceptable under extreme conditions, and pre-revolutionary France seems to have qualified as such a case. The French monarchy had been rotten to the core, vitiated by its blind pursuit of 'pleasure' and its fetishistic attitude to inherited rank. It was, Ferguson noted, fraught with 'imbecilities and difficulties…in every department'.[156] He did not sound very worried when he wrote to John Mcpherson in 1790 that the French were 'bussy translating their Monarchy into a Democracy'.[157]

---

idea in that work. See, for example, *History*, pp. 12, 419, 449. Ferguson also remains committed in this later work to the belief elaborated in his earlier work that historical progress is, by and large, asymptotic. *History*, p. 170.

[148] Charles Camic, *Experience and Enlightenment; Socialisation for Cultural Change in Eighteenth Century Scotland*, Chicago: University of Chicago Press, 1983, pp. 55-6.

[149] Kettler, *Social and Political Thought of Adam Ferguson*, p. 7.

[150] These subjects were entitled: 'Of the Being of God' and 'Of the Attributes of God'.

[151] As pointed out by John Brewer. 'Conjectural History, Sociology and Social Change', p. 18.

[152] See Pascal, 'Property and Society', pp.174-5; D. Kettler, 'Ferguson's Principles; Constitution in Permanence', *Studies in Burke and His Time*, Vol 19, 1978, pp. 208-22, p. 209; Lois Whitney, *Primitivism and the Idea of Progress*, Baltimore: The Johns Hopkins Press, 1934, p.153.

[153] As Thomas Schofield has noted: 'The commencement of the French revolution was greeted among governing circles in Britain with a mixture of surprise, regret and self-satisfaction, but not hostility'. Schofield, 'Conservative Political Thought in Britain', p. 602.

[154] The revolutionaries were 'struck with democracy as with a Spark of Electricity or a Stroke of Lightening and have continued charged even since'. Letter to Alexander Carlyle, October 2, 1797, *Correspondence*, No. 332, II, p. 423.

[155] Letter to John Mcpherson, January 19, 1790, No. 265, *Correspondence*, II, p. 337; Kettler, *Social and Political Thought of Adam Ferguson*, p. 94.

[156] Oz-Salzberger, *Translating the Enlightenment*, p. 104.

[157] Letter to John Macpherson, July 31, 1790, *Correspondence*, No. 269, II, p. 340.

Nevertheless, like many others, his complacency would eventually turn to dismay when it became clear that the Jacobins ruled by terror.[158] Though he continued to insist that the French court had been corrupt and therefore deserving of overthrow (writing that he was glad to see the demise of the 'frivolous corrupted pretenders to aristocracy')[159] he regarded the Jacobins as architects of 'a tyranny more bloody and terrible than any that is known in the history of mankind.'[160] In addition, France was increasingly regarded as a fearsome 'Hydra' who threatened the security of Britain as well as the rest of Europe. Ferguson thought that under Napoleon (the new Caesar) the Republic could only survive by aggressive militaristic imperialism.[161] By the mid to late 1790's he regarded the French republic as epitomising two evils, '[large scale] Democracy and Atheism'.[162] Together they represented in Ferguson's mind 'Antichrist himself'.[163]

A number of other shifts are worth mentioning. Firstly, Ferguson seems much more amenable in his early work to the idea of a broadened franchise. In the *Institutes* he entertains the idea that 'the inferior class' should be given veto power over the 'determinations of the aristocracy' or else be given the right to choose 'those who are to act for them'.[164] This theme, at least in its explicit applications, is absent from the later works.

Further, Ferguson seems to have withdrawn his support for *Ossian* in his later years. In a letter he wrote to Henry Mackenzie in the late 1790s he distanced himself from Macpherson, admitting that he had long suspected the latter of taking 'liberties' in the production of the epic poems.[165] Towards the end of his life he also seems to be less committed to republican values and the dangers of imperialism, advocating harsh military action in relation to the American rebels, opposing Irish independence and refusing to support the Yorkshire reform movement led by Christopher Wyvill. In general, his attitude to all plans of reform seemed to harden with the years and with exposure to the realities of political change.[166]

---

[158] 'Of the French Revolution with its Actual and Still Impending Consequences in Europe', *Collection of Essays*, No. 14, p. 134.

[159] Letter to John Macpherson, July 15, 1799, *Correspondence*, No. 354, II. p. 455.

[160] 'Of the French Revolution with its Actual and Still Impending Consequences in Europe', *Collection of Essays*, No. 14, pp. 134-5.

[161] Kettler, *Social and Political Thought of Adam Ferguson*, p. 94; Letter to John Macpherson, March 1796, *Correspondence*, No. 308, II. pp. 384-5.

[162] Letter to Alexander Carlyle, November 23, 1796, *Correspondence*, II, No. 322, p. 408.The French army 'must have foreign Ennemies to devour or will devour at home'. Letter to John Mcpherson, September 26, 1797, *Correspondence*, II, No. 331, p. 420.

[163] Letter to Alexander Carlyle, November 23, 1796, *Correspondence*, No. 322, I, p. 408. Nevertheless he declared himself impressed by Bonaparte's institution of the Legion of Honour '[a]s a proper incentive system for all military establishments, including the British'. Fagg, *Biographical Introduction, Correspondence*, I, p. lxxxii. See Letter to Henry Dundas, August 2, 1802, *Correspondence*, No. 369, pp. 480-1.

[164] *Institutes*, pp. 272-3.

[165] Letter to Henry MacKenzie, 26 March, 1798, *Correspondence*, No. 337, II, pp. 430-1.

[166] Though it should be noted that Ferguson's attitude to rapid reform and the 'overthrow' of institutions was always negative. See, for example, *Institutes*, pp. 293-4. Ferguson was not the only British thinker whose enthusiasm for republicanism was dampened by the American and French revolutions. According to Mark Philp, these events 'anathematised republican rhetoric' and 'locked the

Overall, though, there is a reasonable degree of coherence in Ferguson's thought. Despite the vast breadth (and occasional incompatibility) of his inspirational sources, the basic contours of his world-view are reasonably stable. The problem for Ferguson scholars is to locate accurately its parameters. Like a number of other Ferguson commentators,[167] Alan Smith has also noted this consistency of views throughout yet he also observes that Ferguson requires his readers to do some heavy conceptual work of their own; to mentally glue his individual ideas together into a coherent system. 'While Ferguson takes great care in formulating each observation, he leaves the system to be culled out by the reader.'[168] This is a fair assessment of the task set before any reader of Ferguson. In addition, Ferguson, by his own admission, is careless about citing his sources[169] and his style is rambling and prolix. Consequently there is a good deal of legwork to be performed. Having done that, the pieces tend to fall neatly into place. In a sense, then, this book is an attempt to organise and arrange these pieces more systematically and to counter claims that his thought lacks any system.

Although Ferguson nowhere expounds a synthetic theory of history his writings may be thought of as a collection of 'first principles' loosely connected by 'a historical narrative'.[170] He is striving towards a sociological science of history; historical in being 'a collection of facts in description or narration' and scientific in 'identifying general rules...to explain particulars'.[171] Ferguson's conception of social science is connected to his meta-theory of nature's equilibrium. It is an extremely complex edifice that reflects his desire to avoid representing the world in tidy, abstract simplicity and to describe it as he believes it really is, in all its complexity, variety and apparent disorderliness. His explanation for the evolution and maintenance of human institutions defies reduction to a few neat variables. Instead a multiplicity of forces is portrayed as instrumental in the process, among them appetites, short-term rationality, habit, conflict and adversity, environmental factors, and even human weakness. The various forces are highly interactive and Ferguson denies the appropriateness of separating them as discrete variables.

Though there are identifiable laws governing the social world, they are myriad and can usually only be appreciated at a distance. Human affairs cannot be comprehended under a few simple laws. There are always exceptions and the role of environment, culture and free will often intervene to obscure the picture. Ferguson finds that most of his friends, colleagues and adversaries are too anxious to oversimplify in favour of a favourite system.

British state into a dogged resistance to popular participation'. Mark Philp, 'English Republicanism in the 1790s', *The Journal of Political Philosophy*, Vol. 6 (30), 1998, pp. 235-62, p. 270.

[167] See, for example, Willke, *The Historical Thought of Adam Ferguson, passim*. David Kettler notes that 'Ferguson never changed the general tendency of his opinions'. *Social and Political Thought of Adam Ferguson*, p.153. According to Lois Whitney, Ferguson's commitment to the conception of a 'great chain of being' is present in all his works, including the last. Whitney, *Primitivism and the Idea of Progress*, pp.150-1.

[168] Smith, *The Political Philosophy of Adam Ferguson*, pp. 24-5.

[169] *P.I.*, p. 8; *Essay*, p. 66.

[170] Bryson, *Man and Society*, pp. 41-2.

[171] *Institutes*, pp. 2-3.

> In collecting the materials of history, we are seldom willing to put up with our subject
> merely as we find it. We are loth to be embarrassed with a multiplicity of particulars,
> and apparent inconsistencies. In theory we profess the investigation of general
> principles; and in order to bring the matter of our inquiries within the reach of our
> comprehension, are disposed to adopt any system.[172]

The popular enlightenment mechanistic analogy used to depict social order is rejected in favour of a more supple, organic model which better represents Ferguson's view of social order as variable, dramatic and discordant and yet ultimately integrated. The 'beauty' of society's order 'is not of a quiescent kind'. Rather, 'the whole is alive...in action [and] perpetually changing.'[173] This desire for realism sacrifices elegant simplicity to a qualified and elaborate messiness. The effect is compounded by Ferguson's use of a disparate range of sources in his attempts to theorise about the world about him. He perceives the world through an intricate prism resulting in a kind of patchwork effect which Ferguson himself obliquely acknowledges.[174]

Alan Smith notes, quite rightly, that given the 'diversity and complexity of the corpus...it is not surprising that his body of thought has been widely misinterpreted, though often in ways that do capture some one side of [his] thought'.[175] The pastiche quality of Ferguson's philosophy can be exceedingly misleading. His reader must be at all times conscious that in expounding any particular idea Ferguson may begin by adopting the ideas of one authority, abandon them at the point where they no longer cohere with his world view and proceed to incorporate others. In the case of his teleology, for example, the initial inspiration is Aristotelian,[176] soon abandoned for Newtonianism tempered with Christianity and Stoicism. Another case in point is Ferguson's treatment of self-interest which concedes some significant ground to Smith, and even Mandeville, while holding steadily to certain Christian/Stoic principles.

It is only in the absence of a carefully mapped topography of filiation boundaries that Ferguson's philosophy appears inconsistent. As Jean Willke puts it so sensitively, 'Ferguson's writing is like a mosaic — a beautiful one' with 'many lights and shades and facets' which 'come together in an orderly and intelligible whole.'[177] To appreciate Ferguson fully and to avoid an unjust interpretation of Ferguson as jumbled and confused the reader must pay close attention to these various 'lights and shades'.

Ferguson's commitments are not all mutually exclusive, as some scholars have suggested.[178] His philosophy should, rather, be thought of as complex and

---

[172] *Essay*, p. 21.

[173] *P.I.*, p. 174

[174] *P I.*, pp. 7-8. It was Kettler who first noted this 'patchwork' effect. *The Social and Political Thought of Adam Ferguson*, p. 7.

[175] Smith, *The Political Philosophy of Adam Ferguson,* p. 13.

[176] *P.I.,* p. 312.

[177] Jean Willke, *The Historical Thought of Adam Ferguson*, Unpublished Doctoral Dissertation, Washington D.C: The Catholic University of America, 1962, p. 223.

[178] See, for example, Bernstein, 'Ferguson and Progress', p. 100; Kettler, *Social and Political Thought of Adam Ferguson*, p. 293 and 'Constitution in Permanence', p.213; Charles Camic refers to Ferguson's

composite. Ferguson employs whatever means are 'at hand', using ideas and sources creatively, never hesitating to modify them whenever it seems appropriate and always ready to discard them should other means appear more useful. He is a creative adaptor. 'Polymath' is probably too grand a term for someone who regarded himself more modestly as a 'glean[er]' drawing on the 'inexhaustible field of reflection' laid down by ancient and modern authors and on which he seeks to build.[179] Yet Ferguson was rarely confined by his influences[180] but used them to forge his own unique moral, sociological and historical vision designed along utilitarian rather than aesthetic lines.

2. INFLUENCES

In order to understand Ferguson's place in the history of ideas it is important to appreciate his inspirational sources. As has been noted, these influences were numerous and varied and although his key sources were classical there are many modern influences present in Ferguson's writings. Of his classical influences, the dominant were Stoic, specifically Roman Stoic, a debt he explicitly and repeatedly acknowledges.[181] Except for its fatalistic aspects (which he nevertheless occasionally, albeit softly, endorses) he liked almost everything about Stoicism, from its religious and moral content to its practical advice for living. Ferguson's particular favourites were Marcus Aurelius and Epictetus whom he regarded with intense reverence[182] and they were important authorities on matters moral and theological. Ferguson thought that 'the better part of Roman law was derived' from Stoic doctrine and insisted that it was a source to which 'jurisprudence must ever recur.'[183] So much the Stoic was Ferguson that he commonly referred to himself as

---

'conflicting commitments' (Camic, *Experience and Enlightenment*, p. 54) while Kettler, with specific reference to the progress/decline issue, argues that Ferguson's response 'could in no way be seen to form part of a coherent pattern of ideas'. *Social and Political Thought of Adam Ferguson*, p. 222.

[179] *P.I.* p. viii.

[180] Willke, *The Historical Thought of Adam Ferguson*, p. 228.

[181] See, for example, *P.I.*, pp. 7-8. Norbert Waszek rightly notes that Ferguson's Stoicism follows the Roman accretions. N. Waszek, *Mans Social Nature*, pp. 154-5. See also J. Small, 'Biographical Sketch of Adam Ferguson', *Edinburgh Review*, Vol.75 (255), 1867, pp. 48-85; Lawrence Castiglione, 'Introduction' to the 1973 reprint of *Principles of Moral and Political Science*, New York: AMS Press Incorporated, 1973; Kettler, 'Constitution in Permanence', p. 211 and by the same author, *Social and Political Thought of Adam Ferguson*, pp. 141, 156, 182.

[182] In the *Principles*, Ferguson cites Marcus Aurelius and Epictetus as the finest expositors ever of religious piety, noting that 'such sentiments of a sublime religion may be justly considered as the highest attainments of created intelligence'. Marcus is judged to have attained a species of 'god-like eminence'. *P.I.*, pp. 312, 331-2. Though Ferguson singled out Marcus and Epictetus particularly, he admired all the Stoic philosophers. An awareness of Stoicism probably came to Ferguson via Shaftesbury and Hutcheson. while Montesquieu's fondness for Stoicism undoubtedly reinforced his attraction to its teachings. Montesquieu, *Laws*, 5. 24. 10, pp. 465-466. Ferguson wrote that 'this sect has been revered by those who were acquainted with its real spirit, Lord Shaftesbury, Montesquieu...Mr. Hutchison (sic) and many others'. *P.I.*, p. 8. Although Ferguson's most admired mentors were disciples of Stoicism, the particular variation he proffers is his alone.

[183] *P.I.*, p. 8

'the Old Roman' while the Edinburgh Review dubbed him 'the Scottish Cato'.[184] Ferguson was not the only member of the Scottish literati to be influenced by Stoicism. Smith, for example, has long been regarded as an adherent.[185] Stoicism enjoyed a popular revival in eighteenth century Scotland and the Christian-Stoic synthesis was widely embraced.[186] But none of Ferguson's contemporaries relied so heavily on Stoicism for interpreting social life, particularly where Nature's apparent evils and contradictions were concerned.

Like Ferguson in his own time, Marcus Aurelius represented a 'transitional phase of thought' in Stoicism. There is less emphasis on self-sufficiency and a greater readiness to reflect on our need for improvement. Rather than focusing on the classic Stoic virtue of pride, Marcus Aurelius' emphasis on service and benevolence reflects an anticipation of the Christian virtue of humility which Ferguson takes up.[187] There are also residual traces of the pantheism of Stoicism in Ferguson. Christianity, of course, owes a large debt to Stoicism. The 'Holy Spirit' of Christian theology presents itself originally as the 'creative fire' or spirit of the universe in Stoic theology while Christ is described in the fourth gospel as the *logos*, a Stoic term meaning word or reason. The belief that we are God's offspring is also held jointly by Christians and Stoics, as is the doctrine of a final conflagration. The practice of asceticism is common to both, both systems are perfectibilist and both venerate sages as exemplars of perfection.[188] Francis Hutcheson (Marcus Aurelius' translator and a key Fergusonian influence) resolved all virtue into benevolence, the philosophical counterpart of Christian love, while Marcus Aurelius stressed the importance of the solidary virtues of '*humanitas*' (benevolence), '*sympathia*' (our organic relationship to one another) and communalism.[189] 'Nature', he wrote, 'has constituted rational beings for their own mutual benefit, each to help his fellows according to their worth, and in no wise to do them hurt.'[190] He stressed that selflessness was its own reward[191] and believed that we were created expressly to serve the 'common welfare' and to perform 'deeds of kindness'[192] Both Epictetus

---

[184] To his friend, George Dempster, he was known as 'my modern Epictetus'. Fagg, *Adam Ferguson: Scottish Cato*, p. 264.

[185] See Waszek, *Man's Social Nature*, Chapter 4, and, by the same author, 'Two Concepts of Morality: The Distinction of Adam Smith's Ethics and its Stoic Origin', *Journal of the History of Ideas*, Vol. 44 (4), 1984, pp. 591-606. See also MacFie and Raphael, Introduction to *TMS*, pp. 5-10. I have suggested elsewhere that Smith was far less the Stoic than Ferguson. Hill, 'Ferguson and Smith on Human Nature', *passim*.

[186] M.A. Stewart, 'The Origins of the Scottish Greek Chairs', in *Owls to Athens: Essays on Classical Subjects*, E.M. Craik (ed), Oxford, Clarendon Press, 1990, p. 399 and, by the same author, M.A. Stewart, 'The Stoic Legacy in the Early Scottish Enlightenment', in M.J. Osler (ed), *Atoms, Pneuma and Tranquillity*, Cambridge: Cambridge University Press, 1991. See also Sher, *Church and University*, esp. Chapter 8 and Waszek, *Man's Social Nature, passim*.

[187] Maxwell Staniforth, 'Introduction' to Marcus Aurelius, *Meditations*, Translated and with an Introduction by Maxwell Staniforth, London: Penguin, 1964, p. 21.

[188] Staniforth, 'Introduction to *Meditations*', pp. 23-6.

[189] D.D.Raphael and A.Macfie, Introduction to *TMS*, pp. 6-7.

[190] Marcus Aurelius, *Meditations*, 9.1. p. 137.

[191] Marcus Aurelius, *Meditations*, 11.4. p. 166.

[192] Marcus Aurelius, *Meditations,* 9.42, p. 149.

and Marcus also held a profound faith in a benign universe in which nothing was ill or evil and where everything, despite appearances, accorded with the divine master-plan. Ferguson shared in all these beliefs.[193]

It is important to be aware that Ferguson is less attracted to the resignation dimension commonly associated with Stoicism (and more dominant in Greek Stoicism) than to the more ardent *Roman* Stoic civic virtues of political vigour and martial valour. Though they are fairly ambiguous on this point, the Stoics seem to have been neither consistent pantheists nor thoroughgoing determinists.[194] Accordingly they regarded social criticism and service as one of their most important roles. Stoicism, particularly in its late Roman days, is less a philosophy of endurance than a philosophy of activism and personal responsibility[195] that is intended to galvanise its adherents into political action. The cultivation of Stoic *apatheia* applies only to events outside our control. Marcus wrote, for example, that a person 'does not sin by commission alone, but often by omission'[196] and his programme of social and legal reform, as well as his considerable military service, is testament to this belief. The resignation and activist dimensions of Roman Stoic thought are reconciled by the fact that the Stoic order is law-driven. Epictetus and Marcus both argued that virtue consists in the acceptance and performance of duties confluent with the secondary identity or station assigned to individuals by Zeus.

> [Y]our purpose is...to return to your country, to relieve the fear of your kinsmen, to do the duties of a citizen yourself, to marry, bring up children, hold the customary offices. For you did not come into the world to select unusually fine places, I ween, but to live and go about your business in the place where you were born and were enrolled as a citizen.[197]

It was expected that sapients would participate in public life unless some practical difficulty prevented them.[198] They did not believe that they were relieved of any civic duty, quite the opposite.[199] The inclination to participate in public life flows naturally from our desire to 'safeguard and protect' our fellow human

---

[193] *P.I.*, pp. 312-13.

[194] As A.A. Long has argued, 'Stoic determinism does not exclude a coherent theory of voluntary human action [or] moral responsibility'. 'Freedom and Determinism in the Stoic Theory of Human Action', in A. A. Long, (ed.), *Problems in Stoicism*, London: The Althone Press, 1971, p. 174.

[195] Passmore, *Perfectibility of Man*, p. 57. Epictetus, *Enchiridion*, translated by George Long, New York: Prometheus Books, 1991, 5. p. 14.

[196] Marcus Aurelius, *Meditations*, 9. 5. p. 139; Philip Noyen, 'Marcus Aurelius: The Greatest Practitioner of Stoicism', *Antiquite Classique*, Vol.24, 1955, pp. 372-83, p. 378. See also, Epictetus, *Discourses as Reported by Arrian, the Manual and Fragments*, with an English translation by W.A. Oldfather in 2 Vols, London: Harvard University Press, 1989, 2.10. 1-2, p. 275 and Lisa Hill, 'The First Wave of Feminism: Were the Stoics Feminists?', *History of Political Thought*, Vol. 22 (1) 2001, pp. 12-40.

[197] Epictetus, *Discourses*, 2.23. 36-40, p. 417.

[198] M. Griffin, *Seneca, A Philosopher in Politics*, Oxford: Clarendon Press, 1976, p. 331.

[199] *Cosmopolitai* were generally regarded as a link between the immediate community and the wider world due to the fact that they appeared to be 'unusually resilient and self controlled, unusually independent of immediate social approval because they were understood to have a special insight into the laws of the *cosmos*'. S.R.L. Clarke, 'The City of the Wise', *Apeiron*, Vol. 20 (1), 1987, pp. 63-80, p. 74.

beings.[200] Seneca stressed the importance of participation in public affairs while Panaetius encouraged *cosmopolitai*, to behave like any other 'citizen', to enjoy 'the common bond of speech and life', to form and partake in 'public assemblies' and to provide for the material needs of himself, his family and for those others 'he holds dear'.[201] Those Stoics unable to contribute directly to public life (for example, the slave Epictetus) sought to participate indirectly by exerting their influence over elites, commenting on statecraft and public policy and denouncing bad governments.[202] Each assigned station has its attached duties and these, Epictetus suggests, should be observed scrupulously.[203] The assiduous execution of 'daily duties' is virtuous and within the reach of the ordinary person.[204] For the Stoics, virtue is always manifested in particular instances. Specific social roles are associated with particular obligations and 'appropriate actions' *(kathekonta)* and the correct performance of such duties gives rise to a secondary order of virtue, admittedly inferior to the virtue attendant on wisdom, but laudable nevertheless.[205]

But it should be noted that, for the good Stoic, when the eternal laws of Zeus conflict with the worldly laws of 'Caesar' the former always take precedence.[206] Ferguson seems to have struggled with this most important Stoic tenet. Though in some respects he embraces the idea of the *cosmopolis* and a universal siblinghood of rational souls, we shall see that, when pushed, his patriotic and local sympathies take precedence.

In any case, other primary sources were Moderate Scottish Presbyterianism and such important figures as Hugo Grotius, Isaac Newton,[207] Francis Bacon, Lord Shaftesbury, Francis Hutcheson, Charles-Louis Montesquieu,[208] Aristotle, Tacitus, Polybius, Thucydides, and Cicero. The latter was employed as a kind of *de facto* Stoic source. Ferguson makes it clear that Cicero will be recognised mainly in his role as an expositor of (early and middle) Stoicism.[209] Shaftesbury and Hutcheson were both disciples of Roman Stoicism[210] though Ferguson seems to go directly to

---

[200] Cicero, *De Finibus Bonorum et Malorum*, with an English translation by H. Rackham, London, William Heinemann Ltd, 1961, III. p. 68.

[201] Epictetus, *Discourses*, 2.10. 7-13. p. 277.

[202] For a fuller discussion see Lisa Hill, 'The Two Republicae of the Roman Stoics', *Citizenship Studies*, Vol. 4 (1) 2000, pp. 65-79.

[203] Epictetus, *Discourses*, 2.10. 7-13. p. 277.

[204] E.V. Arnold, *Roman Stoicism*, New York: The Humanities Press, 1958, p. 305.

[205] Christopher Gill, 'Personhood and Personality: The Four Person*ae* Theory in Cicero, *De Officiis* I', *Oxford Studies in Ancient Philosophy*, Vol. 6, 1988, pp. 169-200, p. 175.

[206] I. Xenakis, *Epictetus Philosopher-Therapist*, Martinus Nijhoff, The Hague, 1969, p. 126. For a fuller discussion of this point see also Hill, 'The Two Republicae of the Roman Stoics'.

[207] For examples of Ferguson's unreserved praise for Newton see, *P.I.* pp. 200, 312.

[208] For Ferguson's profound admiration of Montesquieu see, for example, *Essay*, p. 66 and 'Biographical Account of the late Dr.Joseph Black', *Royal Society of Edinburgh Transactions*, Edinburgh, Vol. V. (3), 1801, (hereafter referred to as 'Dr.Black') pp.101-117, p. 102. For more details on Ferguson's debt to Montesquieu see Chapters 4 and 9.

[209] *P.I.*, p. 8.

[210] Hutcheson translated the *Meditations* into English. Sher, *Church and University*, p.118. Shaftesbury was well acquainted with the work of both Epictetus and Marcus Aurelius. W.A.Oldfather, 'Introduction to Epictetus', in Epictetus, *Discourses*, p. xxviii. Ferguson shared with Hutcheson a desire to 'mould teenage boys' in the principles of moderate Christianity and Stoicism. R.B. Sher, 'Professors of

the original source for inspiration. Nevertheless, the work of Hutcheson particularly, must have made an impression on Ferguson, particularly since their theodicies share so much in common.[211]

There also appears to be a great deal of Machiavelli in Ferguson and scholars tend to take for granted his influence[212] despite Ferguson's more or less complete refusal to cite him, let alone acknowledge that he ever existed.[213] Machiavelli's thought may have come to Ferguson indirectly. James Harrington popularised Machiavelli's thought and brought it to public attention in the seventeenth century. Mandeville (on whom Ferguson expended much critical energy)[214] also transferred Machiavellian thought to the British public, while Montesquieu (who, it has been claimed, borrowed freely from Machiavelli without proper acknowledgment)[215] is another likely source. But it is also possible that much of the influence attributed to Machiavelli came from the same place Machiavelli found it, namely, Tacitus, Cicero and other classical authorities.

The influence of Rousseau, whose ideas it would have been hard to avoid in the eighteenth century, seems certain even though Ferguson cites him only twice, once on a point of agreement and another, in order to contradict him.[216] There would have been much in Rousseau to irritate him,[217] and Ferguson often seems to be writing in opposition to him. Yet, there are also many parallels in their thinking. Both were preoccupied with civic virtue, 'effeminacy' and the moral and civic costs of progress.[218] Both freely cited Montesquieu,[219] admired Stoicism,[220] believed in the

---

Virtue: The Social History of the Edinburgh Moral Philosophy Chair in the Eighteenth Century', in M.A. Stewart. (ed.), *Studies in the Philosophy of the Scottish Enlightenment,* Oxford: Clarendon Press, 1990, p.119.

[211] For further discussion of Hutcheson's theodicy, see James Moore, 'Hutcheson's Theodicy: The Argument and the Contexts of *A System of Moral Philosophy*', in *The Scottish Enlightenment*, Paul Wood, (ed.), Rochester: University of Rochester Press, 2000. The theodicies of Shaftesbury and Gottfried Leibniz would also have been influences difficult for Ferguson to avoid.

[212] See Kettler, *Social and Political Thought of Adam Ferguson,* p. 7; J.G.A. Pocock, *The Machiavellian Moment*, Princeton: Princeton Univesity Press, 1975, pp. 499-500; Willke, *The Historical Thought of Adam Ferguson*, p.226; Smith, *Adam Ferguson,* p. 391; Forbes, 'Introduction' to *Essay,* pp. xxviii, xxxi.

[213] For a rare exception see *History*, p. 4.

[214] For Ferguson's disapproval of Mandeville see *Essay*, pp. 36-7 and 'Principle of Moral Estimation', *Collection of Essays*, No. 25, p. 231.

[215] Duncan Forbes, 'Scientific Whiggism: Adam Smith and John Millar', *Cambridge Journal*, Vol. 6, 1954, pp. 643-70, p. 660. Montesquieu does, in fact, acknowledge Machiavelli on one occasion as a 'great man'. *Laws*, 1. 6. 5, p. 77. Yet on a second occasion he refers to 'Machiavellianism' disparagingly. *Laws*, 4. 20, p. 389. For remarks on the relationship of Machiavelli to Montesquieu see William Mullen, 'Republics for Expansion: The School of Rome', *Arion*, Vol. 3, 1976, pp. 298-364.

[216] *Essay*, pp. 116, 11. On the belief that Ferguson failed to acknowledge agreement with Rousseau on any point, John Bernstein has rejected the likelihood of Rousseau's having influenced him. J.A. Bernstein, 'Adam Ferguson and the Idea of Progress', *Studies in Burke and His Time*, 19 (2), 1978, pp. 99-118.

[217] Such as his contractarianism; primitivism; emphasis on the importance of an intrusive, regulatory state; view that human needs are naturally sated by the 'simple necessities' available in the state of nature; insistence that the surest sign of good government is population growth; belief that all constitutions have a natural tendency to degenerate and his promulgation of the diffusionist theory of civilisation.

[218] See Rousseau, 'Discourse on the Origin of Inequality', in *Social Contract and Discourses*, p. 57.

innate goodness of humankind,[221] disparaged over-extension[222] centralisation,[223] imperialism and the use of mercenaries,[224] and both proposed early theories of alienation.[225] They also expressed concerns about the growing role in modern life of private interest to the detriment of a concern for the public sphere.[226] Indeed, most of Ferguson's thinking seems to hover in the middle ground between Smith's progressivism, modernism, liberalism and laissez-faire-ism and Rousseau's romantic, egalitarian and *dirigiste* tendencies.

Aside from other Scottish literati like Robertson, Kames, Carlyle and Stuart,[227] Ferguson's good friends Adam Smith and David Hume were also important influences both negative and positive. In some respects he regarded himself as their adversary, frequently railing against them with grudging admiration but sometimes conceding significant ground to them, as will be shown. In particular, he was less convinced than either of them that progress was generally positive. He opposed their perceived utilitarianism and disagreed with their dislike of social conflict. Whereas Smith's attitude to civic virtue and the role of beneficence in social life provoked Ferguson, it was Hume's hedonism and metaphysical and epistemological scepticism that seemed to bother him most, believing as he did that it inevitably led to two of the greatest human errors, atheism and fatalism. These disagreements, as well as those he had with Rousseau, are particularly important in illuminating Ferguson's status as a transitional thinker. Opposition to the egoism of Hobbes, Locke and Mandeville is also a consistent theme, as it was to most thinkers within the Scottish Enlightenment.

It is a commonplace in Fergusonian scholarship to suggest that Ferguson's writings are troubled by contradictions born of his many ambivalences, coupled with his use of a too disparate range of sources. Some see the problem as lack of underlying system[228] while others see his so-called 'conflicting commitments' as being related to his simultaneous embrace of modern and antique values.[229] The

---

[219] For example, following Montesquieu, Rousseau argued that 'the wise legislator does not begin by laying down laws good in themselves, but by investigating the fitness of the people, for which they are destined, to receive them. Rousseau, *Social Contract*, p.17 and also pp. 250-5.

[220] K. F. Roche, *Rousseau: Stoic and Romantic*, London: Methuen, 1974.

[221] As did all the other major figures of the Scottish Enlightenment. Rousseau, 'Discourse on the Origin of Inequality', in *Social Contract and Discourses*, p. 118.

[222] Rousseau, *Social Contract*, pp. 219-21.

[223] Rousseau, *Social Contract*, pp. 263-4.

[224] Rousseau, *A Discourse on Political Economy*, in *Social Contract and Discourses*, pp. 157, 158.

[225] 'This alienation or self-estrangement theme is found earlier than Ferguson's *Essay*, in Rousseau's *Discourse on the Origin of Inequality*, but in Ferguson, the treatment is different' due to an emphasis on the division of labour which is lacking in Rousseau. Forbes, 'Introduction' to *Essay*, p. xxxi.

[226] Rousseau, *Social Contract*, pp. 265-6.

[227] According to Anand Chitnis: 'There were primarily five literati who dominated the social philosophy of their age...David Hume, Adam Smith, William Robertson, Adam Ferguson, and John Millar'. Anand Chitnis, *The Scottish Enlightenment*, London: Croom Helm Ltd., 1976, p. 92.

[228] For example, John Bernstein suggests that Ferguson was 'too unsystematic as a philosopher of history for anyone else to be able to systematise perceptions he left disjointed and hard to reconcile with one another'. Bernstein, 'Adam Ferguson and the Idea of Progess', p.100.

[229] Kettler, *The Social and Political Thought of Adam Ferguson*, p.293, and, by the same author; 'Constitution in Permanence', p.209, pp.221-2; K.G. Ballestrem, 'Sources of the Materialist Conception

suggestion is that his project is incoherent and therefore a failure, or at least a partial one.

Ferguson is undeniably ambivalent about developments in the 'polished' age but his position can be shown to be basically coherent. Notwithstanding the very real tensions, and occasional contradictions, a good deal of his apparent incoherence is attributable to the complexity of his approach coupled with his often disorderly writing style.

Ferguson attempted to synthesise classical orientations towards the common good with the newly revived ethic of benevolence — as expounded by such thinkers as Cumberland, Shaftesbury and Hutcheson — with modern conditions and the even newer ethic of private interest which, since it existed, and seemed to be quite useful, had to be accounted for.[230] In pursuing this task, Ferguson finds himself caught up in a protracted battle, not only with Hobbes and Mandeville, but also with Smith and Hume whom he regards (perhaps unjustly) as representatives of Epicureanism. For Ferguson, Epicureanism was the cause of the corruption of Rome (and therefore, by implication, it was having the same effect upon Britain) via its reduction of ethics to a hedonism of pleasure and pain, an inattention to the public sphere, its restriction of 'goodness' to private affairs and finally, its denial of Providence.[231]

Ferguson's writings are frequently the scene of a protracted replay of the ancient battle between Stoicism and Epicureanism.[232] Indeed, this is a key sub-text of his ethics, as will be shown. Although he agrees with them in many respects, Ferguson must avoid coming fully on to the moral and epistemological terrain of his adversaries, some of whom, he believes, underestimate the costs of progress and misguidedly celebrate the breakdown of traditional social life. He must therefore devise a new kind of philosophy that accommodates benevolence and civic virtue while fulfilling the practical function of being able to define the best form of political society for modern times.[233] In this regard, therefore, rather than being 'typical' of the 'Scottish School', as has sometimes been suggested,[234] Ferguson's philosophy can be distinguished from those of Scottish contemporaries.[235]

---

of History in the History of Ideas', *Studies in Soviet Thought*, Vol. 26 (1) 1983, pp. 3-9, p. 7; Camic, *Experience and Enlightenment*, pp. 54-5.

[230] Smith, *The Political Philosophy of Adam Ferguson*, p. 35.

[231] *History*, pp. 169-70. For further discussion see Sher, *Church and University*, p.180.

[232] See, for example, *Institutes*, pp. 137-9, *P.II.*, pp. 3-5.

[233] Smith, *The Political Philosophy of Adam Ferguson*, p. 35. For Waszek, Ferguson's thought is 'directed towards the intellectual past [but] is [also] highly original and points towards the future' in exploring what happens to community under the stress of modernity. *Man's Social Nature*, p.140.

[234] Bryson, *Man and Society*, pp. 30-52. Bryson is correct in saying that Ferguson is concerned with a similar 'set of ideas' as his Scottish contemporaries but overlooks that his manner of dealing with those same ideas is often distinct. Jane Fagg, Ferguson's biographer, likewise submits that 'Ferguson was typical of the literati... only [his] work in America with the Carlisle Peace Commission, his birth on the borders of the highlands, and his ability to speak Gaelic set him apart'. Fagg, *Adam Ferguson: Scottish Cato*, pp. 333-4. See also Lehmann, *Adam Ferguson*, p. 235; A. Silver, 'Friendship in Commercial Society: Eighteenth-Century Social Theory and Modern Sociology', *American Journal of Sociology*, Vol 95 (6), pp. 1474-1504, 1990, p.1481; and Pascal, 'Herder and the Scottish Historical School', p. 27.

[235] See, for example, 'Principle of Moral Estimation', *Collection of Essays*, No. 25, *passim*, which features a critique of Smith's and Hume's ethics. For a discussion of Ferguson's main points of

In exploring Ferguson's social thought we are able to notice those precise points at which Ferguson attempts his bridge or synthesis of seemingly incompatible traditions. In his discourse on 'pneumatics', for example, the moment is located at the point where Ferguson has to decide how he will respond to Smith's views on self-interest and beneficence; how to defend his civic humanism against the strong arguments of his adversary, and, indeed, his own commitment to empirical science. Another of these moments is detectable in Ferguson's discussion of the decline of nations when he simultaneously entertains a 'modern' optimism about the commercial age with a Stoic remorse at the loss of civic virtue and corporate sentiments which accompanies progress. It is through a careful identification of these 'watershed' moments, and of Ferguson's attempted reconciliation of any resulting dissonance, that we are able to trace his forging of this new space. In the end Ferguson achieves an awkwardly harmonious position; awkward, not so much in being dissonant, but simply in its sheer complexity.

---

disagreement with Hume see *Institutes*, p.156 and Kettler, *The Social and Political Thought of Adam Ferguson* p. 453.

CHAPTER 3

FERGUSON'S THEOLOGY/ONTOLOGY

It is extremely important to understand Ferguson's attempts to build a social science in the context of his prior theological and moral commitments. The study of society had yet to be separated from the subject of moral philosophy and yet Ferguson's science of humanity seems secular. The bridge he creates to unite the opposing universes of religion and science is achieved via his belief that God's will is expressed in the workings of efficient or secondary causes rather than through direct divine intervention.[236] The world is the product of design, and the observable order of regularity in human affairs is the direct result of this design and purpose in nature.[237] Since Ferguson's God is a distant, non-interventionist 'General Providence', the world requires inbuilt laws to maintain an 'order of things, which in a state of counteraction and apparent disturbance, mutually regulate and balance one another'. This balance in human affairs is achieved largely through unintended consequences or the law of heterogeneity of ends; in other words, through natural social laws of spontaneous order. This spontaneous order arrangement is at the core of Ferguson's entire social science and, from his own point of view, it is the Providentialist superstructure that makes his system work. His reliance on Providence is partly a function of his deep faith in a designing God but is also partly related to the fact that neither he nor anyone else had yet come up with a convincing non-teleological theory of evolution or evolutionary psychology for him to draw upon. Nevertheless, from a more modern point of view, his system still works well as a proper social science even after the Providentialism has been removed, because the main arena of social order activity is on the level of efficient causes. The universe is designed and yet no immediate agency is ascribed to what happens within it. Things happen because of impersonal, invariable and self-regulating laws of nature, not because of God's special interventions. God has ordained nature to operate by secondary causes and to know the laws of nature is to apprehend the decrees of God.[238] Reliance on secondary (efficient) causes is not, therefore, incompatible with a Providential view of motion.

Yet, it has been suggested that the notion of design is 'explicitly rejected by the Scots' and that their social 'theory provides an explanation of the origin of complex social structures without the need to posit the existence of a directing intelligence.'

---

[236] 'That the author of nature though himself omnipotent acts in every department by the intervention of secondary causes...The secondary cause is an instrument in the hand of man by which to effect his [God's] purpose in many instances'. 'Of Cause and Effect, Ends and Means, Order, Combination and Design', *Collection of Essays*, No. 13, p. 124.

[237] See, for example, *P.II.*, p. 27. *P.I*, pp. 53, 180; *Essay*, pp. 89-90.

[238] A view held also by Newton. J. E. McGuire 'Force, Active Principles and Newton's Invisible Realm', *Ambix*, Vol. 15, 1968, pp. 154-208, pp. 202-7.

Ferguson's theory, along that of his fellow Scots, is thus conceived as some variant of 'adaptive evolution'.[239] While it is true that, for Ferguson, design is redundant from the standpoint of human actors it is not at the social systems level. And although it is accurate, in a narrow sense, to define Ferguson's approach as evolutionistic, it is really evolution *by design* (though not by *human* design). *Causally,* Ferguson's theory is a two-tiered arrangement comprising the individuo-psychic or efficient causes level, and the social systems or final causes level. He is very keen to impress upon his reader that his system is driven by the notion of Final Causes, firmly rejecting as implausible any explanation that relies on efficient causation or the operation of 'physical powers' alone.[240]

1. FERGUSON'S PERSONAL CONVICTIONS: COMPETING VIEWS

Scholarly opinion is divided over the nature of Ferguson's theology. Some portray his philosophy as Deistic, or as reflecting the disappointments of a lapsed Christian.[241] Others, either implicitly, or explicitly, portray his project as secular or purely materialist in nature.[242] The enthusiasm of some scholars to cast Ferguson as the first 'sociologist' seems to have resulted in a tendency to present his views anachronistically. This study aims to show that Ferguson's whole edifice of social order, and the complex of natural laws which generate it, must be understood in relation to his closely held Christian-Stoic beliefs about design, purpose and destination.

It has been asserted that Ferguson's is an essentially secular enterprise, characterised by a 'deeply ingrained secularism despite its surface piety'.[243] The implication here, presumably, is that Ferguson's 'surface piety' is merely a cover to

---

[239] Hamowy, *Spontaneous Order*, pp. 3-4. Hayek also implicitly elides the Providentialist underpinnings of Ferguson's vision. See D. Simpson, 'Joseph Schumpeter and the Austrian School of Economics', *Journal of Economic Studies*, Vol. 10, (4), 1983, pp.15-28, p. 26.

[240] For example, *Essay*, p. 12; *P.I.*, p. 312 and *P.II.*, p. 27.

[241] Jean Willke concludes that, in his maturity, Ferguson was a 'thorough-going deist'. Willke, *Historical Thought of Adam Ferguson*, p.34. See also, G.L. McDowell, 'Commerce, Virtue and Politics: Adam Ferguson's Constitutionalism', *Review of Politics*,Vol. 45 (4), 1983, pp. 536-52. Andrew Skinner has detected in Ferguson's philosophy a belief in 'a Divine Rational Intelligence'. Andrew Skinner, 'Economics and History-The Scottish Enlightenment', *The Scottish Journal of Political Economy*, Vol. 12, 1965, pp. 1-22, p. 22. For the idea that Ferguson was a lapsed Christian see Peter Gay, *The Enlightenment: An Interpretation*, in 2 Vols, London: Weidenfeld and Nicholson, 1970, Vol. 2, p. 336. According to Sher, '(t)he fact that Ferguson left the ministry in the 1750s has led scholars unfamiliar with the intricacies of Scottish ecclesiastical affairs' to incorrectly assume this view. Sher, *Church and University*, p. 125.

[242] Some materialist or secularist interpretations follow: Duncan Forbes, in his 'Introduction' to Ferguson's *Essay* (p. xviii.) describes the latter's analysis of conflict as 'utterly matter of fact, dry and secular'. The German historian Breysig characterised Ferguson as 'a pure empiricist, free from both theological and intellectual teleological' assumptions. Lehmann, 'Review', p. 177. See also Pascal, 'Herder and the Scottish Historical School', p. 27; Ferrarotti, 'Civil Society and State Structures in Creative Tension', pp. 11-12; Meek 'The Scottish Contribution to Marxist Sociology', pp. 34-45; D. Zaret, 'From Political Philosophy to Social Theory', *Journal of the History of the Behavioural Sciences*, Vol. 17, 1981, pp. 153-73.

[243] Kettler, *Social and Political Thought of Adam Ferguson*, p. 131.

secure publication and prevent the alienation of readers. Most of Ferguson's contemporaries were well aware that charges of heresy or impiety could still be damaging even in enlightened, eighteenth century Scotland. The hanging in 1697 of Thomas Aikenhead would have been vivid in their minds (Aikenhead was a Edinburgh University student and the last person to be executed for heresy in Britain). More recently, and closer to home, Hume had suffered as a result of his scepticism when the Kirk successfully blocked his applications for Chairs, first in 1745 at the University of Edinburgh (Moral Philosophy) and subsequently in 1752 at the University of Glasgow (Logic and Rhetoric).[244]

Yet Ferguson is openly critical of orthodox religion whenever the subject arises[245] and his 'Introduction' to the *Principles* contains a declaration of his intention to limit his theological conclusions to those suggested by 'common sense'.[246] Though his theological education had been mainly Christian Calvinist in nature[247] he is explicit in his preference for natural religion. To those who would question his decision to 'restrict his argument...to the topics of mere natural religion and ', Ferguson replies unambiguously:

> This being the foundation of every superstructure whether in morality or religion, and therefore to be separately treated, he considered as that part of the work which was allotted to him. Farther institutions may improve, but cannot supersede what the Almighty has revealed in his works, and in the suggestions of reason to man...And what the Author of our nature has so taught must be considered as the test of every subsequent institution that is offered as coming from him.[248]

All of Ferguson's theological conclusions are gleaned, not from Scriptures or established religious doctrine, but from the works of nature. 'True religion' consists in the 'study of nature, by which we are led to substitute a wise providence operating by physical causes' for 'phantoms that terrify, or amuse the ignorant.'[249]

---

[244] Broadie, *The Scottish Enlightenment*, pp. 33-5.

[245] Ferguson makes no attempt to hide his dislike of revealed religion and at no point does he describe himself as a Christian. See *P.I.*, p. vii; *Institutes*, pp. 235-6; and *The Morality of Stage Plays Seriously Considered*, Edinburgh, 1757, p. 5. Even so, the *Biographical Dictionary of Eminent Scotsmen* reported that Ferguson, having been '(b)red in the tenets of the church of Scotland...was a respectful believer in the truths of revelation. *A Biographical Dictionary of Eminent Scotsmen*, Vol. II, Edinburgh: Blackie and Son, 1864, p. 201.

[246] There is little or no significant orthodox Christian content in Ferguson's writings except where his philosophy is specifically intended for the education of youth. Kettler, *Social and Political Thought of Adam Ferguson*, p. 153. But, even in such material, his critique of religious 'casuistry' is clearly in evidence. See, for example, *Institutes*, pp. 235, 164. For the most part, Ferguson either ignores or indirectly criticises revealed and established religion. For example: 'Under the title of *religion* we admire and love the conceivable perfections of the supreme Being: But bigotry and superstition may assume the name of religion, and substitute acts of oppression and cruelty towards men for act of duty towards God. We must not, therefore, trust to whatever may bear the name of religion or conscience, or to what may have a temporary vogue in the world for our direction in the paths of a just and manly virtue'. *P.II.*, p. 320. Ferguson's emphasis. See also *P.I.*, p. vii.. He also refers to the 'very fatal effects' which accompany 'the abuse of religion'. and applauds provisions made in the Twelve Tables to permit 'every family' freedom 'to worship the gods in their own way'. *Institutes*, p. 216; *History*, p. 12.

[247] Kettler, *Social and Political Thought of Adam Ferguson*, p. 171.

[248] *P.I.*, pp. vii-viii.

[249] *Essay*, pp. 89-90.

If Ferguson's so-called 'surface piety' were only a cover, then he makes much more of it than he would have needed in order to protect himself. In any case, and as will be shown, much of his system is logically dependent (at least from his own point of view) on the principle of design and purpose in nature.

It should be noted that capturing accurately Ferguson's theological position is no easy task given the astounding array of categories and permutations for religious belief that emerged during the Enlightenment period[250] where evasion and obfuscation on this topic seems to have been almost fashionable. At the same time, any ambiguity is just as likely traceable to the fact that Ferguson's theology was composite, sometimes awkwardly so, and often implied rather than explicit. For this reason, it seems the more fruitful option to limit the discussion to identifying those core theological tenets which are operational and indispensable within his philosophy, such as the existence of God, the idea of design and especially *purpose* in nature, the doctrine of free will and the denial of the existence of evil.

Unfortunately there is little, if any, systematic attempt to establish a theological framework in Ferguson's analysis. Rather it is scattered and implied throughout. Once collated, the following picture emerges. In a broad sense his theology is probably best described as Christian-Stoic but in its details it is a composite of Newtonian and Aristotelian theology (for his views on the problem of causation);[251] Stoicism (with its commitment to theodicy, civic and other-regarding values, universalism and the belief that the philosopher's mission is to discern the laws of nature in order that we might conform to them);[252] and Christianity, in the form expounded and transmitted to Ferguson via Francis Hutcheson (for its perfectibilism, its avowal of the doctrines of genesis, design and free-will and the resolution of all virtues into benevolence, the philosophical equivalent of Christian love).[253] Ferguson was influenced by Hutcheson's introduction of 'liberal and naturalistic interpretations' to Calvinist theology and the latter's sympathies were clearly with the moderates or 'liberals.'[254] There is, naturally, some tenet overlap in these sources such as a common Christian and Newtonian belief in genesis.

---

[250] J. Viner, *The Role of Providence in the Social Order,* Philadelphia: American Philosophical Society, p. 13.

[251] Ferguson sees these two sources as fully consistent. *P.I.,* p. 312. For further discussion of Newtonian theology see: M.A. Hoskin, 'Newton, Providence and the Universe of Stars', *Journal of the History of Astronomy,* Vol. 8, 1977, pp. 77-101; P. Casini, 'Newton: The Classical Scholia', *History of Science,* Vol. 22, 1984, pp. 1-23; James E. Force, 'Hume and the Relation of Science to Religion Among Certain Members of the Royal Society', *Journal of the History of Ideas,* Vol. 45 (4), 1984, pp. 517-53, p. 523; D. Kubrin, 'Newton and the Cyclical Cosmos: Providence and the Mechanical Philosophy', *Journal of the History of Ideas,* Vol. 28 (3), 1967, pp. 325-46; J. Gascgoigne, 'From Bentley to the Victorians: The Rise and Fall of Newtonian Natural Theology', *Science in Context,* Vol. 2 (2), 1988, pp. 219-56 and G. W. Trompf, 'On Newtonian History', in Stephen Gaukroger, (ed.), *The Uses of Antiquity,* Amsterdam: Kluwer Academic Publishers, 1991, pp. 213-49.

[252] 'The will of God' is 'declared' or reflected in 'the order established in his works'. *P.I.,* pp. 166-7. See also *P.I.,* pp. vii, 312, 338.

[253] Raphael and Macfie, 'Introduction' to *TMS,* p. 6. For a discussion of Hutcheson's influence on Ferguson see Sher, *Church and University,* p.167 and T.D. Campbell, 'Francis Hutcheson: "Father of the Scottish Enlightenment"', in R.H. Campbell and A. S.Skinner, (eds), *The Origins and Nature of the Scottish Enlightenment,* Edinburgh: John Donald Publishers, 1982.

[254] Willke, *Historical Thought of Adam Ferguson,* p. 34.

Richard Sher's conclusion that Ferguson's writings are profoundly Christian-Stoic in nature thus seems the most convincing[255] though they could just as easily be described more generally as those of a Deist.[256] John Haldane, who attacked Ferguson publicly for his views on the theatre, described him as an 'avowed deist...companion to the wicked...a vile blasphemer and maligner of our Lord and his apostles'.[257] Certainly, Ferguson shared with Smith and Hume an abhorrence of religious 'bigotry and superstition'[258] but he was only a minor rebel. Even though he resigned his commission as chaplain to the Black Watch Regiment with the vow that he would have 'little further connection with the Clergy of Scotland', he never demitted and remained active in promoting Moderate causes in the General Assembly of the Church of Scotland.[259] It is probable that Ferguson's motives here were more strategic than anything else. The Church of Scotland exerted great influence over Scottish society. No doubt he regarded it as an important vehicle for prosecuting his ideas about the best way forward for Scotland. In any case, overall, his theological disposition was generally mild, reflecting a tolerant forbearance that sometimes bordered on indifference to the religious controversies of his time.

2. THEODICY, CAUSATION AND DESIGN

Theodicy is perhaps the keynote of Ferguson's belief system. Charles Camic notes, quite rightly, that despite Ferguson's having abandoned, consciously, 'the essentials of his Christian heritage...his works, alone among those of the enlighteners' sought to explain the mystery of God's permission of evil.[260] A great deal of his thought is devoted to this task and in his chapter in the *Principles* entitled 'Of the Origin of

---

[255] Sher, *Church and University*, pp. 177; pp. 324-8. Ferguson's combination of Stoic natural religion with orthodox Christianity is not as problematic as it at first appears. According to Jacob Viner "natural theology" was not an innovation. It had been freely accepted in Catholicism from at least the late Middle Ages as a supplement and reinforcement of revealed doctrine. It found early acceptance in Anglicanism'. J. Viner, *The Role of Providence*, p. 12.

[256] This term is somewhat imprecise since 'Deists would embrace the existence and some of the attributes of deity, and often a humanitarian ethic, but held divergent opinions about the soul, immortality and last judgement'. M.A. Stewart, 'Religion and Rational Theology', in Alexander Broadie (ed.) *The Scottish Enlightenment*, Cambridge; Cambridge University Press, 2003, p. 33.

[257] John Haldane, 'The Player's Scourge', cited in Fagg, *Biographical Introduction*, p. xxvii. Ferguson's involvement in the controversy surrounding John Home's play, *Douglas,* brought him into open conflict with the Church. Ferguson participated in and attended rehearsals and readings of the play. He also published a pamphlet (*The Morality of Stage Plays Seriously Considered*) criticising the Presbytery of Edinburgh's condemnation of plays. Fagg, *Biographical Introduction*, p. xxviii.

[258] *P.II.*, p. 320. See also *P.I.*, pp. 304-5.

[259] Fagg, *Biographical Introduction*, p. xxix. Such causes involved defending Hume and other 'infidel' thinkers against attacks from conservative elements within the Church of Scotland as well as writing 'pamphlets on controversial topics such as *Douglas* [and] the militia'. According to Richard Sher, '[b]y the time of his academic retirement in the mid-17802, Ferguson had acquired a reputation as one of the managers of the Moderate interest in the church'. Sher, *Church and University*, pp. 71-2, 99, 125.

[260] Camic, *Experience and Enlightenment*, p. 61.

Evil' he states explicitly that it is an attempt to 'justify the ways of God to men'.[261] Obliquely identifying himself as a theist, he opposes his adversary, 'the atheist', by arguing that apparent evil, rather than negating the existence of God manifestly attests to it.[262] Those of an intelligent and 'grateful' disposition will understand that 'every circumstance or event in the order of nature...serve[s] to manifest, and to extol the supreme wisdom and goodness of God'.[263] Everything exists for a reason; nothing in the universe is truly evil for all of creation performs some positive role in the benign master plan. Marcus argued along similar lines in the *Meditations* that even 'roguery' and 'impudence' are 'necessary to the world'[264] just as 'sickness, death, slander, intrigue, and all the other things that delight or trouble foolish men' are 'normal'.[265] He instructed pessimists who contemplated the apparent evils of life with 'mistrust' to remember that this 'is but Nature's way; and in the ways of Nature there is no evil to be found'.[266] The universe was to Marcus a single, integrated and monistic unit, driven by a benign impulse.

> Always think of the universe as one living organism, with a single substance and a single soul; and observe how all things...are moved by its single impulse, and all play their part in the causation of every event that happens.[267]

Ferguson notes that even the belief in 'polytheism', though one of 'the great and prevailing errors of the human mind', is nevertheless a blessing because it contributes to moral knowledge and eventually leads us to a belief in one God.[268] 'Complaints of moral evil' in people, are likewise really 'the symptoms of a progressive or improving nature'.[269]

Ferguson bases his belief in the existence of God, not on the authority of the Scriptures, but on inferences drawn (albeit heroically) from the empirical world. These are: the causal argument; the argument from design; the cosmological argument, the moral argument and the argument from universal consent.[270]

The teleological argument, which was a common Protestant variant on the design argument, suggests that, since all created life seems to be purposeful, so it must have been designed.[271] The design argument posits the existence of an original unmoved

---

[261] Ferguson expresses this intention by quoting beneath his chapter title Milton's famous passage from *Paradise Lost*: 'What in me is dark, Illumine; what is low, raise and support; That, to the height of this great argument, I may assert eternal Providence; And justify the ways of God to men'. *P.I.*, p. 172.

[262] *P.I.*, pp. 172-203.

[263] *P.I.*, p. 187.

[264] Marcus Aurelius, *Meditations*, 9. 42. p. 148. Ferguson makes the identical argument that the follies of rogues and knaves provide better incentive to good conduct than the 'mild and shining examples'. 'Of Things That Are or May Be', *Collection of Essays*, No. 27 (1), p. 229.

[265] Marcus Aurelius, *Meditations*, 4. 44. p. 73.

[266] Marcus Aurelius, *Meditations*, 2. 17. p. 51.

[267] Marcus Aurelius, *Meditations*, 4. 40. p.73.

[268] *P.I.*, p. 168.

[269] *Institutes*, p. 124.

[270] For a summary of these arguments see Alan Richardson and John Bowden, (eds), *A New Dictionary of Christian Theology*, London: SCM Press Ltd, 1983, pp. 37-9.

[271] *Institutes*, p. 117. 'Who ever doubted that the eye was made to see, the ear to hear, the teeth to grind and the stomach to digest the food and so of innumerable instances which, tho various, are still analogous and argue in the power intelligent invention, boundless continual analogy and the combination

mover to account for the order and symmetry of the natural world.[272] The moral argument (which is a component of the design argument) states that since the universe has produced ethical animals (humans) there must be a transcendent moral source to account for this moral nature.[273] The cosmological argument, meanwhile, posits the world as caused by a first, non-contingent cause. Ferguson's theory of progress (which he bases on the principle of change) finds its explanation in the action of an unchanged originator of change.[274] Finally, he invokes the more modern, anthropological argument known as 'the argument from the common consent of humankind'. A belief in the existence of God is universal throughout the globe and across diverse cultures, therefore such a belief must be natural, that is, innate. Since the human constitution is designed, then God's existence is probable.[275]

A different, though equally heroic, train of assumptions leads Ferguson to a belief in the immortality of the soul. Here he combines a kind of spiritual conjecturalism with some basic facts of life; the immortality of the human soul is inferred from the simple fact of our having been created in the first place and thereafter supplied with the means for survival. The will to create implies the will to preserve; therefore the assumption of there being an afterlife seems reasonable.[276] But it is worth noting that Ferguson's tone here is qualified and cautious. He is 'very careful', as Kettler notes, 'not to insist too strenuously on the possibility of immortality'.[277]

Turning to the *substance* of his religious beliefs, Ferguson seems to have been deliberately ambiguous about identifying his religious bias precisely, however he makes it plain that he is neither atheist nor agnostic.[278] At the same time he leaves no

---

of parts to a beneficent and salutary end'. 'Of Things that Are or May Be' (Part 1), *Collection of Essays*, No. 27, p. 220. See also: 'Of the Intellectual or Conscious Powers', *Collection of Essays*, No. 31, p. 266 and passim.

[272] *P.I.*, p. 338. Ferguson asserts that the first thing we know about God is 'that he acts from design and means to obtain an End'. 'What may be Affirmed or Apprehended of the Supreme Creative Being', *Collection of Essays*, No. 2, p. 8.

[273] *Institutes*, p. 122.

[274] 'The succession of powers and productions or cause and effect cannot be eternal. There must have been a power underived or which had nothing prior to itself'. 'Of the Intellectual or Conscious Powers', *Collection of Essays*, No. 31, p. 263. 'From the first cause all is derived'. 'Of Cause and Effect, Ends and Means, Order, Combination and Design', *ibid*, No. 13, p. 120. Further, '[t]he unerring mind does now what it always did, and is incapable of change; because to change would be to deviate from what is best'. *P.I.*, p. 180.

[275] *Institutes,* pp. 114-16.

[276] *P.I.*, p. 330-2.

[277] Kettler, *Social and Political Thought of Adam Ferguson*, p. 174-5.

[278] It would have been unusual for Ferguson to be an atheist during this time. Deism was far more common. Norman Hampson, *The Enlightenment*, London: Penguin, 1982, p. 131. In fact, Ferguson likens the atheist to a thief who is intent on undermining the peace of mind of others. 'Of Cause and Effect, Ends and Means, Order, Combination and Design', *Collection of Essays*, No. 13, p. 127. It seems clear that Ferguson's published beliefs were sincere. It is reported that his last words addressed to his daughters from his deathbed were: 'There *is* another world', *Dictionary of National Biography*, Leslie Stephen and Sidney Lee (eds.), Vol. VI, London: Oxford University Press, 1917. The inscription he chose for his own gravestone was: 'I have seen the works of God: it is now your turn: do you behold them and rejoice.' Ferguson expressed a profound piety in his private letters. To his close friend, John Macpherson, he wrote: 'The Intelligence that Conducts the universe is here present and intimately know[s] what we think

doubt that he finds little attraction in Christian practices and doctrine except where they coincide with Stoic natural religion.[279] Ferguson indicates his commitment to the following coincidental tenets: the existence of a benevolent 'Providence'; the limited extent of human control over events; the reality of objective ethical standards; the priority of the public over private good and a commitment to the supreme value of benevolence. The most conspicuous exception to this general rule is Ferguson's embrace of the Ciceronian/Christian doctrine of free will which is underplayed (and seemingly absent) in the teachings of Stoicism. But his repudiation of Scriptural authority, rejection of the Calvinist doctrine that salvation depends on the grace of God,[280] denial of Special Providence and complete rejection of the concept of sin, original or otherwise, distances him from Christianity considerably.[281]

The closest Ferguson comes to categorically identifying his private religious convictions is when he describes himself, in passing, as a 'theist.'[282] This would, at best, commit him to nothing more than a belief in one God who stands in some kind of direct relationship with human beings. His writings do betray a conception of God more closely akin to that of Stoicism than Christianity. The terms 'God' and 'nature' are used interchangeably and his conception of our relationship to God echoes the pantheistic elements of Stoicism. Like the Stoics, Ferguson identifies God with Nature.[283] At other times 'He' is 'the Author of Nature', 'the Almighty'[284] or simply 'God'[285] but *never* a personal one.[286] The terms are used interchangeably, reflecting Ferguson's sense of ease in combining Christian and Stoic ideas.

Despite our ability to identify the principal tenets of Ferguson's theology, the bulk of his exposition is taken up with the world of appearances in line with his own view that the pursuit of 'metaphysics' is, by its nature, a futile enterprise. This does not represent a scepticism on Ferguson's part, rather, certain things, such as the

---

and do. May he never be Absent from our thoughts'. Letter to John MacPherson, April 29, 1800, *Correspondence*, No. 360, II. p. 466.

[279] Montesquieu expressed a similar dual attachment in the *Laws*, 5. 24. 10, pp. 465-6.

[280] As opposed to the independent efforts of human agents. According to Kettler this 'heroic theme…emerged in Ferguson's writings at least in part as a defence against anti-heroic emphases of Calvinist Christianity'. Kettler, *Social and Political Thought of Adam Ferguson*, p. 176.

[281] This is not really as radical a position as it first appears since, according to Lucien Goldman, during the Enlightenment period '[f]eeling oneself a Christian no longer entailed acceptance of all the dogmas established and recognised by the Church. Membership of the Church committed one only to those affirmations and articles of faith that one explicitly recognised oneself'. Lucien Goldman, *The Philosophy of the Enlightenment*, London: Routledge and Kegan Paul, 1973, p. 57. Similarly, Anthony Waterman notes that 'it is a mistake to imagine that natural theology would have been regarded, in eighteenth century Britain, as in anyway opposed to or even inconsistent with Christianity. A.M.C. Waterman, 'Economics as Theology: Adam Smith's *Wealth of Nations*', *Southern Economic Journal*, Vol. 68 (4), 2002, pp. 907-21, p. 919.

[282] *P.I.*, p. 172.

[283] *P.I.*, p. vii. Quoting Marcus Aurelius, Ferguson waxes pantheistic with uncharacteristic abandon: 'O beautiful order of nature! Whatever thy seasons bring, shall be fruit, neither too early nor too late for me'. *P.I.*, p. 312.

[284] *P.I.*, p. vii.

[285] *P.I.*, p. 53.

[286] *P.I.*, p. 338.

goodness and 'existence of God' are self-evident. Ferguson calls such beliefs 'ultimate facts'. These 'facts' are really articles of faith that do not, for epistemological reasons, admit of investigation.[287] Certain key propositions are given without being too vigorously defended: God exists, the world is the product of design and the observable order of regularity in human affairs is a direct result of this design and purpose in nature.[288] Ferguson's optimism is marked throughout, inspired by Marcus Aurelius' dictum that 'We have no reason...to believe that it was possible for God to make the universe better than he has done'.[289]

Ferguson does not, therefore, take on board any of Hume's critical theological arguments except to contradict them in passing. He attacks Hume on the question of cause by invoking Aristotle and the Stoics and defends the argument from design on the grounds of faith. That the universe had a First Cause is an 'ultimate fact' and that it exhibits all the characteristics of Design is also an 'ultimate fact' and ultimate facts need no other verification than that conferred by our sensory experience of them.[290] Ferguson contradicts Hume's claim that 'effect is correlative to cause and they are inseparable' on the grounds that 'there may be existence without any cause external to itself' (a First Cause or original unmoved mover).[291] Hume's reduction of all causes to efficiency does not make sense, at least not to Ferguson. After all, without some conception of 'an End, the whole fabrick of successive means would fall to the ground.'[292]

The existence of God is confirmed by our universal belief in his existence. This belief must be endogenous, Ferguson reasons, and the abstract speculations of 'sceptics' cannot 'derogate' from such powerful empirical evidence.[293] Then, as if determined to miss Hume's point altogether, Ferguson declares that '[s]ceptics have not denied the reality of these perceptions; they have rather complained of them, as the foundation of general and vulgar errors.' The belief in God is a 'natural sensation' for which there is no need to find a 'reason' apart from that of its obvious veracity.[294] Ferguson then goes on to acknowledge the existence of a belief in 'a plurality of Gods' but seems unable to offer any convincing explanation for this contradictory evidence apart from the observation that it represents a 'corruption' of right thinking.[295] At first sight this appears to be nothing more than blatant ethnocentrism but it could just as easily be related to Ferguson's Stoic leanings. The Stoics recognised diversity of religious belief but thought all cultures worshipped the same (albeit single) God by different names.

---

[287] *Institutes*, pp. 8-9; *Essay*, p. 12.

[288] *P.I.*, pp. 173-5; *Essay*, p. 12.

[289] *P.I.*, p. 338.

[290] *Institutes*, p. 117.

[291] *P.I.*, p. 153.

[292] 'Of the Principle of Moral Estimation', *Collection of Essays*, No. 25, p. 214. Francis Hutcheson also subscribed to teleological arguments, though we can, of course, trace them back to Aristotle and the Stoics. Waszek, *Man's Social Nature*, p. 48.

[293] *Institutes*, pp. 114-5.

[294] *Institutes*, p. 116.

[295] *Institutes*, p. 120.

In any case, Hume's arguments are either ignored, contradicted or wilfully misunderstood. Ferguson's endorsement of the argument from design embodies an explicit identification of God's mind with our own in associating the apparent purpose and order of the universe with the type of design evident in human contrivance.[296] His unreconstructed cosmogony and undisguised anthropomorphism signals his complete refusal to engage with Hume in any meaningful way. His replies to Hume are identical to the kind of arguments Hume attacks in the first place, therefore it makes for a rather uninteresting theological debate between them. Ferguson's theology is noteworthy in the sense that it is a well developed blending of Stoic and Christian thought but it offers few critical or groundbreaking insights such as Hume advanced.

For Ferguson, there is no question of inner self-regulation and growth as the potential source of order. Order was imposed externally at the moment of creation in inbuilt laws of nature. Ferguson's insistence that social order arises spontaneously does not connote a lack of design or purpose in the universe; simply that *human* design (that is, large scale planning) has no role in it. But the theme of a 'divine architect' organising human affairs via entelechy is constantly reiterated.[297] Ferguson's teleology thus deviates from traditional Aristotelian teleology which denied the existence of a Platonic demiurge.[298] It also differs because it is a *transcendent* teleology as opposed to the type of immanent teleology expounded by Aristotle and later Hume.[299] It resembles Western religious teleology, which — unlike the Aristotelian — tends to involve a purpose being imposed externally upon the operations of nature and usually entails ideas of creation. Ferguson's teleology also differs from the Aristotelian in postulating a dynamic, rather than static, universe and which is monistic (designed as an interdependent world system) rather than pluralistic.[300] The earth and all its contents are but part of a universe in which both 'the author' and 'the work is one'.[301]

> The Author of nature…has not so disjoined individuals from one another in any parts of
> his works. There is an affinity and combination of minds, as well as of material

[296] *Institutes,* p. 117.

[297] For example, *P.I.,* p. 53.

[298] Joseph Owens, 'Teleology of Nature in Aristotle', *The Monist,* Vol. 52, 1968, pp. 158-73, p. 163.

[299] Anthony Edel describes the distinction thus: 'The history of philosophy sometimes divides teleologies into transcendent and immanent. In the former, some purpose is imposed from outside upon the operations of the natural world; in the latter there is a plan or design in some sense within it. Western religious teleology is generally transcendent: God, pre-existing the world, creates it and designs the way of things and creatures. Aristotle's teleology is not, of course, like that; moreover, his account includes no Creation, but offers a world eternal in its forms. It would thus be classified as an immanent teleology'. A. Edel, *Aristotle and His Philosophy,* London: Croom Helm, 1982, p. 65. See also Owens, 'Teleology of Nature in Aristotle', p. 170.

[300] Monistic teleologies, such as Ferguson expounds, conceive whole world plans, highly interdependent and interconnected, whereas pluralistic teleologies such as Aristotle's, 'postulate separate systems in the world, each with its own plan; what each system strives to do depends on its nature, but how systems intersect is largely a matter of accident that expresses no single comprehensive plan or nature'. Aristotle's teleology is also anthropocentric in the sense that he perceives 'man' as the highest order of biological existence and that nature is seen to be placed in the service of 'man'. Edel, *Aristotle,* pp. 65-6. This is Ferguson's view also. See, for example, *P.II.,* p. 28.

[301] 'Of the Intellectual or Conscious Powers', *Collection of Essays,* No. 31, pp. 266-7.

substances. The chain of communication extends from one to many, from species to species, and even from world to world, throughout the intellectual as well as material system of nature.[302]

Ferguson's teleology seems to be a composite of Christian, Stoic, Newtonian and Aristotelian influences underpinned by a firm commitment to theodicy.[303]

> The system of nature is sublime in respect to the might of its Author. It is beautiful with respect to the regular fitness of parts for the attainment of their ends, and in respect to the beneficent purpose which they are fitted to serve.

Ferguson also goes on to dispel any misapprehensions that his approach might be purely evolutionist by declaring that all human effort would be meaningless without 'a well-concerted design' and would undoubtedly result in 'disorder, confusion and extreme deformity.'[304] It is a 'great mistake' in thinking 'to supersede the existence of mind and Providence, by tracing the operations of nature to their physical law' than to the 'unerring mind' which contrived them.[305] There is a definable *purpose* to the design; accordingly the most urgent question for the philosopher is to discover the end, or '*de finibus*' of human existence.[306] Ferguson's attitude here is a rejection of Hume's denial of the possibility of 'discerning a divine purpose. For Hume this would involve a vulgar identification of the Creator's mind and methods with our own.[307] In addition, Hume was convinced that even if we could evince the Creator's purpose this knowledge would be of no practical use to a reasonable person.[308] Obviously, Ferguson is of the opinion that such knowledge is not only supremely useful but within our grasp. As for Hume's epistemological objection, Ferguson simply argues that the existence of divine purpose is an incontrovertible or 'ultimate fact' for which there is ample empirical (sensory) evidence.[309]

Despite Hume's best efforts, Ferguson remains convinced that the 'world is governed by the wisdom of God'. A 'wise Providence' operates through 'fixed and determinate laws' of nature.[310] God is a First Cause, a 'General' rather than special 'Providence'[311] who pre-exists a world he created perfect. Because the natural world

---

[302] *P.II.*, p. 324. 'The belief of the existence of God has been universal' and appears to be endogenous or innate. *Institutes*, pp. 114-116.

[303] Kettler notes, quite fairly, that Ferguson 'freely used Aristotelian and Stoic arguments with little regard for philosophical niceties'. *Social and Political Thought of Adam Ferguson*, p. 127.

[304] *P.II.*, p. 27.

[305] *P.I.*, p. 180.

[306] 'Of the Principle of Moral Estimation', *Collection of Essays*, No. 25, p. 214.

[307] Kettler, *Social and Political Thought of Adam Ferguson*, p. 122. Though in fairness to Ferguson, he does show some awareness that this might be a problem. When referring to the 'error' of polytheism he notes, critically, that some 'nations have made up a list of their gods upon a model, taken from the human race, numerous and distinguishable by sex and age, as well as by disposition and rank'. *P.I.*, p. 168.

[308] David Hume, 'Of the Immortality of the Soul', *Essays,* passim; Kettler, *Social and Political Thought of Adam Ferguson*, pp. 122-3.

[309] *Institutes*, pp. 8-9. Kettler, *Social and Political Thought of Adam Ferguson* pp. 123-4.

[310] *P.I.*, pp. 53, 180; *Essay*, pp. 57, 89-90.

[311] The distinction is as follows: 'General Providence' refers to God's action in the original creation of nature. In the beginning God created the material frame of nature and He structured it to function in obedience to the laws of nature which He also created. In contrast to this original creative act of general

is equipped with uniform laws to keep it in motion, direct divine intervention is redundant. Providence works through the efficient causes of physical laws of nature (our instincts in concert with the material forces of nature) to secure spontaneous order and our moral and practical progress, our *telos* or final cause.[312]

3. SOCIAL ORDER AS A PROGRESSIVIST TELEOLOGY[313]

Ferguson agreed with William Robertson that history bears all the marks of design;[314] it has an intelligent structure, which is not arbitrary but orderly. The world's 'beauty' consists in 'the symptoms of intelligence, invention, wisdom and goodness' apparent 'in its every part'.[315] There is a discernible *telos* to all human activity which is moral perfection conceived as an ongoing, asymptotic process. Rather than perceiving everything in created nature as possessing essences striving for self-realisation, as Aristotle had suggested, only 'minds' are destined for progress. This progressive process, once established, possesses an independent momentum. The species is endowed with an immutable progressive instinct as well as other drives that ensure its survival. Human independence and agency are combined with the idea of a Providential order. The material world, the miraculous balance of nature, is the forum or matrix for the expression of these innate drives. Human achievements, (knowledge and the development of our social and political institutions) which simultaneously hone and provide the nursery of our moral evolution, evolve insensibly and by degrees. They are immanent in human nature and in the external conditions carefully contrived by a benevolent Creator. The seeds of human development are planted and the conditions for their fruition secured.[316] God is retired to an evanescent abstraction and the human species becomes the focus of attention as it negotiates its way towards its destiny. Human existence is progressive and dynamic; it has a purpose, and that purpose is also its cause. *Telos* does not simply connote 'aim' or 'purpose'.[317] Strictly speaking it is also the final cause of our development, just as the acorn contains the potential of an oak tree, *causing* it to become an oak tree rather than some other species of tree.[318]

---

providence is 'Special Providence' which refers to a particular act of direct divine intervention that cancels or contravenes the ordinary course of natural operations'. J. E. Force, 'Hume and the Relation of Science to Religion Among Certain Members of the Royal Society', *Journal of the History of Ideas*, Vol. 45 (4), 1984, pp. 517-53, p. 519.

[312] See, for example, *P.I.*, pp. 305, 312; *History*, p. 170.

[313] Though teleological explanations can be traced back to Aristotle, the term 'teleology' is a modern one, apparently coined in eighteenth-century philosophical Latin to denote the study of final causes in nature. The term was absorbed almost immediately into the modern philosophical vocabulary. It is generally applied to any activity that is purposive or goal directed. Owens, 'Teleology of Nature in Aristotle', p.159.

[314] Broadie, *The Scottish Enlightenment*, pp. 57-8.

[315] 'Of Things that Are or May Be' (Part 1), *Collection of Essays*, No. 27, p. 221.

[316] *Essay*, p. 120

[317] Martin Heidegger, *The Question Concerning Technology and Other Essays*, Translated and with an Introduction by William Lovitt, New York: Garland Publishing Inc., 1977, p. 8.

[318] Edel, *Aristotle*, p. 64. Ferguson himself employs this typically Aristotelian acorn/oak tree analogy. *P.I.*, p. 188.

Fergusonian historiography is at once modern because progressivist, yet also theologically conventional in terms of its perfectibilist and teleological aspects. Ferguson conceives the progress and development of the species as the acting out of a divine plan. But because the Creator is a General rather than Special Providence, the burden of responsibility falls principally to mortals. Free will, short-term rationality and conscious agency take centre stage as the species engages in an asymptotic process of self-realisation.[319] Ferguson's entire philosophy embodies an energetic affirmation of our freedom to choose. Everyone, he insists, 'is a voluntary agent'.[320] Ferguson rejects the doctrines of predestination and moral necessity and disputes the application of mechanistic causal explanations to organic life forms, particularly human beings.[321] The 'atheistic fatalism' of Hobbes on the one hand, and the rigid determinism of Descartes, Bacon, Spinoza and Hume, on the other,[322] is resoundingly spurned. This aspect of Ferguson's thought is discussed more fully later on where its full implications for his historiography are explored.

4. A PROVIDENTIALIST SOCIAL SCIENCE?

It could be argued that Ferguson's profoundly Providentialist and teleological approach to the study of society disqualifies it as a significant forerunner of secular social science. There are a number of arguments against such a charge. Though we are accustomed to conceiving social science proper as, by definition, a secular enterprise, there is no reason why we should exclude the possibility of a First Cause to account for the existence of those efficient causes to which the social science directs its attention.[323] As far as the explanatory power of Ferguson's social theory goes, the theological dimension does not drastically affect outcomes because the primary arena of activity is at the individuo-psychic, efficient causes level, as will be shown in more detail presently. For the most part,[324] Ferguson's explanations *depend* neither on First Causes nor on the Special interventions of Providence. Since 'God', for Ferguson, is a 'General' rather than 'Special Providence', order is generated by efficient causes, therefore the model is effectively comparable with secular contemporary accounts like Hume's or twentieth century accounts like F. A. Hayek's. Regarding Hume, the main difference is that whereas Hume does not care to speculate on the *original* and First Cause of these efficient causes, Ferguson does. Both expound two-tiered arrangements, both models are generated by endogenous drives at the efficient causes level, and both depend on the law of the heterogeneity of ends. So long as the main arena of action is located at the efficient causes level,

---

[319] *Essay,* pp. 12-13.

[320] *Institutes,* p. 125.

[321] Whitney, *Primitivism and the Idea of Progress,* p. 148. See *Institutes,* p. 75.

[322] D. P. Sailor, 'Newton's Debt to Cudworth', *Journal of the History of Ideas,* Vol. 49 (4), 1988, pp. 511-16, p. 511.

[323] The real problem is obviously the appeal to *Final* Causes, which precludes any scientific appreciation of behaviour or evolution as open-ended.

[324] Excepting his claims about human defects being deliberately endued in order to secure order and progress. To be discussed.

and so long as these causes issue in positive aggregate outcomes, it qualifies as a proper theory of spontaneous order. Any authentically secular spontaneous order model has four essential features: its undirected character, its gradualism, its inevitability and its universality. All are present in Ferguson's account. The undirected character refers to the individuo-psychic level, not the final causes level which displays all the *apparent* signs of design, especially in its uniformity and inevitability. (Hayek likewise emphasised 'the unintended consequences of *human* action').[325] For Ferguson, world order *is* the product of design whereas for Hume it is *as if* the world is the product of design, so neat is the arrangement.[326]

5. CONCLUDING REMARKS

In Ferguson's early social science the design principle dominates the entire scene. The world is the product of design and its order and progress are Providentially inspired. The optimistic ontology which underpins his system comes originally from Stoicism. The world was created as a harmonious, self-righting unit and '(w)e have no reason...to believe that it was possible for God to make the universe better than he has done'.[327] Ferguson also relies heavily on the influence of Christianity for its avowal of genesis, design, free will and the resolution of all virtues into benevolence. Therefore, whenever we detect a sociological flavour in Ferguson's work, we need to be mindful of the theological context. But this fact need not disqualify Ferguson's insights as anticipatory because his reliance on efficient or secondary causes for maintaining equilibrium clearly foreshadows sociology's much later dependence on latent or sub-rational group processes to explain social order.

---

[325] Roger A. Arnold, 'Hayek and Institutional Evolution' *The Journal of Libertarian Studies*, Vol.4 (4), 1980, pp. 341-51, p. 341. My emphasis.

[326] As Barry observes: 'What is important about the theory of spontaneous order is that the institutions and practices it investigates reveal well-structured social patterns which *appear to be the product of some omniscient designing mind* yet which are in reality the spontaneous co-ordinated outcomes of the actions of, possibly, millions of individuals who had no intention of effecting such overall aggregate orders'. Norman Barry, 'The Tradition of Spontaneous Order', *Literature of Liberty*, Vol. 5 (2), 1982. pp. 7-58, pp. 8-10. My emphasis. See also Edna Ullmann-Margalit, 'Invisible Hand Explanations', *Synthese*, Vol. 39 (2), 1978, pp. 263-91, pp. 268-70. For further discussion see Chapter 6.

[327] *P.I.,* p. 338.

CHAPTER 4

METHOD AND HISTORIOGRAPHY

This chapter examines the methodological aspects of Ferguson's historical, social and moral project. It also defines his aims in pursuing it. Ferguson was concerned to discover the 'dispositions' of our species in a style that could be described as moving towards 'methodological holism'. Insisting, against Hobbes, on the natural sociability of the species[328] he sets out to construct an early social psychology or anthropology, which consists in his marriage of a kind of 'anthropological empiricism' with a conjectural history. Claims that Ferguson's writings represent a proto-Marxist materialist analysis are dealt with briefly while there is some attention paid to the theological and spontaneous dimensions of his historiography.

1. GENERAL APPROACH

The laws of nature, especially those relating to social order, must be understood in order that they might be properly observed. Ferguson wants to discover 'scientifically' and empirically the laws governing human nature ('the laws of [the] animal and intellectual system') and from there to deduce moral principles or guidelines for behaviour.[329] In this, as on many other counts, he emulates the Stoic Epictetus, who conceived the philosopher's mission as one of discovering the laws of our nature in order that we might conform to them and thereby conform to God's will. The result is a procedure simultaneously empirical and normative.

> Before we can ascertain the rules of morality for mankind, the history of man's nature, his dispositions, his specific enjoyments and sufferings, his condition and future prospects, should be known.[330]

It is only through a thorough examination of the human constitution and its conditions that we can attain the self-mastery we need in order to live according to nature.[331] There is an 'established order' of things regulated by 'fixed' 'laws of nature'. This order 'is the proper work of God, the proper study of man, the foundation of skill, wisdom and art.'[332]

---

[328] See, for example, *P.I.,* p. 198.

[329] *Essay*, pp. 8-9. See also 'Of the Different Aspects of Moral Science', *Collection of Essays*, No. 29, p. 251.

[330] *Institutes*, p. 11. See also *P.I.*, p. 5 and Barnes, 'Sociology Before Comte', p. 234.

[331] *P.I.*, p. 3.

[332] *P.I.*, p. 179. This was precisely Hutcheson's approach. Francis Hutcheson, *A System of Moral Philosophy*, in Two Volumes, London: 1755, I: 1.

To the modern reader, the *Essay* looks like a social history of the human species whereas for Ferguson it was equally an exercise in moral philosophy. On the advice of Epictetus, he narrows down the conceptual tools necessary for raising 'the mind to a just sense of divine providence' to '[t]wo things only': 'attention to the course of nature, and a grateful mind.' The role of the philosopher is to infer God's will for herself and, for Ferguson, with his firm commitment to empiricism, there is no better starting point than with our own species' history.[333] The subject of his history is therefore human society, the matrix for the existence, development and progress of individual agents. Like the nineteenth and twentieth century sociologists he foreshadowed, Ferguson sought to create an in-depth study of forms of sociation and the laws that governed them.

Ferguson was careful to stress the distinction between his descriptive history and the normative prescriptions which he saw as logically flowing from it. The term 'law' is used in two senses. 'Physical' laws refer to laws that govern matter and mind, that is, observable uniformities,[334] whereas 'moral laws' are normative. A moral law is a law 'which we desire to have uniformly observed...in consequence of its rectitude, or of the authority from which it proceeds; not in consequence of it being the fact.'[335] This second kind of law is of great interest to Ferguson because, as he says, 'it is of more importance to know the condition to which we ourselves should aspire, than that which our ancestors may be supposed to have left.'[336] Ferguson seems to be suggesting that his project as a 'scientific' historian is subordinate to his mission as a moralist. Yet the two functions are intimately related, the success of the second being almost entirely dependent on the skill with which the first is executed.[337] Ferguson therefore takes seriously the 'scientific' task before him.

Ferguson adopted a type of Newtonian empiricism and combined it with Montesquieu's descriptive and historical method in order to achieve a distinctly sociological effect. He shares in Adam Smith's high regard for Newton, a 'true scientist', who avoided 'vain conjecture' and relied instead on observable data.[338] Ferguson admired Newton's skill in comprehensively accounting for the movements of the planets in terms of two universal laws, those of motion and gravitation.[339] He strove to comprehend 'man's' nature or constitution under universal laws or first

---

[333] *Essay*, pp. 14-16. 'To know human nature...we must avail ourselves not only of the consciousness...of a single mind, but, more at large also, of the varieties that are presented in the history of mankind'. *P.I.,* p. 49.

[334] 'The physical laws of nature may be collected from a sufficient number of particulars, which, though differing in circumstances, and diversified in their appearances, suggest a general fact common to many bodies'. *P.I.,* p. 115. Or '[a] physical law of nature is a general state of what is uniform or common in the order of things, and is addressed to the powers of perception and sagacity'. *P.I.,* pp. 159-60.

[335] *Institutes* pp. 78-9. The same strict distinction is made elsewhere: 'We are not now inquiring what men ought to do, but what is the ordinary tract in which they proceed'. *P.I.,* p. 263.

[336] *Essay*, p. 16.

[337] *P.I.,* p. 5.

[338] *P.I.,* pp. 116-117; Smith, 'The History of Astronomy', in Adam Smith, *Essays on Philosophical Subjects*, I.S. Ross, (ed.), Oxford: Clarendon Press, 1980, pp. 97-105. For Ferguson's general aversion to 'hypothesis and vain conjecture' see also *Joseph Black*, p. 111.

[339] *Institutes*, II. 2. passim.

principles on the basis of observed uniformities and without recourse to the Scriptures or the special interventions of a personal God. This, he believes, is the true test of the philosopher.[340]

The key to understanding the world and its workings is to study the material world as it actually is, not as we would wish it to be. Ferguson reproaches any 'unscientific' historian who 'substitutes hypothesis instead of reality' thereby 'confound[ing] the provinces of imagination and reason, of poetry and science.'[341] His ambition is to approximate in social science the method of 'physical science', namely, to discover 'the actual state of things'.[342] God's will is communicated to us through his works, nature being the privileged ontological and epistemological reference point.[343] Ferguson's predecessors, the British empiricists and Hutcheson, had built up their moral philosophies from a similar epistemological framework, that is, by importing Newtonian and Baconian principles of 'natural science' into the study of morality.[344] Equally, Ferguson's approach can be thought of as a reaction to Cartesian a priorism with its reliance on 'supposition upon supposition, without any evidence of reality'.[345] Everything we need to know about the world is set before us in the great 'volume of nature' which Ferguson conceives democratically as 'open for the information of mankind'.[346] Like the Stoics, Ferguson perceived this task in social terms as an enterprise upon which we are all embarked. 'The world's a system', he remarked, 'and the best we can do is to assist one another in perceiving and communicating its parts and their connection.'[347]

Rejecting the ideas of a state of nature and the conventional distinction between artifice and nature, Ferguson insists that every situation and condition is natural to the species. He consciously attempted to avoid the type of ethnocentrism that was still rife in his time by using as wide a variety of ethnographic sources as were available to him and by adopting an early structural-functionalism.[348] He believed that every society, in whatever state of development (except in cases of despotism) is a desirable state, equally capable of providing the conditions for human flourishing.[349] But he was unable to escape completely from his own unconscious Western ethnocentrism. Convinced of the underlying unity of humanity he was interested in the detection and analysis of cultural universals[350] including the natural

---

[340] *Essay*, pp. 30-1.

[341] *Essay*, p. 8.

[342] *P.I.*, p. 160.

[343] See *P.I.*, pp. 213, pp. 166-7.

[344] Oz-Salzberger, *Translating the Enlightenment,* p. 111.

[345] *P.I.*, p. 118.

[346] *P.I.*, p. 218.

[347] 'Principle of Moral Estimation', *Collection of Essays*, No. 25, p. 204.

[348] For example: 'It is well known that external expressions, whether of moral sentiment or devotion, in the manners or religious observances of men, are, like the words of their language, mere arbitrary signs which custom accordingly may alter: But the sentiments themselves...retain their distinctive quality under all the variations of their external expression'. *P.I.*, p. 223. See also *P.II.*, p. 142.

[349] *Essay*, p. 94. For Ferguson's brief excursus on ethnocentrism see *Essay*, pp. 194-5.

[350] Ferguson notes for example, that a universalisable 'moral science' is achieved by 'abstracting from local forms and observances'. *P.II.*, p. 113.

tendency for all cultures to develop in roughly the same manner. Predictably, European, (particularly British) culture is taken to be the most advanced exemplar and is therefore indicative and predictive of the direction of other cultures in a state of progression.

Although his main unit of concern is society, Ferguson by no means neglects the human constitution. He aims to study 'man's' functioning both individually and in groups in order to deduce normative principles. He thus devotes considerable space to the study of 'pneumatics', the eighteenth century equivalent of psychology.[351] Eighteenth century anthropology was much broader than its contemporary avatar, necessarily entailing both empirical elements and an a priori study of the metaphysical, existential and essential attributes of 'man'. This study inevitably led to a rudimentary study of human psychology or 'knowledge of the soul in general, and of the soul of man in particular'.[352]

But, because he was also interested in establishing law-like social explanations Ferguson combined this study with findings that drew heavily on a wide base of ethnographic data. Ferguson is striving for a kind of proto-anthropology which, in his own terminology, consists in recording the observations of the 'indifferent spectator' — whose concern is with 'external appearances' — and combining it with a more individualistic and introspective 'history of the mind'.[353] A certain degree of self-examination is required in order for Ferguson to understand the 'process by which we internalise…moral, social and intellectual ideas' and acquire 'moral culture'.[354] Generally, though, aside from this introspective supplemental method, he aims to be empirical and to deduce general rules on the basis of observed uniformities. He will attempt to be strictly 'scientific' in his approach and simply report his findings. Of course, there is always the problem of 'ultimate facts' ('facts that cannot be explained by any rule previously known') self-evident truths whose deeper workings are beyond our grasp. Such things must remain articles of faith for 'to require proof *a priori* for every fact, were to suppose that human knowledge requires an infinite series of facts and explanations; which is impossible.' In fact, the cause of 'penetrating appearances…[the] vain desire of accounting for ultimate facts' has 'retarded the progress of science'.[355]

It is far more useful to get on with a thorough study of 'particulars' or observable phenomena rather than attempting to speculate about the origins or causes of

---

[351] Dugald Stewart agreed that the foundation of theoretical history is the study of the progress of the human mind. Mary Fearnley-Sander, 'Philosophical History and the Scottish Reformation: William Robertson and the Knoxian Tradition', *The Historical Journal*, Vol. 33 (2), 1990, pp. 323-38, p. 325. For further discussion see Chapter Five.

[352] This, at least, was how William Smellie defined it in his *Encyclopaedia Britannica*. F. Vidal, 'Psychology in the Eighteenth Century: A View from Encyclopaedias', *History of the Human-Sciences*, 1993, Vol. 6 (1), pp. 89-119, pp. 95-6.

[353] *P.I.*, p. 49. *P.I*, p. 3-6. Not to be confused with Smith's impartial spectator.

[354] Phillipson, 'The Scottish Enlightenment', pp. 20-1.

[355] *Institutes*, pp. 8-9. The existence of a 'moral sense' is, for example, an 'ultimate fact in the constitution of our nature'. It is a 'law' because 'uniform' in its 'operations' and 'nature' but is, at the same time, in 'no way susceptible of explanation or proof'. In the same way, the 'laws of gravitation, cohesion, magnetism, electricity, fluidity [and] elasticity' are also ultimate facts.. *P.II.*, p. 128.

things.[356] Ferguson condemns both Berkeley's and Hume's scepticism (idealism) about the reliability of the senses for representing the material world, in favour of Thomas Reid's common sense realism. The science of disclosing the details of 'external existence' is tenable and 'reality of knowledge...may be safely assumed' because perception is, in the main, veridical; that is to say, the senses *can* be relied upon to faithfully reflect the external world. Ferguson considers himself a follower of Reid's method in his determination to 'remov[e] the mist of hypothesis and metaphor' and simply seek out and 'state the facts'. Scientific progress requires that we focus on the 'applications and consequences' of natural laws, rather than their 'origins'. Thus, his study of the human constitution, is about *observing* rather than 'explain[ing], the laws of conception and will'. Epistemological and metaphysical scepticism is not only pointless,[357] but represents an obstacle to the type of social science Ferguson wishes to pursue, namely a systematic folk or pre-theoretical type of psychology in which human minds and the *noumena* of the external world are taken as fundamental explanatory concepts rather than as objects to be problematised, deconstructed or analysed away.[358] 'Real knowledge' (ultimate facts notwithstanding) is both possible and desirable of attainment. Against sceptics like Hume, Ferguson finds it perfectly reasonable, not only to trust the reports of our senses but also to make reasonable assumptions based on the regular and observable tendencies they record (in other words, induction). Responding to one of Hume's most famous examples, he suggests, '[t]he sun, even by a person who never saw him rise or set, may be supposed, from the course he holds, to have risen in the east, and to set in the west'. Thus, we can, for example, safely assume that sociable peace, rather than an isolated and chaotic state of war is the original condition of our species since a) we have no 'proof' that the 'first ages' were a scene of perpetual war and b) in most societies, even the most barbarous, people tend to get along fairly peaceably 'until some occasion of quarrel' arises.[359]

In a similar vein, Ferguson resolves at the outset of the *Essay* to strictly avoid any kind of metaphysical speculation, any discussion of religious subjects, such as the nature or attributes of God or the spiritual destiny of 'mankind', other than that which is directly inferable from experience. He insists that he is not going to waste his time on such matters and resigns himself to ignorance on epistemological grounds.[360] In this, too, he emulates Bacon[361] though it should be noted that, at times, his resolve fails. Even so, taken in context, Ferguson's social scientific ambitions are impressive. As Duncan Forbes rightly notes:

> Had anyone before Ferguson, with the exception of Montesquieu, so totally and explicitly resisted the temptation to indulge in imaginative and conjectural

---

[356] *Essay*, p. 29.

[357] *P.I.*, pp. 75-76.

[358] Ferguson does admit that 'scepticism' is useful for 'restraining credulity' which is 'one species of error'. Nevertheless, 'carried to extreme [it] would discourage the search of truth, suspend the progress of knowledge, and become a species of palsy of all the mental powers'. *P.I.,* p. 91.

[359] *P.I.*, p. 198.

[360] *Essay*, pp. 36-7. *P.I.*, p. 320.

[361] Ferguson admired Bacon profoundly. *Institutes*, p. xvii. By the 1730s Bacon's science was an 'integral part of the curriculum' of all Scottish universities. Wood, 'The Natural History of Man', p. 90.

reconstruction of the origin of society, and to go behind, not just the family, but the group, the 'troops and companies' in which man is always found.[362]

For Ferguson, the key to human psychology lies, not in the study of isolated individuals, ('in some imaginary state of nature') but in the study of 'man' as a social being. The examples of feral children, (for example Memmie la Blanche, the Wild Girl of Champagne and Wild Peter of Hanover who was sent to John Arbuthnot to be studied)[363] routinely paraded as spectacles for the curious gaze of polite society, are dismissed as aberrations that not only tell us nothing about human science but inevitably give 'rise to many wild suppositions'. Ferguson advises those of his colleagues with anthropological ambitions to start with the far more sensible proposition that '[m]ankind are to be taken in groups, as they have always subsisted.' He ridicules attempts to 'penetrate the secrets of nature' through locating some imaginary 'source of existence', and reminds us that humanity 'has always appeared within the reach of our own observation, and in the records of history'.[364] We have always been social and have always existed in a state of progression. Hobbes' and Rousseau's error is dismissed with good-natured raillery. 'Until we are told by whom the state of nature was done away, and a new one substituted, we must continue to suppose that this is the work of man himself'.[365] The key to understanding humanity is right before us; the evidence everywhere in the normal and everyday modes of existence. It is from the 'ordinary course of things', says Ferguson, 'that the laws of nature are collected'. Though the 'new and strange may amuse the imagination...the affectation of novelty' is apt to mislead the cause of 'science'.[366]

The Hobbesian (and later Rousseauian) construct of a 'state of nature' is condemned as both unrealistic and useless, even as an analytical tool not only because Ferguson is not looking for justifications by which to establish abstract principles of obligation and authority but for empirical reasons also. There never was a state of nature for humans have always lived in some form of civil society. Contrary to Rousseau's assertion that 'nature' has taken 'little care' to 'unite' and make 'sociable' human beings,[367] our 'mixed disposition to friendship or enmity'

---

[362] Forbes concludes: 'It cannot be said of Vico, Mandeville, or Rousseau...nor can it be said of Hume'. 'Introduction' to *Essay*, p. xvi.

[363] C. Fox, R. Porter and R. Wokler, *Inventing Human Science: Eighteenth Century Domains*, Berkeley: University of California Press, 1995, p. 12. The story of Memmie la Blanche was made known in a book published in Edinburgh in 1762 (*Account of a Savage Girl found in the Woods of Champagne*, Edinburgh, 1762). Eriksson, 'The First Formulation of Sociology', p. 268. Ferguson was thus undoubtedly aware of the case.

[364] *Essay*, p. 8. Montesquieu set the example for Ferguson here in his attempt to displace state of nature theories with the argument that principles of social order could only be deduced from social realities. Strasser, *Normative Structure of Sociology*, p. 42. Nevertheless his break with state of nature theories was never as decisive as Ferguson's.

[365] *P.I.*, pp. 199. Hume also ridiculed the notion of a state of nature describing it as 'a mere fiction, not unlike that of the golden age which poets have invented'. David Hume, *A Treatise of Human Nature*, Analytical Index by L.A. Selby-Bigge, Second Edition with Text Revised and Notes by P.H. Nidditch, Oxford: Oxford University Press, 1976, 3. 2. 2, p. 493.

[366] *P.I.*, p. 5.

[367] Rousseau, 'Discourse on the Origin of Inequality', in *Social Contract and Discourses*, p. 70.

and our capacity for 'reason...language and articulate sounds' are clear evidence of our natural sociability.[368] Indeed, 'the atmosphere of society...is the element in which the human mind must draw the first breath of intelligence itself [and] the vital air by which the celestial fire of moral sentiment is kindled'.[369] Human behaviour can only be understood socially. Indeed, Ferguson suggests that individuals reared in isolation are not really human.[370] Ferguson demonstrates the incoherence of the Enlightenment conception of individualism in its metaphysical variant by showing how all forms of existence are 'necessarily forms of social existence'.[371] All 'natural' impulses have social reference and humanity is always and everywhere in its natural state. 'If we are asked...Where the state of nature is to be found? we may answer, It is here; and it matters not whether we are understood to speak in the Island of Great Britain, at the Cape of Good Hope, or the Straits of Magellan.' Every situation and condition is natural to the human species. The distinction between artifice and nature is thus meaningless since we are born to create and contrive and have always done so.[372]

Ferguson approached his project with a relatively open mind, invoking evidence from a comprehensive range of cultures and ethnic groups[373] gleaned from an equally impressive array of ethnographic sources. He refers to his sources as 'both the earliest and the latest accounts collected from every quarter of the earth'.[374] His Roman *History* draws on 'the remains' of almost every ancient history available at the time and among his contemporary 'anthropological' sources were: Buffon's *Natural History*, *Halley's Tables*, Lowthorp's *Abridgement of Philosophical Transactions*, Wallace's *Numbers of Mankind*, Hume's *Populousness of Nations*, Lafitau's *Moeurs des Sauvages Ameriquains*,[375] Abulgaze's *Geneological History of the Tartars*, Chardin's *Travels*, Marsden's *History of Sumatra*, Colden's *History of Five Nations*, Charlevoix's *History of New France*, D'Arvieux's *History of the Wild Arabs*, Rubruquis' *Travels*, Carceri's, *Voyage Around the World*, Strahlenberg's *Historical-Geographical Description of the North and Eastern Part of Europe and Asia*, Jones's *Dissertations on Asia* and Kolbe's *The Present State of the Cape of Good Hope*.[376]

Despite the heterogeneity of his sources, Ferguson's aim was not to invoke an anthropology of difference but to achieve general explanation. He continuously

---

[368] *Essay*, p. 9.

[369] *P.I.*, pp. 268-9.

[370] *Essay*, p.23: 'Send him to the desert alone, he is a plant torn from its roots: the form indeed may remain, but every faculty droops and withers; the human personage and the human character cease to exist'.

[371] Ted Benton, 'How Many Sociologies?', *Sociological Review*, Vol. 26, 1978, pp. 217-36, p. 226.

[372] *Essay*, pp. 12-14. Hume was in complete agreement on this point. See *Treatise*, 3.2.1, p. 484.

[373] 'European, Samoide, Tartar, Hindoo, Negro and American' are the six discrete 'racial' groups identified, though occasionally he seems to treat 'Arab' people as a distinct 'racial' group as well. *Essay*, pp. 106-18; *Institutes*, p. 20.

[374] *Essay*, p. 9.

[375] Lafitau is considered to be the 'father of social anthropology'. Eriksson, 'The First Formulation of Sociology', p. 256.

[376] For a full list of Ferguson's ethnographic sources see 'Bibliography', Section 2.

emphasises the uniformities in general terms, while admitting the differences which are adduced to the exercise of free will and the presence of environmental diversity. Beneficence, for example, is a universal passion though its 'arbitrary expressions are the different rites established in different countries'.[377]

2. NATURAL OR CONJECTURAL HISTORY: A STADIAL THESIS

Ferguson's is a history painted in broad brushstrokes tracing human progress in the arts, in customs and mores and in political and legal institutions. But it is fairly disorderly, lacking dates and actual chronology and composed, instead, of a series of impressions tracing the analogous 'infancy' of the species through to its 'maturity'.[378] It should be remembered that 'history' in the eighteenth century was considerably less rigorous than it is today. Ferguson's own definition of history as 'a collection of facts in description or narration' is precisely what he delivers to his reader.[379]

Ferguson's history is a conscious homage to the style of Montesquieu whom he praised lavishly.[380] He emulates the latter's methodological empiricism, based his entire system on his endorsement of Aristotle's assumption of the natural sociability of humanity;[381] shared the former's belief in the immutability and uniformity of human nature;[382] agreed that social laws were generated via the human constitution;[383] adopted his taxonomy of political forms and effective political condition (focusing upon such issues as Machiavellian civic virtue and the elements of a stable constitution); recognised the role of environmental factors in shaping the latter and concerned himself with the causes of, and solutions to, the decline of nations. Like Montesquieu, Ferguson's unit of analysis is society, and his concern lies in the identification of the general laws that govern it and the explanation of causal relations between social facts. He thereby takes to heart Montesquieu's famous dictum that history is not explained by singular events but by underlying causes and law-like relationships.

> It is not Fortune who governs the world, as we see from the history of the Romans...There are general causes, moral or physical, which operate in every monarchy, raise it, maintain it, or overthrow it. All that occurs is subject to these causes; and if a particular cause, like the accidental result of a battle, has ruined a state, there

---

[377] *Institutes,* pp. 224-5. Humans are universally characterised as 'being united in society, and concerned in what relates to their fellow-creatures'. They also 'universally admire qualities which constitute or procure the good of mankind; as, wisdom, justice, courage and temperance'. *Institutes,* p. 38.

[378] *Essay,* p. 10.

[379] Bryson, *Man and Society,* p. 255.

[380] Bryson, *Man and Society,* p. 51. Ferguson (over-generously) attributed to Montesquieu 'the original of what I am now'. *Essay,* p. 66.

[381] Grotius is also another likely source for this view.

[382] Chitnis, *The Scottish Enlightenment,* p. 95-6.

[383] Montesquieu, *Laws,* 1. 1. 2., p. 6. Grotius also conceived human nature as the source of social laws and therefore order. '[T]he very nature of man', he wrote, 'is the mother of the law of nature'. Hugo Grotius, *Prolegomena,* to *The Life and Works of Hugo Grotius,* W.S.M. Knight, London: Sweet & Maxwell Ltd., 1925, Section 16.

was a general cause which made the downfall of the this state ensue from a single battle. In a word, the principal impulse draws with it all the particular occurrences.[384]

Another important source for Ferguson (as well as other Scottish historians of the time) was Samuel Pufendorf. Like his Scottish imitators, he saw the emergence of private property as a key factor in the development of societies. Secondly, he seems to have been the first to propose a stadial theory of progress.[385] Scots like Smith, Millar, Kames, Robertson and Ferguson took up this idea with enthusiasm.

Turning to Ferguson's historiography, the key aspect to be noted is that it is quite modern in offering a progressivist, perfectibilist, spontaneous and law-driven conception of human affairs. Attacking the rationalistic device of contract as the 'chief principle of historical explanation'[386] Ferguson appeals to an evolutionistic perfectionism which relies instead on endogenous and unconscious causes. The laws of spontaneous order secure, not only our vital social institutions, but our practical and moral progress as a species through time. Order in our institutions, mores and living conditions is not simply maintained; our species is also propelled perpetually towards its practical and moral evolution. History is a process of natural (albeit soft) determinism, generated by endogenous human characteristics and moderated by human will and agency. Yet Ferguson's 'progressive teleology' also emphasises our species' self-creation, and its place as the highest form of created being. It is, therefore, highly anthropocentric. Ferguson begins his *Essay* by laying out two of his most important assumptions. Firstly, that our progress is far more advanced than that 'of any other animal' and secondly, that whereas other species merely advance individually from a state of 'infancy to manhood', humans advance collectively, in a natural and teleological sequence, from 'rudeness' through to 'civilisation'.[387]

In order to prove that the human experience is subject to laws of spontaneous order Ferguson wants to show that our history is subject to uniform laws, that it has a logical structure, and that society has progressed naturally and predictably from a rude to a polished state in accordance with the species' 'naturally' progressive tendencies. Historical progress refers to a kind of developmental change from one social structure to another. Montesquieu was the first to explore these kinds of social categories but, as Ronald Meek has noted, there is no clear indication that he regarded these different structures as 'successive stages of development through which societies normally progressed over time'.[388] Yet, if Ferguson was indeed influenced by Montesquieu in this matter this is probably what Ferguson took him to mean. Ferguson does see the stages as successive, sequential and universally inevitable for all cultures, as did other thinkers like Smith and Millar. For example, Millar agreed with Ferguson that the 'similarity' of human 'wants' coupled with the

---

[384] Charles-Louis Montesquieu, *Consideration of the Causes of the Greatness of the Romans and Their Decline*, New York: David Lowenthal, 1969, Chapter xviii.

[385] Salzberger, 'Introduction' to *Essay*, p. xiii.

[386] Lehman, *Adam Ferguson*, p. 237.

[387] *Essay*, pp. 7, 10-11.

[388] Ronald Meek, *Social Science and the Ignoble Savage*, Cambridge: Cambridge University Press, 1976, p. 35.

similarity of 'faculties by which those wants are supplied, has everywhere produced a remarkable uniformity in the several stages of [humanity's] progression'.[389]

There is a natural and sequentially linear order to history which Ferguson presents in the form of a tri-stadial thesis. A fundamental pattern or general law revealed by Ferguson's comparative anthropology is the natural and universal tendency for all cultures to progress sequentially through several discrete stages from 'savage' (hunters and gatherers) through to 'barbarous' (agricultural) and finally to 'polished' (commercial) social forms.[390] These forms, the divine blueprint of our progress, inhere in 'human nature'.[391]

This important 'discovery' leads Ferguson to establish (along with Smith, Millar, Robertson, Stewart, Kames, Stuart and other Scots)[392] a natural or 'conjectural' history, to use the term Ferguson's pupil, Dugald Stewart, would later coin to describe their approach.[393] Such a history is natural insofar as it seeks to reveal the tendency of human development notwithstanding the interference of influential individuals or historical 'accidents'. It is conjectural because this development can still be mapped out in the absence of complete data particularly where there is data from comparable societies to fill the gaps and complete the picture. Conjectural history thus frequently (though not exclusively) embodies a comparative approach.[394] Ferguson's use of the comparative method is said to have laid the foundation for the comparative method employed in later sociology.[395]

Ferguson tells us that we may 'form a just notion of our progress from the cradle' by examining 'those who are still in the period of life we mean to describe'. The present condition of Native Americans, for example, tells us all we need to know about the origins of European — and indeed all other peoples — for '[i]t is in their present condition, that we are to behold, as in a mirrour, the features of our own progenitors'.[396] The conjectural method allows for the filling of gaps with inferences drawn from actual human tendencies. For example, the social instincts exhibited by

---

[389] Millar, *Origin of the Distinction of Ranks*, p. 176.

[390] *Essay*, pp. 80-105.

[391] Even constitutions appropriate for the age are conceived teleologically: 'The seeds of every form are lodged in human nature; they spring up and ripen with the season'. *Essay*, p. 120.

[392] For a fuller discussion on the conjectural histories of other Scottish contemporaries see Christopher J. Berry, *Social Theory of the Scottish Enlightenment*, Edinburgh: Edinburgh University Press, 1997, pp. 61-70.

[393] Dugald Stewart, 'Account of the Life and Writings of Adam Smith, LL D,' I.S. Ross (ed.) in Adam Smith, *Essays on Philosophical Subjects*, W.P.D.Wightman and J.C.Bryce (eds), Oxford: Oxford University Press, 1980, pp. 292-3.

[394] J.C. Wilsher, 'Power Follows Property — Social and Economic Interpretations in British Historical Writing in the Eighteenth and Early Nineteenth Centuries', *Journal of Social History*, Vol. 16, 1983, pp. 7-26, p. 10. In the absence of comparative data or direct evidence, reasonable conjecture is considered to be an acceptable substitute. This, at least, was Stewart's view. Salim Rashid, *The Myth of Adam Smith*, Cheltenham: Edward Elgar, 1998, pp. 54-5.

[395] Frederick J. Teggert, *Theory of History,* New Haven, Conn.: Yale University Press, 1925, p. 89, cited in Hamowy, *Social and Political Thought of Adam Ferguson*, p. 127.

[396] *Essay*, p. 80.

contemporary 'man' are not new but have always been present in the human frame; since human nature is constant, humans must always have been social.[397]

Ferguson's inspiration for the use of this method seems to have come originally, not from Turgot, as might be expected, but from 'Greek and Roman historians' like Thucydides and Tacitus who had found 'in the customs of barbarous nations...the more ancient manners of Greece'.[398] A secondary, more modern, source of inspiration may have been Cadwallader Colden, the first American writer to employ the comparative method. Colden's *History of Five Indian Nations* was published in 1727 and was cited by Ferguson.

But this application of the comparative approach is about as far as Ferguson is prepared to go in terms of reconstructing history. One difficulty of the conjectural approach is that it tends to be verificationist in the sense that the proof of human destiny, as inferred from human tendencies and history, is uncritically adopted as scientific. The other problem with Ferguson's adoption of the comparative approach is that it seems to have involved him in a methodological contradiction by causing him to inadvertently invoke a kind of methodological primitivism, something which, as a progressivist, he would ordinarily have wished to avoid. When Ferguson asserts that our nature is best exemplified by those living in savage and barbarous conditions, he is seems to be implying that behaviour is somehow more 'natural' in such situations[399] thereby contradicting his other premise that all states and stages are equally natural. In addition, the conjectural approach is highly ethnocentric. It universalises 'human nature' in the image of Western culture and assimilates 'all the non-Western peoples into a single progressive series reaching its apogee in Western civilisation'.[400] Such an approach may be usefully contrasted with Rousseau's thoroughly anti-perfectionist primitivism. Here too a three-stage paradigm is employed, comprising a pre-social primitive state, a transitional state of barbarism and finally civilised society. Rousseau's ideal is not the pre-social state, as is often supposed, but the transitional period characterised by self-sufficiency, rudimentary forms of sociability and the 'expansion of the human faculties'. Here, there is maintained 'a just mean between the indolence of the primitive state and the petulant activity of our *amour-propre.*' This, he notes, is the state in which most 'savages' are found, a fact which 'seems to prove that men were meant to remain in it'. Any 'subsequent advances' have achieved nothing more than 'the decrepitude of the species'.[401]

---

[397] *Essay,* p. 21. For John Brewer, Ferguson's use of conjectural historiography represents a constraint on 'his anticipation of nineteenth century sociology' because 'it led to a concern with the prospects of civil society which easily encouraged the use of civic humanist discourse'. Although I would argue that Ferguson's concern with corruption inspired his most profoundly sociological observations, there is also merit in Brewer's suggestion that 'this alternative discourse pulls Ferguson back from expanding and developing' them to their fullest potential. Brewer, 'Adam Ferguson and the Division of Labour', pp. 22-3.

[398] *Essay,* pp. 78-80. As noted by K.E. Bock, 'The Comparative Method of Anthropology', *Comparative Studies in Society and History,* Vol. 8, 1965-6, pp. 269-280, p. 271.

[399] *Essay,* p. 23.

[400] R. Nisbet, *History of the Idea of Progress,* London: Heinemann, 1980, p. 149.

[401] Rousseau, 'Discourse on the Origin of Inequality', in *Social Contract and Discourses,* p. 91.

Nevertheless Ferguson's use of the conjectural method was still relatively critical and self-aware. He cautioned that it was a valid method only so long as its practitioners understood that they operated at all times under the constraint that they themselves were also *subjects* of history and therefore inescapable products of particular historical and cultural circumstances. They would thus be, not only culturally prejudiced, but also epistemologically limited in their understanding.[402]

Unlike the 'Four Stages' means of subsistence schema (hunting, pastoral, agricultural and commercial) adopted by Smith and Millar, the categories in Ferguson's three-stage paradigm are based on social structure as well as economic condition. The terms 'savage', 'barbarous' and 'polished' refer to the level of laws, government, 'proficiency in liberal and mechanical arts, in literature and in commerce'.[403] Ferguson wants to base his categories on social, as well as economic characteristics because his bias is towards social and political, rather than economic condition,[404] hence John Pocock's designation of Ferguson's analysis as 'perhaps the most Machiavellian of the Scottish disquisitions of this theme.'[405] Ferguson's focus is normative and political whereas Smith and Millar sought to use a purely descriptive approach in order to identify economic types.[406] For example, in describing modes of subsistence in savage societies Ferguson is more interested in developing a moral theory about the relative position of women within them (which he likens to slavery) than in analysing the economic aspects of the modes themselves.[407]

Stage theory plays an important role in Ferguson's perfectibilism in the sense that the stages are conceived teleologically with increasing 'civilisation' as a kind of asymptotic goal. This makes Ferguson typical of many eighteenth century minds, for

---

[402] 'Our method, notwithstanding, too frequently is to rest the whole on conjecture; to impute every advantage of our own nature to those arts which we ourselves possess; and to imagine, that a mere negation of all our virtues is a sufficient description of man in his original state. We are ourselves the supposed standards of politeness and civilisation; and where our own features do not appear, we apprehend, that there is nothing which deserves to be known. But it is probable that here, as in many other cases, we are ill qualified, from our supposed knowledge of causes, to prognosticate effects, or to determine what must have been the properties and operations, even of our own nature, in the absence of those circumstances in which we have seen it engaged'. *Essay*, p. 75.

[403] Whether there was to be a fourth stage is an open question. David Kettler's assertion (*Social and Political Thought of Adam Ferguson*, p. 229) that Ferguson conceives 'despotism' as the fourth stage of history is questioned. Taxonomically speaking, despotism is not a developmental social stage, but a type of political constitution. *Analysis*, pp. 54-5. Ferguson outlines no fourth stage of history but this does not mean that he expected none, only that he avoided 'vain conjecture.' This misunderstanding may have arisen from the fact that Montesquieu (a key Fergusonian source) identified despotic rule as both a type of constitution and a developmental stage.

[404] D. MacRae, 'Adam Ferguson: Sociologist', *New Society*, Vol. 24, 1966, pp. 792-4. For a further discussion of the stadial thesis see H. Hellenbrand, 'Not to Destroy But to Fulfil: Jefferson, Indians and Republican Dispensation', *Seventeenth Century Studies*, Vol. 18 (4), 1985, pp. 523-48; Meek, *Social Science and the Ignoble Savage*, p. 154 and by the same author; 'The Scottish Contribution to Marxist Sociology', pp. 34-45 and K.G. Ballestrem, 'Sources of the Materialist Conception of History in the History of Ideas, *Studies in Soviet Thought*, Vol. 26 (1), 1983, pp. 3-9.

[405] J.G.A. Pocock, *The Machiavellian Moment*, Princeton: Princeton University Press, 1975, p. 499.

[406] See *P.I.*, p. 252 where Ferguson makes explicit that his categories are not strictly economic.

[407] For a short treatment of this discussion see: J.G.A. Pocock, *Barbarism and Religion,* Cambridge: Cambridge University Press, 1999, Vol. 2, pp. 335-7.

whom the retreat from incivility represented a gradual march towards perfection. The term 'civilisation' which Ferguson seems to have been the first to use in English, 'connotes both a fundamental process of history and the end result of that process'.[408]

3. FERGUSON AS A PROTO-MARXIST?

Ferguson's unique developmental categories make it difficult to conceive how his views could have been linked to a proto-materialist and even proto-Marxist historiography (as was attempted by a number of pioneering Ferguson scholars) more difficult even than with Smith or Millar whose categories are clearly economic. Roy Pascal, as a typical example, claims that the main theme of the *Essay* is that society 'owes its form and development to the structure and development of private property, and that the mode of this social development is one of progress through internal contradictions, through the struggle between classes with an antagonistic relationship to property'.[409] Such a misreading is due, according to Forbes, to an insufficient knowledge of 'the eighteenth century background'.[410] Ferguson frequently assures us that 'subordination' or 'rank distinctions' are not only perfectly natural[411] but also necessary to the functioning of commercial societies.[412] Subordination is deemed 'valuable' and there is 'nothing debasing' in being either a seller or hirer of labour.[413] It is therefore probably a distortion to perceive in the *Essay* a fully developed proto-Marxist theory of class struggle though there are certainly some important aspects in common. Ferguson's history *does* have dialectical aspects and he *does* anticipate a pluralist theory of class conflict but these dialectical effects are limited to political and constitutional

---

[408] 'The evolutionary assumption is explicit in the works of other Scottish colleagues of Ferguson — such as James Dunbar's *Essays on the History of Mankind in Rude and Cultivated Ages* (1780) and John Logan's *Elements of the Philosophy of History* (1781) — who treat of violence as the antithesis of civil society and assume, optimistically, that it is on the wane in modern civil societies'. Keane, *Civil Society. Old Images*, p. 119.

[409] Pascal, 'Property and Society', p. 178; Hamowy, *Spontaneous Order*, p. 22; R. Meek, 'Smith, Turgot and the 'Four Stages' Theory', *History of Political Economy*, Vol. 1, 1971, pp. 9-27 and by the same author, 'The Scottish Contribution to Marxist Sociology', pp. 34-50; Swingewood, 'Origins of Sociology', p. 171.

[410] Forbes, 'Introduction' to *Essay*, p. xxv.

[411] For example, '[t]here is a principle of subordination in the difference of natural talents' as well as in the adventitious '[mal]distribution of property, power and dependence'. 'Separation of Departments', *Collection of Essays*, No. 6, p. 143.

[412] *Essay,* pp. 63-4. See also Forbes, Introduction to *Essay*, p. xxv. William Robertson also took the view that 'there can be no Society, where there is no Subordination'. Cited in Daniele Francesconi, 'William Robertson on Historical Causation and Unintended Consequences', *Cromohs*, Vol. 4, 1999, pp. 1-18, p. 8. Note, incidentally, how Ferguson disagrees with Smith that people are born with equal talents. For Smith's views here see *An Inquiry Into the Nature and Causes of the Wealth of Nations*, R.H. Campbell, and A.S. Skinner, (eds), Oxford: Clarendon Press, 1979 (hereafter cited as *WN*), I.ii.4., p. 28.

[413] Ferguson adds that it is only in the 'Vices' of sellers and hirers of labour that he finds cause for criticism. These vices are: 'Envy and Rapacity on the part of the Poor, Arrogance and Licentiousness on the part of the rich'. 'Of the Separation of Departments', *Collection of Essays*, No. 15, p. 165.

arrangements.[414] By the same token, Ferguson's assertion that 'property is a matter of progress'[415] upon which these materialist interpretations hinge, is by no means equivalent to the statement, 'progress is a matter of property'.[416] Ferguson is simply observing the manner in which property relations alter as civilisations progress; the property relations themselves do not propel history though they do play some part. In his remarks immediately preceding the passage in question Ferguson observes that private property is unknown in the savage age whereas for the barbarian it is 'a principal object of care' though not yet regulated by government. When Ferguson tells us that 'property is a matter of progress' he is not identifying property itself as an agent of change. He is merely noting that private property does not emerge until the 'barbarous' age when people have acquired the legal and technical apparatus to support its possession.[417] Ferguson is also reiterating here his view that avidity, a psychogenetic urge, is an important factor in the progress of the species. 'The mechanic and commercial arts took their rise from the love of property, and were encouraged by the prospect of safety and gain'.[418] Property itself does not propel change; rather the love of it, avidity, indirectly does. This is not to deny the relevance of material factors to Ferguson's analysis. He is undoubtedly *partially* the materialist. The most important thing to remember is that the materialist dimension of his thought is not the sole, but merely one of the many, determinants of social change, as will be shown. In addition it is a *secondary* propellant of history, the primary ones being psychogenetic in nature, as will also be shown. In any case, Donald Winch reports a 'steady retreat' from such materialist interpretations of Scottish thought in recent years.[419]

4. SPONTANEOUS ORDER HISTORIOGRAPHY AND THE MYTH OF THE ORIGINAL LEGISLATOR

Durkheim once remarked that no social science was possible until theories of great legislators had been discarded.[420] The legislator myth, which can be traced back to Plato,[421] flourished during the eighteenth century and according to Duncan Forbes, 'its destruction was perhaps the most original and daring *coup* of the social science

---

[414] For a fuller discussion see Chapter 7.

[415] *Essay*, p. 81.

[416] As first noted by Duncan Forbes. 'Introduction' to *Essay*, p. xxv.

[417] *Essay*, pp. 81-2.

[418] *Essay,* p. 164.

[419] D. Winch, 'Adam Smith's 'Enduring Particular Result'', in I. Hont, and M. Ignatieff, (eds), *Wealth and Virtue*, p. 259. For a further discussion of this debate see A. Skinner, 'A Scottish Contribution to Marxist Sociology', I. Bradly, and M. Howard, (eds), *Classical and Marxian Political Economy: Essays in Honour of Ronald L. Meek*, London: 1982, pp. 79-114 and Chapter 10 of this book.

[420] Emile Durkheim, *Montesquieu and Rousseau*, Ann Arbor: University of Michigan Press, 1960, p. 12.

[421] J. T. Valauri, 'Social Order and the Limits of Law', *Duke Law Journal*, Vol. 3 (3), June, 1981, pp. 607-18, p. 610.

of the Scottish Enlightenment'.[422] A fundamental premise of Ferguson's historiography is that history is rarely moved by single visionaries but is a spontaneous process generated socially, sub-rationally and gradually. Significantly, the progress of the species is more or less uniform and this cannot be attributed to cultural contact or the transmission or copying of the ideas of one or a few ingenious individuals. As Ferguson notes, 'why seek from abroad the origin of arts, of which every society, having the principles in itself, only requires a favourable occasion to bring them to light?'[423] After all, '[m]atters have proceeded so far, without the aid of foreign examples, or the direction of schools'.[424] Our progressive drives, 'ambition' and 'self-preservation', are instinctive and, since human nature is uniform, it stands to reason that cultures will progress in roughly the same manner. 'It is not so surprising', for instance, 'that poetry should be the first species of composition in every nation'.[425] Every nation, 'however aided by lights from abroad', possesses 'the fabrics of science and art to erect for [itself]'.[426] Though chance and good fortune frequently play a part in progress, such 'accidents' are ultimately irrelevant; without them we would still make roughly the same progress.[427] Primordial creative imperatives, as well as basic species needs, are constant, therefore we should expect to find some cross-cultural uniformities, all things being equal, that is, provided the cultures being compared are at the same stage in their natural development and enjoy relative domestic 'political felicity'. Even where 'nations actually borrow from their neighbours, they probably borrow only what they are nearly in a condition to have invented themselves'. Certain inventions are coeval with particular social forms and a new advance is unlikely to arise before its proper time, that is, 'till the way be prepared by the introduction of similar circumstances'.[428]

Ferguson is probably addressing the authors of the *Encyclopedie* with their diffusionist theory of civilisation. On this view, civilisation was conceived as having been transmitted sequentially from nation to nation from its original source in Egypt.[429] It was a commonplace of seventeenth-century learning that the Greeks obtained much of their knowledge from the Egyptians and this doctrine remained

---

[422] Forbes, 'Introduction' to *Essay*, p. xxiv. Millar also subscribed to this view. John Millar, *The Origins of the Distinctions of Ranks*, reprinted in W.C. Lehmann, *John Millar of Glasgow 1733-1801*, London: Cambridge University Press, 1960, pp. 177-8.

[423] *Essay*, p. 162.

[424] *Essay*, p. 168.

[425] *Essay*, p. 165.

[426] *P.I.*, pp. 283, 42.

[427] *Essay*, pp. 162. Hume argues along similar lines in one of his essays that real advances are social products while 'what depends upon a few persons is, in great measure, to be ascribed to chance'. Moreover, socially produced changes are always the more sensible and are better suited to existing conditions whereas the innovations of 'single persons...are more influenced by whim, folly, or caprice than by general passions or interests'. Hume, 'The Rise of Arts and Sciences', *Essays*, p. 112.

[428] *Essay*, pp. 162-3.

[429] Forbes, 'Introduction' to *Essay*, p. xxiv. James Burnett (Lord Monboddo) was also a proponent of this view. J. Gascoigne, 'The Wisdom of the Egyptians', in S. Gaukroger, ed., *The Uses of Antiquity*, p. 204. So was Rousseau. 'Discourse on the Moral Effects of the Arts and Sciences', p. 8 and 'Discourse on Inequality', pp. 61-2, in *Social Contract and Discourses*.

popular until the early part of the nineteenth century.[430] But Ferguson counsels us 'to receive, with caution, the traditional histories of ancient legislators, and founders of states', reminding us that history is, by and large, a spontaneous affair generated by the accumulated acts of innumerable actors through time. Contrary to popular history, the governments of Rome and Sparta 'took [their] rise from the situation and genius of the people, not from the projects of single men'.[431] Moreover, Ferguson insists with Smith that these arrangements are, paradoxically, far more likely to secure human prosperity than any deliberate planning on the part of people.[432] Montesquieu made similar arguments admonishing legislators to respect the delicate concatenation of elements which have produced whatever the 'spirit' of a nation is at any particular moment in time, 'for we do nothing better than what we do freely and by following our natural genius'.[433] Ferguson believes that there is an order of nature independent of human will which does not require, and may even be impugned by, the interventions of 'men of system' labouring under delusions of constructivist grandeur. Hayek was later to imitate this antipathy with similar arguments about the superiority of spontaneous systems of dispersed knowledge and individuated desires.[434]

One of Ferguson's objections to the rationalist assumptions of 'traditional' historians is that they rely on mythic conceptions of human capabilities. None of us commands the requisite genius, foresight or practical ability to bend and shape history at will. And to Ferguson's sceptical mind, 'traditional' historiographies entertain unreasonable expectations of people's tolerance for rapid change. The scenario of entire populations complacently acceding to every 'improvement' dreamed up by legislators is preposterous.[435] Ferguson shares with Smith, Hume, Millar and Stuart in an aversion to 'system' and the utopian schemes of self-important legislators. Smith, for example, famously derided the hubris of the social engineer who 'fancies himself the only wise and worthy man in the Commonwealth' and arrogantly assumes 'that his fellow citizens should accommodate [themselves] to him and not he to they'. Using the analogy of a chess game, Smith rebuked the 'conceit' of any legislator who 'imagine[s] that he can arrange the different pieces' without appreciating that 'in the great chess board of human society, every single piece has a principle of motion of its own altogether different from that which the legislature might chuse to impress upon it'.[436] In a similar vein John Millar argued

---

[430] Many eighteenth century Deists also held to the diffusionist thesis. R. Emerson, 'Peter Gay and the Heavenly City', *Journal of the History of Ideas*, Vol. 28, (3), 1967, pp. 383-402, p. 391. For further discussion see M. Bernal, *Black Athena,* London: Free Association Books, 1987, Vol. 1, pp. 121-60.

[431] *Essay*, p. 121.

[432] Smith, *WN*. I. IV. v.b.43. p. 540.

[433] Montesquieu, *Laws*, 3. 19. 5. p. 310.

[434] See, for example, F.A. Hayek, *The Fatal Conceit*, edited by W.W. Bartley, London: Routledge, 1989, pp. 84-5.

[435] *Essay*, p. 120.

[436] Smith, *TMS*, p. 234. Hume likewise rejected all large-scale 'plans of government' such as Plato's *Republic* and Thomas More's *Utopia* as 'plainly imaginary'. But he made an exception in the case of Harrington's 'Commonwealth of Oceana', which he described as 'the only valuable model of a commonwealth, that has yet been offered to the public'. Hume,'Idea of a Perfect Commonwealth', *Essays*, p. 514.

that 'no system, be it ever so perfect in itself, can yet be expected to acquire stability, or to produce good order and submission, unless it coincides with the general voice of the community'.[437] Gilbert Stuart agreed, suggesting that subscribers to Great Legislator myths have it the wrong way around:

> It is from no preconceived plan, but from circumstances that exist in real life and affairs, that legislators and politicians acquire an ascendancy among men. It was the actual condition of their times, not projects suggested by philosophy and speculation, that directed the conduct of Lycurgus and Solon.[438]

Hume was similarly convinced of the irrationalist basis of society. The whole notion of a deliberate social contract based on the suggestions of instrumental rationality is untenable. '[T]is impossible in [humanity's] wild and uncultivated state, that by study and reflexion alone, they should ever be able to attain' such 'knowledge'.[439]

Human affairs cannot be contained within neat master plans because they are messy, tumultuous and causally complex. The 'congregation of men' is neither static nor 'quiescent' but is dynamic, continually rearranging itself into a 'general result' which is both 'salutary and just' by a process of 'balance, counterpoise and mutual correction'.[440] Accordingly, the artificial interventions of legislators are usually misguided. We must never forget that history is, properly understood, a spontaneous business.

5. CONCLUDING REMARKS

Because of his belief in spontaneous order, Ferguson seems to think that the way we are, in general terms, will reflect the way we should be ideally. In other words, he requires the descriptive to define the normative. This is not as banal or tautological as it at first appears because his aim in this instance is to correct rationalistic (and even superstitious) errors that may have perverted the 'natural' course of behaviour. In order to draw out the universal tendencies of human behaviour, he combines empirical, introspective, and conjectural approaches to arrive at what he believes is a faithful portrait of ideal human conduct. The results of these efforts are reflected in the following chapters.

Methodologically speaking, Ferguson did not really give us a strictly empirical or quantitative science of society with well-defined boundaries because his project is still bound up in the methodologies of the distinctively eighteenth century disciplines of pneumatics, moral philosophy and politics. His ability to deliver a more fully developed social science is probably hampered by his self-appointed task of using social science to forge a new kind of moral science. Even so, his determination to take social science seriously yields some pioneering and

---

[437] John Millar, *An Historical View of the English Government from the Settlement of the Saxons in Britain to the Accession of the House of Stuart*, Four Volumes, Glasgow: 1787-1803, III., p. 329.

[438] Gilbert Stuart, *A View of Society in Europe*, Edinburgh: Bell and Murray, 1778, pp. 54-5.

[439] Hume, *Treatise*, II. iii, p. 486.

[440] *P.II.*, pp. 511-12.

distinctively sociological insights, particularly in regard to his absorption with social facts and his attempt to frame a plausible alternative to traditional historiographies. In working towards an historically grounded understanding of social, political, moral and cultural phenomena Ferguson's work constitutes an early form of historical sociology.[441]

---

[441] As also noted by Lehmann, *Adam Ferguson*, pp. 247-8.

CHAPTER 5

FERGUSON'S FACULTY AND MORAL PSYCHOLOGY

It is clear that Ferguson did not study psychology as it has been understood since the first half of this century, namely, as an experimental discipline, fully separated from philosophy and concerned with such issues as sensory discrimination, acoustics, vision, cognition and memory. Certainly, there are practically no references to Ferguson in modern psychology, therefore posterity has correctly treated his system as a faculty psychology written by a moral philosopher and historian.[442]

Ferguson had little interest in propounding 'psychology' even as it was understood in the eighteenth century. Whereas eighteenth century psychology is usually seen as a continuation of John Locke's work in *An Essay Concerning Human Understanding* (1690)[443] Ferguson's efforts can be understood as a general reaction to the kind of metaphysical hair-splitting promulgated by Locke and a more specific reaction to his empiricism (idealism). Ferguson agrees with Reid that the senses are capable of reporting accurately on the world and that it is far more useful to get on with analysing the contents of these reports than with endless epistemological questions about their character and veracity. Ferguson wanted to understand the human *constitution* and its interactions with the social world, not the human *mind*.[444] He once wrote to Edward Gibbon, 'my trade is the study of human nature.'[445] Ferguson's interest is thus a sociological rather than strictly individualised one but in order to understand what makes *society* tick, he must first understand the movements of its constituent parts. The order of the human world must be understood, not only at the social systems level but also at the individuo-psychic level. The individual should be studied *in her social context*. Ferguson's psychology of the human passions is thus a vital corollary to his social science[446] Since humans are part of the natural world it must be possible to study human nature scientifically. Just like the material world, the human constitution is governed by observable laws.[447] Indeed, the study of pneumatics overlaps with that of anatomy and physiology.[448]

---

[442] See, for example, J. Pierce, 'The Scottish Common Sense School and Individual Psychology', *Journal of Individual Psychology*, Vol. 31, 1975, pp. 137-149, p. 140.

[443] Vidal, 'Psychology in the Eighteenth Century', p. 90.

[444] Though he often uses the word 'mind' when referring to the constitution or faculties.

[445] Letter to Edward Gibbon, April 18, 1776, *Correspondence*, No. 88, I. p. 141.

[446] As Haakonssen has also noted in respect to the psychologies of Smith and Hume. Knud Haakonssen, *The Science of the Legislator: The Natural Jurisprudence of David Hume and Adam Smith*, Cambridge: Cambridge University Press, 1981, p. 6.

[447] *Essay*, pp. 8-9.

[448] *Analysis*, p. 7.

Part of Ferguson's originality lies in his stress on the importance of our aggressive, competitive and conflictual drives[449] and his sophisticated treatment of the nature/nurture debate which he frames in a manner similar to that which continues to rage in psychology and other disciplines. Further, his psychology is eccentric in its resistance to the utilitarian tendencies of emerging contemporary systems; its rejection of Hume's and Smith's device of sympathy as the mechanism which generates moral judgement[450] and its insistence that the exercise of benevolence is a) a cause of social order and a powerful species survival feature and b) the chief source of happiness. His theory of the human powers is thus set up in opposition to (real or perceived) proto-liberal hedonists like Mandeville, Smith and Hume and in this regard his work signposts a critical point in the emergence of liberal and commercial sensibilities. His task is to plausibly defend the passion of benevolence against its perceived enemies without recourse to the Scriptures, religious sophistry or primitivistic sentimentality.

Ferguson's work can also be seen as a reaction to the claims of French Materialists like Montesquieu whose 'Scientific Materialism' consisted in the attempt to describe living organisms and their processes strictly as machines and in terms of physical and chemical events. Julien de La Mettrie, another French materialist, argued in *L'homme Machine*, (1748) that humans were machine-like both physically and mentally.[451] La Mettrie saw the body as a system of parts, each activated by its own principle of self-movement. On this view, 'there is no soul independent of the body'[452] and, like animals, we are purely hedonistic. By the middle of the nineteenth century such an approach to the study of living organisms was the norm.[453] To Ferguson's mind, the 'materialists' had committed the unpardonable error of 'treating of man as of an engine' rather than the mysterious, complex creature that 'he' is, with all 'his' impenetrable emotions, reactions, judgements, faculties and moral sentiments.[454] Further, the human body is an integrated system, animated by a single engine, the soul or 'mind'.

1. GENERAL APPROACH

Psychology is not for Ferguson a medical endeavour. Nor is it scientifically biological. And he has almost no interest in psycho-pathologies of behaviour. It is the normal, 'healthy' course of human action which absorbs him because this constitutes the *social* patterns he is really interested in identifying and explaining. There is no formal science and no application of experimental method but there *is* a

---

[449] Explored more fully in Chapter 8.

[450] As noticed also by John Robertson. 'The Scottish Contribution to the Enlightenment', p. 48.

[451] M. Wertheimer, *A Brief History of Psychology*, New York: Holt, Rhinehart and Winston, 1970, p. 20.

[452] John P. Wright, 'Materialism and the Life Soul in Eighteenth Century Scottish Physiology', in *The Scottish Enlightenment*, Paul Wood (ed.), Rochester: University of Rochester Press, 2000, p. 182.

[453] Wertheimer, *A Brief History of Psychology*, p. 20.

[454] Montesquieu actually refers to the human body as a 'machine' throughout the *Laws* See, for example, 3. 14. 12, p. 242 and 3. 14, 2, p. 234.

sustained attempt to systematically identify and enumerate the various primordial 'dispositions' of the species on the basis of observed uniformities and from there to deduce certain 'general rules'. While Ferguson does show some interest in subjects like perception, reflexes, learning, memory, and philosophy of mind, it is cursory and displays little originality for the period. He is a psychologist only in the very loose sense that his work constitutes a 'formal study of human beings' through a process of enumerating and examining motive forces.[455]

Aside from its role in his social science, Ferguson's pneumatics also plays an important role in his moral system. He proceeded according to the belief that 'pneumatics' is the bedrock of moral philosophy. The apprehension of mind (self-knowledge) is essential in order to ascertain correct morals and thereby live properly and pursue moral perfection.[456] Significantly, Ferguson wants to frame his findings within a Providential teleology. Knowledge of ourselves reveals God's intentions for us and therefore normative guidelines for action.[457] We are at once part of, subject to, and beneficiaries of a divine master plan. The philosopher's task is to perceive and communicate this plan to others. Heeding the advice encapsulated in Pope's famous couplet, ('Know then Thyself, presume not God to scan. The proper study of mankind is man') Ferguson bases his approach on the premise that God's will is expressed in every part of our constitution, even the baser self-preserving parts, all of which deserve serious study. His faculty psychology is therefore an integral component of his theodicy. Notwithstanding the Stoic precedent, Ferguson must have been impressed by Francis Hutcheson's earlier attempt to account for every human drive and passion in terms of a benign master plan geared towards human happiness.

The method for Ferguson's mainly descriptive faculty psychology is a combination of general theory (based on observation and anthropological narrative)

---

[455] According to David Hothersall's definition of faculty psychology. D. Hothersall, *History of Psychology*: Philadelphia: Temple University Press, 1985, p. 21.

[456] *Institutes*, p. 11. The same point is reiterated in 'Joseph Black', p. 109 and in the *Principles*, *I*. p. 1. This approach seems to have originated with Francis Bacon (Wood 'The Natural History of Man', pp. 94-5) though Aristotle had also argued that 'we must study the soul of man' in order 'to understand what moral goodness is'. Aristotle, *Ethics*, translated by J.A.K. Thomson, London: Penguin, 1976, Book I. xiii. p. 87. It should be remembered that in the eighteenth century moral philosophy included what we would today define as psychology. Viner, *The Role of Providence*, p.78. For a general discussion of the psychology of the 'Common Sense' school see Philip Flynn 'Scottish Philosophers, Scotch Reviewers, and the Science of Mind', *The Dalhousie Review*, Vol. 68, 1988, pp. 259-83. See also Pierce, 'The Scottish Common Sense School and Individual Psychology', pp. 137-49.

[457] But such should not be taken to mean that Ferguson approaches the genuinely prescient psychology of Nicolas Malebranche who also conceived human behaviour as efficient causes of God's transcendent will. Reed, 'Theory, Concept and Experiment', p. 342. Whereas Ferguson identifies our faculties and passions as these efficient causes, Malebranche was articulating an almost fully developed theory of the power of the unconscious mind. Ferguson's approach is also a long way away from the nascent 'science' of psychiatry promulgated by Diderot, Holbach, Marat, and Hartley because he has limited himself to working within a theological framework; the study of human beings has not been fully naturalised because to Ferguson's mind there is far more to human beings than matter and cells. For further discussion on the transition of the perception of mental illness from a metaphysical to a physiological event see Sergio Moravia, 'The Enlightenment and the Sciences of Man', *History of Science*, Vol. 18, 1980, pp. 247-68, pp. 263-4.

and personal introspection.[458] By conjoining both methods he believes he is best able to penetrate the human psyche while avoiding the methodological traps of subjectivity[459] and the epistemological dead-ends of empiricism and scepticism. By 'introspection' Ferguson simply means intuitive introspection or pure self-observation. In order to avoid a prioriism, he appeals to the principle of consciousness whenever empirical anthropology fails to deliver answers. Mere conjecture is subordinate to the supreme authority of our consciousness of 'facts'. Knowledge of our species flows directly from self-knowledge.[460]

2. FERGUSON'S CONTRIBUTION TO THE EIGHTEENTH CENTURY NATURE/NURTURE DEBATE.

Although Ferguson insists that 'man' is, after all, part of the natural world and therefore another animal, subject to all the conditions that govern animal life[461] he also insists that we are a *special* kind of animal, therefore there are limits to the use of other species to comprehend our own.[462] Our mixed and special nature makes it difficult to appreciate where nature and artifice begin and end.

The key to comprehending human nature lies in something that distinguishes us from other animals; our progressive urge, 'a desire of perfection' which leads us to invent, contrive and make judgements about things. Our species possesses animal instinct but it is also characterised by the qualities of mind, the ability to imagine and pursue ends and a desire for progress and moral perfection;[463] characteristics we normally conceive of as learned. Ferguson, too, understands them as *partly* learned but it is our *propensity* to acquire them that is innate.[464] Instincts are not only less reliable in humans than they are in other species,[465] but they can only take us so far. 'Man' is destined for 'friendship', immortality and union with the mind of God. 'He' is sublime, formed to 'reason' and make moral judgements and is therefore equipped with the requisite higher faculties to support this elevated nature.[466] Such species *hubris*, was of course, an eighteenth century commonplace[467] but it originates with Aristotle's chain of being schema.

---

[458] *P.I.,* p. 49.

[459] *P.I.,* pp. 6-7.

[460] *P.I.,* p. 4.

[461] *Essay,* pp.48-9.

[462] *Essay,* pp. 11-12.

[463] *Essay,* pp. 12-14. 'To the mere animal, the Author of nature appears to have said, "Such I have made you, and such you shall be, and no more". To man, "I have given you intelligence and freedom; I have not set bounds to what you may attain"'. *P.I.,* 54. See also *P.II.,* pp. 324. Rousseau also held that humans are unique among the animals in possessing a 'faculty of self-improvement'. 'Discourse on the Origin of Inequality', in *Social Contract and Discourses,* p. 60.

[464] *Essay,* pp. 16-17.

[465] *P.I.,* p. 32; *P.I.,* p. 133.

[466] *Essay,* pp. 176, 16.

[467] See for example, Adam Smith, *Essays on Philosophical Subjects,* P.D. Wightman and J.C.Bryce (eds),With Dugald Stewart's Account of Adam Smith, I.S.Ross, (ed.) Oxford: Oxford University Press, 1980, p. 136.

As individuals we possess two sets of faculty powers, those of the understanding (cognitive) and those of the will (active).[468] On the one hand we are characterised by consciousness, sense and perception, reasoning and foresight, memory, imagination and abstraction. These are our rational, cognitive powers. On the other there are the animal or active powers governed by the following laws: the law of self-preservation; the law of society and the law of estimation or progression.[469] But the highly dynamic and interactive nature of our genetic makeup is consistently stressed.[470] The animal powers (which perform most of the ordering legwork in Ferguson's scheme) draw on the rational powers for support. Ferguson's model is further complicated by the fact that all urges are expressed either as conflict ('opposition') or as co-operation ('union'). But whether we are competing or co-operating with our fellows, the action is always social. There are times, for example, when even violence may be classed as social behaviour.[471]

Ferguson is particularly preoccupied with the relationship between the rational and instinctive sides of our natures as evidenced by the fact that Part I of the *Essay* is almost entirely devoted to exploring such issues. But this is really only to show that since humanity has always been social, it follows that all drives have social reference. For this reason there is no point in attempting to separate the animal and intellectual faculties. Ferguson saw no substantive distinction between artifice and nature since he deemed *all* human activity natural.[472] Instincts are always overlaid with equally natural yet socially constructed behaviours. We are destined to create and contrive; the instincts of artifice are innate. The rational and instinctive faculties mutually support each other and are inextricably linked.[473] This, Ferguson opines with unabashed anthropocentricism, is what makes humans superior to other species.[474] 'Consciousness', combined with our natural ability to make judgements, gives rise to 'conscience', by which our species is distinguished, and which is 'the lamp of God in the soul of man'.[475] But it is extremely important to be aware that these views on reason only apply to what might be described as short-term,

---

[468] *P.I.*, p. 68.

[469] *Institutes*, pp. 86-90; *P.I.*, III, 'Of Mans Progressive Nature' and pp. 26-36, 42, 56, 167, 174-5; 'Of the Laws of Nature in the Department of Active Man', *Collection of Essays*, No. 30, p. 259. See Bryson, *Man and Society*, Chapter 2, for further discussion.

[470] *Institutes*, p. 87.

[471] As is shown in more detail in Chapter 7.

[472] See, for example, 'Of Nature and Art', *Collection of Essays,* No. 28, pp. 245-250.

[473] 'Of Perfection and Happiness', *Collection of Essays*, No. 1, p. 3. Hume took a more extreme view, arguing that 'Reason...is no motive to action and directs only the impulse received from appetite or inclination, by showing us the means of attaining happiness or avoiding misery'. David Hume, *Enquiries Concerning Human Understanding and Concerning the Principles of Morals*, Reprinted from the 1777 Edition with Introduction and Analytical Index by L.A. Selby-Bigge and Text Revised and Notes by P. H. Nidditch, Oxford: Clarendon Press, 1992, Appendix 1. 246. p. 294.

[474] *Essay*, pp. 16-7, 10. See also Ferguson, *Analysis of Pneumatics and Moral Philosophy For the Use of Students in the College of Edinburgh*, (hereafter cited as *Analysis*) Edinburgh: A. Kincaid and Bell, 1776, pp. 7-12.

[475] 'Of the Laws of Nature in the Department of Active Man', *Collection of Essays*, No. 30, p. 259.

individual-level rationality. Like Smith he is highly critical of rational planning on the large-scale, social level.[476]

Unlike Mandeville and the French Materialists, who focused their attention on instinct as the underlying cause of all human action, Ferguson is more willing to ascribe to the species some apprehension of its telic destiny. People are not exactly like other animals. The 'brutes' always behave identically and are, moreover, *means* directed. When an animal eats, for example, it does so for the purpose of eating, not for the final purpose of good health, sustenance or the conservation of energy for planned exertions. Humans, on the other hand, possess consciousness and foresight, and often act in pursuit of *ends* such as these.[477]

People, if they so desire, may acquaint themselves with the final *moral* cause towards which they are instinctively propelled as efficient causes. By so doing the individual takes a proactive role in the perfective process.[478] Obviously, however, Ferguson perceives that a good many of our practical achievements are achieved unconsciously and instinctively. He seems to be saying that order and perfection may be achieved either consciously or unintentionally. Our practical and immediate survival functions are more likely to be secured through the operations of instinct and/or short-term rationality, whereas our perfective urges seem to involve consciousness, choice, and will on the part of agents. We are not simply primitive organisms responding blindly to attractions and aversions (as Mandeville had implied) but are rational beings capable of acting consciously upon our world. Reason is itself an original faculty derived 'from the Author of our being'. Ferguson rejects the distinction 'promiscuously' made between reason and instinct because humans are distinguished from other animals by their capacity to combine both sets of faculties in the execution of any given action.[479] Ferguson shows how the faculties of reason and instinct mutually assist one another. The 'promptings of the heart' do not necessarily oppose the functions of the understanding, and success in ventures is most likely when the two faculties are co-operating.[480] For example, ambition is an instinctive drive but it also entails volition in terms of the choice of its objects and the means employed for attaining them. This idea of the fusion of the various faculties is best demonstrated in Ferguson's discussion of our capacity for language, where he poses the rhetorical question, is speech 'natural to man?' After replying in the affirmative, a second question arises: How is it that languages are so diverse — after all — 'instinct is uniform in its effects'.[481] The answer lies in the latitude of choice and creativity exercised by people and in the 'variety of their external pursuits and attainments'.[482] Similarly, in moral affairs, there exists 'a felicity of conduct...in which it is difficult to distinguish the promptitude of the head from the ardour and sensibility of the heart. When both are united they constitute superiority

---

[476] For a more in-depth discussion of this point see Chapter 6.

[477] *P.I.*, p. 61.

[478] *P.II.*, p. 36.

[479] *P.I.*, pp. 60-1.

[480] *Essay*, p. 33.

[481] *P.I.*, p. 41. *Essay*, pp. 9-10, 16.

[482] *P.I.*, p. 49.

of mind'.[483] It is not always clear how the separate faculties of reason and instinct interact in Ferguson and his ambiguity on this count may well have been intentional. After all, we are creatures animated by a host of dynamically interdependent motive forces.[484]

But what really sets human intelligence apart from that of other species is its consciousness of the possibilities for 'unremitting' improvement.[485] Events are not determined and we are entirely responsible for our own actions.[486] The mind/body debate is, no doubt, of great import to those of a philosophical bent but hardly relevant to the type of social science Ferguson is trying to establish.

> The distinction betwixt mind and body is followed by consequences of the greatest importance; but the facts to which we now refer, are not founded on any tenets whatever. They are equally true, whether we admit or reject the distinction in question, or whether we suppose, that this living agent is formed of one, or is an assemblage of separate natures. And the materialist, by treating of man as of an engine, cannot make any change in the state of his history. He is a being, who, by a multiplicity of visible organs, performs a variety of functions.[487]

Ferguson stresses that it is not enough to explain human development purely in terms of drives and intentions. Though institutions originate in the instincts of people, their development is partially cultural. Political establishments, for example, while natural to 'man', are also 'the natural result of his experience'.[488] Establishments are consolidated with time, the force of convention and the accumulated genius of generations. The role of instinct in human affairs is further blurred and attenuated by other contributory factors such as habit, environment and our rational faculties. Our original instincts are refined and modified through habit and experience, conflict, trial and error. We learn through experience and experimentation; our 'intelligent faculties are tried and whetted in pursuing appearances to reality'.[489] Ferguson even refers to learning situations which modern sociologists now label the 'conditioned response', 'emotional transfer' and 'repression'.[490]

The important thing to bear in mind is that Ferguson conceives 'human nature' as a simultaneously cultural and ahistorical product. Subjects are always situated but may be abstracted in a limited, genetic sense. Ferguson agreed with Montesquieu that we are all born with similar genetic material, with Hume in the constancy of 'human nature',[491] and with Machiavelli 'men have, and always have had, the same

---

[483] *Essay*, p. 33.

[484] *Institutes*, p. 110.

[485] *P.I.*, p. 200.

[486] *P.I.*, p. 202.

[487] *Essay*, p. 49.

[488] *P.II.*, p. 268.

[489] *P.I.*, p. 177.

[490] Bryson, *Man and Society*, p. 142. For a fuller discussion see Chapter 8.

[491] A. Skinner 'Economics and History — The Scottish Enlightenment', *Scottish Journal of Political Economy*, Vol. 12, February, 1965, pp. 1-22, p. 5.

passions'.[492] Cross-cultural variations result from external conditions and from our peculiar responses to such conditions (free will). Yet the influence of genetics is prior to that of environment. Ferguson is very clear that '[we] have not any sufficient reason to believe that men, of remote ages and nations, differ from one another otherwise than by habits acquired in a different manner of life'.[493] This emphasis on the primacy of nature over culture is reminiscent of Stoicism.

3. HEALTHY ARCHETYPES, THE 'PNEUMATIC' CONSTITUTION OF THE . SPECIES AND ROLE OF PNEUMATICS IN SOCIAL ORDER

Substantively speaking, the first thing to be noted about Ferguson's study of the human powers is that it is teleological.[494] The faculties are always defined in terms of their *purpose*.[495] This is because the Providential order of the Creator is achieved unintentionally via efficient causes (i.e. subrational drives). Social order and physical survival are secured by 'the necessities of man's animal nature'.[496] But, unlike other animals, people are destined for far more than mere animal survival[497] and this is reflected in the telic bent of their psychological make-up. We are born vulnerable and in need of the assistance of others because we are *destined* to live in society[498] and desirous and capable of communication for the same reason;[499] ambitious because *destined* to advance;[500] discerning because 'formed' to make moral distinctions; self-preserving because *destined* to survive, flourish and prosper;[501] introspective and intelligent because *destined* to know ourselves;[502]

---

[492] Niccolo Machiavelli, *The Discourses*, Edited and with an Introduction by Bernard Crick, Suffolk: Penguin, 1998, 3. ?? 43. p. 517

[493] *P.I.*, p. 221; *Essay*, pp. 12-15.

[494] An entity has a teleological function when it has use or contributes to the 'attainment of some end or purpose of some system or user'. William G. Wimstatt 'Teleology and the Logical Structure of Function Statements', *Studies in History and Philosophy of Science*, Vol. 3 (1), 1972, pp. 1-80, pp. 4-5.

[495] 'Who ever doubted that the eye was made to see, the ear to hear, the mouth to receive, and the teeth to grind his food; that the foot was made to step on the ground; the hand to grasp, or enable him to seize and apply things proper for his use'. 'Of Things that are or May Be' (Part 1), *Collection of Essays*, No. 27, p. 220. See also. *P.I.*, p. 165. Hutcheson's faculty psychology was also teleological; indeed faculty psychologies are, by nature, essentially teleological. D.W. Howe 'The Political Psychology of the Federalist', *William and Mary Quarterly*, Vol. 44, July, 1987, pp. 484-507, p. 488.

[496] *P.I.*, p.256.

[497] 'Of Nature and Art' *Collection of Essays*, No. 28, p. 246.

[498] *P.I.*, p. 29. Margaret Reesor notes: 'Cicero attributes to the Stoics generally the statement that men were born in order that they might help one another'. M. Reesor, *The Political Theory of the Old and Middle Stoa*, New York: J.J. Augustin, 1951, p. 21.

[499] *P.I.*, p. 47.

[500] 'Of the Laws of Nature in the Department of Active Man', *Collection of Essays*, No. 30, p. 258; *Essay*, pp. 12-13.

[501] *Essay*, p. 16.

[502] *P.I.* p. 9. '[T]o know himself,and his place in the system of nature, is the specific lot and prerogative of man'. *P.I.*, 306. *'In the game of human life, the inventor knew well how to accommodate the players'*. *P.I.*, p.187; 'Of Cause and Effect, Ends and Means, Order, Combination and Design', *Collection of Essays*, No. 13, p. 129;'Of Things that are or May Be', *Collection of Essays*, No. 27 (2),

magnanimous, tenacious, wise and resilient because *destined* to struggle;[503] belligerent because *destined* to develop through conflict;[504] and habitual because '*destined*' to 'improve by exercise'.[505]

Initially, this type of reasoning strikes the reader as circular. Ferguson seems to be arguing tautologically, for example, in his discourse on the reasons for human inventiveness when he suggests that '[t]he final cause appears to be, that [our] talent for invention should be employed'.[506] What is really meant is that humanity is destined to *prosper* through the exercise of such powers. The final cause is not merely that these powers be employed for their own sake but that they be employed in order that the species survives, flourishes, and develops.

The primary forces of human activity are located in our psychic constitutions. Social organisation is immanent in a 'human nature' which is universal[507] and immutable. As with Aristotelian teleology, the 'soul' or mind (Ferguson uses the terms interchangeably) is the organising principle of life.[508] At the same time, Ferguson seems to anticipate the structuralism of Levi-Strauss in expounding a theory of order based on non-cognitive or sub-rational universal mental structures which issue in complex, large-scale, patterns of order.[509]

It is important to appreciate that Ferguson's pneumatic system is intended to mesh with and serve his Providential explanation for the causes of social order. The 'Divine Architect's' ends are secured, not through direct intervention in human affairs, but indirectly in and through laws of nature, in this case through laws governing human behaviour, which are innate. Teleologically speaking, the seeds of social order are located in (designed) human psychic or biogenetic conditions.[510] Although Ferguson's teleology has been defined as transcendent it is not a contradiction to identify *potential* as immanent in human nature. This type of arrangement is fully consistent with teleological explanations which refer traditionally to formal and secondary causes.

---

p. 238. All of these faculties as teleologically conceived can be found in Stoic thought. Reesor, *Old and Middle Stoa*, p. 32.

[503] *Essay*, pp. 45-8.

[504] See, for example, *Essay*, pp. 24-9, 62-63.

[505] *P.I.*, p. 202.

[506] *Institutes*, p. 17.

[507] The belief in human uniformity shared by Ferguson, Montequieu and Machiavelli is traceable to Stoicism. Patricia Springborg, *Western Republicanism and the Oriental Prince*, Oxford: Polity Press, 1991, p. 47.

[508] Owens, 'Teleology of Nature', p. 162.

[509] By structuralism is meant: 'the systematic attempt to uncover deep universal mental structures as these manifest themselves in kinship and larger social structures, in literature, philosophy and mathematics, and in the unconscious psychological patterns that motivate human behaviour'. E. Kurzweil, (ed.), *The Age of Structuralism: Levi Strauss to Foucault*, New York: Columbia University Press, 1980, p. 1. For a fuller discussion see Chapter Six.

[510] For example, true progress 'proceed(s) from a principal of advancement in the subject itself.' *P.I.*, p. 190. See also Bryson, 'Some Eighteenth Century Conceptions', p. 413.

Ferguson's conception of Providence as directing the universe through the secondary means of uniform laws was common by the seventeenth-century.[511] Grotius had conceived human nature as the source of social laws and therefore order[512] while Cambridge Platonists such as Glanville and Witchcote conceived natural laws as mentally inherent;[513] in other words God works indirectly through endowed human drives rather than intervening directly in human affairs.[514] Aristotle also conceived all human behaviour as endogenously generated or as deriving from the soul. The soul or mind is entelechy,[515] the organising principle containing the seeds of our potential. The soul, on this view, is cause in three senses. It is the cause of motion, it is the final cause of its body and it is also its substance. The body exists for the sake of the soul and the soul is the final cause of its body. Like everything in nature we are driven by internal forces to achieve, sustain and defend 'the form which is the law of our being'[516] and this is the cause of all motion and order in human life.

Ferguson combines elements of Aristotelian entelechy with a more modern, progressive conception of human nature through conceiving our innate progressive equipment as a blueprint for the species, not for individuals apart, consequently progress, despite the mortality of individuals, is open-ended. 'The order of nature is preserved by succession, not by perpetuity of life'.[517] In this way, each individual, in each generation, contributes to the long-term perfection of the species.[518]

4. THE INTERNAL LIFE OF LIBERALISM: SOCIABILITY AND THE LIBERAL PSYCHE

One of the most important aspects of Ferguson's work is his insistence on (and detailed defence of) the sociable passions. It was Ferguson's belief that 'men are happy in proportion as they love mankind'. Contra Hobbes and his realist imitators, the individual's relationship to society is not restrictive, repressive, static or merely causal, but positive, beneficial, dynamic and improving.[519] Ferguson stands in opposition to the axiom which would later dominate psychoanalytical psychology, namely that society (via the superego) represents a limitation on the individual and

---

[511] John Gascoigne, 'The Wisdom of the Egyptians and the Secularisation of History in the Age of Newton' in S.Gaukroger, (ed.), *The Uses of Antiquity*, Dordrecht: Kluwer Academic Publishers, 1991, p. 172.

[512] '[T]he very nature of man', he wrote, 'is the mother of the law of nature'.

[513] Whitney, *Primitivism and the Idea of Progress*, pp. 13-14.

[514] Kames, by contrast, described this view of the universe as a 'gross absurdity' and believed in a personal God, a Special Providence, a 'Father of us all'. W.C. Lehmann, *Henry Home, Lord Kames, and the Scottish Enlightenment: A Study in National Character and in the History of Ideas*, The Hague: Martinuss Nijhoff, 1971, p. 277.

[515] H. Driesch, *The History and Theory of Vitalism*, London: Macmillan, 1914, p.18.

[516] E. E. Spicer, *Aristotle's Conception of the Soul*, London: University of London Press, 1934, pp. 134-41.

[517] *Institutes*, p. 126.

[518] *Essay*, pp. 10.

[519] Pierce, 'Common Sense School', pp. 140-1.

that the socialisation process is violent to the extent that it demands 'repression, denial, sublimation, and the use of other defence mechanisms'.[520] To Ferguson's mind there is no natural conflict between individual and society because the social state is a fundamentally congenial and enabling one.[521]

> It is here that a man is made to forget his weakness, his cares of safety, and his subsistence; and to act from those passions which make him discover his force. It is here he finds that his arrows fly swifter than the eagle, and his weapons wound deeper than the paw of the lion...From this source are derived, not only the force, but the very existence of his happiest emotions; not only the better part, but almost the whole of his rational nature.[522]

Perhaps the most interesting aspect of Ferguson's pneumatics was its signposting of an important moment in the history of liberalism; the point at which the social role of beneficence came to be seriously questioned and the corresponding role of 'interest' legitimated. Ferguson's defence of beneficence and the solidary life draws our attention to his protracted dispute with Smith and Hume over what kind of moral order is best suited to a commercialising nation. In Ferguson we witness a classically oriented mind struggling earnestly to cope with the rapid changes brought on by progress. His response defines his particular place in the history of political thought and maps the boundaries of the new space he attempts to create. But it is here where he seems to be at his most conflicted and awkward; where his project of liberal-Stoicism seems to falter most for he never seems able to reconcile his loyalties.

Whereas Smith, in his writings, moves confidently towards (what was to become) the liberal philosophical tradition, Ferguson is caught by his divided loyalties to two traditions: one utilitarian, individualistic and market oriented (emergent liberalism); the other idealistic, religious, romantic, and communal (Stoicism). Ferguson is attempting to imagine a political society in which interest, competition, benevolence and classical communitarianism coincide and in this sense his writings may be thought of as an attempt to reconcile classical civic humanism with actual modern conditions.[523] Ferguson provides a window into a transitional phase in the development of Western political philosophy because of his strong resistance to utilitarianism and his accompanying insistence that benevolence, rather than pleasure, is the chief source of human happiness.[524] Both Smith and Hume, for example, rejected the notion of a universal benevolence which Ferguson had adopted from Hutcheson and Shaftesbury.[525] Indeed, Hutcheson had accused Hume

---

[520] Adler, *The Individual Psychology of Alfred Adler*, pp. 7-8, 146-7.

[521] Pierce, 'Common Sense School', pp. 140-2.

[522] *Essay*, p. 23.

[523] To put it in terms first framed by Allan Smith. *The Political Philosophy of Adam Ferguson*, p. 35.

[524] Forbes, Introduction to *Essay*, p. xxviii.

[525] Hume asserted that 'there is no such passion in human minds, as love of mankind'. *Treatise*, II. ii. 1, p. 481. For further discussion see Evan Radcliffe, 'Revolutionary Writing, Moral Philosophy, and Universal Benevolence in the Eighteenth Century', *Journal of the History of Ideas*, Vol. 54 (2) April, 1993, pp. 221-40. Though Hume took an anti-Stoic line, he seems to have identified himself more with Scepticism than with Epicureanism. For a detailed discussion of Hume's prejudices here see M.A. Stewart, 'The Stoic Legacy in the early Scottish Enlightenment' in Osler, *Atoms, Pneuma and Tranquillity*, pp. 273-96.

of 'lacking warmth in the cause of virtue'.[526] This is not to suggest for a moment that Smith and Hume denied that humans were sociable, for on this point all three were firmly united. They simply disagreed on the question of what mechanisms (motive forces) generated this sociability.

One of Ferguson's key problems is to reconcile the alleged primacy of benevolence with the 'naturalness' of progress. Seventeenth-century primitivists had argued that, since people are naturally benevolent, and since there is little contemporary evidence of benevolence, this confirms the theory of degeneration.[527] Because Ferguson eschews primitivism and argues for the naturalness of progress, it befalls him to explain the apparent primacy of interest in the new, and 'natural' commercial or 'polished' age.[528] In other words he must justify his simultaneous adherence to progress and benevolence in the face of the seemingly contradictory evidence in order to maintain a coherent position.

The tremendous effort Ferguson devoted to this task reflects the intensity of his concern over this problem. In some respects, he seems to be struggling to work out his own views as he goes along. God could not have been wrong in endowing us with some of our more venal sentiments yet His incorporation of benevolence into our constitutions must be significant. To Ferguson's way of thinking, the Creator's work should not require any justification. The problem must lie with his adversaries' interpretations of it and this is where he directs his attention. His critique of interest was not, of course, an innovation. Late seventeenth century thinkers such as Charles Davenant and earlier eighteenth century minds like Bolingbroke and Brown had been there before him[529] while Lawrence Dickey has drawn our attention to the 'neo-puritan revival' in late eighteenth century England which directed its critical energies to the rampant 'conspicuous consumption' of the 1750s and onwards.[530] But Ferguson does not build upon these critiques of luxury, commerce, and interest because he does not share in their unqualified condemnation of market society. Further, Ferguson's quarrel is not with earlier supporters of interest as the all-embracing principle, such as La Rochefoucauld and Helvetius,[531] but with Mandeville and with his contemporaries and colleagues, Smith and Hume, with

---

[526] Hutcheson cited in Broadie, *The Scottish Enlightenment*, p. 35.

[527] Whitney, *Primitivism and the Idea of Progress*, p. 22.

[528] For a more detailed discussion of the moral problem of interest in the eighteenth-century see Thomas A. Horne, 'Envy and Commercial Society: Mandeville and Smith on "Private Vices, Public Benefits"', *Political Theory*, Vol. 8-9, November, 1981, pp. 551-69. The political applications of interest in exacting rational and predictable behaviour are canvassed in J. A.W. Gunn, 'Interest Will Not Lie: A Seventeenth Century Political Maxim', *Journal of the History of Ideas*, Vol. 29 (4), 1968, pp. 551-564. See also, A. O. Hirschman, *The Passions and the Interests*, New Jersey: Princeton University Press, 1977, passim and Myers, *The Soul of Modern Economic Man*, passim.

[529] John Sekora, *Luxury*, London: Johns Hopkins University Press, 1977, p. 93. Yet, Ferguson does not refer to any of these earlier critiques. Even Gibbon was not entirely hostile to greed and luxury. He distinguished between 'harmless and harmful luxury'. Sekora, *Luxury*, p. 103. For Mandeville's views here about the hypocrisy of contemporaries who disparaged material progress while enjoying its material benefits see Malcolm Jack, 'Progress and Corruption in the Eighteenth Century; Mandeville's "Private Vices, Public Benefits"', *Journal of the History of Ideas*, Vol. 37 (2), 1976, pp. 369-76, p. 373.

[530] L. Dickey, 'Historicising the "Adam Smith Problem": Conceptual, Historiographic, and Textual Issues', *The Journal of Modern History*, Vol. 58, 1986, pp. 579-609. p. 606.

[531] Hirschman, *The Passions and the Interests*, pp. 42-3.

whom he also shared a good deal of common ground. In fact, it almost seems as though the more he thinks about the problem of beneficence the more he concedes to them.

Ferguson approved of Smith's abilities as a political economist[532] but had reservations about his moral philosophy, particularly its dependence on 'sympathy' and its marginalisation of the positive classical virtues, especially beneficence, in accounting for both the maintenance of social harmony and the survival of the species. But it should be noted that Ferguson has a tendency to vulgarise Smith's position by focusing on the allusions to self-interest and 'self-love' at the expense of the equally important dimensions of self-command, propriety and prudence. There is also a tendency to caricature the subtle dynamic between 'sympathy' and the judgements of the impartial spectator as purely hedonistic, relativistic and utilitarian.[533]

Significantly, Ferguson does not dismiss self-interest (or, his preferred term, 'self-preservation') out of hand. He agrees with Shaftesbury, Kames, Hutcheson and Rousseau[534] that humans possess two sets of 'instinctive propensities'. One set refers to our 'animal preservation, and to the continuance of [the] race', the other 'lead[s] to society.' Ferguson acknowledges the usefulness of 'interest', but rejects the primacy accorded it by Smith in the survival of the species.[535] For Ferguson, not only is benevolence *not* superfluous but it is just as much a survival mechanism as interest and self-preservation.[536] Order derives from a variety of drives some of which are other-regarding. The human constitution is far more complex and contradictory than most thinkers will allow.[537] Hume, for example, suggested that people are mainly driven by the peaceful pursuit of pleasure. Ferguson disagreed. People do pursue pleasure, but they also pursue and enjoy the challenging,

---

[532] Ferguson, *P II.*, p. 427; Smith, *Correspondence*, p. 193. At the conclusion of the 1775-76 teaching session Ferguson recommended his students to Smith as an authority on 'Political Oeconomy'. Richard Sher, 'Adam Ferguson, Adam Smith, and the Problem of National Defense' *Journal of Modern History*, Vol. 61, (2), 1989, pp. 240-68, p. 258.

[533] See, for example, 'Principle of Moral Estimation' *Collection of Essays*, No. 25, pp. 209-10. It should be noted, nevertheless, that Ferguson is aware that Smith's theory is saved from complete relativism by his acknowledged dependence on the judgements of an ideal spectator, 'a well informed and impartial observer'. But this is pointed out by Ferguson only to show that Smith's theory is, as a consequence, incoherent. Kettler, *Social and Political Thought of Adam Ferguson*, p. 114; *P.II.*, pp. 123-6.

[534] R. A. Leigh, 'Rousseau and the Scottish Enlightenment', *Contributions to Political Economy*, 1986, Vol. 5, pp. 1-21, p. 7.

[535] The 'self-preservation and propagation of the species' is secured by 'original and immediate instincts. Hunger, thirst, the passion which unites the two sexes, the love of pleasure and the dread of pain. *TMS.*, II. i. 5. 10, pp. 77-8. Ferguson agreed that these drives secure our *physical* preservation, however he does not regard this as the 'great end of nature'; our species is destined for much more, namely, the perfection of the moral personality. Ferguson attributes to Hume the belief that 'morality is founded on utility and that virtue is only a cow that gives milk of a particular sort'. 'Principle of Moral Estimation' *Collection of Essays*, No. 25, p. 205. See also Ferguson's critique of Smith's theory of sympathy where he disparages Smith's substitution of 'sympathy' for genuine moral sentiments. ibid. For Smith's views on the role of beneficence see, *TMS* II. ii. 3. 3, p. 86.

[536] *P.I.*, p. 29. Hume argued that the legal order, though socially beneficial, does 'not arise from a view to the public good' but has its exclusive and 'real origin' in 'self-love'. *Treatise*, III. ii. vi, pp. 528-9.

[537] *Essay*, p. 8.

conflictual and hazardous. Mandeville's contention that we are not naturally sociable but only teachable, (and that, given our inherent selfishness, this teaching necessarily entails hypocrisy)[538] is also confronted.

Ferguson defends his civic bent against what he perceives as the threatening encroachment of the values of commercialism and individualism[539] nevertheless his response to Mandeville, Smith and Hume, reflects a hard-edged pragmatism not too far removed from that of his adversaries.

Smith's is the most important system in this story, not only because his legacy has been more enduring but also because his views seem to have provoked Ferguson into attempting to frame a plausible alternative. Though it was Smith who ultimately prevailed in this battle of ideological wits, Ferguson's opposition to Smith has value in signposting the move away from pre-commercial public values like beneficence,[540] charity, philanthropy and chivalry towards the dispassionate and impartial rationalities of liberal justice. Though Smith was neither the only, nor the first, to explain why beneficence (the philosophical equivalent of Christian love) was no longer indispensable to the functioning of modern market society, his was, arguably, the most subtle account to date of the impracticality of benevolence as the basis for social life. According to Smith, self-preservation is the primary responsibility suggested to us by nature. Such is taken as proof of God's love for us, and 'His' desire to secure for us our physical security, prosperity and continuation as a species.[541] Benevolence and the other-regarding passions could never be relied upon to secure the welfare of a being so thoroughly dependent on things external to it.[542] Society is bound together, not by 'mutual love or affection' but from 'a sense of its utility'. Beneficence, though agreeable, is only the 'ornament which embellishes, not the foundation which supports' the edifice of society. Rather, it is calm, dispassionate and invariable justice which serves that vital function.[543] Our greater interest in ourselves first, our nearest and dearest afterwards, and strangers little at all, is both inevitable and 'natural'.[544] 'What', asks Smith rhetorically, 'can be added to the happiness of the man who is in health, who is out of debt, and has a clear conscience?'[545] Physical and social survival, pleasure, the avoidance of pain, the eradication of 'social anxiety'[546] and the pursuit of the 'natural joy of prosperity'.[547]

---

[538] Louis Dumont, *From Mandeville to Marx*, Chicago: University of Chicago Press, 1977, p. 68. For Mandeville, 'the imaginary Notions that Men may be virtuous without self-denial are a vast Inlet to Hypocrisy'. Bernard Mandeville, 'A Search into the Nature of Society', *The Fable of the Bees or Private Vices, Publick Benefits*, in Two Volumes, edited by F.B.Kaye, Oxford: Oxford University Press, 1924, I. p. 331.

[539] See, for example, *P.II.*, pp. 28-9.

[540] Which manifests variously as 'friendship, gratitude, liberality, or charity'. *P.II.*, p. 373.

[541] *TMS*, VII. ii. 1.15-6, p. 272; II. i. 5.10, p. 77; VI. ii. i.1, p. 219.

[542] *TMS*, VII. ii.3. 18, p. 305.

[543] *TMS*, II. 3. 2, pp. 85-6.

[544] *TMS*, III. 3. 9. p. 140.

[545] *TMS*, I. iii. 1. 7, p. 45.

[546] To borrow an apt turn of phrase from Nicholas Philippson. N. Phillipson, 'Adam Smith as Civic Moralist', in Hont, I. and Ignatieff, M. (eds), *Wealth and Virtue: The Shaping of Political Economy in the Scottish Enlightenment*, Cambridge: Cambridge University Press, 1983, p. 185.

[547] *TMS*, III. 3. 9, p. 139.

These are the ends of life and seem to constitute a large part of human happiness for Smith.

Smith's work represents an important turning point in the construction of the separative self. He emphasised and justified private interest, contingent values, personal liberty, the priority of rights over duties, prudence over beneficence and wealth over virtue by confirming their naturalness. Others had been there before him but Smith was among the first of the moderns to deny the viciousness of our self-regarding tendencies and here lay the power of his contribution.[548]

4.1   Ferguson's Response

Though Mandeville is really Ferguson's chief rival, it is Ferguson's relationship to Smith that is most interesting here, mainly because Ferguson was persuaded by much of what Smith had to say. He begins his defence of benevolence by attacking his easier-to-deal-with adversary (Mandeville) who had identified self-interest as the primary cause of society. Society, Ferguson avers, does not have a single cause, and even if it did, it would not be 'self-interest.' Only a misguided mind would think of reducing the highly complex human personality to a single set of selfish motives.[549]

The case of Smith is less straightforward. Though Smith agreed that the exercise of beneficence was not only enjoyable for its own sake but constituted the perfection of virtue, he disagreed as to how useful it was to the maintenance of commercial societies. Ferguson, for his part, conceded that self-interest produced many positive unintended consequences and was 'more constant, and more uniform' in its effects, but insisted that 'love and compassion' were not mere 'ornaments' but rather 'the most powerful principles in the human breast'. And contrary to 'the prevailing opinion that the happiness of a man consists in possessing the greatest possible share of riches, preferments, and honours', true happiness is really a product of (or, at least, synonymous with the exercise of) benevolence.[550] People are united by the instincts of 'kindness and affection' and such instincts give rise to a universal and natural 'right' to both receive and extend friendship and consideration.[551] Humans are the only species capable of subordinating 'personal interest or safety' to the rewards of 'friendship'.[552] Agents are judged virtuous, not in proportion to their wisdom or avowed beliefs, but in terms of their willingness to act in response to obligations. Our principal happiness lies in the active service of others. A human is are, 'by nature, the member of a community: and when considered in this capacity, the individual appears to be no longer made for himself. He must forego his happiness and his freedom, where these interfere with the good of society'.[553] Ferguson is not trying to prove that human beings are purely altruistic but rather that

---

[548] For a fuller explanation of this point see: L. Hill, 'The Liberal Psyche, *Homo Economicus* and Different Voices', *Journal of Applied Philosophy,* Vol. 13 (1), Spring, 1999, pp. 21-46.

[549] *Essay*, p. 35-7.

[550] *Essay*, pp. 38-9 and n. 9.

[551] *Essay*, p. 38.

[552] *Essay*, p. 207.

[553] *Essay*, p. 59.

the other-regarding drives are natural and therefore important species survival mechanisms. Further, virtue is not, as is commonly thought, 'disinterested' because '[e]very emotion of the heart' is as enjoyable and satisfying as the 'gratification of selfish desire'.[554] Anticipating and commenting upon the imminent publication of Smith's *Wealth of Nations*, Ferguson admonished its author 'not to consider [commerce and wealth] as making the sum of national felicity, or the principal object of any state'.[555] Smith's account of justice as a negative virtue also jars against Ferguson's insistence that justice is a positive virtue that demands more than a modest exercise of good sense and abstention from harm. Just as Rousseau lamented the displacement of '[s]incere friendship, real esteem, and perfect confidence' with the 'uniform and deceitful veil of politeness' that passed for civility in the 'enlightened' age,[556] so Ferguson considered the new and more temperate forms of social interaction which Smith celebrated. Care of the self, 'retirement from public affairs', and devotion to the 'virtues' of prudence and propriety do not deserve those 'applauses of moderation and virtue' all too commonly witnessed in polite society.[557]

But there are some key points of agreement, one of them being that all of our psychological apparatus is Providential, consequently it would be presumptuous of anyone to find fault in it.[558] 'Man' has a 'mixt nature', says Ferguson, and, since God has created us, no instincts are redundant, nor should any be repressed. Why should we attempt to 'repress one sett (sic) of animal enjoyments, and authorise another'?[559] Ferguson advises the 'poor man' who 'complains of his lot', not to resign himself to the situation, but to seek a worldly solution. 'Providence has given you, and to all other men, a set of wants; and it is the will of providence that you proceed to supply them: Be diligent, industrious, and frugal'.[560] Along similar lines Smith asserted that by acting contrary to natural dictates we 'obstruct...the scheme which the Author of nature has established for the happiness and perfection of the world, and...declare ourselves...the enemies of God'.[561] Superficially, Ferguson's position seems almost identical to Smith's, but in Ferguson there is far less emphasis on the egoism which underpins the former's system. Ferguson does not deny the existence of selfish desire, he merely argues that it is one of a host of drives operating within us and that, hierarchically, the selfish are always subordinate to the sociable drives. Ferguson thus counters the real or perceived hedonism, not only of Smith but of Hobbes, Locke, Mandeville and Hume as well.[562]

---

[554] *Essay*, p. 55.

[555] *Essay,* p. 140.

[556] Rousseau, 'A Discourse on the Moral Effects of the Arts and Sciences', in Rousseau, *Social Contract and Discourses*, pp. 6-7.

[557] *Essay*, p. 243.

[558] Viner, *The Role of Providence*, p. 81.

[559] *P.II.*, p. 383.

[560] *P.II.*, p. 61.

[561] Smith, *TMS*, III.5.7, p. 166.

[562] For example, Locke says that: 'Things are good or evil, only in reference to pleasure or pain'. *An Essay Concerning Human Understanding*, Edited and with a Foreword by P.H Nidditch, Oxford, Clarendon Press, 1979, XX. 2. p. 229.

Ferguson's commitment to beneficence is more philosophical than sentimental or pious. Benevolence is just as much a human survival feature as interest, therefore we misinterpret Nature when we deny the dominance of the other-regarding passions. 'No one' Ferguson avers, 'has yet been so bold as to maintain...[t]hat a mother, in presenting the breast to her child, has a view only to some future returns of advantage to herself'. The love of parents is utterly disinterested yet this purely other-regarding passion is the basis of society and ensures its ongoing survival.[563] Benevolence is not the only 'disinterested' passion either. 'Hatred, indignation, and rage, frequently urge [people] to act in opposition to their known interest, and even to hazard their lives, without any hopes of compensation in any future returns of preferment or profit'.[564] Hobbesian moral individualism is methodologically suspect because it ignores the empirical evidence about group altruism and its species adaptivity; the harsher and more threatening the external conditions, the stronger the bands of society.[565]

5. LIBERAL MORALITY: BENEFICENCE, ACTIVISM AND THE PROTESTANT WORK ETHIC

Still wedded to solidary notions of 'the good', Ferguson also wants to defend the naturalness of the self-regarding drives in order to develop a pragmatic ethical system suited to mass societies characterised by markets, increasing levels of differentiation and a new (and apparently unavoidable) type of strangership. He laments the passing of feudal morality and yet embraces progress because it is 'natural'. Smith, by contrast, has no regrets about the displacement of feudal norms of interaction based on chivalry, spontaneous trust, altruism and friendship, with those regulated by the more reliable mechanisms of contract and the social physics of sympathy. The traditional (and precarious) Christian virtues of charity and humility are also gladly exchanged for the dispassionate but more dependable virtues of market life.

Yet for both of them, the morally indifferent imperatives of self-interest and acquisitiveness have many positive unanticipated benefits. Consumerism and the sociology of work become important themes here as do issues relating to the transition from mechanical to organic forms of social solidarity. Despite his critique of modern trends, Ferguson is also a *defender* of commercialism. It generates a

---

[563] *P.I.*, p. 29. Ferguson emphasises that *both* the self and other regarding drives are species survival mechanisms: 'The general tendency of benevolence, like that of the animal propensities, is to preserve the human race, and to render man useful to his fellow creatures...while the selfish principles co-operate to the preservation of the whole, by preserving...the safety of individuals apart, benevolence' works to the 'general' good. *P.II.*, p. 19. See also *P.II.*, p. 122, for more on the social utility of beneficence.

[564] *Essay*, pp. 20-1.

[565] *Essay*, p. 24: 'Men are so far from valuing society on account of its mere external conveniences, that they are commonly most attached where those conveniences are least frequent: and are the most faithful, where the tribute of their allegiance is paid in blood.' *Essay*, pp. 23-4. Notwithstanding its utility beneficence is also an end in itself whereas for Smith 'self-preservation and the propagation of the species' are 'the great ends' of human existence. *TMS.*, II. i. 5. 10. p. 77.

number of worthy secondary virtues, unleashes creative powers and, under ideal conditions, may even be a preventative of corruption.

5.1   Interest as Productive of Secondary Virtues

Despite Ferguson's distaste for interest he never aligns himself with the puritanical asceticism of such thinkers as John Brown whose *Estimate of the Manners and Principles of the Times* (1757) epitomised the response to Britain's foreign and domestic problems of the eighteenth century. In it, blame is laid squarely at the feet of the commercial classes with their love of interest and luxury.[566] For Ferguson to follow through with this line of reasoning would be to compromise his theodicy, and display a naivety which did not belong to him. He therefore decides to imitate Montesquieu's example[567] in suggesting that personal wealth, as a function of avidity, reflects a prosperous, prudent and well-governed society characterised by 'the security of property, and a regular administration of justice,' which are 'the appurtenances of public virtue'.[568] On an individual level, Ferguson notes (albeit with qualified enthusiasm) that participation in commercial life may encourage a host of secondary virtues, among them frugality, sobriety, punctuality, faithfulness, enterprise and industry.[569] Though its possession alone does not constitute or secure virtue[570] the attainment of wealth, along with its *proper use,* demands the exercise of a number of secondary virtues. Ferguson may be regarded as an early prophet of the 'work ethic' in hinting at an indirect relationship between self-interest and virtue.[571] '[T]he habit of regular industry' is a 'great preservative of...innocence, and a principal constituent of happiness'.[572] Though material wealth is the object of those 'in the pursuits of fortune' nevertheless 'their exertions are productive of 'industry and ingenuity...sobriety and fortitude'.[573] Wealth 'attended with education' and 'the virtues of industry, sobriety and frugality, which nature has prescribed as the means of attainment' afford conditions whereby 'the industrious are furnished with exercises improving to the genius of man.'[574] These qualities are reminiscent of the Stoic virtue of propriety and the Epicurean virtue of prudence embraced with such

---

[566] Sekora, *Luxury,* p. 93. These problems were typified by the example of the 'South Sea Bubble' scandal in 1720, which ruined thousands.

[567] Montesquieu argued that 'the spirit of commerce brings with it the spirit of frugality, economy, moderation, work, wisdom, tranquillity, order and rule'. Montesquieu, *Laws,* 1. 5. 6. p. 48.

[568] *P.II.,* p. 500. Adam Smith expressed similar views. *WN,* II. iii. 36. pp. 345-6.

[569] *Essay,* pp. 138-9; *P.II.,* p. 500: Smith makes a similar argument for the secondary virtue-generating effects of self-interest in the *Lectures on Jurisprudence,* Edited by R.L. Meek, D.D. Raphael and L.G. Stein, Oxford: Oxford University Press, 1978, (B), 326-7, pp. 538-9 and *TMS,* VII. ii. 3. 16. p. 304. The pursuit of 'fortune' could lead to the practise of frugality, industry and application'; qualities which characterise the 'prudent' agent. Smith *TMS,* IV. 2. 8. pp. 189-90.

[570] Indeed, it generally has the reverse effect. 'Increase of wealth does not proportionally increase enjoyment. It often leads to sensuality, dissipation, sloth, pride and disdain'. *Institutes,* pp. 145-6.

[571] Bernstein, 'Adam Ferguson and the Idea of Progress', p. 112.

[572] *P.II.,* p. 372.

[573] *P.II.,* p. 326-7.

[574] *P.I.,* pp. 254-5.

enthusiasm by Adam Smith. The Stoics admitted that the pursuit of advantage is 'rational' and that wealth and virtue attaches to what is civically appropriate.[575] Ferguson agrees that self-preservation is rational and beneficial to society provided the individual bears always in mind that 'he is, by nature... a member of society'. Such agents 'will find subjects only of satisfaction and triumph' in the care of themselves.[576] Philosophy teaches that 'virtue alone is happiness', yet it is also true that 'the proper use of [a person's] fortune is a virtue, and therefore a part...in that very happiness on which he is taught to rely.' Happiness is denied to 'whoever neglects the proper oeconomy of his affairs'.[577] Ferguson also agrees with Smith that individuals, though social and other-regarding, are nevertheless naturally self-managing. For example, 'no person able to earn his own bread should be maintained gratuitously.'[578]

But Ferguson seems unable to shake off his ambivalence. Despite his apparent enthusiasm for the secondary virtues at other times he makes little effort to hide his contempt for them.

> Among traders, punctuality and fair dealing is the standard of estimation, and in the cant language of merchants, a good man means a person that is solvent, and full able as well as willing to fulfil his engagements.[579]

And further, 'nor is the person *altogether* contemptible, who is fair in his dealings only that he may be rich.[580]

5.2   Creative Potential of Self-Interest

Though Ferguson denies emphatically that self-interest is the sole, or even dominant, motive of conduct he readily acknowledges its myriad benefits. Interest is, apparently, a key source of a good deal of the very useful social, economic and political institutions known to our species while the market economy provides a stimulating environment for activities which enhance productivity.

Self-interest, via its wealth-generating capacity, is inadvertently, a creator and preserver of individual liberty. Ferguson notes that '[l]iberty, in one sense, appears to be the portion of polished nations alone'.[581] This observation echoes Montesquieu's postulate of a causal relationship between liberty and advanced commercialism, though the latter believed that liberty inspired commerce rather than

---

[575] Waszek, 'Two Concepts of Morality', p. 603. For example, Epictetus thought that personal interest and piety had a tendency to coincide. *Enchiridion,* 31. p. 30. It should be recognised that 'rationality' is understood here in a pre-Cartesian and specifically Stoic sense. Because we all partake of the divine spirit and are all of one substance it would make no sense for Nature to permit the neglect of a part of 'herself'. See, for example, Marcus Aurelius, *Meditations*, 11.1. p. 165.

[576] *Essay*, p. 55.

[577] *P.II.*, p. 341.

[578] *Institutes*, p.227.

[579] *P.I.*, p. 302

[580] *P.I.*, p. 253. My emphasis.

[581] *Essay*, p. 247.

the reverse, as Ferguson argued.[582] For Ferguson good public policy and rule of law flow indirectly from a 'people, possessed of wealth, and become jealous of their properties'. Citizens of polished nations, alone, conceive 'the project of emancipation, and have proceeded, under favour of an importance recently gained, still farther to enlarge their pretensions, and to dispute the prerogatives which their sovereign had been in use to employ'.[583] Commerce, in creating more varied roles, relationships, bustle, and interactions between people, enhances scientific advances[584] and the 'commercial arts' inspire inventiveness and enlarge knowledge.[585] Smith and Hume thought that the wealth generated by commerce improved and 'softened' the manners of a nation.[586] Ferguson agreed with this latter observation but was not altogether convinced that this softening was a positive development.

In any case, even though Ferguson regards commerce as a fundamentally 'sordid' business[587] this does not prevent him from appreciating its positive unintended effects. He adopts a kind of functionalist's view of commercial activity; the unintended consequences of economic self-interest and commerce are far more beneficial than any conscious attempt at public service could ever be. Though the 'principle of trade is private interest, the farthest possible removed from public spirit', the wealth generated by interest 'is a benefit to the state'. Paradoxically 'private interest in trade operates with the least erring direction for the public benefit, and is secure of its purpose, where public councils would mistake or miss of their aim'.[588] Smith's trickle down effect is endorsed. Though 'the object in commerce is to make the individual rich', felicitously, 'the more he gains for himself, the more he augments the wealth of his country'.[589] Francis Hutcheson had also approved of any commercial activity that was socially useful. Consequently he supported the institutions of private property, money lending, and the division of labour.[590] The Scots were not, of course, the only early modern thinkers to suggest that the pursuit of commerce could be innocent or productive (as Albert Hirschman has amply and long since demonstrated)[591] but they were probably the first set of thinkers to do so systematically.

---

[582] A 'nation, made comfortable by peace and liberty, freed from destructive prejudices, would be inclined to become commercial'. Montesquieu, *Laws*, 19. 3. 27, p. 328.

[583] *Essay*, p. 247.

[584] *Essay*, p. 175.

[585] *P.I.*, pp. 250-1.

[586] See, for example, Hume, *Essays* II, 'Of Refinement in the Arts', p. 274.

[587] *Essay*, p. 92.

[588] *P.II.*, p. 425.

[589] *Essay*, p. 139.

[590] See Goldsmith, 'Mandeville and the Scottish Enlightenment', p. 600.

[591] Hirschman, *Passions and Interests*, pp. 53-63.

5.3   Ambition and Activism

A further noteworthy dimension of Ferguson's psychology is his stress upon the naturalness of human dynamism, reflecting his hostility to the hedonistic equation of pleasure with leisure and respite. Ferguson's inspiration for this emphasis seems have originated with Tacitus, Machiavelli and Roman Stoicism. He believed that our active powers could successfully relieve the existing evils in society and that apathy and inactivity were the first steps towards corruption and the decline of nations.

Commerce has a positive, cathartic aspect. The market economy is an outlet for our creative and restless urges. We are active creatures always in need of something to do. Idleness and repose are actually uncomfortable states because we were made to struggle and strive.[592] Ferguson seems to share in Machiavelli's concern with the vice of *ozio*. *Ozio*, which roughly translates as a combination of idleness and effeminacy, results when no proper accommodation is made for the exercise of our incessant desire for acquisition and improvement.[593] But commerce could never constitute virtuous activity, and commercial agents don't actually produce anything of a *primary* nature. Even so, commerce and the market economy provide a stimulating environment for activities that indirectly enhance the productivity and wealth of nations.[594] Commerce also provides opportunities for the exercise of interest which is highly productive in commercial and industrial enterprises and has led to almost every major advance or innovation of civilisations.[595] The phenomenon which Thorstein Veblen was later to identify as 'invidious comparison' is foreshadowed in Ferguson's claim that once necessity has been sated, 'ambition' spurs the 'inferior ranks of men' to gain 'the advantages which they observe in the possessions of the rich'. In the process they are inadvertently 'excited to promote...the wealth of their country'[596] and to cultivate a number of laudable 'qualities of the human soul' such as 'elevation of mind'.[597] At this point Ferguson blurs the distinction between interest and ambition. In fact, he never systematically defines their relationship. Here, he seems to be using the terms interchangeably, whereas elsewhere, he defines interest as a combination of ambition and self-preservation. In any case, the parallels with Smith are striking here.

Activity is praised above all, especially in the form of 'ambition' and competition. Ambition is defined as a generalised desire for excellence which may be expressed beneficently, consciously and socially, on the one hand, as well as personally and unconsciously, on the other.[598] Even personal ambition is laudable because it is productive of motion. Conversely, leisured luxury and refinement are

---

[592] *Essay*, pp. 13; 43-59.

[593] Springborg, *Western Republicanism,* p. 224.

[594] *P.II.*, pp. 424-5.

[595] *Essay*, p. 35.

[596] *P.II.*, p. 371.

[597] *Essay*, p. 244.

[598] Occasionally, however, Ferguson still uses 'ambition' in the more narrow, negative sense. See, for example, *P. I.*, p. 34.

resoundingly detracted with Ferguson reserving special condemnation for the frivolous pursuits of the leisured class.[599]

Ferguson adopts Machiavelli's observation that our species is of a fundamentally restless nature. The perpetual expansion of our needs causes us to 'find fault with the present, praise the past, and long for the future.'[600] It is in our nature to act upon the world, to improve it and to remove any obstacles and inconveniences to our own happiness. People are 'not formed to acquiesce in any precise situation'.[601] Reiterating Machiavelli's disapproval of the Christian emphasis on resignation,[602] and in his only direct criticism of Stoicism, Ferguson contradicts the view 'that all external situations are equal; and that the perfect man would be equally happy in the bull of Phalaris, as on a bed of roses'. It is 'unhappy to neglect any means' that might secure a person's 'happiness'.[603] But Ferguson is well aware that this is only Stoicism coarsely understood[604] therefore his criticism is probably directed towards the popular conception rather than to Stoicism itself. Marcus Aurelius, whose particular brand of (Late) Stoicism emphasised activism over apathy, is upheld as the ideal active agent, able to recognise those circumstances beyond his control while actively pursuing those duties and obligations within his immediate command. Living according to nature entails the knack of striking a proper balance between recognising and observing natural laws while consciously exercising our Providentially inspired, active powers.[605]

Activism is particularly approved of whenever it stands in relation to social necessity. The civic humanist themes of civic and martial virtue resonate here. So too does the Stoic injunction to recognise and perform whatever duties are confluent with assigned stations, especially in our 'higher' moral 'engagements'. It is in the pursuit of these higher engagements that we 'acquire or... preserve [our] virtues'.[606] We must be active, strive continually and employ our rational powers but within the prudent limits defined by Stoicism. Wisdom consists in an intelligent indifference to all external conditions and events outside the reasonable control of the individual. Stoicism requires the recognition of the obligation to perform whatever duties fall to us but it also carries with it the notion of human excellence; of our potential to rise above our physical nature and accommodate our heroic urges. The outlook of 'fatalists', says Ferguson, is absurd. People are, by nature, active beings who thrive in struggle and in overcoming difficulties.[607] Contrary to the Old Testament

---

[599] See, for example, *Essay*, pp. 238-40.

[600] Machiavelli, *Discourses*, 2. Preface, p. 268.

[601] *P.II.*, p. 99.

[602] Machiavelli, *The Discourses,*2. 2. p. 278.

[603] Bernstein, 'Ferguson and the Idea of Progress', p. 110; *P.II.*, pp. 68-9.

[604] Since he condemns the common misapprehension of Stoicism as synonymous with 'stupidity', or sluggishness. *P.I.,* p. 7.

[605] This was the particular wisdom and virtue of Marcus Aurelius. *P.I.*, p. 336.

[606] *Essay,* p. 242. Epictetus decreed: 'But whoso nobly yields unto necessity, We hold him wise and skill'd in things divine'. *Enchiridion*, L. II. p. 44.

[607] *P.II.*, p. 54.

conception of labour as a hateful consequence of the Fall,[608] humans are not naturally averse to labour. In fact our greatest happiness consists in work and activity'.[609] Any state of leisure is to be strictly avoided because our species detests boredom. Work itself is enjoyable, even essential, to psychic well-being.[610] 'It is a wretched opinion that happiness consists in a freedom from trouble, or in having nothing to do.'[611]

The dominant and most irresistible human drive in the human constitution is that of 'ambition'. Under the influence of this 'propensity' people are so irresistibly compelled to act creatively that they 'forego any pleasure, or endure any pain'.[612] By the early eighteenth century the definition of 'interest' had shifted its focus from the sum of human aspirations to a more narrowly defined concern with economic advantage[613] and this is the sense adopted by Ferguson. The narrowing of the definition of 'interest' warrants Ferguson's provision of the new, more general, category of aspirations identified as 'ambition'. Though Ferguson is not always consistent here it seems that ambition differs from self-preservation because its objects (whether conscious or unconscious) are more various, and may be purely altruistic or moral in nature. Interest is largely confined to the care of the body whereas ambition is generally directed towards progress, whether moral, intellectual or technical. The operations of interest and ambition sometimes overlap; at other times, an action, such as the care of property, might be the result of ambition and self-preservation combined. Ambition is a native urge yet it also involves the moral and rational faculties and this is another attribute distinguishing it from self-preservation. Ambition (which sometimes incorporates self-preservation) is the source of all humanity's major achievements whether economic, scientific, artistic or intellectual. Rather than conceiving ambition in disparaging terms,[614] Ferguson defines it in more positive, Machiavellian, terms as an instinct for perpetual striving, the incessant and insatiable 'desire of something better than is possessed at present'. Ambition is insatiable need inspiring and impelling us towards ever-more progress. '[I]t is the continual increase of riches, not any measure attained, that keeps the craving imagination at ease'.[615] The effects of ambition are marked in all aspects of human life. It prompts us to pursue and secure property, to erect political, legal and

---

[608] Or even a Calvinist conception of labour as an indication of electedness. In Genesis 3 it is written that God told Adam: 'Cursed is the ground for your sake; In toil you shall eat from it all the days of your life...In the sweat of your face you shall eat bread'. Genesis 3, 17-19, The Holy Bible, p. 3.

[609] P.I,. p. 175.

[610] P.II., p. 87.

[611] Institutes, p. 155.

[612] In so saying, Pierce suggests, Ferguson anticipates Alfred Adler's concept of the 'subordination of drives'. Pierce, 'Scottish Common Sense School', p. 143.

[613] Hirschman, Passions and Interests, pp. 32-3.

[614] Smith associated 'ambition' with emulation, envy and vanity. See, for example, TMS, I. iii. 2. i, p. 50. It is defined more narrowly as the desire for eminence, of 'real superiority, of leading and directing the judgements and conduct of other people'. TMS, VII. iv. 25, p. 336. But Ferguson treats emulation as something separate and distinct from ambition. Institutes, pp. 93-5.

[615] Essay, p. 138; P.I., pp. 244-5.

social 'establishments... for the peace and good order of society' and is the cause of all our advances in science, knowledge, art and 'philosophy'.[616]

Ambition is key to understanding Ferguson's perfectibilism and his attempt to defend an enlightenment faith in progress within a teleological and providential framework; it is 'the specific principle of advancement' and is never exhausted.[617] Yet Ferguson inveighs against the expansion of *voluptuous* desires because under 'natural' conditions the appetitive 'wants of nature are easily supplied' and 'confined within narrow limits'.[618] The unlimited expansion of needs associated with uncorrupted ambition should be directed towards the 'higher and better pursuits of human life'. Though ambition operates alongside interest in 'the concerns of mere animal life' (subsistence) its operations are more consequential in the superior realm of the practical and moral progress of the species itself. Ambition may occasionally mislead us to pursue unworthy objects such as 'the possession of wealth' and 'power' nevertheless Ferguson is confident 'that intelligent beings, sooner or later...are destined to perceive the true path of ambition'[619] which leads us to cultivate the 'social dispositions', the ultimate route to virtue and happiness.[620] Ferguson sees the progressive urge as 'ceaseless', 'universal' and *the* primary motive force.[621] The healthiest goals are those which are social in nature and which emphasise co-operation. Ambition does not stem from a desire to overcome deep-seated insecurities or feelings of inferiority but is, rather, an expression of a more benign form of perfectionism characterised by a desire to effect union with the mind of God.[622]

6. CONCLUDING REMARKS

Despite the teleology and Providentialism, Ferguson's insistence on the fundamental sociability of the species, and the manner in which this fact affects individualised drives, helped to make space for the later development of social science proper. So does his confrontation of French Materialism and exploration of the nature/nurture controversy. His further insistence that the other-regarding urge is both natural and adaptive also shows great prescience.

Ferguson's interest in the animating principles of human life constitutes an early sociology of emotion while his objections to the implicit hedonism of early liberalism illuminates a critical moment in the development of liberal culture. In particular, his disagreements with Smith and Hume offer insights into an important ideological crossroads in the history of ideas. Ferguson's achievement lies partly in his acuity as an observer of the effects of modernity and market ethics on social life

---

[616] *P.I.*, p. 207.

[617] *P.I.*, p. 235.

[618] *P.II.*, p. 342.

[619] *P.I.*, pp. 235-9.

[620] *Essay*, pp. 56-7.

[621] Pierce, 'Scottish Common Sense School', pp. 142-3.

[622] To be discussed further in Chapter 11 passim. See also pp. 120-1.

and his preparedness to deal with the constraints of *actual* economic and social conditions. This preparedness allows him to evade the rigid, puritanical asceticism of earlier critiques of self-interest and commercial life and to appreciate the positive effects of progress.

CHAPTER 6

FERGUSON'S "INVISIBLE HAND"

The Theory of Spontaneous Order

1. BACKGROUND

The concept of spontaneously generated order is interpolated throughout Ferguson's entire corpus and is the core theoretical schema for most of his writings. Spontaneous generation or 'invisible hand' models are, of course, fundamental to the emergence of modern social science though it should be noted that Ferguson was not the first thinker to develop an anti-rationalist[623] account of the manner in which social order emerges spontaneously from the seemingly random behaviours of individual actors. Such ideas are traceable in embryonic form to Bernard Mandeville and Giambattista Vico in the early eighteenth century,[624] to Luis Molina and the Salamanca School in the sixteenth century[625] and as far back as the fourth century B.C in the works of Chuang Tzu, a Chinese intellectual.[626] But Ferguson is ranked among the cluster of European thinkers to first formulate a theory of spontaneous order, the others being Montesquieu, David Hume, Adam Smith, Thomas Reid, Gilbert Stuart, William Robertson and John Millar. Further, Ferguson's analysis was the most exhaustive, systematic and explicit statement to date of the way in which social patterns, order and progress emerge spontaneously from the seemingly random, private actions of individuals through time.[627] Rather than being the result of conscious planning and design, social order is the product of sub-rational, internal

---

[623] By which is meant Cartesian rationalism. F.A. Hayek makes the following distinction between a post- and pre-Cartesian conception of reason: 'To the medieval thinkers reason had meant mainly a capacity to recognise truth, especially moral truth, when they met it, rather than a capacity of deductive reasoning from explicit premises'. F.A.Hayek, 'Kinds of Rationalism', *Studies in Philosophy, Politics, and Economics*, London: Routledge & Kegan Paul, 1967, p 84.

[624] According to Duncan Forbes, John Bernstein and Ian Ross, Ferguson was unlikely to have been influenced by the work of Vico. Duncan Forbes, 'Scientific Whiggism: Adam Smith and John Millar' *Cambridge Journal*, Vol.VI, 1954, pp.643-70, p. 658; Bernstein, 'Adam Ferguson and the Idea of Progress', p. 104; I. Ross, Foreword to R. Hamowy, *The Scottish Enlightenment and the Theory of Spontaneous Order*, Carbondale: Southern Illinois University Press, 1987, p.ix.

[625] Barry, 'The Tradition of Spontaneous Order', pp. 12-14 and Lee Cronk, 'Spontaneous Order Analysis and Anthropology', *Cultural Dynamics*, Vol. 1 (3), 1988, pp. 282-308, p. 283.

[626] Ian Ross, 'Forward' to Hamowy, *Spontaneous Order*, p. ix and *passim*. For more sources on the topic of spontaneous order see Bibliography, Section 5.

[627] See, Cronk, 'Spontaneous Order Analysis', p. 284 and Hayek, 'The Results of Human Actions', P. 97.

processes. This theory is known to have influenced directly the later thinking of such important sociological figures as Hegel, Durkheim, Hayek and Polanyi, among others.

2. GENERAL DISCUSSION

Ferguson's approach explicitly contradicts the kind of rationalist and contractarian views of history which flourished up to and around Ferguson's time.[628] Discarding notions of an original contract, great legislator myths, and the diffusionist theory of civilisation, Ferguson posits instead an irrationalist theory of history and social order and presages structural functionalist explanations of the development and maintenance of social institutions, patterns and mores. He shows how the propagation of the species, the origin and maintenance of the family, the division of labour, language, technological and artistic advances, and the organised state are all unintended consequences of individual actions. Rationality and long-term, deliberate planning play only a minor role in the unfolding of human history. For human agents, there can be no Archimedean perspective on the totality of human affairs. Events taking place at the social systems or final causes level are the exclusive concern of God and relate to the big picture or social systems level, while the less demanding responsibilities associated with efficient causes are delegated to human agents. The two tiers are connected in a kind of magnetic relationship of irresistible attraction. 'Providence' has so arranged things that, however apparently random our actions on the efficient level, order, happiness and moral progress are secured on the Final Causes or social systems level. Institutions develop gradually, shaped unconsciously by human hands and forged by motives entirely unrelated to their eventual results. In the two-tiered model, the first tier is represented by the individual goal level, the second by the social systems level. The arrangement is best described as a form of 'Providentialist functionalism' whereby underlying mental structures give rise to a universal pattern of social, cultural, technological and political structures.

Spontaneous order analysis, as Ronald Hamowy (following Hayek) defines it, describes how highly ordered social arrangements emerge and persist from the unintended consequences of countless individual actions performed through time.[629] Key social institutions, whether political, linguistic, economic or legal, embody the collective intelligence of our species. Michael Polanyi seems to have been the first to coin the term 'spontaneous order' in 1950[630] while F.A. Hayek popularised it in

---

[628] Lehmann, *Adam Ferguson*, p. 93.

[629] Hamowy, *Spontaneous Order*, pp. 3-4; Cronk's and Hayek's definitions of spontaneous order hinge on the detection of 'regularities and predictabilities' in social processes. Cronk, 'Spontaneous Order', p. 282; Hayek, 'Rules and Order', p. 11. Richard Vernon canvasses the different senses in which 'unintended consequences' has been used by a variety of thinkers in his article: 'Unintended Consequences', *Political Theory,* Vol. 7 (1), February, 1979, pp. 57-73.

[630] Michael Polanyi, *The Logic of Liberty: Reflections and Rejoinders*, London: Kegan Paul, 1951, p. 112. See also A. Bognor, 'The Structure of Social Processes: A Commentary on the Sociology of Elias Norbert', *Sociology*, Vol. 20 (3), August, 1986, pp. 387-411, p. 391 and F.A. Hayek, 'Kinds of Rationalism', *Studies in Philosophy, Politics and Economics*, London: Routledge Kegan Paul, 1967.

1960 when he defined spontaneous order analysis as any 'systematic social theory' that accounts 'for the manner in which an order or regularity could form itself among those actions which none of the acting persons had intended'.[631] Others have employed such terms as '*autopoiesis*', 'self-organisation,'[632] the 'law of the heterogeneity of ends',[633] the unanticipated consequences of purposive social action',[634] 'the unintended social outcome of individual actions'[635] and finally 'invisible-hand explanations,'[636] a phrase inspired, originally, by Adam Smith's comment that the individual pursuing private egoistic goals is 'led as if by an invisible hand to promote an end which was no part of his intention'.[637] Invisible-hand explanations must be restricted to explanations of social phenomena and should hinge on human agency but not on human design. Therefore spontaneous order analysis refers only to the type of explanation that accounts for the unintended consequences of individual actions which issue in adaptive rather than maladaptive social patterns and order.[638] The four essential features of spontaneous order models — its undirected character, its 'gradualism', its inevitability and, finally, its uniformity or universality throughout cultures[639] — are all present in Ferguson's account.

Though Ferguson never articulates his belief in spontaneous order synthetically the notion underpins and is diffused throughout his entire system of thought. It should be noted that he did not use the term 'spontaneous order' but referred instead to 'the results of human action, but not the execution of any human design', a phrase that Frederick Hayek later took up with enthusiasm.[640] The term 'spontaneous order', though seemingly anachronistic, is a useful shorthand because Ferguson's exposition contains all the ingredients of the more familiar modern accounts. Like Hayek, Ferguson conceives order as undirected, unintentional, gradual, inevitable and generated at the efficient or individuo-psychic level. And although Ferguson stresses that order is Providentially inspired, his Providence is 'General' rather than 'Special' and the order he imagines in no way depends on the special interventions of God. Rather, order is secured at the micro level via the uncoordinated actions of free agents.

---

[631] Cited in Hamowy, *Spontaneous Order*, p. ix.

[632] Bognor, 'Structure of Social Processes', p. 391.

[633] Forbes 'Scientific Whiggism', p. 655.

[634] Robert K. Merton, 'The Unintended Consequences of Purposive Social Action', *American Sociological Review*, Vol. 1, 1938, pp. 894-904.

[635] Schneider, *The Scottish Moralists*, p. xxxi.

[636] R. Nozick, 'The State of Nature', in *Anarchy, State and Utopia*, Oxford: Basil Blackwell, 1974, pp. 18-19. The term 'indirection' is also associated with spontaneous order type explanations. Hamowy, *Spontaneous Order*, p. 12.

[637] Smith, *WN*, IV. ii. 9, p. 456. The same phrase is repeated in *The Theory of Moral Sentiments*. IV. i. 10. p. 184.

[638] Ullmann-Margalit, 'Invisible-Hand Explanations', pp. 265-8.

[639] Lehmann, 'Review', p. 176.

[640] As Hayek himself explicitly acknowledged. For a detailed treatment of the influence of the Scottish School in general on Hayek's theories of spontaneous order, see Christina Petsoulas, *Hayek's Liberalism and its Origins, His Idea of Spontaneous Order and the Scottish Enlightenment*. New York: Routledge, 2001.

Explaining how we achieve our complex social structures and the general equilibrium of society, Ferguson outlines the basic physics of his natural order in his now famous passage:

> Mankind, in following the present sense of their minds, in striving to remove inconveniences, or to gain apparent and contiguous advantages, arrive at ends which even their imagination could not anticipate; and pass on, like other animals, in the track of their nature, without perceiving its end...Every step and every movement of the multitude, even in what are termed the enlightened ages, are made with equal blindness to the future; and nations stumble upon establishments, which are indeed *the result of human action, but not the execution of any human design.*[641]

The ordering process is regulated by 'laws of nature' operating within and between individuals and in the external conditions of human life. Order or 'equilibrium' is the product of all laws of nature combined and they are laws in the sense of their being uniformly observable.[642] The notion of order is explicitly predicated, in turn, on notions of design and purpose in nature. That is to say, it is a Providential teleology. Providential teleologies were, of course, commonplace in the eighteenth century but few, if any, embodied such deep sociological insights.

The operations of spontaneous order secure the emergence and maintenance of the various key institutions, or evolutionary universals, of society: the division of labour, cultural and technical achievements, marriage and the family, language and regular government. Ferguson's explanation for the evolution of human institutions is highly complex. A multiplicity of interactive variables is portrayed as instrumental in the process. These include instinct, short-term rationality, habit, conflict and adversity, environmental factors, private property and even, curiously, human defects.

The processes of human history, the development of all human institutions, the 'natural' progress of our species; all are attributable to the deployment, via human agency, of the law of unintended consequences. The seemingly random, egoistic actions of individuals, in reality, form part of a wider beneficent pattern originally orchestrated by 'Providence' and apparently geared towards human happiness and prosperity. Each separate human action contributes to the equilibrium and harmony of human society which operates with the smooth efficiency of a well-designed machine. Pre-Enlightenment rationalism is rejected and the 'wisdom' of exceptional legislators, normally given as the source of rules and the legal order, is displaced by the 'hidden wisdom immanent in a dispersed and evolutionary system'.[643] Anticipating William Graham Sumner's application of the principle of natural selection to the development or folkways and mores,[644] Ferguson notes that practical 'know-how' and tacit knowledge refined through the ages ensures the gradual emergence of workable traditions and institutions. Developments are the product of short-term rationality but possess no rationality (from the human perspective, at

---

[641] Ferguson, *Essay*, p. 119. My emphasis.

[642] *Institutes*, p. 4.

[643] Barry, 'The Tradition of Spontaneous Order', p. 9.

[644] Lehmann, Adam Ferguson, p. 250; W. G. Sumner, *Folkways: A Study of the Sociological Importance of Usages, Manners, Customs, Mores and Morals*, Boston: Ginn, 1906. Though, unlike Sumner, Ferguson was not a moral relativist.

least) in the broader sense. Progress occurs only in society through the operation of the principles of 'union' and 'dissension' (co-operation and conflict),[645] ambition, and self-preservation, all of which issue in unplanned social, economic and political institutions and 'group ways'.[646]

Since the happiness of people is the final end of spontaneous order, Ferguson's approach could be described as a kind of 'system-utilitarianism', a term used by John Gray to describe Hayek's much later model.[647] But to characterise Ferguson's version of this model as pure system-utilitarianism would be to elide its conceptual mainstay, namely, its Providential dimension. Whereas Hayek posited the possibility of wholly secular systems of spontaneous order, the emergence of which can be accounted for in terms of a process of open-ended natural selection, for Ferguson the logic of spontaneous order rests on the 'fact' of design. The observable order of regularity in human affairs is the direct result of this design and purpose in nature.[648] Balance and order is achieved largely through indirection or the 'law of heterogeneity of ends'.[649] Institutions develop gradually, shaped unconsciously by human hands and forged by motives entirely unrelated to their eventual results. For Ferguson, a human is an animal (albeit a special one) reacting intuitively via passions, instincts or short-term rational imperatives. Whereas some writers on this subject posit the dichotomy Ferguson confronts as one of instinct versus rationality, it is really one of long-term versus short term rationality, the latter *inspired* by instinct. Every aspect of Nature's order is 'calculated for the preservation of the whole'. We are not always conscious of our role is securing this order because '[t]hings the most remote, are made to concur to the same salutary purposes'.[650] As people work sub-rationally to secure social order, their capacity to do so depends upon their enjoyment of a minimum level of negative liberty. This 'protected domain'[651] aspect is comparable to the bounds of 'natural liberty' in Adam Smith's equilibrium model.[652]

The 'law' of the heterogeneity of ends is at work in every aspect of human existence. Each of our self-regarding, short-term goals yields felicitous yet completely unforeseen results: the instinctive drive for subsistence results in the accumulation of wealth and inadvertently leads to technical improvements in production; the development of private property leads to the emergence of legal and political establishments; the herding instinct develops, over time, into nationalistic sentiments and thereafter leads to the emergence of sovereign states and so on. Its

---

[645] *Essay*, p. 21.

[646] Lehmann, 'Review', p. 174.

[647] John Gray, *Liberalisms: Essays in Political Philosophy,* London: Routledge & Kegan Paul, 1989, p. 92. 'System-utilitarianism' is contrasted with the more rationalistic nature of Benthamite act-utilitarianism. See also by the same author, *Hayek on Liberty*, Oxford: Basil Blackwell, 1985, p. 59.

[648] 'Of Cause and Effect, Ends and Means, Order, Combination and Design', *Collection of Essays,* No. 13, p. 120.

[649] A phrase coined by Duncan Forbes to describe the manner in which individuals, pursuing private short-term goals, inadvertently secure social order. Forbes, 'Scientific Whiggism', p. 655.

[650] *Institutes*, p. 126.

[651] The term 'protected domain' is originally Hayek's.

[652] Smith, *WN*, I. X. c. 59. p. 157; II. ii. 94. p. 324 and II. iv. Ix. 50, p. 687.

law-like operations are nowhere better exemplified than in Ferguson's discussion of subjects relating to human reproduction.

3. THE HETEROGENEITY OF ENDS: POPULATION AND PROPAGATION OF THE SPECIES

Along with many other eighteenth century minds, Ferguson took a particular interest in the problem of population and in the related issues of procreation and marriage. His views on the subject were informed by his firm belief in the law of unintended consequences and an accompanying faith in a kind of spontaneous free market of social relations. These views probably developed in direct response to Montesquieu's advocacy of legislative measures to encourage population levels. (Like many of his contemporaries, Montesquieu was convinced that France was depopulating).[653]

By the time Ferguson arrived at the problem the use of legislative and rationalistic means to stimulate population growth had seen a long history. According to Ferguson such methods have never worked, paradoxically, because they were *designed* to do so. Passion, ('the mutual inclination of the sexes') not reason, is what ensures the preservation of the species. Sexual desire is the efficient cause, and is based in instinct, whereas propagation is the final cause and therefore the exclusive province of the Creator. The business of procreation could not be conducted otherwise, so vital a function would never be entrusted 'to the precarious will' of human agents. Legislative attempts to interfere in this process not only impugn the laws of spontaneous order, but violate the liberties of naturally self-governing agents.

> The sovereign, who charged himself with the care of the people, seemed to consider a state into which mankind are powerfully led, by the most irresistible calls of affection, passion and desire, as a kind of workhouse into which they must be driven by the goad and the whip.[654]

Ferguson introduces a central aspect of his analysis (and one which also characterises Smith's model); the more crucial to the flourishing of our species is the function or institution, the less likely it is to be left to the tenuous will and judgement of single agents. Families, for example, are the constitutive units of society, the 'establishments most indispensably necessary to the existence and preservation of the kind'. Propagation is 'to the race, what the vital motion of the heart is to the individual' therefore the Creator wisely elects to avoid consigning 'the preservation of nature's works' to the precarious judgement 'of those most clearly concerned'.[655] In this respect, 'man' is an animal in the full extent of that designation'.[656] Much earlier, Aristotle had argued along similar lines that

---

[653] For a fuller discussion see Mason, 'Ferguson and Montesquieu', p. 196; Montesquieu, *Laws*, 4. 23. 21, pp. 441-51.

[654] *History*, p. 419.

[655] *P.I.*, pp. 28. See also, *P.I.*, p. 201.

[656] *Essay*, p. 48.

procreation was a purely instinctive activity, ('not of choice') but which had a vital function quite distinct from the manifest motive which drove it, namely, the survival of the species.[657]

Efficient causes are restricted to purely temporal desires and inclinations, whereas sustainable population levels, upon which the survival of the species depends, is the sole province of the Creator. That is to say, we can be trusted to 'mate' and to pursue other limited functions relating to self-preservation but we are not to be entrusted with the perpetuation and long-term prosperity of our species. There is no necessity, nor room, for human intervention midway. As Ferguson puts it so neatly:

> Charged with the care of his preservation, admonished by a sense of pleaure or pain, and guarded by an instinctive fear of death, nature has not intrusted [humanity's] safety to the mere vigilance of his understanding, nor to the government of his uncertain reflections.[658]

The best governments can do is provide the right conditions for population growth, namely, a secure foundation for prosperity and a strong defence of individual rights. 'Nature' can be trusted to take care of the rest.[659]

The institutions of marriage and the family are also described as the incidental products of conditions created in nature. Ferguson notes the relative vulnerability of human offspring and the prolonged period requisite for rearing, constraints which necessitate the formation of small, secure, stable units or groupings based on kinship, in other words, the family.[660] Hutcheson had already made this argument in *A System of Moral Philosophy*[661] (published posthumously in 1755) and Hume agreed. The family is the product of 'the natural appetite betwixt the sexes' coupled with the necessity of caring for the inevitable results of that attraction.[662] For his part, Ferguson has the Creator deliberately implanting defects in the human frame (in this instance, weakness and vulnerability) to ensure 'His' own hindermost aims, in this case, the institutionalisation of the family. Ferguson explains how the natural vulnerability of human infants, and of the female in labour, give rise to the evolution of the family unit.

> That the birth of a man is more painful and hazardous; that the state of his infancy is more helpless, and of longer duration, than is exemplified in the case of any other species, may be ranked with the apparent comparative defects of his animal nature: But this circumstance, we may venture to affirm, like many others of his seeming defects, is

---

[657] D.N. Robinson, *Aristotle's Psychology*, New York: Columbia University Press, 1989, p. 120.

[658] *Essay*, pp. 48-9.

[659] *Essay*, pp. 133-41. See also *Institutes*, pp. 24-5. Hume arrived at a similar conclusion. Robertson, 'The Scottish Enlightenment at the Limits of the Civic Tradition', Hont and Ignatieff,. (eds), pp. 164-5.

[660] *P.I.*, pp. 27-9. This notion of society being rooted in the human desire for procreation is found in Stoic thought, specifically in that of Panaetius via Cicero. Cicero, *De Officius*, with an English translation by Walter Miller, London: Harvard University Press, 1990, I. 12, pp. 13-15.

[661] According to Hutcheson, 'tender parental affection' is evoked by the 'lasting imbecility of our younger years'. Francis Hutcheson, *A System of Moral Philosophy, in Three Books,* 2 Vols., Glasgow and London: R. Foulis et al., 1755, 1. I.i.2, p. 3.

[662] Hume, *A Treatise of Human Nature*, 3. 2. 2. p. 486.

of a piece with that superior destination, which remains to be fulfilled in the subsequent history of mankind.[663]

Significantly, this passage suggests that human defects are conceived in teleological terms. Our weaknesses are deliberately endued by the Creator for the express purpose of securing our happiness and prosperity. Ferguson's insistence that human defects are deliberately and *purposefully* endued is powerful counter-evidence of any purely evolutionist interpretation of his thought. He agrees with the pronouncement of Marcus Cato in Cicero's *de Finibus* that the will to create implies the will to preserve. '[I]t could not be consistent that nature should both intend offspring to be produced and make no provision for them to be lovingly tended when born'.[664] In this case, the defects associated with birth and child rearing create mutual dependencies and strong ties of affection which generate, in turn, the enduring social bonds upon which the security of our species depends. The seemingly adverse circumstances of birth contain 'the germ of that social connection, which man is destined to have with his kind'. Human sociability is thus assured and the matrix (society) for our progressive destiny secured.[665]

Ferguson prefigures Thomas Malthus in a related discussion on population levels when he tells us that population increases are a spontaneous by-product of material prosperity.[666] Yet human endeavours to increase prosperity 'arise' from a different and unrelated motive, namely, present ease and comfort, which is 'intended for the benefit of those who exist, not to procure the increase of their numbers'.[667] Population growth is the unintended consequence of self-interest and a desire for personal security. Deliberate attempts to stimulate population growth invariably fail; indeed they 'frustrate' and 'mislead' the process. Similarly, attempts to discourage growth would also be misguided for humans always 'people up to their resources; and the aid of government is required not to improve on the laws of propagation, but to bestow security and plenty'. When well-meaning legislators propose to interfere in the delicate balance of nature they are in grave danger of 'hurting an interest they cannot greatly promote, and of making breaches they cannot repair'. When people are free to go about their business unhindered by artificial policy 'they may follow

---

[663] *P.I.*, p. 28.

[664] Cicero, *De Finibus*, 3. 62, p. 283.

[665] *P.I.*, pp. 27-30. Polybius (a key historical source for Ferguson) also located human sociability in human weakness. Polybius, *The Rise of the Roman Empire*, Translated by Ian Scott-Kilvert, Selected with an Introduction by F.W. Walbank, London: Penguin, 1979, 6.5, pp. 305-6. Cicero argued (similarly. speaking again through Marcus Cato) that the natural affection experienced within the nuclear family develops into a more generalised affection for our fellow human beings, thereby reinforcing our social bonds. Cicero, *De Finibus*, 3.62-8, pp. 281-9. Notwithstanding the teleological dimension, Ferguson's observations here anticipate the Attachment Theory of Suttie and Bowlby. Attachment Theory asserts that 'sociality is not merely suggested by child-parent relations but is innate in them, and in that sense the human capacity for social relations is derived from biologically based needs'. Barbalet, *Emotion, Social Theory and Social Structure*, p. 141.

[666] *Essay*, p. 135. Condorcet came to the same conclusion before Malthus. But other Scottish thinkers, such as Millar and Kames, argued the opposite; that prosperity and luxury worked to reduce population. Forbes, 'Scientific Whiggism', p. 650.

[667] *Essay*, p. 135.

the propensities of nature with a more signal effect, than any which the councils of state could devise'.[668]

Liberty is thus essential for the natural growth of populations.[669] The population laws of the Roman military tyrant Octavius are to Ferguson both repugnant and counterproductive. It could only 'be said' of [Octavius] and of other 'sovereigns' who presume to interfere in the laws of social equilibrium, 'that they administer the poison while they are devising the remedy, and bring a damp and a palsy on the principles of life, while they endeavour, by external applications to the skin, to restore the bloom of a decayed and sickly body'. The important task of maintaining sustainable population levels must never be delegated to the unreliable and often capricious 'wisdom of sovereigns, or...single men'.[670]

Ferguson notices that unintended consequences have ripple effects, generating in turn, more and more positive, unintended consequences. The most important among them are the following.

4. LANGUAGE

Ferguson echoes Mandeville in observing that language developed out of the actions of countless individuals who neither intended nor even entirely comprehended the incredible complexity of their own creation.[671] The species is seen to embody an extraordinary genius which no individual could possess. Language is a social product and we should regard with scepticism the misapprehensions of those 'poets' who taught that speech was originally transmitted 'by some founder of rationality and civilisation'. Contractarian and rationalistic explanations for the origins of language are roundly dismissed with Ferguson declaring 'that both associating and speaking, in however rude a form, are coeval with the species of man'.[672]

Language serves a number of key telic functions in Ferguson's scheme. Speech allows us to preserve our shared history in the form of oral folklore which, in turn, stirs our 'passions' and enhances communal sentiments.[673] Since speech is subject to so much regional variation it helps to preserve community boundaries. But this does not prevent it from serving the further function of aiding the diffusion of knowledge

---

[668] *Essay,* p. 136. See also *Institutes,* p. 246. Smith made a similar argument in the *Wealth of Nations* (I. viii. 38-43, pp. 97-9) and Aristotle had arrived at the same conclusion much earlier. L. Robin, *Greek Thought and the Origins of the Scientific Spirit,* New York: Russell and Russell, 1967, p. 272. Malthus agreed that state interference in population control was unnecessary and would only exacerbate any existing problems. Thomas Malthus, 'A Summary View of the Principle of Population', in *Three Essays on Population,* New York: Mentor Books, 1960, p. 37. Montesquieu, by way of contrast, thought that, in certain cases, state interference in 'the Propagation of the Species' was warranted. *Laws,* 4. 23. 16-28, pp. 437-54.

[669] *Essay,* pp. 131, 139.

[670] *Essay,* pp. 136.

[671] For a discussion of Mandeville's work here see F.B. Kaye, 'Mandeville on the Origin of Language', *Modern Language Notes,* Vol. 39. (1), pp. 136-142.

[672] *P.I.,* pp. 43.

[673] *Essay,* p. 76. Grobman, 'Adam Ferguson's Influence on Folklore Research: the Analysis of Methodology and the Oral Epic', *Southern Folklore Quarterly,* Vol. 38, 1974, pp. 11-22.

and invention across and between cultures. Through language, '[d]iscoveries of science, models of invention, or attainments of genius, wherever they may have originated, find their way into the world, and become the property of mankind'. Language helps us to preserve existing accomplishments and to share new ones while our capacity to master foreign dialects enables us 'to retain the knowledge of what has ceased to be spoken for many ages past'.[674] Ferguson notes the unplanned (from the human perspective at least) contribution that language has made to the general progress of humankind. 'Man's specific talent for expression and communication ...serves...to reunite the efforts of mankind to one common purpose of advancement in the progress of intelligence'.[675] Ferguson agrees with Aristotle that it is language that makes us both fit and destined for life in a polity.[676] The universality of language confirms our *destiny* to live in society[677] and society, in turn, leads inevitably to political society.[678] The faculty of speech was incorporated into our essential make-up for a specific purpose, namely, to enable us to live and co-operate together in order to, in turn, survive, prosper and progress. Humans are the only species destined for political life since humankind alone is capable of speech. Since speech is universal, 'peculiar to man' and natural[679] all people, but people only, will partake of political life.

The case of spoken language exemplifies the intimate symbiosis of nature and artifice which is a key Fergusonian principle. The propensity for speech is innate and yet it is, at the same time, 'the first and most wonderful production of human genius...*In this the created mind is itself a creator'.*[680] All of human progress is a social event and the invention of language serves as an invaluable catalyst to this process. Fergusonian perfectibilism is conceived as a process of self-creation for the species yet it is also enacted within a telic framework defined and shaped by divinely implanted propensities and instincts.

5. TECHNICAL ACHIEVEMENTS AND THE DIVISION OF LABOUR

According to Ferguson, invention, or the refinement of the 'mechanical arts', is a powerful determinant of social evolution. Yet inventions themselves are rarely the outcome of conscious intentions. On the contrary, they are usually the incidental effects of people striving to secure their personal wants. Where people are 'protected' and free to pursue their own employments 'devices' naturally 'accumulate'.[681] Our desire to overcome adversity and remove practical obstacles

---

[674] *P.I.,* p. 47. This argument seems to contradict Ferguson's other comments about the limited role of cultural diffusion in the progress of nations. See below.

[675] *P.I.,* p. 36.

[676] Aristotle, *Politics: The Athenian Constitution,* Edited and with an Introduction by John Warrington, London: Heron Books, 1959, 1. 1. 1253a, p. 7.

[677] *P.I.,* pp. 47, 269.

[678] *P.II.,* p. 244.

[679] *Institutes,* p. 44; *P.I.,* pp. 40-1.

[680] *P.I.,* p. 287. My

[681] *Essay,* pp. 161-3.

from our path gives rise to new technologies. Invention is a function of a particular psychological need in people for action and 'occupations'. Our species has an innate aversion to inactivity and boredom.[682] It is in our nature, Ferguson asserts in Machiavellian tones, to pit our resources against odds and to wrestle with nature.[683]

Ferguson's exposition of the nature, development and effects of specialisation is a central focus of his theory of spontaneous order. He begins by implicitly challenging Adam Smith's explanation of the source of specialisation. Smith had located the origin of the division of labour in a peculiar human instinct to 'truck barter and exchange'.[684] Ferguson, by contrast, bases the tendency to specialise labour functions upon natural human diversity coupled with certain environmental factors, namely the enormous variety of situations and obstacles confronted in the range of human experience.[685] Typically the process is one of gradual evolution, based on small, successive improvements over time rather than on any long-term planning on the part of actors.[686]

The division of labour is central to human progress, since it is productive of wealth and prosperity. Specialisation also brings with it certain unforeseen, though essential, social institutions. Professional specialisation leads inevitably to a *social* division of labour and therefore social classes which, rather than being harmful to society, are vitally important to its functioning. The system of structured inequalities acts as a stimulant to the market by providing workers with a long-range work incentive. Class envy and emulation is crucial for keeping commercial economies in motion.[687]

6. FERGUSON'S ASSAULT ON CONTRACTARIANISM: THE EMERGENCE OF THE STATE

In their respective expositions of spontaneous order, Smith, Hume, Millar, Stuart, and Ferguson share in common an energetic rejection of the type of contractarianism found in early modern political philosophy. This rejection signposts — indeed it makes possible — the transition to modern social science.[688] For Ferguson, human instinct, individual psychology, habit, custom and convention, material circumstances and conflict all play a role in the development of formal government. His discourse on the origins of the state discards all rationalistic notions of a state of nature and of any social or political contract. Contrary to Rousseau's postulate of pre-social 'man' living independent, '[s]olitary, indolent' and 'dispersed among other animals',[689] Ferguson insists that humans have always lived in groups.[690] As he

---

[682] *Institutes*, p. 155.

[683] *Essay*, pp. 44-9. See also *Institutes,* p. 268, *P.I.,* pp. 250, 267-8

[684] Smith, *WN*, I. p. 25.

[685] *P.I.,* p. 246.

[686] *Essay*, p. 174.

[687] *Essay*, p. 225.

[688] Vernon, 'Unintended Consequences', p. 58. Eriksson, 'The First Formulation of Sociology', pp. 254-5.

[689] Rousseau, 'Discourse on Inequality', in *Social Contract and Discourses*, pp. 58, 54.

quite sensibly points out, Rousseau could not have been right because, by his own reasoning 'men must have been already together in society, in order to form any compact, and must have been in the practice to move in a body, before they have concerted together for any purpose whatever'.[691]

Ferguson thus explicitly rejects Rousseau's attempt to 'discover the natural man' and his assumption that the state of society is an impediment to such knowledge.[692] He further rejects the rationalist constructivism of Descartes which has its source in the Aristotelian division between *physis* (nature) and *nomos* (convention). Ferguson designates this distinction a false dichotomy describing a class of phenomena occupying an intermediary space between nature and artifice, the products, simultaneously, of *physis* and *nomos*.[693]

Society derives from instinct, from principles of 'union' and 'dissension' while its formal institutions have an informal and spontaneous origin.

> In these happy, though informal proceedings, where age alone gives a place in the council; where youth, ardour, and valour in the field, give a title to the station of leader; where the whole community is assembled on any alarming occasion, we may venture to say, that we have found the origin of the senate, the executive power, and the assembly of the people; institutions for which ancient legislators have been so much renowned.[694]

Simultaneously rebuking Western cultural hubris and a more general species hubris, Ferguson notes that, while we are apt to ascribe the achievements of other species 'to the wisdom of nature' (instinct) those of civilised humans 'are ascribed to themselves, and are supposed to indicate a capacity superior to that of rude minds'.[695] Institutions are coeval with our species because we instinctively develop them. Such apparently artificial structures as regular government are, in fact, perfectly natural, for they are immanent in the divine plan, that is to say, they are immanent in a Providentially arranged human nature.[696] Ferguson reintroduces his eccentric 'defects' argument to the discussion by asserting that political establishments, do not arise from instincts as such, but from their defects. Government arises exigently in order to offset the negative spillovers of our natural greed and belligerence. 'As the commercial arts originate in the necessity of man's animal nature, the arts which may be termed political originate in the wants and defects of instinctive society.'[697]

The state emerges, not from a conscious desire for political order, but to counter the abuses created by the pursuit of private property. With typical pragmatism Ferguson notes that, despite our natural sociability, there are times when we must be *forced* to be sociable. Our natural tendency towards 'invidious comparison' creates

---

[690] *Essay*, p. 21.

[691] *P.II.*, p. 244.

[692] Rousseau, 'A Discourse on the Origin of Inequality', in *Social Contract and Discourses*, pp. 43-5; Ferguson, *Essay,* p. 11.

[693] 'Of the terms that we employ in treating of human affairs, those of natural and unnatural are the least determinate in their meaning'*Essay*, p.15

[694] *Essay.* p. 84.

[695] *Essay*, pp. 173-4.

[696] *P.I.*, p. 256; *P.II.*, pp. 244-5; *Essay*, p. 120.

[697] *P.I.*, p. 256.

enmity between people and formal government comes about in order to protect citizens and their private property.[698] The state also exists to offset another adverse effect of private property, namely, the possibilities for oppression created by the rank distinctions to which private property gives rise. Regular government emerges 'not to establish subordination, but to correct the abuse of subordination already established'.[699] Hume also thought that positive justice emerged in order to protect and regulate the use of private property.[700]

But Ferguson does not permit nature's apparent defects to tarnish the name of the Creator for they have been *deliberately* incorporated in the human constitution by God so as to encourage people to develop their faculties through conflict and adversity.[701] But since the Creator is beneficent, 'He' has also conveniently supplied the species with an antidote for the negative spillovers of an otherwise useful instinct by endowing it with a native urge to erect formal government.[702] Civil society is a function of human needs, whereas formal government is a direct response to the evils arising from private property. These arrangements are part of a wider, self-righting, system of spontaneous order. Our seemingly adventitious institutions are, in reality, the products of indirection and even our psychological make-up embodies an intricate self-regulating mechanism such as has just been described. Ferguson seems to be building on the Aristotelian argument that the state is natural because it originates in human needs. There is also a sense in which he is imitating the former's teleologically causal explanation of its origins. For Aristotle the state is 'prior to the family and to the individual' because it is the final cause of everything that came before it as part of its final existence. The development of the state is inevitable and the primitive forms that predate it (and are part of its coming into being) are *caused* by their *telos* (ie the state itself).[703]

The idea of human defects as deliberately implanted by 'Providence' for higher ends is a commonplace in Ferguson's writings and fits neatly within his whole conception of the positive social function of conflict and adversity. It also stands as powerful evidence in support of a Providentialist/teleological interpretation of Fergusonian spontaneous order in the sense that such an argument would have no logical place in a purely evolutionistic scheme.[704]

Ferguson emphasises the polygenesis of our key institutions and the absence of any long-term human design in their development. The symmetry and complexity of government, the harmonious accommodation of its various components, could not conceivably have been the work of a single legislator, however wise. Good constitutions always reflect and embody the collective wisdom of generations of actors who have shaped it piecemeal and dialectically through centuries of

---

[698] *Essay*, pp. 81, 95-8. See also Ferrarotti, 'Civil Society and State Structures', p. 14.

[699] *P.I.*, p. 262; *Institutes*, p. 40. See also Zaret, 'From Political Philosophy to Social Theory', p. 159.

[700] Hume, *Treatise*, 3. 2. 2. p. 489.

[701] *Institutes*, pp. 22-4.

[702] *P.II.*, pp. 496, 244; *P.I.*, p. 256 and *Remarks*, p. 3.

[703] Robinson, *Aristotle's Psychology*, p. 120.

[704] Indeed, Ferguson frequently links the idea of defects with the design principle. See, for example, *P.I.*, p. 177 and Chapter 11 of this volume.

adaptation, conflict and compromise. Accordingly, Ferguson shares in Burke's (and Smith's) aversion to any kind of rapid change or revolutionary spirit.[705] This would disrupt 'Nature' whose *modus operandi* is exclusively sub-rational and evolutionistic. 'No constitution is formed by concert, no government is copied from a plan'. People 'proceed from one form of government to another, by easy transitions'.[706] Although Ferguson concedes that, once established, some institutions (in this case free constitutions) may be deliberately 'preserved by the vigilance, activity, and zeal, of single men',[707] government is ultimately the unintended effect of conflict originating in human defects. In turn, the unintended effects of government are enhanced security and social welfare and greater liberty for all. These complex causal relationships result in conditions that bear all the marks of conscious human design, yet for Ferguson, nothing could be farther from the truth.

7. HISTORY AS A BLIND PROCESS

An important element of Ferguson's approach was the belief that rationality and deliberate planning played only a minor role in the unfolding of history. Instead, short-term goals pursued at the micro level, powered by drives and reinforced by habit, achieve, in the long term, never-dreamed-of results. It would be impossible to pinpoint the precise moment of any institution's genesis for two reasons: firstly, establishments are rarely, if ever, the issue of a single identifiable actor, and secondly, they are inspired by instinct and are therefore coeval with the human species.[708] Inventions evolve gradually and are social rather than individual products. As in the case of language, for example, 'no single genius, however vast, is equal to the invention of a language'.[709] The human species achieves unimagined results which could never have been effected by single persons or even single generations.

The process of human improvement occurs, not in identifiably discrete or revolutionary steps, but with imperceptible gradualness as group-ways and social structures slowly adapt and respond to human needs. Human agency is expressed in a gradual, incremental, fashion and in the business of day-to-day survival. Institutions develop insensibly and by degrees, the product of countless individual actions through time. Ferguson's approach thus anticipates Hegel's theory of the cunning of reason; indeed Hegel was well acquainted with Ferguson's work.[710]

Ferguson tells us that the 'forms of society...arise...from the instincts, not from the speculations of men'. Genetic urges, are, in turn, moulded 'by the circumstances

---

[705] *Institutes*, p. 274; *P.II.*, pp. 291, 496-7; *Remarks*, pp. 23-4; Smith, *TMS*, pp. 231-4.

[706] *Essay*, p. 120.

[707] *Essay*, p. 130.

[708] *Essay,* pp. 118-20, 21-3.

[709] *P.I.*, p. 42. Nevertheless Ferguson acknowledges the occasional contribution of the 'singular genius'. *P.I.*, p. 36

[710] Even so, Hegel only mentions Ferguson 'in passing'. Waszek, *The Scottish Enlightenment,* pp, 21, 103-4 Hegel is also thought to have been influenced by Smith's 'invisible hand' formulation. John B. Davis, 'Smith's Cunning of Reason', *International Journal of Social Economics*, Vol. 16. (6) 1989, pp. 50-68.

in which they are placed'. Ironically, Ferguson quotes Cromwell (a revolutionary) in making his point that it is our blindness to effects which best secures social order. A 'man never mounts higher, than when he knows not whither he is going'.[711] The Aristotelian influence is prominent here with a distinction made between higher and lower ends or final and efficient causes. 'The efficient cause', Ferguson tells us, 'is the energy or power producing an effect. The final cause is the end or purpose for which an effect is produced'.[712] In practice, this means that people find 'lasting improvements in the pursuit of temporary expedients'. As with Smith's, the formulation is low on human rationality and like Smith, Ferguson draws clear boundaries between the individual and social systems tiers by insisting that, with a few exceptions, interference by individuals or the state in the latter sphere of activity should be strictly avoided. Such attempts merely resemble the farcical efforts of the 'fly in the fable, who admired its success, in turning the wheel, and in moving the carriage' whereas in fact 'he has only accompanied what was already in motion...and waved with his fan, to give speed to the winds'.[713] Our daily needs are neither the concern 'of national councils' nor of 'those who act for the community' but are best entrusted to the hands of private individuals. After all, 'private interest is a better patron of commerce and plenty, than the refinements of state'.[714] We should attend only to our daily concerns and restrict our efforts to objects within our immediate control.[715] The supply of daily necessities requires only 'care, industry, and skill, which are the virtues of a private station; not superior genius, fortitude, liberality and elevation of mind — the virtues of those who are to rule the world'. Accordingly, the 'commercial arts...are properly the distinctive pursuit or concern of individuals, and are best conducted on motives of separate interest and private advancement'.[716] Ferguson thus shares in Smith's views on the minimal negative state,[717] though his ideal state is probably less minimal than Smith's.

The broader framework for this conceptual distinction between micro-psychological and macro-institutional realms is originally Stoic. Stoicism enjoins us to restrict our attention to concerns immediately within our control and resign our will, in larger matters, to the wisdom of God.[718] A substantial precedent can also be traced to the Calvinist faith in the causal power of the passions and sub-rational drives, Providentially understood.[719]

[711] *Essay*, p. 119.

[712] *Institutes*, pp. 5, 17.

[713] *Essay*, p. 137; Smith, *TMS*, II. i. 5. 10. pp. 77-8.

[714] *Essay*, p. 139.

[715] *P.I.*, p. 4.

[716] *P.I.*, p. 244.

[717] See also *Essay*, p. 139.

[718] 'Men are charged only with the care of ...doing what is right...Events are reserved to God'. Ferguson, *Analysis*, p. 27

[719] For a fuller discussion on the influence of Calvinist anti-rationalism and unintentionality see David Allan, *Virtue, Learning and the Scottish Enlightenment*, Edinburgh: Edinburgh University Press, 1993, pp. 212-15.

8. EVOLUTIONISM

Along with Hume, Millar, Robertson, and Smith, Ferguson conceives the development of social institutions as a painstakingly slow affair based on imperceptible improvements.[720] The process is one of 'adaptive evolution'[721] but it should not be assumed that it is a purely evolutionary process devoid, in Ferguson's mind, of telic meaning. Rather than anticipating some kind of open-ended, evolutionary theory of progress (such as Hayek's) Ferguson's model locates itself in the 'chain of being' tradition because it is anthropocentric; is predicated on the design principle and refers, ultimately, to final causes.[722] In addition, Ferguson's model is not really evolutionistic in the Darwinian sense, though, according to Lois Whitney, it comes very close.[723] Ferguson writes:

> The genius of variation, which is so eminent in comparing different species of being together, is carried onto the economy with which the same species, in respect to the individuals that compose it, is continually changing; and the generations that were and are, hasten to make way for those which are yet to come.[724]

This is as near as Ferguson comes to articulating any kind of precursory theory of evolution. He argues, not only for the immutability of the species,[725] but for the distinctiveness of the human race and there is no hint of an evolvement from other species.[726] In the 1773 edition of the *Essay* he makes the following significant note.

> The attainments of the parent do not descend in the blood of his children, nor is the progress of man to be considered as a physical mutation of the species. The individual, in every age, has the same race to run from infancy to manhood, and every infant, or ignorant person, now, is the model of what man was in his original state.[727]

Ferguson's model is evolutionistic only in the sense that practices and institutions develop gradually, comparable with what Hayek would later describe as *institutional* social Darwinism, notwithstanding the teleological element which is peculiar to Ferguson.[728]

Ferguson infers our progressiveness from the principle of change[729] and endorses Marcus Aurelius' dictum that 'Nature's highest happiness lies in changing the things that are, and forming new things after their kind. Whatever is, is in some sense the

---

[720] See Hume, *Treatise*, 3. 2. 2. p. 493; Millar, *The Distinction of Ranks*, pp. 238, 255, 278; Adam Smith, *Lectures on Jurisprudence*, R.L. Meek, D.D. Raphael and L.G. Stein (eds), Oxford: Oxford University Press, 1978 (hereafter cited as *LJ*), B, p. 406.

[721] Hamowy, 'Progress and Commerce', p. 77.

[722] *P.I.*, pp. 174-8, 165. See also Whitney, *Primitivism and the Idea of Progress*, p. 145.

[723] Whitney, *Primitivism and the Idea of Progress*, pp. 151-2. There were inklings of evolutionism already emerging in scientific treatises of the time. For example, Maupertuis's *Essai de Cosmologie* (1741) alludes to the idea of 'survival of the fittest'.

[724] *P.I.*, p. 174.

[725] *P.I.*, pp. 167-8.

[726] *P.I.*, pp. 48, 61; *P.II.*, p. 410; *Essay*, pp. 11-2, 16.

[727] *Essay*, 'Variants', p. 265.

[728] Hayek, *Rules and Order*, p. 23.

[729] *P.I.*, p. 190.

seed of what is to emerge from it'.[730] But Ferguson stresses that the principle of change does not alone necessarily connote the potentiality for progress; after all, inanimate objects are subject to change from external causes. Genuine organic progress is always generated endogenously.[731]

Ferguson observes the principle of change at work in all life processes[732] and imagines creation as an ongoing, rather than simultaneous, event.[733] The evolution of institutions and mores is linear and perfectibilist. Change is inevitable, therefore all institutions are, by nature, time and culture bound.[734] Humanity's stupendous achievements are the work of individuals in the immediate sense, though properly attributable to the genius of God from the long view.[735] Knowledge and experience accumulated and handed down through the ages assumes a quality of perfection seemingly inconsistent with the imperfect nature of humanity. This appearance is also a function of the painstakingly slow pace of improvements, the origins of which are obscured by time.[736] Ferguson remarks with awe that 'the speculative mind is apt to look back with amazement from the height it has gained...the summit of which he could scarcely have believed himself to have ascended without supernatural aid'.[737] We simply pursue our 'wants' but inadvertently obtain something higher; our practical and moral perfection. Ferguson and Burke agreed that the evolution of our most important achievements is necessarily slow, unfolding at its own 'natural' pace.[738] This gradualism led them both to a position of social conservatism and to a concomitant rejection of any kind of revolutionary change. Radical reform should be avoided wherever possible because predicting 'all the consequences' and 'effects' of any 'innovation' is well 'above the reach of human wisdom'.[739]

9. SPONTANEOUS ORDER AS TELEOLOGY

Ferguson's system is best described as a kind of Providential teleology[740] but he is keen to affirm its 'scientific' credentials. He insists that his faith in spontaneous order is not a priori but is based on the empirical evidence. Every modern and ancient history speaks of universal, underlying social patterns as does all the anthropological evidence available.[741]

---

[730] Marcus Aurelius, *Meditations*, 4. 36. p. 72.

[731] *P.I.*, pp. 313, 174; *P.I.*, pp. 190-1

[732] *P.I.*, p. 190.

[733] Whitney, *Primitivism and the Idea of Progress*, p. 151; *P.I.*, p. 175.

[734] 'Of the Separation of Departments', *Collection of Essays*, No. 15, p. 150.

[735] *P.I.*, p. 53.

[736] *Essay*, pp. 119, 163.

[737] *P.I.*, p. 43.

[738] Whitney, *Primitivism and the Idea of Progress*, p. 153; *Essay*, pp. 12-13.

[739] *P.II.*, p. 498.

[740] John Bernstein describes Ferguson's as a 'Providential teleology' though he limits this observation to the *Principles*. 'Adam Ferguson and the Idea of Progress', p. 113

[741] See, for example, *Essay*, pp. 74, 96-7, 183.

Ferguson agrees with Marcus that the world is a single, closed, self-regulating unit.[742] The reason why human life operates spontaneously (that is, on the level of efficient causes) is that our powers of reason are too frail to secure the ends of Providence which Ferguson infers as being, in the short term, to live according to our nature, the 'happy instruments of providence',[743] so that we can achieve, in the long term, our 'superior destination' which is union with the mind of God via a process of moral perfection.[744] This notion of end defined as mind seeking moral goodness and 'the indications of supreme intelligence' comes jointly from Socrates, Epictetus and Marcus Aurelius[745] and fulfils the minimum requirement of teleology in the strict classical sense that any teleological formulation must, by definition, refer to God as unrealised perfection.[746] Our efforts for this unrealisable union with God is the cause of all motion and order in the universe.[747]

History bears all the marks of design. It has an intelligent structure which is not arbitrary but orderly and composed. 'The system of nature' does not 'merely' consist of 'cause and effect but of ends and means' which point to 'an intelligence of wisdom and goodness in the first cause'.[748] There is a discernible *telos* which is moral perfection conceived as an ongoing, asymptotic process.[749] But rather than perceiving *everything* in created nature as possessing essences striving for self-realisation, as Aristotle had suggested, humans alone are destined for progress.[750] This progressive process, once established, possesses an independent momentum. The species is endowed with an immutable progressive instinct as well as other supportive drives that ensure its survival. Human independence and agency are combined with the idea of a Providential order. The material world, with its miraculous symmetry, is the forum or matrix for the expression of these innate drives. Human achievements such as the accumulation of knowledge and our social and political institutions, simultaneously hone and provide the nursery for our moral evolution. They are immanent in human nature and in the external conditions carefully contrived by a benevolent Creator. The seeds of human development are planted and the conditions for their fruition secured.

The designs of the Creator are not ensured through continuous intervention. God, the 'divine architect', is merely a First Cause, a General Providence, investing human beings with certain immutable instincts and propensities (even defects) in order to guarantee the unfolding of the divine blueprint through the ages. This point of view, that is, of God representing an abstract First Cause and little more, is consistent with the rest of Ferguson's theology which places great emphasis on the universe as a perfectly designed monistic unit requiring no external maintenance.

---

[742] Marcus Aurelius, *Meditations*, 4. 40, p. 73.

[743] *Essay*, p. 264.

[744] *P.I.*, pp. 28, 329-30; *P.II.*, p. 403.

[745] *P.I.*, pp. 312-3.

[746] G.E.M. Joad, 'The Problem of Change: Teleology and Mechanism', *Guide to Philosophy*, London: Victor Gollancz, 1937, pp. 202-3.

[747] *P.I.*, pp. 184-5; Joad, 'The Problem of Change', p. 203.

[748] 'Of Cause and Effect', *Collection of Essays*, No. 13, p. 121.

[749] *P.I.*, pp. 184-5.

[750] *Essay*, pp. 10-14.

God is retired, reduced to an absent, evanescent abstraction,[751] and the human species becomes the focus of attention as it negotiates its way towards its destiny.

10. PROGRESS AND PERFECTIBILITY

The final aspect to be noted about Ferguson's theory of spontaneous order is that it represents a progressivist and perfectibilist view of history. Order in our institutions, mores and living conditions is not simply maintained; our species is also propelled perpetually towards its practical and moral evolution.[752] Though teleology and progressivism are normally thought of as incompatible, Ferguson uniquely synthesises classical teleology with a more modern conception of progress.

Our species is caught up in a continuous, asymptotic, perfective process.[753] Its 'emblem is a passing stream, not a stagnating pool'.[754] This process is purposeful; we are *destined* to progress. Human existence has a purpose, and that purpose is also its cause. Ferguson even uses the Aristotelian analogy of seeds containing and causing the realisation of potential in order to expound his teleology. The seeds of full human potential, like that of trees, are given at birth.[755] Marcus Aurelius invoked the metaphor of seeds to illustrate his theory of change[756] while Seneca used the analogy of the human embryo to describe our development as the gradual conversion of potentiality into actuality.[757] But unlike these closed and static models, Ferguson's teleology is dynamic and progressive. His strategy for combining classical entelechy with a genuinely progressive conception of human nature is to conceive our innate progressive equipment as a blueprint for the species, not for individuals apart. As individuals we possess identical genetic material with potential that is limited only by our brief life spans. But because we are habitual, communicating, social animals, able to benefit from the gains of past generations through the transmission and institutionalisation of knowledge, every individual is able to both augment and benefit from the wisdom and achievements of the community through time. In this manner, each individual, in each generation, contributes to the long-term perfection of the species.[758]

---

[751] 'The author is invisible but his operation is manifest'. 'Of Things that are or May Be', *Collection of Essays*, No. 27 (1) p. 224

[752] It has been suggested that Ferguson's history contains 'no tincture of the perfectibility thesis found in Comte or Godwin'. A. S. Skinner, 'Adam Ferguson: The History of Civil Society', *Political Studies*, Vol. 15, 1967, pp. 219-21, p. 220 For opponents of this reading (other than myself) see: John Veitch, 'Philosophy in the Scottish Universities', *Mind*, Vol. 2 (6) April, 1877, p. 217; Kettler, *Social and Political Thought of Adam Ferguson*, p. 122; Bernstein, 'Ferguson and the Idea of Progress', *passim*, and Pierce, 'The Scottish Common Sense School', pp. 142-3.

[753] *P.I.* p. 47; *Essay*, pp. 204-5.

[754] *Essay*, p. 13.

[755] *P.I.*, p. 184; See also *P.I.*, p. 190.

[756] Marcus Aurelius, *Meditations*, 4. 36. p. 72.

[757] Robert Nisbet, *History of the Idea of Progress*, London: Heinemann, 1980, p. 45. Seneca's analogy was to be used by various thinkers, from St Augustine to Comte, for the next nineteen hundred years.

[758] *Essay*, pp. 10-11; *P.I.*, pp. 36, 194; 'Of Cause and Effect, Ends and Means, Order, Combination and Design', *Collection of Essays*, No. 13, p. 123.

We act upon the world and assume a good deal of responsibility for the kinds of progress we make.[759] The Roman Stoic conception of responsibility is combined with a Christian/Ciceronian belief in the moral independence of agents to establish the centrality of the concept of free will within Ferguson's teleology. Though no single agent is capable of altering events, each individual person plays an efficacious role in the process.[760] Even so, this agency is enacted within the framework of a Providentially ordained, natural order. Human progress is more or less predictable and assumes certain universal forms which argue a concerted plan. Notwithstanding the telic aspect, this approach is an anticipation of nineteenth and twentieth century structural-functionalism, with its emphasis on totalities over elements and deep over surface structures; its detection of universal codes and abstract rules; and, finally, its assumption that humans possess 'an innate, genetically transmitted and determined mechanism that acts as a structuring force' which limits the potential range of such structures.[761]

The idea of purpose in design is persistently affirmed and our progress evinces a divine purpose.[762] Despite the use of the analogy of seeds, with their finite potential, Ferguson's model is not deterministic. Progress is teleological in the sense that the grand design of the species is pre-determined by the Creator and fulfilled through human striving. History is a process of natural determinism, generated by endogenous human characteristics but expressed and moderated by human will and agency.[763] Ferguson's 'progressive teleology' is also anthropocentric in emphasising our species' self-creation and its place as the highest form of created being.[764]

Perfection can be a simultaneously prosaic or divine pursuit, consequently the species becomes more perfect in its institutions, inventions and customs as it strives for union with the mind of God. Our progressive urges do not distinguish between the sublime and the banal, the absolute or the relative, but are expressed as a generalised desire for excellence.[765] Ferguson sees our more ordinary advances as matrixes for the pursuit of moral perfection. History is propelled, unintentionally, by our constant drive to improve ourselves and our material circumstances. This process is unremitting because perfection is an impossible achievement.[766] As with Aristotelian teleology, God is conceived as the magnet of the universe, unattainable yet perpetually drawing us towards 'Him' and compelling us to strive and evolve.[767] Progress is a process of unending striving for union with the Divine Architect. In

---

[759] In particular, we exercise considerable latitude in terms of the content and rate of progress. *P.I.*, p. 314; *P.II.*, pp. 54-5

[760] *P.I.*, p. 202.

[761] Michael Lane, *Structuralism*, London: Jonathan Cape, 1970, pp. 14-15.

[762] Namely our moral self-realisation, expressed in the service of the community and in mutual beneficence. *P.II.*, pp. 28-9

[763] Jean Willke also offers an interpretation of Ferguson's history similar to that presented here. Willke, *Historical Thought of Adam Ferguson*, passim

[764] I have borrowed the term 'progressive teleology' from David Kettler. Kettler, *Social and Political Thought of Adam Ferguson*, p. 130

[765] *Institutes*, p. 90.

[766] *P.II.*, p. 403.

[767] Joad, *Philosophy*, pp. 202-3.

this regard, then, Ferguson's teleology is an eccentric one because it is not deterministic and because his conception of perfection is focused on means rather than ends.[768]

11. CONCLUDING REMARKS

Ferguson was one of the first thinkers to develop a systematic theory to explain how the sub-rational and self-regarding behaviours of individuals could form themselves spontaneously through time into adaptive social patterns and progressive order. Less well known than the invisible-hand doctrine of his friend and colleague, Adam Smith, Ferguson's is yet more detailed and penetrating.

Though he works from the argument from design, Ferguson nevertheless gives us a detailed and sophisticated proto-sociology of social order by describing how natural laws penetrate every aspect of human life. Our institutions, security, survival, prosperity, happiness, moral progress and even history itself are all attributable to natural laws of equilibrium working through human agents and their interactions with the material world. Society has an intelligent structure transcending the ability of individuals apart yet reflecting the Providentially inspired genius of our species through time. What Ferguson seems to have elaborated is a kind of 'Providentialist functionalism'[769] that reveals a universal pattern of underlying mental structures that manifest in social, cultural, technological and political structures. Ferguson offers us a model based on the design principle but which also anticipates the orientations of nineteenth century sociology and in this regard his work represents a critical phase in the development of social science.

---

[768] For a fuller discussion of this point see Chapter 11.

[769] Thanks to John Gray for the suggestion of this phrase.

CHAPTER 7

FERGUSON'S EARLY CONFLICT THEORY

This chapter focuses upon Ferguson's highly original work in the area of conflict theory; work which is partly responsible for his modern reputation as 'Father of Sociology'.[770] Ferguson's was probably the most developed treatment to date of the positive, ordering properties of conflict[771] and his discussion has many prescient aspects. It anticipates nineteenth and twentieth century conflict theory in positing conflict as an authentic medium, even *form*, of sociation and it embodies an early dialectical historiography.

Ferguson relies heavily upon conflict in his explanation of historical processes and in the securing of social order. Conflict generates many positive unintended consequences: it prevents social ossification; leads to the formation of the state, formal defence institutions and large-scale communities; it plays a pivotal role in the development of the moral personality; it preserves the balance of powers in government and prevents the encroachment of despotism and it contributes to the maintenance of social stability and cohesion. Conflict is thus fundamental to the flourishing of human societies and the march towards civilisation.[772] Because conflict achieves all of this in a spontaneous fashion, it plays an important role in Ferguson's discreditation of contractarian accounts of the emergence of civil society. But, despite the genuine originality of his approach, it is worth remembering that Ferguson finds his inspiration in sources like Tacitus and Machiavelli. His brief but apparently enjoyable career as chaplain to the Black Watch Regiment[773] is also likely to have shaped his positive attitude to 'opposition'.

1. GENERAL DISCUSSION

It has been said that Ferguson's exposition of conflict 'set him off from the conventional position of his century',[774] while Duncan Forbes has described it as the Scottish Enlightenment at its most 'tough minded' representing 'the highwater mark of social realism in the eighteenth century.'[775] Though Ferguson agreed with Shaftesbury, Hutcheson, and most of the Scottish literati that Hobbes' morbid and one-dimensional view of human nature was incorrect, he differs somewhat in his

---

[770] See, for example, Lehmann, *Adam Ferguson*, pp. 98-106; Barnes 'Sociology Before Comte', p. 235; Strasser, *Normative Structure of Sociology*, p. 52.

[771] Lehmann, *Adam Ferguson*, pp. 189-90.

[772] Forbes, 'Introduction' to *Essay*, p. xviii.

[773] Kettler, *The Social and Political Thought of Adam Ferguson*, p. 45.

[774] Bryson, *Man and Society*, p. 49.

[775] Forbes, 'Introduction' to *Essay*, pp. xvii.

simultaneous embrace of a key Hobbesian assumption, namely 'man's' essential belligerence. Part of Ferguson's agenda is to challenge the false dichotomy promulgated by contractarians of tranquil society, on the one hand, and violent, isolated chaos on the other. Rather, we are social beings with belligerent tendencies. He also confronts the Aristotelian (and later Hobbesian) premise that the key purpose of society is stability and social harmony. Rather, 'some circumstances in the lot of mankind' prompt us to be social, while others prompt us 'to war and dissension.'[776] Ferguson never claims that aggression is either our preferred or principal preoccupation,[777] But he does insist that conflict is just as natural as tranquillity and may even be equally desirable.

2. ENDOGENOUS SOURCES OF CONFLICT

For Ferguson, the underlying causes of conflict are to be found, partially in external conditions, but primarily in the human psyche. Notwithstanding the universality of envy and covetousness (other galvanisers of conflict), the human species is naturally restless and conflict, in its extreme form (war) provides it with one of its principal occupations. We 'appear to have in [our] minds the seeds of animosity, and to embrace the occasions of mutual opposition, with alacrity and pleasure.'[778] These drives are both universal and innate, known as they are to 'every savage' and 'every boy...at his play.' We even 'exult in the midst of alarms that seem to threaten [our] being.' Indeed, our possession of such respectable virtues as 'magnanimity, fortitude, and wisdom' confirms our destiny to 'struggle' in adversity.[779]

The Stoic principle of 'union' cannot by itself account for every aspect of human affairs. We are, to be sure, social animals, yet we are also driven by the principle of 'dissension.'[780] People are both mutual and factious by nature.[781] We are 'disposed to separate' yet always 'found in divisions and compartments, under the denomination of families, tribes, or hordes'.[782] Ferguson contradicts Hobbes' postulate of the fundamental violence of humanity on the grounds that it is based on a selective perception of our constitution. His response to the contemporary debate that raged over whether humanity' was essentially co-operative and social or solitary and belligerent was to dismiss the whole argument as fixated upon a false dichotomy generated, in turn, by the fiction that there ever was a pre-social state of war and lawlessness.[783] Instead, our species has always been social and has always been motivated by two sets of drives, those of 'union and opposition'. Rather than attempting to reduce all drives to a single motive, Ferguson contends that 'in treating

---

[776] *Essay*, p. 24. These 'circumstances' are those that subsist in human nature, otherwise known as drives.

[777] *Essay*, pp. 148-9.

[778] *Essay*, p. 25.

[779] *Essay*, pp. 48.

[780] *Essay*, p. 21-5.

[781] *Institutes*, p. 22.

[782] *P.II.*, p. 293.

[783] *P.I.*, pp. 197-9. 'The state of nature' is at once 'a state of war' and of 'amity'. *Essay*, p. 21.

of human affairs' we ought to take every facet of our nature into consideration.[784] But what Ferguson means by the phrase 'human affairs' is really 'male affairs'. Women are almost completely invisible in this highly masculinist account of the human constitution.[785]

Ferguson's dualistic taxonomy of motives is linked to his conclusion that our species has a tendency to form itself into cliques and loyal units. Our instincts impel us to form cohesive units but they also dictate the means for preserving these units. Instinctive belligerence and competitiveness, rather than destroying society, are really its preservatives. Thus 'union and dissension' are not binary opposites, as Hobbes had maintained,[786] but are closely related. Our sociability inspires us to form cliques while our natural belligerence, inspired by corporate sentiments, helps to preserve them.[787]

Forestalling accusations that his embrace of conflict and violence might contradict other claims about the importance of the social passions and the existence of a benevolent Providence orchestrating events to our advantage and preservation, Ferguson concedes that, initially, 'Nature, in this instance, appears to disregard the safety and peace of her works, and to adopt a destructive policy.' The rationale he goes on to provide, namely that human life is finite and death inevitable, is basically Stoic in nature.[788] Ferguson endorses and expands the observation of Marcus Aurelius that the universe is in a perpetual state of flux and renewal.[789] Change, expiration, regeneration; all accord with the divine Masterplan. Our natural belligerence has a teleological aspect, having been deliberately incorporated as a self-preserving mechanism. If that same drive leads to our death, then that too is part of ever-rejuvenating 'Nature'. As Ferguson says, we were not made to live forever. Even 'the longest liver must' die.'[790] The injuries and fatalities tallied in the course of our boisterous 'amusements' are perfectly normal, even benign events. A premature death on the battlefield is also a natural death, simply another 'distemper...by which the author of nature has appointed our exit from human life.'[791] It is the survival of our species, not the survival of individuals apart which really counts and since conflict leads us to form co-operative, nurturing society, which in turn, hones the moral personality and preserves the species through time, its advantages are perceived to far outweigh its defects. We must think in *species*, not individual terms, Ferguson insists, if we are to penetrate the mysteries of our

---

[784] *Essay*, p. 21.

[785] According to Oz-Salzberger, Ferguson's 'idea of cognition and moral growth was political' and since he clearly perceives politics as an exclusively male activity, his observations on moral and psychological development is 'strictly limited to the strong sex'. Oz-Salzberger, *Translating the Enlightenment*, pp. 114-15.

[786] Thomas Hobbes, *Leviathan*, Edited and with an Introduction by C.B. MacPherson, Ringwood: Penguin 1981, I, xiii, pp. 184-88.

[787] Montesquieu had also opposed Hobbes in this 'binary opposites' matter but the former's position differs from Ferguson's in its contractarian tendencies. Montesquieu, *Laws*, 1.1. 2. pp. 6-7.

[788] *P.I.*, pp. 16-17.

[789] Marcus Aurelius, *Meditations*, 6. 15. p. 93.

[790] *P.I.*, pp. 17; 323. *Essay*, pp. 28-9.

[791] *Essay*, p. 29.

Creator's permission of violence. Introducing the somewhat ruthless analogy of expendable plant life, Ferguson suggests that progress, through self-creation, involves risk, and inevitably the death, of some of its agents. By way of compensation, the Creator provides an abundance of supplicants for progress in order to offset any apparent waste that results. Rather than negating the existence of a benevolent, designing mind, the appearance of disturbance, agitation and transformation, manifestly attests to it.[792]

In describing his theory of social order Ferguson always emphasises that the vicissitudes and mess of life are part of its essential harmony, at least from the long view. In this manner, he is able to perform the difficult balancing act of maintaining, simultaneously, a Stoic optimism about the essential 'rightness' of the universe, oppose his chief adversary Hobbes, and still satisfy his empiricist ambitions by acknowledging the more unpleasant facts of life. Harmony and equilibrium in human affairs may be achieved, paradoxically, through disharmony and apparent disequilibrium.[793]

3. WAR

Ferguson consciously emulates Tacitus' and Machiavelli's moral approach to war by emphasising its positive aspects. It was Tacitus who taught that it was the love of 'danger itself' rather than the material and social 'rewards of courage' that inspired belligerent activism.[794] And following Machiavelli, Ferguson does not attempt to persuade us that belligerence is in itself virtuous but shows, rather, that 'virtue stands in special relation to necessity and that necessity frequently involves war and conflict.'[795] Ferguson seems to agree with Machiavelli that we must live in the real world. The vices of others frequently demand the sacrifice of our virtuous pretensions to the exigencies of necessity.[796] There are times when war is unavoidable and even desirable. Only a fool considers 'the time of necessary war among nations as a period of misery, or the time of peace as, of course, a season of happiness.'[797] Indeed, wars can represent periods of intense productivity and creativity for those involved[798] while just war (that is, war in defence of home territory) is not only virtuous activity but, for many, an avocation, even a form of recreation or play.[799]

---

[792] *P.I.*, pp. 332-3.

[793] *P.I.*, pp. 18-19.

[794] *Essay*, p. 47.

[795] As Springborg has suggested with respect to Machiavelli. Springborg, *Western Republicanism,* p.221. Ferguson, *Essay*, pp. 23-4.

[796] Niccolo Machiavelli, *The Prince*, Translated and with an Introduction by George Bull, London: Penguin, 1981, 15. p. 91.

[797] *P.II.*, p. 502.

[798] 'Their wars, and their treaties, their mutual jealousies, and the establishments which they devise in view to each other, constitute more than half the occupations of mankind, and furnish materials for their greatest and most improving exertions'. *Essay*, p. 116.

[799] *Essay*, pp. 47-8; 104.The 'disciplined soldier...contends against an enemy with an alacrity and even gaiety of spirit'. *P.II.*, p. 503.

Ferguson recovers Tacitus' conviction that war is purgative and therefore beneficial.[800] He also anticipates the theory of repression by suggesting that the suppression of instinctive belligerence is not only damaging to the 'passive sufferer' but may lead to still greater violence.[801] Conflict, and even violence, are conceived as performing perfectly natural, even useful and laudable functions in human affairs. In times of war this is doubly so.

War suggests the necessity of regular government or 'departments of state' and ensures its ongoing survival by preserving solidarity between its members. It is possible, Ferguson explains, to establish tenuous commercial relationships without formal conventions, but it would be impossible for people to live in security without some sort of government.[802] Ferguson agrees with Machiavelli that war strengthens social bonds; it necessitates the formation of smaller social groupings into larger aggregates[803] while the sense of common danger unites communities still further. The perception of external common enemies results in communities which are 'faithful, disinterested (and) generous.'[804]

The institution of private property is closely bound up in the process because government evolves only in those communities marked by 'collusions of private interest.' Nations characterised by private ownership, and therefore high levels of material prosperity, are vulnerable to the avaricious advances of their neighbours. This constant threat of invasion leads to the formation of organised defence institutions which entails the formation of larger communal units and, inevitably, the state.[805] As Ferguson says:

> Without the rivalship of nations, and the practice of war, civil society itself could scarcely have found an object, or a form. Mankind might have traded without any formal convention, but they cannot be safe without a national concert. The necessity of a public defence, has given rise to many departments of state, and the intellectual talents of men have found their busiest scene in wielding their national forces.[806]

Nation-states are therefore (in part at least) unintended consequences of conflict. We need our fellow 'men' and the affection of those closest to us, but also, paradoxically, their rivalry. Though Ferguson conceded that 'internal tranquillity' could be a 'blessing'[807] and admitted that conflict was not always positive, he was

---

[800] Tacitus is also a source for Ferguson's views on the socially binding effects of war. Tacitus, *The Agricola and the Germania*, Translated and with an Introduction by H. Mattingly, London: Penguin, 1970, passim.

[801] *P.II*, pp. 502-3.

[802] *Essay*, p. 26.

[803] *Discourses,* 1. 1. pp. 100-1.

[804] *Essay*, pp. 99, 26-9.

[805] Ferrarotti, 'Civil Society and State Structures', p. 14. This line of thought is not to be confused with any kind of social contract born of a chaotic state of nature. This formation is inevitable, grounded in instincts, teleologically conceived.

[806] *Essay*, p. 28.

[807] *P.II.*, p. 502; *Essay,* pp. 149-50.

firmly committed to the view that war and conflict are catalysts for all forms of government.

4. FACTIONAL CONFLICT AND CONSTITUTIONAL GOVERNMENT: ANTICIPATIONS OF A PLURALIST THEORY OF CONFLICT

According to Hermann Strasser, Ferguson rates as 'the single most important precursor of the theory of class conflict'[808] while Ludwig Gumplowicz identified Ferguson as the first significant exponent of the 'group struggle' theory of social development.[809] Conflict is of particular service in helping to form and preserve free constitutions. The emergence of limited constitutional government is a function of 'class' or factional conflict.[810] Factions clash over the efforts 'to withstand the encroachments of sovereignty' upon the property and rights of individuals which, in turn, gives rise to the necessity of government restrained by law. Rules and laws emerge from this ongoing struggle to preserve individual liberty from the encroachments of rulers.[811] Out of this dialectical process Ferguson anticipates an exponential accumulation of 'wise establishments' advantageous to 'Liberty and Just Government.'[812] After 'free' constitutions have been established, they must be continually preserved and, again, this is achieved through conflict. A free constitution is maintained, moulded and preserved, inadvertently, through conflict. Self-interest (in this case, the individual's desire to preserve her/his own liberty) and class resentment are inadvertently harnessed in the service of securing the public good. Faction, motivated by self-interest, preserves liberty which is 'maintained by the continued differences and oppositions of numbers, not by their concurring zeal in behalf of equitable government.'[813] Though 'the spirit of faction' is generally destructive in small scale republics it is a vital guard against corruption and 'servility' in monarchies.[814] Perhaps the most significant aspect of Ferguson's analysis is the fact that governmental forms are perceived as being determined by class structure. 'Forms of government', he tell us, 'take their rise, chiefly from the manner in which the members of a state have been originally classed.'[815]

It has been suggested that Ferguson's discussion of party faction and the perils of political harmony represents a critical, running commentary on Hume[816] who had written that factions exacerbate social conflict, undermine the rule of law and 'subvert government.'[817] Hume certainly had good reason to be wary of the effects

---

[808] Strasser, *The Normative Structure of Sociology*, p. 56.

[809] Barnes, 'Sociology before Comte', p. 235.

[810] *Essay*, 124-5, 128; Hamoway, 'Progress and Commerce', p. 73.

[811] *Essay*, pp. 247-57.

[812] *Reflections*, p. 2.

[813] *Essay*, pp. 124-4.

[814] *Institutes*, p. 289.

[815] *Essay*, p. 131. Herman Strasser's brief but excellent review of Ferguson's achievement has been paraphrased here. Strasser, *The Normative Structure of Sociology*, pp. 56-57.

[816] Forbes, 'Introduction' to *Essay*, p. xxxvi.

[817] David Hume, 'Of Parties in General', *Essays*, p. 55.

of faction. According to John Stuart Shaw, factional conflict was particularly wild and venomous, not only in pre-Union Scotland but also in post-Union England, the latter with a 'disproportionately severe...impact on Scottish affairs'.[818] Hume's 'ideal commonwealth' is one in which wealth inequalities are minimised with a view to reducing 'party strife'[819] whereas Ferguson welcomed the inevitable ructions which accompany these perfectly legitimate wealth inequalities. Hume positively associated the polished age with political stability. The 'vulgar arts' of commerce and manufactures beget 'laws, order, police, discipline' and improve statecraft. Under the influence of this knowledge, governors become milder, less severe and therefore less likely to incite subjects/citizens to rebellion. 'Factions are...less inveterate, revolutions less tragical, authority less severe, and seditions less frequent. Even foreign wars abate of their cruelty.'[820] Ferguson is all for civilisation and the domestication of violence and he agrees that manners and mores are considerably softened in the polished age but he is sceptical about Hume's claim that this is always and necessarily a good thing. In particular, he objects to both Hume's and Smith's preoccupation with the desirability of political tranquillity. Ferguson saw tranquillity as potentially hazardous and disagreed that faction was destructive. In fact, faction and free government are causally linked and therefore inseparable.[821] Without the disputes arising from faction, free government is threatened by the potential for despotism. '[L]iberty is never in greater danger than it is when we measure national felicity...by the...mere tranquillity' that a ruler 'may bestow.'[822] Ferguson endorses the argument first set out by Polybius in the *Rise of the Roman Empire* that the Romans maintained free constitutions 'not...by means of abstract reasoning, but rather through the lessons learned from many struggles and difficulties' and through the adoption of reforms indicated by 'the light of experience'.[823] Rejecting all utopian, total and unitary forms of rule Ferguson argues that 'independence' and 'opposition of interest' must be maintained and cultivated at all times.[824]

Far from being a sign of stability, political quiescence hides a sinister truth: '[T]he turbulence of free states is contrasted with the seeming tranquillity of despotical government.'[825] The appearance of disturbance indicates the *existence*, rather than absence of rule of law and the protection of such rights as free speech and right of protest. Ferguson admonishes as misguided anyone who would seek to reconcile the 'animosities' and 'opinions of men' for '[n]othing... but corruption can suppress the debates that subsist among men of integrity.' It is far better for a political community to suffer unrest than for its individual citizens to be denied an

---

[818] Shaw, *Political History of Eighteenth Century Scotland*, p. 18.
[819] Hume, 'Idea of a Perfect Commonwealth', *Essays*, p. 514.
[820] Hume, 'Of Refinement in the Arts', *Essays*, p. 274.
[821] Hamowy, 'Progress and Commerce', pp. 74-5.
[822] *Essay,* p. 255.
[823] Polybius, *Rise of the Roman Empire,* 6. 10. p. 311.
[824] *Essay*, p. 61.
[825] *P.II.*, p. 510.

active role in public affairs.[826] Indeed, 'our very praise of unanimity' is 'a danger to liberty.'[827] Ferguson might have had Smith and Hume in mind when he expostulated:

> We have reason to dread the political refinements of ordinary men, when we consider, that repose, or inaction itself, is in a great measure their object; and that they would frequently model their governments, not merely to prevent injustice and error, but to prevent agitation and bustle and by the barriers they raise against the evil actions of men, would prevent them from acting at all. Every dispute of a free people, in the opinion of such politicians, amounts to disorder, and a breach of the national peace...Men of superior genius sometimes seem to imagine, that the vulgar have no title to act, or to think.[828]

Liberty and its achievement is always an awkward business, frequently giving 'rise to complaints But this gives no cause for the despotical and corrupt alternatives since it is an observable fact that the 'best constitutions of government are attended with inconvenience.'[829] The popular use of architectural and mechanistic analogies to describe 'order in civil society' is questionable because buildings and machines are 'inanimate and dead.' Society, by contrast, is 'living and active', therefore there is great danger in employing this kind of analogy to establish a constitutional ideal. For Ferguson the inorganic analogy is synonymous with 'obedience, secrecy', political slavery and oligarchy whereas the organic model he prefers sets up 'commotion and action' as ideals, rather than pathologies.[830] People are at their most creative and progressive, not in sequestered contemplation, but surrounded by competitors, adversaries and allies and embroiled in all manner of 'ferments', wars and factional disputes.[831]

Ferguson differs from Hume in his approach to conflict partly because of his ambivalence about progress. Hume is far more enthusiastic about the social and political benefits of the commercial stage. Life in 'ancient nations' is in most important respects 'inferior' to that in the modern. It is happier because more calm, predictable and pacific. War was more brutal, ubiquitous and furious in ancient orders, regimes more unstable, and tyranny more common.[832] On the one hand, Ferguson welcomes the more civilised expressions of 'opposition' witnessed in modern times, however, he is worried that too much order will lead to inertia. He seems to have appreciated the importance of what were to become central tenets of twentieth century conflict theory, namely, that excessive consensus can be detrimental by inhibiting 'adaptation to change' and encouraging 'maladjustive inertia', tendencies which could 'precipitate the disintegration of a group'.[833]

---

[826] *Essay*, pp. 62-3.

[827] *Essay*, p. 252.

[828] *Essay*, p. 209.

[829] *Essay*, p. 255.

[830] *Essay*, p. 254, n. 97.

[831] *Essay*, p. 170.

[832] Hume, 'Populousness of Ancient Nations', *Essays*, pp. 404-6

[833] Pierre L. Van Den Bergh, 'Dialectic and Functionalism: Towards a Theoretical Synthesis', *Sociological Theory*, W.L. Wallace (ed.), Chicago: Aldine Publishing Company, 1969, p. 210; *Essay*, p. 252.

In increasingly complex, 'modern,' societies such as interested Ferguson, political compromise is hammered out dialectically between competing factions. This dissonant process results, propitiously, in just laws that are the product of compromise and the participation and commitment of each section of society. Statutes enacted in this manner operate like treaties, 'the resolutions of a people determined to be free'.[834] But Ferguson is not entirely original here. Machiavelli had made an almost identical (though less well-developed) argument before him. There is even a section in the *Discourses* entitled 'That Discord Between the Plebs and the Senate of Rome made this Republic both Free and Powerful' in which Machiavelli argues that, provided a people are free from corruption, tumults are, at worst, harmless and may, in fact, do some good towards preserving free constitutions.[835] Similarly, Ferguson suggests that factional conflicts are educative and productive of political efficacy. '[T]he rivalship of separate communities and the agitations of a free people, are the principles of political life, and the school of men.' Faction is good because it is a preventative of that fatal precursor to political corruption, apathy, or to use Ferguson's terms, (paraphrasing Plutarch) that 'complaisance, by which men submit their opinions without examination.'[836] Though factional 'divisions...seem to endanger' the very existence of society, in fact it is faction that preserves its vitality by providing postures and roles for 'the scene that is prepared for the instruction of its members.'[837] Ferguson even endorses Plutarch's suggestion that legislators should deliberately encourage factional dispute.[838]

Ferguson's complacency about conflict ran deep, sometimes verging on naivety. Rejecting the standard argument that 'a promiscuous use of arms' would be dangerous to the security of the state Ferguson indicates that he has no fear of arming a populace riven with factional conflict. Any attempt to deprive particular groups of what he regards as a most fundamental right and duty (i.e. military service) will merely 'serve to foment and embitter their divisions'. It is one thing to have a 'difference of opinion' but quite another and more serious 'ground of animosity' to furnish 'unequal treatment and inferior privilege.' Ferguson admits that 'familiarity with arms' may, to a limited degree 'render private quarrels and popular riots more bloody', however he insists 'that a few domestic inconveniences' should not 'deter us from the necessary steps' of defence against foreign enemies. And anyway, under the new civility whereby violence is regulated by 'proper laws and an active policy', such 'inconveniencies' are likely to be entirely preventable.[839]

---

[834] *Essay*, p. 249.

[835] Machiavelli, *Discourses* 1. 4. p. 113. See also Bernard Crick's illuminating commentary on this subject in the 'Introduction', pp. 33-37. Roy Branson suggests that Ferguson influenced Madison in this regard. Roy Branson, 'James Madison and the Scottish Enlightenment', *Journal of the History of Ideas*, Vol. 40, 1979, pp. 235-50, pp. 248-9.

[836] *Essay*, p. 63.

[837] *P.I*, p. 267.

[838] Ferguson paraphrases Plutarch here: '[G]ood citizens should be led to dispute'. *Essay*, p. 63.

[839] *Reflections*, 21-29. For a fuller discussion of Ferguson's attitude to national defence see: Richard Sher, 'Adam Ferguson, Adam Smith and the Problem of National Defense', *Journal of Modern History*, Vol. 61 (2) 1989, pp. 240-68. See also, by the same author, *Church and University*, pp. 213-41.

5. SPORT AND PLAY

Ferguson's rejection of the traditional hedonistic opposition of pleasure and pain is most pronounced in his discussion of sport and competition. Not only is play an end in itself but it has a number of vital latent functions. Contrary to the distorted sensibilities of hedonists and other 'effeminate' types, activities involving effort, struggle, even pain, are perfectly congenial to the active nature of 'man'.

> How many are there to whom war itself is a pastime, who chuse the life of a soldier, exposed to dangers and continued fatigues; of a mariner, in conflict with every hardship, and bereft of every conveniency; of a politician, whose sport is the conduct of parties and factions; and who, rather than be idle, will do the business of men and of nations for whom he has not the smallest regard. Such men do not chuse pain as preferable to pleasure, but are incited by a restless disposition to make continued exertions of capacity and resolution; they triumph in the midst of their struggles; they droop, and they languish, when the occasion of their labour has ceased.[840]

Our species is not only instinctively bellicose but inherently competitive as indicated, for example, in our games and sports which are often the very 'image of war.' Indeed, the natural urges at play are precisely the same for both sportsman and the soldier.[841] Such games as 'shooting at mark', gaming, even poaching and other forms of 'pursuit'[842] are a rehearsal for military dexterity.[843] This observation (that play frequently mirrors the state of war) is reminiscent of Machiavelli's observation in the *Discourses* that the sport of hunting 'teaches one a host of... things that are essential in warfare.'[844] But there is also a remarkable anticipation of twentieth century sociology of sport here. For Ferguson, as for Norbert Elias and Eric Dunning, sport represents a 'controlled decontrolling of restraints on emotions' whereby emotion is at once aroused and satisfied. Organised games serve to offset the 'stifling effects of the routinised organisation of social relations' within developing and therefore increasingly ordered societies. Sport is a 'mimetic' activity. Genuinely dangerous situations are enacted or imitated in order to arouse emotional responses associated with warfare but 'in 'safe' forms without the risks attached to the real thing.'[845] Sports provide 'outlets for emotions, impulses and tensions' and make space 'for the socially approved arousal of moderate excitement behaviour in public.'[846] Especially dangerous sports provide a socially sanctioned theatre for the expression of such masculine values as 'courage; strength and dominance' while giving physical expression to other approved social values like

---

[840] *Essay*, p. 47.

[841] *Essay*, pp. 28, 45-7.

[842] '[P]ursuit in Ferguson's civic language, is not limited to the quest for material improvement. It is hunt, war and play as much as labour, arts, or commerce, which for Ferguson marked the realisation of men's true nature'. Oz-Salzberger, *Translating the Enlightenment*, p. 115.

[843] Indeed, Ferguson goes so far as to suggest that, were it possible to estimate the numbers of England's poachers, one could 'compute the present Strength of our country'. *Reflections,* pp. 16-17.

[844] Machiavelli, *Discourses*, 3. 39. p. 511. Machiavelli, in turn, cites his debt to Xenophon.

[845] Robert Van Krieken, *Norbert Elias,* London: Routledge, 1997, p. 129.

[846] N. Elias and E. Dunning, *Quest for Excitement: Sport and Leisure in the Civilising Process,* Oxford: Blackwell, 1986, p. 65; Van Krieken, *Norbert Elias*, pp. 127; 129.

competition, team effort, and fair play. In this context, aggression and aggressive *transgression* provide opportunities for 'reflecting' upon and reinforcing these values. Sport domesticates potentially dangerous impulses and channels the need for physical aggression into a relatively benign but satisfying symbolic form, a 'metaphor for otherwise unacknowledged aspects of experience...the chaotic, uninhibited and uncontrollable competition which lurks beneath the apparently co-operative surface.'[847]

Though Ferguson does not, of course, use the same terminology he nevertheless anticipates all these ideas in his own observations. For example:

> Every animal is made to delight in the exercise of his natural talents and forces: The lion and the tyger sport with the paw; the horse delights to commit his mane to the wind, and forgets his pasture to try his speed in the field; the bull even before his brow is armed, and the lamb while yet an emblem of innocence, have a disposition to strike with the forehead, and anticipate, in play, the conflicts they are doomed to sustain. Man too is disposed to opposition, and to employ the forces of his nature against an equal antagonist; he loves to bring his reason, his eloquence, his courage, even his bodily strength, to the proof. His sports are frequently an image of war; sweat and blood are freely expended in play; and fractures or death are often made to terminate the pastimes of idleness and festivity.[848]

Internal conflict and controlled competition between insider groups can be just as beneficial to social cohesion as conflict between insider and outsider groups. Ferguson believed that the greater the level of social intimacy, the more intense the conflict within the groups. Conflict enables the groups to discharge suppressed and potentially destructive hostilities between members and thereby re-establish unity and cohesion.[849]

6. PROGRESS AND CIVILISATION

Ferguson saw conflict as a key generator of history. Indeed he was convinced that some form of conflict is a prerequisite for any significant social change. Civil society is itself a product of conflict because it emerges as a necessary safeguard against both internal and external conflict. Ferguson's approach thus shares much in common with dialectic (Marxian) conflict theory. To begin with, both models see social change as evolutionary and as an 'ascensional spiral towards progress.' Secondly, the dialectical notion of evolution assumes that 'a given state of the social system presupposes all previous states, and hence, contains them, if only in residual or modified form.' Finally, both are fundamentally equilibrium models.[850] Ferguson expounds a kind of 'conflict structuralism' in which conflict is understood as at once integrative and positively disruptive. What is so interesting about Ferguson's

---

[847] Jeremy MacClancy (ed), *Sport, Identity and Ethnicity*, Oxford: Berg Publishers, 1996, pp. 3, 7.

[848] *Essay*, p. 28. See also *Reflections*, pp. 17-18.

[849] This kind of 'safety-valve' theory of conflict was also outlined by Simmel and the German ethnologist Heinrich Schurtz who referred to 'institutionalised outlets for hostilities and drives ordinarily suppressed by the group' as a means for protecting social life from their otherwise potentially destructive impact. Coser, *Functions of Social Conflict*, p. 41.

[850] Van Den Bergh, 'Dialectic and Functionalism', pp. 210-11.

dualism here is that it pre-emptively responds to a complaint Ralf Dahrendorf was later to voice about mid-twentieth century sociology, namely, that it had failed to produce a synthetic social theory which accommodated both functionalist (consensus) and dialectic (disruptive) sociologies of conflict.[851] Ferguson's fully developed theory of spontaneous order, (incorporating latent and manifest functions) achieved what later sociologies were still struggling towards: a theory in which conflict plays a dual role as an important agent of equilibrium, on the one hand, and a key generator of change, on the other.

Ferguson was alert to the problem of lack of excitement in societies that were becoming increasingly unexciting. In particular, how would a commercialising — and therefore 'softening' — nation like Britain cope with the management of human aggression? Ferguson was also acutely aware of the role played by specialisation in the transition from barbarism to civilisation, from a warrior culture dominated by codes of chivalry, to a market culture based on legal rules, 'cool' virtues and a strict division between work and leisure. Could human boisterousness and belligerence be contained within the relative dullness of polite society? Ferguson did not believe sports alone could perform this function (he believed that militias would also serve this purpose)[852] but he did perceive in sports a valuable outlet for our otherwise potentially destructive urges.

The process which Elias was later to refer to as 'sportisation', is a key mechanism in the civilising process, to the extent that it compensates for 'the control and restraint of overt emotionality' demanded of modern subjects by permitting a 'more regulated expression of aggressive emotions and impulses.'[853] The gradual process of controlling and mitigating all forms of violence is an important aspect of Ferguson's theory of progress. While conflict is generally positive, unbridled violence must be taken under control and either sublimated or harnessed in the service of community. For John Keane, the eighteenth century push for civilisation was about 'resolving the permanent problem of discharging, defusing and sublimating violence.'[854] Ferguson is an important observer of this push although he was distinguished by his insistence on the positive aspects of conflict urges. Savagery and barbarity are dispelled by the development of 'regular government and political subordination.' Nations are properly described as 'polished' when violence has come to be regulated, channelled and checked. Ferguson sees mature statehood as synonymous with the exclusive and legitimate deployment of violence. The modern state is superior to the barbarous because in it '[q]uarrelling' is regulated by 'rules' rather than 'the immediate dictates of passion, which ended in words of reproach, in violence, and blows.'[855] The modern state is also superior to the extent that it has learned to constrain the brutality and destructiveness of pre-commercial party politics:

---

[851] Lewis A. Coser, *Continuities in the Study of Social Conflict*, New York: The Free Press, 1970, p. 4.

[852] For a fuller discussion of Ferguson's views on this topic see John Robertson, *The Scottish Enlightenment and the Militia Issue*, Edinburgh: John Donald, 1985, pp. 88-91, 200-22.

[853] Elias and Dunning, *Quest for Excitement*, pp. 60-90.

[854] John Keane, *Civil Society*, pp. 117-19.

[855] *Essay*, p. 188.

> When they took arms in the division of faction, the prevailing party supported itself by expelling their opponents, by proscriptions, and bloodshed. The usurper endeavoured to maintain his station by the most violent and prompt executions. He was opposed, in his turn, by conspiracies and assassinations, in which the most respectable citizens were ready to use the dagger.

The conduct of war is also vastly improved in modern times. Previously, '[c]ities were razed, or inslaved; the captive sold, mutilated or condemned to die' whereas now it is conducted according to laws, 'treaties and cartels.' Civility has penetrated the social fabric so thoroughly that people have learned to 'mingl[e] politeness with the use of the sword.' Civilised societies operate according to doctrines of just war (or so Ferguson likes to believe) whereby force is used solely in the name of 'justice' and the legitimate defence of 'national rights.'[856]

7. SOCIAL INTIMACY AND CIVIC VIRTUE

Like Rousseau, Ferguson is concerned at the effects of progress and the refinement of manners on moral character. Rousseau lamented the manner in which polite society dampened and masked ardent sentiments, including those of patriotism and hostility towards out-groups. He wrote: 'We do not grossly outrage even our enemies but artfully calumniate them. Our hatred of other nations diminishes, but patriotism dies with it.'[857]

Ferguson agreed, though for different and, arguably, better-developed reasons. Conflict has moral and educative aspects. Our natural belligerence serves a valuable function in the formation of the moral personality by 'furnish[ing] a scene for the exercise of our greatest abilities.' These qualities 'are sentiments of generosity and self-denial that animate the warrior in defence of his country.'[858] Ferguson accords with Thucydides' view that war is a kind of school for virtue, especially civic virtue.[859] War, adversity, indeed any situation involving adversity, incidentally refines not only the martial, but also the social, emotional and intellectual faculties. The formulation is strikingly teleological with Ferguson suggesting that such conditions are deliberately orchestrated by the Creator as part of the process of human development.[860] Conflict, in honing our critical faculties, helps to preserve civic virtue because the practice of war has led to the refinement of martial vigour and statecraft.[861]

---

[856] *Essay*, pp. 189-190; *Reflections*, p. 8..

[857] Rousseau, 'A Discourse on the Moral Effect of the Arts and Sciences', in *Social Contract and Discourses*, p. 7.

[858] *Essay*, p. 28.

[859] Though Adam Smith also made reference to the ennobling hardships of war, it was not for him a consistent theme. Smith, *TMS*, VI. iii, 6. p. 239.

[860] *P.II.*, pp. 507-9.

[861] *Essay*, pp. 28-29, 149.

War provides the perfect occasion for the exercise of our active powers and may enhance the social virtues. The horrors of war are offset by socially useful 'passions of another sort'.

> Sentiments of affection and friendship mix with animosity; the active and strenuous become the guardians of their society; and violence itself is, in their case, an exertion of generosity as well as courage.

Violence becomes socially productive when exercised by the 'patriot and warrior' for in such circumstances it results in 'the most illustrious career of human virtue.'[862] War is not always malevolent. On the contrary, it frequently occasions the exercise of 'the best qualities of men.'[863] The apparent variance between Ferguson's benevolent ethics and his unambiguous views on conflict is particularly striking at this point. But, in typical fashion, he reconciles the dissonance with the familiar device of a paradox. Our apparently contradictory nature, simultaneously sociable and hostile, is really two sides of the same coin. There is a direct correlation between the strength of our social passions and the lengths to which we are prepared to go in order to defend them and this is nowhere better exemplified than in the actions of the 'true' warrior whose very violence is 'sancti[fied]' and made sociable by its reference to the safety of his compatriots.[864] External pressures are beneficial to the maintenance of social life. '[T]he assaults of an enemy have been frequently useful to nations, by uniting their members more firmly together, and by preventing the secessions and actual separations in which their civil discord might otherwise terminate.'[865] Ferguson opines that 'it is vain to expect that we can give to the multitude of a people a sense of union among themselves, without admitting hostility to those who oppose them'.[866] Garry Wills refers to this irony of human nature as 'the Ferguson paradox' noting that Jefferson used the idea to demonstrate 'that Indians love by showing that they hate.'[867] Ferguson may have in mind the highland clan system when his speaks nostalgically of those '[s]mall and simple tribes, who in their domestic society have the firmest union, are in their state of opposition as separate nations, frequently animated with the most implacable hatred.'[868] Similar arguments are found in Cicero: What we might otherwise perceive as 'brutality and savagery' when 'restrained by the uniting bonds of society' become productive and praiseworthy 'courage.'[869] Shaftesbury made similar arguments in relation to political faction. '[T]he very Spirit of Faction', he wrote, while seemingly anti-social, actually arises from the imperatives for 'social Love, and common Affection', albeit in an 'irregular' form. Contrary to the common perception of party

---

[862] *Essay.* p. 29.

[863] *Essay,* p. 25.

[864] *Essay,* p. 104.

[865] *Essay,* p. 26.

[866] *Essay,* p. 29.

[867] Garry Wills, *Inventing America*, New York: Doubleday, 1978, p. 289.

[868] *Essay,* p. 25; Waszek, *Man's Social Nature,* pp. 162-3.

[869] Cicero, *De Officiis,* 1. 44. 157. p. 161.

politics as the province of purely self-interested actors, '[o]f all characters' it is really 'the thorough selfish one [that] is the least forward in taking party.'[870]

8. COMPLICATIONS AND TENSIONS

Because of Ferguson's Providentialism and, in particular, his emphasis on the virtue of beneficence, John Bernstein has suggested that 'Ferguson's admiration for the qualities revealed in conflict constitute a problem for his moral philosophy...which he never adequately confronted.'[871] But Ferguson is able to answer his critic by aligning his celebration of our belligerent and aggressive drives with a number of important Stoic virtues. These are not the quiet Greek-Stoic virtues of pacifism and *apatheia* but the more ardent Roman-Stoic civic virtues of political vigour and martial valour. Conflict has civic and moral utility; even violence is shown to stand in special relation to necessity and the mandatory performance of duties confluent with assigned station. It should also be remembered that Ferguson is striving for a kind of empirical social science and is unwilling to put 'system' before the observable facts. In other words, even if he were an advocate of Stoic quietism he would not allow any of his moral prejudices to interfere with his mission as an early 'social scientist'. It is for this reason that he counsels his reader to beware of confusing the Hobbesian debate with the moral question of whether we are essentially good or evil creatures. Our social nature does not necessarily preclude violence and our violence does not make us evil. Our inherent sociability is an observable, empirical fact, a law relating to our physical nature. It has no moral dimension and is not contradicted by the presence of conflict.[872]

For Fania Oz-Salzberger, Ferguson's simultaneous commitment to Stoic values and conflict represents a 'glaring contradiction' which he is 'quite simply, unwilling to solve.'[873] Others have argued that Ferguson's insistence on the compatibility of the principles of 'union and dissension' represents a significant departure from Stoic principles.[874] David Kettler sees this 'departure' as reflecting Ferguson's response to 'the dubious respectability of the Stoic teachings among the educated men of his time'[875] but such an explanation is unconvincing in light of Ferguson's manifest and frequently advertised enthusiasm for Stoicism.[876] Norbert Waszek, meanwhile, relates Ferguson's alleged departure from Stoicism to his first-hand experience with the clan system, which, it is argued, must have brought home the positive social

---

[870] Anthony Ashley Cooper, (Lord Shaftesbury) 'An Essay on the Freedom of Wit and Humour', *Characteristics of Men, Manners, Opinions, Times Etc,* Edited and with an Introduction by John M. Robertson, in 2 Vols, London: Grant Richards, I, pp. 76-7.

[871] Bernstein, 'Adam Ferguson and The Idea of Progress', p. 108.

[872] 'To be in society is the physical state of the species, not the moral distinction of any particular man. It is the state of those who quarrel, as well as those who agree'. *P.II.*, p. 24.

[873] Oz-Salzberger, *Translating the Enlightenment*, p. 116.

[874] Waszek, *Man's Social Nature*, 161-63; Kettler, *Social and Political Thought of Adam Ferguson*, p. 156.

[875] Kettler, *Social and Political Thought of Adam Ferguson*, p. 156.

[876] *P.I.*, p. 7.

value of belligerence.[877] This is a better explanation, however, it also makes the assumption that belligerence cannot be accommodated within Stoicism. It should be remembered that Ferguson is a disciple of Roman, not Greek Stoicism. The former placed less emphasis on resignation, with a greater stress on the exercise of the active powers and the performance of duties associated with citizenship. The highest of these is, of course, military service in the defence of homelands. Once he has decided on the inevitability of conflict Ferguson is then able to link violence back to necessity and duty and thereby realign himself with Stoicism.[878]

9. CONCLUDING REMARKS

It has been noted that Ferguson's treatment of the role of conflict has been hailed as one of the first steps towards nineteenth and twentieth century sociology. While it is true that there is little in Ferguson that is not reiterated and fully developed by later thinkers like Coser, Elias and Marx, his real achievement lies in providing a bridge between the religious and ancient worlds and modern, secular and sociological concerns. This synthesis is nowhere better exemplified than in his 'Providential functionalism' whereby a genuinely functionalist and progressivist sociology of conflict is articulated within a teleological, theistic framework. Ferguson artfully translates his nostalgia for pre-commercial forms of sociation and his admiration for the virtues celebrated by thinkers like Tacitus and Machiavelli into something that is distinctively fresh and sociological.

---

[877] Waszek, *Man's Social Nature*, pp. 162-63.

[878] For further discussion of the relationship between war, duty and pacificism in Roman Stoicism see Hill, 'The Two Republicae of the Roman Stoics', pp. 65-79.

CHAPTER 8

HABIT

Ferguson's interest in the social role of habit stems from his more general interest in exploring the sub-rational, unconscious and emotional dimensions of human existence and in developing his theory that tacit processes and drives are capable of generating social order. Specifically, he wants to understand and explain how the norms, structures and institutions initially generated by passions become entrenched over time. The exercise of the passions is not random but rather organised and organisable, as individualised acts are formed into an intelligible system. Ferguson's attempts to understand the ways in which acquired culture intersects with the natural laws of Providence reflects his layered approach to social science. It also enables us to see why his conservatism ran so deep and that his aversion to radical change was, in fact, a carefully reasoned position.

Habit performs some heavy work in the maintenance of social life and the generation of spontaneous order. Ferguson demonstrates its importance by devoting five sections of the *Principles* to its effects.[879]

1. GENERAL DISCUSSION

Ferguson is numbered among the long line of thinkers, stretching back to ancient Greek times, to place particular emphasis upon the importance of habit in human affairs.[880] By habit Ferguson means the mechanisms by which we become socialised, what we would now variously refer to as group-ways, tacit knowledge, moral and social culture, norms and mores. His Scottish contemporaries also shared his interest and have been identified as seminal figures in the anthropology of folkways, influencing the early American social scientist William Graham Sumner (1840-1910) in the writing of *Folkways*.[881] Hume, Reid, Millar and Kames showed great interest in the topic[882] as did other Enlightenment thinkers like Helvetius, Rousseau,

---

[879] Ch. III, Sections ii, iii, iv, v, vi and vii of the *Principles, I*. William Lehmann provides a good exposition of Ferguson's treatment of habit in *Adam Ferguson*, (pp. 52-53, 67-77) as does David Kettler in *Social and Political Thought of Adam Ferguson*. The present chapter owes something to both.

[880] Charles Camic, 'The Matter of Habit', *American Journal of Sociology*, Vol. 91 (5), March 1986, 1039-87, p. 1047. Aristotle, Aquinas, Duns Scotus and William Ockham are just some of them. O. Fuchs, *The Psychology of Habit According to William Ockham*, St. Bonaventure, N.Y.: The Franciscan Institute, 1952, pp. xiii-xvii.

[881] Donald Pickens, 'Scottish Common sense Philosophy and Folkways', *Journal of Thought*, Vol. 22, 1987, pp. 39-44.

[882] Christopher J. Berry, 'Sociality and Socialisation' in Alexander Broadie (ed.) *The Scottish Enlightenment*, Cambridge: Cambridge University Press, 2003, pp. 243-57.

Condorcet and Kant.[883] But the study of habit did not become widespread or systematic until the nineteenth and early twentieth century, when it came to interest psychologists.[884]

In his discussion of the subject Ferguson attempts to demonstrate the inadequacy of the Aristotelian distinction between *physis* and *nomos* by arguing that habits are inherent tendencies, forged socially. Habit is shown to perform a number of vital functions in the maintenance of social order. It serves as 'God's' guarantee that all our important advances will be preserved and enshrined, thereby allowing our species to progress and flourish; it contributes to our moral development and acts as a form of social control; it enhances social cohesion and preserves the matrix of human happiness and virtue, society. Ferguson's treatment of habit is noteworthy because it embodies what appears to be a precursory kind of functionalism in distinguishing between the latent and manifest functions of mores and habits. It also (incidentally) foreshadows Freud's theories of emotional transference and childhood complexes and Pavlov's work on the conditioned response.

In exploring the progress of our species, Ferguson identifies three laws governing our progressive nature. The first is that progress is subject to the proper and judicious exercise of the faculties. The second is that 'ambition' is the inspiration and engine of progress and the third is that our original responses are reinforced by habit. The latter two are of greatest importance 'as they enter into the consideration of every pursuit and attainment, of which they are the fruit or the incitement.' Ambition initiates progress while habit retains and supports the gains of ambition. Habit is defined as 'that, by which the good or bad actions of men, remain with them, and become part of their characters.'[885] Ferguson was optimistic that, on the level of individual psychology, habit would tend to 'fix a disposition' to what is 'good' rather than 'evil' due to the fact that it has a 'tendency' to 'narrow the scope of aberration and mistake'.[886] Ferguson makes clear that this 'pliancy' is a species trait and survival feature, not an individual or personal knack of turning '[one]self into different shapes, with respect to... opinions... inclinations, or faculties.'[887]

2. PRACTICAL FUNCTION OF HABIT

Habits allow us to institutionalise socially useful practices, preserving the adaptive capacity of communities and making further developments possible. Without habit or tradition there would be no accumulation of our species' informal achievements

---

[883] Camic, 'The Matter of Habit', pp. 1047-8. Unlike Ferguson, Kant did not regard habit and custom in positive terms but stressed the need for the emancipation of individuals from habit through the exercise of autonomous rationality. Jeffrey Minson, 'Men and Manners: Kantian Humanism, Rhetoric and the History of Ethics', *Economy and Society*, Vol. 18 (1), February, 1989, pp. 191-220, pp. 202-6.

[884] Such as, William James and Samuel Butler in the nineteenth century and in the early twentieth experimental psychologists like Knight Dunlap, the author of *Habits. Their Making and Unmaking*, New York: Liveright Publishing Corporation, 1939.

[885] *P.I.*, p. 208

[886] *P.I.*, p. 234.

[887] *P.I.*, p. 232.

through time and consequently the laws of social order would have relevance to only the most elementary aspects of life such as propagation and basic survival. Many of the hard-won results of indirection such as language, art, technical know-how and statecraft would be lost and each new generation would need to re-invent itself. Through habit and folkways, the achievements and knowledge gained by individuals or previous generations is retained, affording 'us the ready and spontaneous use of it when acquired.'[888] Habit serves as our collective memory. Without it human progress would be impossible. Habit is therefore essential, both for our practical progress as a species, and for our moral development, individually and collectively. In a similar vein, William James would later write that '[h]abit is the enormous flywheel of society, its most precious conservative agent.[889]

Habit makes life more harmonious, more orderly, more predictable and therefore more psychologically and practically comfortable. A world without habit is chaotic and disconcerting, 'a scene of inextricable confusion and uncertainty.'[890] Habit protects us from our own impetuosity or 'the wavering and fluctuation of mind' and enables us to negotiate the contingencies of life through its capacity to create, in Charles Camic's words, 'a stable inner core that affords immunity from external sensations and impetuous appetites.'[891]

Because habit has a happy tendency to preserve our species' attainments, it saves us a good deal of time and trouble in the practical and moral decisions of daily life. It serves as a sort of ergonomic shorthand which allows us to 'proceed by a kind of spontaneous effort...often without premeditation or intended exertion.'[892] Habit hones our active powers to the point where they become reflexive or 'mechanical.'[893] Indeed 'every passion of the human mind' is enhanced and reinforced through 'acquaintance and habitude.[894] Because habit makes any task easier and more pleasant to perform, it reduces our inclination to avoid life's more onerous tasks.[895] Hume made a similar argument in the *Treatise* when he noted that 'nothing has a greater effect both to encrease and diminish our passions, to convert pleasure into pain, and pain into pleasure, than custom and repetition'.[896]

---

[888] *P.I.*, p. 234.

[889] 'It alone is what keeps us all within the bounds of ordinance and saves the children of fortune from the envious uprisings of the poor. It alone prevents the hardest and most repulsive walks of life from being deserted by those brought up to tread therein. It keeps the fisherman and the deck-hand at sea through the winter; it holds the miner in his darkness, and nails the countryman to his log-cabin and his lonely farm through all the months of snow; it protects us from invasion by the natives of the desert and the frozen zone. It dooms us all to fight out the battle of life upon the lines of our nurture or our early choice, and to make the best of a pursuit that disagrees, because there is not other for which we are fitted, and it is too late to begin again. It keeps different social strata from mixing'. William James, *The Principles of Psychology,* in 3 Vols, Cambridge MA: Harvard University Press, 1981, Vol. 1, p. 125.

[890] *P.I.*, p. 208.

[891] Camic, 'The Matter of Habit', p. 1046. See this article for a more detailed historical treatment of habit in sociology.

[892] *P.I.*, p. 234.

[893] *P.I.*, pp. 224-5.

[894] *Essay*, p. 23.

[895] *P.I.*, pp. 211-12.

[896] Hume, *Treatise*, 3. 3. 5. p. 422.

3. SOCIAL AND MORAL FUNCTIONS OF HABIT

Although humans are born with instincts, there is no strictly pre-social human nature because instinct cannot be abstracted from social life,[897] therefore native urges are 'always overlaid' with socially acquired habits.[898] Susan Shott has noted that Ferguson, along with other Scottish thinkers such as Smith and Millar, was a precursor of the 'symbolic-interactionst' assumption that society is 'antecedent to the individual' and that 'self and mind develop through interaction with others'. Accordingly, 'self-control is a product of social control.'[899] Our ability to experience shame and to be susceptible to the opinions of those around us positively conditions our behaviour. Habit therefore plays a part in the maintenance of the moral sentiments. Social sanctions reward virtuous, and discourage vicious impulses, and inevitably these impulses become reflexive. Instinctive parental affection, for example, intensifies with the experience of intimacy. Our natural affection for others is enhanced by shared experiences.[900] Through habit and the social sanctions of shaming and valorising, instinctive belligerence is magically transmogrified into socially useful courage. Courage is, accordingly, a simultaneously pre-social and social product. Although '[v]ehement passions of animosity or attachment are the first exertions of vigour in [a persons] breast', at the same time, 'courage [is] the gift of society to man'.[901]

While habit 'is not numbered among the original propensities of human nature' it is a 'law' of our nature that 'whatever the living nature is able to perform without impairing its organs, if persisted in, will reproduce a habit.' The tendency to form habits is 'acquired' insofar as it is a 'disposition which results from already having acted'.[902] Nevertheless it is a tendency towards which we are highly 'susceptible'[903] in having arisen from a genuinely instinctive capacity to learn and advance through experience. Humans differ from other animals in the sense that our instincts are not infallible,[904] consequently, in order to fill any gaps created by the fallibility of instinct, 'Nature' endows us with an urge, peculiar to our species, to form habits. Characteristically, Ferguson's discourse on habit is highly teleological. We are

---

[897] 'Human nature nowhere exists in the abstract'. *P.II.*, p. 419; *Essay*, pp. 9-10.

[898] Lehmann, *Adam Ferguson*, pp. 68-9.

[899] Susan Shott, 'Society, Self and Mind in Moral Philosophy', *Journal of the History of Behavioural Sciences*, Vol. 12, 1976, pp. 39-46, p. 39. Shott also asserts that '(c)oncepts nearly equivalent to Mead's notions of "role-taking", the "generalised other", and the "I"-"me" relationship are employed by the Scottish Moralists in their discussions of social and moral conduct'. Susan Shott, 'The Development of Sociological Theory in America; A Sociology of Knowledge Interpretation', in Larry T. Reynolds and Janice M. Reynolds, (eds), *The Sociology of Sociology,* New York: McKay, 1970, p. 18. Symbolic interactionism developed in first few decades of the twentieth century. It focused upon the ways in which 'meanings emerge through interaction' and emphasised 'the ways in which human beings are distinctly symbol manipulating animals'. G. Marshall, *Oxford Dictionary of Sociology,* Oxford: Oxford University Press, 1998, p. 657.

[900] *Essay*, pp. 22-4.

[901] *Essay*, p. 23.

[902] *P.I.*, pp. 209-10.

[903] *Essay*, pp. 16-17

[904] *Institutes*, p. 111.

habitual because our 'Maker has '*destined*' us to improve on our 'natural' faculties through repetition and experience[905] and we are '*destined* to act from observation and experience.'[906] The design principle dominates. The conditions of nature are arranged in an orderly, regular, fashion so as to suggest and promote habitual behaviour. Further, the 'stability' and 'regularity' that habit introduces to social life has been 'beneficently provided'.[907]

Habit is crucial to our quest for moral perfection since it permits us to retain and enhance any progress made. Ethical choices only become internalised in the moral personality once they become habitual.[908] It is a 'law of [humanity's] nature to improve himself and '[t]his', Ferguson opines, 'is probably the most interesting fact that occurs in the history of man...he is intrusted to himself, as the clay is intrusted to the hands of the potter.'[909] Rationalistic and consciously generated forms of knowledge are 'ineffectual' in shaping opinion compared to the effects of the tacit and practical knowledge represented in custom.[910] It is only in society, via the medium of habit, that the moral personality is able to emerge. Since choices are only possible in the presence of other agents, the development of our moral potential outside society is unthinkable.[911]

Habit is a faculty (an 'inclination, facility, and power of performance') which is sometimes put to use in counteracting the baser tendencies of our instinctive urges.[912] It is inherent in the human frame, part of 'the social nature of man, to desire praise, and to shun blame'.[913] Standards of merit, ethics, national sentiments, the sentiments governing our social and emotional relationships, sexual mores. All are the result of habit and all have social reference in 'turning ...upon the fitness or unfitness of the individual to fill his place in society, as a part well adapted to such a whole'.[914] Values and utilities are to a great extent, socially constructed. 'Riches, power and even pleasure, are coveted...only when they are considered as the marks of eminence or rank'.[915] In this sense, then, social norms and values are shaped by and depend upon inter-subjective validation.[916] Though moral judgements have their

---

[905] *P.I.*, p. 202.

[906] *Institutes*, p. 111. My emphasis.

[907] *P.I.*, pp. 217-18.

[908] *P.I.*, p. 208.

[909] *P.I.*, p. 225.

[910] *Essay*, p. 119-21; *P.I.*, p.219. James Murphy captures Ferguson's position in this way: '[W]e begin with natural potentialities, custom shapes these potentialities into habit, and through rational reflection we order our habits in light of our moral ideals'. James Bernard Murphy, 'Nature, Custom and Stipulation in the Semiotic of John Poinset', *Semiotica*, Vol. 82 (1-2), 1990, pp. 33-68, p. 44.

[911] Reesor, *The Old and Middle Stoa*, p. 12.

[912] *P.I.*, p. 131.

[913] *Institutes*, p. 218.

[914] *P.I.*, p. 125. Adam Smith's ideas on the development of the social self are particularly well developed. Shott, 'Society, Self and Mind' p. 42.

[915] *Institutes,* p. 90.

[916] *P.I.*, pp. 126-7.

source in an innate moral sense, they are reinforced by mutual affective responses.[917] Ferguson thus partially pre-empts Durkheim's much later, (secularised) exposition of morality, in defining it as a group product.[918]

Yet Ferguson's emphasis upon the role of habit in morality should not be interpreted as utilitarian or subjective in orientation. A utilitarian strain is detectable, however Ferguson clearly believed in the reality of objective moral standards[919] and was openly hostile to the brand of utilitarian ethics Hume and Smith were perceived to proffer.[920] He is extremely careful to draw a distinction between mores, on the one hand, and morality on the other.

> In matters indifferent, we ought to observe the manners of our country, as we speak of
> its language or wear its dress. In matters important, we ought to choose what is for the
> good of mankind, in opposition to opinion and custom.[921]

'True' morality is found neither in the Scriptures nor in whatever passes for propriety in society. Rather, it inheres in the individual mind, via a moral sense, explicitly provided for this purpose.[922] Afterwards custom and habit reinforce the conclusions of this moral sense and correct any digressions from its intuitions. Deplorable moral customs do exist but their existence alone does not, necessarily, confirm their rectitude. Some products of spontaneous order are manifestly vicious and such 'depravities' are to be regarded as errors, the unavoidable cost of free will. Ferguson distances himself from Hume and Smith by insisting that virtue exists independent of the judgements of an impartial spectator and outside the sympathetic responses of a community with whom one identifies.[923]

Custom and habit enhance social cohesion through generating shared experiences and perceptions and they continually remind people of the advantages of association.[924] Similarly, 'habits of thinking' promote institutional stability. In government, for example, habit engenders stability through promoting shared authority values.[925] Habit is a key integrating factor in our social life.[926] Consensus of opinion, for example, no matter how absurd that opinion might be, is a valuable social tool. Ferguson argues along functionalist lines that the substantive content of the custom or convention is irrelevant. Indeed, he seems to suggest that most social conventions *are* ridiculous and irrational anyway. Their universal observance is

---

[917] *P.II.*, p. 128. Such a view is originally Hutchesonian. Susan M. Purviance, 'Intersubjectivity and Sociable Relations in the Philosophy of Francis Hutcheson' in J. Dwyer, and R.B. Sher (eds), *Sociability and Society in Eighteenth Century Scotland*, Edinburgh: The Mercat Press, 1993, pp. 24-5.

[918] Strasser, *The Normative Structure of Sociology*, p. 48.

[919] *Essay*, p. 36.

[920] See 'Principle of Moral Estimation', No. 25, *Collection of Essays*, passim.

[921] *Institutes*, p.168

[922] 'Of the Distinctions on Which we Act in Human Life', *Collection of Essays,* No. 18, pp. 164-5.

[923] Smith, *Adam Ferguson*, p. 40.

[924] *Essay,* pp. 22-3. Hume makes the identical argument in the *Treatise:* 'In a little time, custom and habit operating on the tender minds of the children, makes them sensible of the advantages, which they may reap from society'. 3. 2. 2. p. 486.

[925] *P.I.*, p. 215. John Millar later wrote that class distinctions were perpetuated and maintained via habit. Millar, *An Historical View of the English Government,* pp. 290-2.

[926] Kettler, *Social and Political Thought of Adam Ferguson*, p. 195.

what really counts since it is the existence of the agreement itself, rather than its immediate significance, which is performing all the valuable social legwork.[927] Durkheim would later identify this as the principle of 'affective maximisation' whereby 'social bonds are based on intense positive affective arousal'. In the normal course of social life people will seek arrangements that maximise this arousal.[928]

Ferguson takes a precursory functionalist's view of cultural variations in support of his claims of an immutable, universal, human nature. Though customs vary cross culturally, their social function is invariable.

> It is the form of respect in Europe to uncover the head: In Japan, we are told, the corresponding form is to drop the slipper, or to uncover the foot. The physical action in these instances is different, but the moral action is the same. It is an act of attention and respect.[929]

Ferguson stresses that his comments on cultural variations are not an invitation to indulge in ethical utilitarianism. Despite local variations, moral laws governing human action are eternal and invariable.[930] Humans possess 'natures of which the essence is permanent,' and yet which are 'qualified for indefinite variety of situations.'[931] Internal drives are moulded and affected by external conditions yet they remain at the core of change. The human world is a scene of great diversification, nevertheless, the operations of our universal 'human qualities' are of greater interest to social science since they possess greater explanatory power.[932]

The notion of an explicit social contract is a myth but *tacit* compact (which does exist) is what is effectively brought into existence by custom and habit.

> Civil society is not improperly termed a state of convention; for although men are actually in society together, before they enter into any form of bargain or compact; yet, every step that is made, in the concourse of numbers, tends to convention. Every practice continued into custom, is fairly interpreted as the faith of parties plighted for the observance of it; and the members of every society, even of the shortest duration, become invested with rights, or subjected to obligations, founded in some species of contract express or tacit.[933]

Ferguson also notes that since there is no 'original right of one person to command another, except so far as is necessary to restrain him from harm', custom and 'convention' is 'the only principle' from which 'a right to command can accrue to one, or an obligation to obey can be incurred by another.'[934] Hume agreed, arguing against the claims of the Jacobites that 'long possession' rather than right of

---

[927] *P.I.*, p. 218.

[928] Thoits, 'Sociology of Emotion', p. 337.

[929] *P.II.*, p. 142.

[930] *Institutes*, p. 162.

[931] *P.I.*, p. 322.

[932] Essay, p. 16. Montesquieu also accounted for the existence of cultural universals in terms of 'natural laws'. *Laws*, 1. 1. 1., p. 1. See also *Persian Letters*, Translated with an Introduction and Notes by C.J. Betts, London: Penguin, 1973.

[933] *P.II.*, p. 270. Neither does the 'consent of ancestors, with whom a practice originated, bind their posterity'. *P.II.*, p. 234.

[934] *P.II.*, p. 290. See also *P.II.*, p. 245.

succession, was what made government legitimate.[935] But Ferguson makes an important qualification here, namely, that convention alone does not confer legitimacy. Specifically, those who live under conditions of oppression, however well established, cannot be said to have consented to it and should consider themselves 'free to procure relief' by whatever means necessary.[936]

4. EMOTIONAL TRANSFERENCE, THE CONDITIONED RESPONSE AND CHILDHOOD COMPLEXES

Switching from an anthropological to a more 'psychological' tone, Ferguson goes on to describe, with great prescience, the phenomena we now label emotional transference, the conditioned response and childhood complexes.[937] These are not, of course, his terms, though his own are explicit enough to leave no doubt as to his exceptional prescience.

> In this manner, we not only attach qualities to subjects, with which they have not any real connection in the ordinary course of things; but we also attach feeling and emotion of mind to things which are not, in reality, objects of such feeling....Passions are...communicated from one person to another by contagion without any communication of thought, or knowledge of the cause; and the person, to whom the passion is communicated, may mistake for the object of it some trifling incident or circumstance which happens to accompany the emotion. If the nurse should shriek, or give signs of horror, while a rat or a mouse is passing on the floor, her child being infected with terror, may from thenceforward attach similar emotions to the appearance of a similar cause...the most ungovernable feelings of horror are incurred on the presentment of things harmless or useful...Of one person...the hair will stand on end on the appearance of a cat; of another...he will sicken and faint at the smell of cheese, or the sight of a particular joint of meat. Such capricious fears or aversions are commonly termed antipathies, and probably must have originated in early childhood, or under the effects of disease; and acquire the force of habit, before the reason of the thing could be questioned.[938]

Petrovich Pavlov's (1849-1936) work in the area of the conditioned reflex could be seen as an exercise in the experimental testing of Ferguson's much earlier hypothesis. But fascinating though these passages are, they are incidental to the larger scheme of things. The phenomena Ferguson describes in them are represented as pathological variations of habit and therefore distractions as far as social order goes. Such perversions of habit detract from its true ordering function. These 'misguided' connections are not like the 'conceptions which are founded upon the ordinary course of things [upon which] we may safely proceed, trusting that nature, being regular and permanent, will persevere in the order she has established.'[939] These latter regular, habitual, events represent authentic experience (that is,

---

[935] Hume, *Treatise*, 2. 2. 10. p. 556.

[936] *P.II.*, p. 234.

[937] William Lehmann was the first to detect this proto-psychology in Ferguson's writings. Lehmann, *Adam Ferguson*, pp. 69-71.

[938] *P.I.*, pp. 137-44.

[939] *P.I.*, p. 133.

experience as intended by the Creator) and secure Nature's equilibrium in our social life. Unavoidably, though, our susceptibility to habituate sometimes leads us in the opposite, socially useless, direction. Ferguson's precursory Freudianism is really an aside on the pitfalls of our susceptibility to habit. In other words, our inherent impressionability may result in reflexive responses that do not have social utility, but are, rather, psychological neuroses which have no useful function at all. In addition, our habitual bent may mislead us into unhealthy behaviour patterns, consequently 'in matters idle or unnecessary [habit] is reckoned a misfortune or a blemish'.[940] On the whole, though, Ferguson thinks that habit will produce socially beneficial results.[941]

5. CONCLUDING REMARKS

The role of habit in Ferguson's conception of spontaneous social order is four-fold: firstly, it serves as the 'Maker's' temporal insurance policy by guaranteeing that any advances made in the past are enshrined in human behaviour to the point where they become reflexive; secondly, being essentially human products, habits permit the exercise of our 'will and choice', play a central role in our moral development and allow our emotions to play their proper role in the maintenance of social life; thirdly, habit solves the abstract problem of identifying the basis for political authority and fourthly, habits enhance communal bonds, permitting and encouraging us to live in the social condition intended for us by Nature. Partly because of the effects of habit, a society underpinned by passions is neither random nor precarious; rather, it is highly ordered, integrated and progressive. Ferguson's sophisticated appreciation of this fact suggests that his aversion to radical social change was probably more scientific than ideological.

---

[940] *P.I.*, p. 21.
[941] *P.I.*, p. 234.

CHAPTER 9

THE ENVIRONMENT

In Ferguson's attempt to compose a complete and integrated theory of social order he was careful not to overlook the role of the physical environment, partly because its harsher aspects were often invoked by his theological adversaries as evidence of a punitive God, but also because of his view that human life is governed by a multitude of forces. Material factors are shown to be highly influential in shaping human behaviour and therefore human history. Ferguson devotes a large section of the *Essay* to a discussion 'Of the Influences of Climate and Situation'[942] and the environmental theme is woven throughout his entire body of work. Montesquieu is thought to have been the first influential writer to explore these issues systematically[943] and he is Ferguson's primary inspiration in this regard.[944] Nevertheless interest in the effect of the environment was widespread in the eighteenth century and claims about the effect of climate on the body and mind, for example, were fairly common.[945]

1. GENERAL DISCUSSION

Ferguson believed that the physical environment is a key agent in the apparatus of spontaneous order and in the progress of the species. Specifically, it serves as the matrix of our development and stimulates progress, either in presenting obstacles, or in providing favourable conditions for the exercise of our creative and industrious faculties. In addition, the physical world, with all its infinite mysteries and

---

[942] *Essay*, pp. 106-118.

[943] Although Montesquieu was not the first thinker to acknowledge the importance of the environment to civilisation he was the most successful publiciser of this idea. Such speculations can be traced back as far as the classical period, most notably to Hippocrates. Clarence J. Glacken, *Traces on the Rhodian Shore*, Berkeley: University of California Press, 1967, pp. 562-8. The Lebanese historian Ibn Khaldoun also predates Montesquieu in terms of these insights, though he does not appear to have had any influence on Ferguson. Khaldoun's *Al Muqaddimah* (*Introduction to History*) was written in the fourteenth century and was published in London in 1680. Like Montesquieu, Khaldoun believed that local climate and topography affected social attitudes. A. Issa, 'Ibn Khaldoun, Montesquieu and the Theory of Climate', *Studi de Sociologia* Vol. 30 (2) 1992, pp. 181-7.

[944] Ferguson acknowledged his debt to Montesquieu on many occasions. See, for example, *Essay*, pp. 66-7. Rousseau's advertence to the importance of climate also comes from Montesquieu. See *Social Contract*, pp, 222, 226, 252.

[945] John Arbuthnot, for example, also made these kinds of observations. Arbuthnot, a Scottish doctor, published in 1731 *An Essay Concerning the Effects of Air on Human Bodies*. Glacken, *Traces on the Rhodian Shore*, pp. 562-4. Similarly Rousseau held to the view that the 'difference of soils, climates and seasons' had introduced 'differences' in 'manner of living'. 'Discourse on the Origin of Inequality' in *Social Contract and Discourses*, p. 85.

symmetries, stimulates our curiosity and provides objects for the exercise and refinement of the intellectual faculties. Finally, certain environments aid prosperity and provide a nursery for civic virtue. In a sense then, Ferguson can be properly thought of as an early human ecologist, human ecology being that branch of social science which attempts 'to link the structure and organisation of a human community to interactions with its localised environment.'[946] Of course, human ecology did not fully emerge as a discrete discipline until the 1920s,[947] nevertheless, Ferguson's anticipation of many of its themes is noteworthy. But it should be noted at the outset that Ferguson is no secular adaptive evolutionist. His views are framed explicitly within a teleological and chain of being framework that relies for its coherence on the principle of design. Accordingly, they tell us as much about his theology as they do about his social science.

There is a sense in which Ferguson's conception of the role of ecological factors defines his understanding of our relationship to God. The world, even at its harshest, is created for our benefit but we are left to negotiate it alone without the aid of divine intervention. At the same time, its richness, marvels and order suggest a designing mind and therefore constantly remind us of God's existence and his ineffable love for us. This underlines that Ferguson's is not a fully developed theory of human ecology. In particular, it differs from late-modern approaches from the point of view of responsibility because humans are not responsible *to* the environment; Ferguson seems to share in the common eighteenth century belief that nature is not only owned by humanity to do with as it wished, but also infinitely replenishible.

2. EFFECTS OF ENVIRONMENT

Ferguson's admiration of Montesquieu is displayed in his attribution of social effects to the physical environment. Montesquieu argued that a country's type of society, its institutions and laws are partly a product of its topography, its climate and soil, and the size of its population.[948] The dynamic between these (and other) factors resulted in the 'spirit' of particular nations.[949] Ferguson noted that there were 'habits of thinking peculiar to nations'[950] and he agreed with Montesquieu that, if one is to insist on the universality of human nature, some explanation must be sought for the enormous variance in laws and customs evident throughout the globe. But it should be noted that Montesquieu placed far more emphasis on difference than Ferguson and was far more willing to derive positive law from social conditions as opposed to human nature.

[946] *The Fontana Dictionary of Modern Thought*, A. Bullock, O. Stallybrass and S. Trombley (eds), London: Fontana, 1989, p. 248.

[947] See J. M. Nazareth, 'Demography and Human Ecology', *Analise Social*, Vol. 28 (4-5) 1993, pp. 879-85. Its birth proper is generally considered to have coincided with the publication of Robert E. Park's groundbreaking article, 'The City', published in the *American Journal of Sociology*, Vol. 20 (1), 1915.

[948] Durkheim, *Montesquieu and Rousseau*, p. 40.

[949] Montesquieu, *Laws*, 3. 19. 4, p. 310.

[950] *P.I.*, p. 214. See also: *Institutes*, pp. 166-7, 38.

Ferguson explains that humans prosper most in certain environments, namely the 'temperate' or 'intermediate' zones'. Whether in the area of commerce, statecraft and the civil arts, war, or the refinement of human 'genius' in literature, 'reason' or the 'fertility' of the imagination, the human 'animal' has always 'attained to the principal honours of his species' in mild climates.[951] Any extreme in temperature is detrimental to human progress and productivity.[952] Conditions should not be so bleak as to render life intolerable, but neither should they be so obliging as to encourage indolence. It is usually the case that 'intermediate degrees of inconvenience in the situation' are best able to 'excite the spirit, and with the hopes of success, encourage its efforts.'[953] Following Montesquieu, Ferguson notes that temperate climates encourage population growth because they bestow 'a greater facility in procuring subsistence'[954] and, like Malthus after him, he believed that birth rates were spontaneously regulated by sustainability. Humans always 'people up to their resources'.[955] Informal customs and formal government policy affecting reproduction and population growth (such as incentives and disincentives to marriage, policies affecting immigration and emigration or prohibitions on practices like abortion and the exposure of infants) are also likely to be made in response to the constraints of the physical environment.[956]

Ferguson thought that Montesquieu was correct in positing a relationship between the size of the population and the civic condition of the polity; if too small the citizenry could be actuated by 'contagious passion';[957] if too large, communal sentiments could not be supported, anomic conditions would result and eventually the ascension of tyrants would be made possible.[958] National character is also shaped by climate. The 'Laplander', for example, has adapted to his environment and is 'hardy, indefatigable...patient...dull...and incapable of change'[959] whereas those who inhabit the 'torrid zones' exhibit a 'mildness' of temperament which inhibits engagement in any activity that might interrupt their 'love of ease and of pleasure'. The 'gentle and pacific disposition' of 'the natives of the East' has made them adaptable and enduring[960] while the ancient Ligurians 'seemed to derive the ferocity of their spirit, as well as the security of their possession, from the rugged and inaccessible nature of their country.'[961]

Although Ferguson's opinions on this subject were not entirely new, they nevertheless aroused objections. Both David Hume and John Millar contradicted his appeal to physical causes to explain manners and temperament. 'The inhabitants of Sparta', Millar asserted, 'are, at present, under the influence of the same physical

---

[951] *Essay*, p. 106.
[952] *Essay*, p. 110.
[953] *Essay*, p. 115.
[954] *Essay*, p. 134.
[955] *Institutes,* pp. 24-5; *Essay*, pp. 137-9.
[956] *Essay*, pp. 134-7.
[957] *Essay*, p. 125.
[958] *Essay*, pp. 256-7.
[959] *Essay*, p. 111.
[960] *Essay*, pp. 108-9.
[961] *History*, p. 62.

circumstances as in the days of Leonidas. The modern Italians live in the country of the ancient Romans' and yet they are barely recognisable as connected in any way.[962] Shrewdly anticipating this kind of criticism, Ferguson argued that national temperament remains constant because environments do, however it is the *objects* of national passions that alter over time and this accounts for the changes Millar later claimed to have detected in regional personality.

> A modern Greek, perhaps, is mischievous, slavish, and cunning, from the same animated temperament that made his ancestor ardent, ingenious, and bold, in the camp, or in the council of his nation. A modern Italian is distinguished by sensibility, quickness, and art, while he employs on trifles the capacity of an ancient Roman; and exhibits now, in the scene of amusement, and in the search of a frivolous applause, that fire, and those passions, with which Gracchus burned in the forum, and shook the assemblies of a severer people.[963]

Disarmingly, Ferguson draws attention to the key deficiency of his analysis which he identifies as its shallowness. He concedes that although we may superficially connect cause and effect regarding environment, we can never really attain a genuine understanding of the nature of the relationship between people and their environments; specifically, we cannot hope to master these mysteries on a strictly scientific or biological level. This requires an acute appreciation of the organic and causal relationship between mind and body which is, unfortunately, well beyond our grasp.[964] Atypically, Ferguson seems to be rebuking Montesquieu here, presumably for the latter's premature conclusion that it is the 'irritability' or 'sensibility' of the nerves and 'fibres' which mediates between the environment and the mind and body.[965]

Despite his protestations about his ability to authoritatively attribute causes, Ferguson still believed we could usefully and validly identify *patterns* of cause and effect, based on the suggestions of contiguity and efficiency, even if we couldn't fully penetrate the secrets of their workings.[966] We can, for example, predict with some confidence, that topographical factors such as 'soil and climate' will determine whether or not a people will be nomadic.[967] Such factors also bear significantly upon the opportunities for a people to establish and preserve nationhood. Physically

---

[962] John Millar, 'Origins of the Distinctions of Ranks', in Lehmann, *John Millar of Glasgow 1735-1801*, pp. 179-80. Lehmann takes the criticism to be levelled at Montesquieu but his target is more likely to have been Ferguson. In any case, Millar identifies Hume's as the proper perspective. For Hume's scepticism 'that men owe anything of their temper or genius to the air, food or climate' see, 'Of National Characters', *Essays*, pp. 197-215. Collini *et al* note that 'Hume's own discussion of these matters laid more stress on pliability, on the part played by custom, imitation, and sympathy, by political institutions and moral as opposed to physical factors in shaping law and manners'. Collini *et al*, *That Noble Science of Politics*, p. 17.

[963] *Essay*, p. 107.

[964] *Essay*, p. 115.

[965] See Montesquieu, *Laws*, 3. 14. 1-2, pp. 231-234.

[966] This typifies Ferguson's general approach to social science. Such relationships are beyond our genuine comprehension, he submits, consequently they are excluded from his brief. Instead he endeavours to pursue a more modest task, one more suited to that of the scientific historian or the 'indifferent spectator' collecting and recording observable data. *Essay*, pp. 8-9; *P.I.*, pp. 49, 176.

[967] *Essay*, p. 96.

discrete territories, for example, are more likely to maintain sovereignty. Nations with seaboard are best able to do so and they will also tend to be the most prosperous since ports facilitate trade.[968]

3. NATURE OR NURTURE?

Ferguson attributes the fascinating multiformity of civilisations (in spite of an allegedly universal human nature) to the vast range of ecological conditions found throughout the planet.[969] We naturally find, therefore, diversity and variations in all kinds of social institutions. '[F]orms of government', for example, 'must be varied, in order to suit the extent, the way of subsistence, the character, and the manners of different nations'.[970] As to the rationale for the creation of these topographical variations in the first place, Ferguson can do no more, initially at least, than to offer the highly anthropocentric observation that 'the author of nature appears to delight in variety'.[971] Indeed, 'variety...appears to be an object or primary end of Creation'.[972]

Notwithstanding his interest in the effects of environment, it should be noted that Ferguson makes a special point of emphasising that it is *inherent* factors (human drives or instincts) not external influences, that are the *primary* motors of history.[973] Here he departs from Montesquieu, whose history, while progressive, does not share with Ferguson's a view of progress as generated by internal drives.[974] Change for Montesquieu is always generated exogenously whereas for Ferguson the external environment can only moderate psychogenetic influences and thereby effect change. But he is no early socio-biologist; the progress he refers to is technological and moral, not biological or genetic. Ferguson's position is more reminiscent of the Aristotelian view that:

> Everything...exists for a final cause, and all those things which are included in the definition of each animal, or which are means to an end or are ends in themselves, come into being through this cause and the rest.[975]

Aristotle goes on to explain what is meant by 'the rest', namely, the efficient causes that bring about secondary modifications in living things. In other words, environmental factors. Ferguson follows suit in giving priority to original drives (which embody our telic blueprint) while reserving a particular place for 'the rest' in his scheme. Any cultural variations not attributable to external conditions are traced

---

[968] *Essay*, pp. 116-17.

[969] *Essay*, pp. 80-1.

[970] *Essay*, p. 63.

[971] *P.I.*, p. 324.

[972] 'Of the Intellectual or Conscious Powers' *Collection of Essays*, No. 31, p. 267.

[973] *P.I.*, p. 235. *Essay*, p. 119.

[974] Lehmann, *Adam Ferguson*, pp. 193-4; Andrew Skinner, 'Natural History in the Age of Adam Smith', p. 41; J.G.A. Pocock, 'Between Machiavelli and Hume: Gibbon as Civic Humanist and Philosophical Historian', *Daedelus*, Vol. 105, 1976, pp. 153-69, p. 155.

[975] Cited in Joad, *Guide to Philosophy*, p. 188.

to the operations of free will.[976] Though Ferguson subscribes to the idea of a universal human nature this is how he accounts for the existence of cross-cultural disparities in laws, customs and institutions.[977]

It would be a gross error to characterise Ferguson's history as essentially materialist in orientation, to see progress as generated purely by economic and environmental forces, as some scholars have done. The way to understand Ferguson's subtle position is to conceive biogenetic forces as generating history and order within the context of particular environments. Our 'instincts' form society however we are 'directed' or influenced 'by the circumstances in which [we] are placed'.[978] Once again, Ferguson produces a complicated explanation by refusing to be drawn into a false dichotomy. He can be thought of as an early 'interactionist', one who sees biological and social factors as working in concert, thereby resolving, at least in his own mind, a dispute (i.e. the nature-nurture debate) that continues to rage until this day.

4. THE ENVIRONMENT, PROGRESS AND PERFECTION

By far the most interesting aspect of Ferguson's discourse on environment is the role he attributes to it in the process of our development, not only as creative and practical beings in quest of scientific and cognitive progress, but as moral agents in a perpetual state of emergence. Typically, Ferguson's 'social science' has a moral purpose. He wants to understand the role played by 'nature' in the getting of wisdom and virtue. It has been noted that Ferguson's conception of virtue is cognitive.[979] The entire system of nature, with all its impediments, hazards, tribulations, mysteries, and deprivations is designed to baffle, illuminate and edify, thereby facilitating our moral progress.

The chain of being, conceived hierarchically with humans in supremacy[980] exists to assist and catalyse our unending efforts at perfection. Human existence is a labyrinth of problems and unrequited needs which the Creator has consciously arranged in order to stimulate human development. The natural world is a series of complex scientific problems to be solved by a species intent on self-perfection.[981] As Ferguson puts it, '[man] becomes powerful in the system of nature, in proportion as he becomes knowing or wise.'[982]

Unlike animals, who possess instincts to direct them in every instance, people are provided with challenging 'privations' which, far from indicating 'a penury in the economy of nature', obligingly provide ideal conditions for the development of the

---

[976] *P.I.*, p. 61.

[977] *P.I.*, pp. 214-15.

[978] *Essay*, p. 119.

[979] See Chapter 11 for a fuller discussion of this point.

[980] *P.II.*, p. 28; 'Of Cause and Effect, Ends and Means, Order, Combination and Design', *Collection of Essays*, No. 13, p. 124.

[981] John Passmore, *The Perfectibility of Man*, London: Gerald Duckworth and Co. Ltd., 1979, pp. 18-19.

[982] *P.II.*, p. 40.

moral personality. Privation is 'proper to the lot of a being, who is... destined to be the artificer of his own fortune'.[983] Apart from the obvious Stoic precedent, Ferguson's views here are highly reminiscent of Pelagianism which opposed the Augustinian doctrine of predestination, affirmed the existence of free will and effectively denied the existence of original sin. On this view, it was not by the infusion of divine grace but by our own active exertions that we achieved salvation.[984]

External or environmental hindrances play a crucial role in the process of self-improvement. Throughout his entire corpus Ferguson takes the originally Stoic view 'that the 'reason and heart of man are best cultivated in arduous situations'.[985] The belief that virtue is honed by, even synonymous with, hardship[986] and that adversity is 'the school of wisdom and virtue' is central to Ferguson's theodicy. Such is immanent in the divine plan. Moreover these 'very wants to which man is born' are 'proofs of goodness in the authority of nature'.[987] To the enlightened individual whose 'apprehension relating to the Providence of God' is supremely lucid '[i]t must appear that a lot, composed of objects to be desired and shunned, is fitted to an active being as the air is fitted to the wing of a bird'.[988]

Life is fraught with perils and obstacles deliberately set in place by the Creator in order to facilitate human development.[989] The species is involved in a marvellous process of self-creation which it experiences through trial and error, activity, conflict, adaptation and choice. Notwithstanding those 'few determinate instincts' that relate to animal self-preservation, 'man' is 'left to follow the dictates of his own observation, discernment and experience.[990] Ferguson addresses the complaint of his imaginary adversary, 'the atheist', who demands to know why a beneficent God would present His favourite creation with a world where every desire is denied 'him' and where not a single one of 'his' needs 'is gratified without delay.' By way of reply Ferguson suggests, somewhat tautologically, that in an alternative, easier world 'every faculty' would 'remain unemployed' and would therefore be superfluous.[991] After all, our 'versatile disposition' equips us for every condition; and even the most inhospitable circumstance is an enlivening opportunity for the exercise of our inclination to 'supply its defects'.[992] Rather than attesting to God's

---

[983] *P.I.*, p. 52.

[984] Pelagius was a British lay theologian influential in the late fourth and early fifth century in Rome, North Africa and Palestine. Richardson and. Bowden, *New Dictionary of Christian Theology*, p. 435. After Ferguson's time, the historian Lucien Febvre (1878-1956) contradicted environmental determinists using similar arguments and by emphasising the activism, 'initiative' and 'mobility' of humans as against 'the passivity of the environment'. Sir Matthew Simmons, *Changing the Face of the Earth*, Oxford: Basil Blackwell, 1989, p. 5.

[985] *Institutes*, p. 268.

[986] *Essay*, pp. 46-7. See also *History*, p. 43.

[987] *P.I.*, pp. 176-81. See also; 'Of Things that are or May Be', *Collection of Essays*, No. 27 (Part 1), p. 228.

[988] *P.I.*, p. 176.

[989] *P.I.*, pp. 176-81; 'Of Things that Are or May Be', *Collection of Essays*, No. 27.

[990] *P.II.*, p. 37; *P.I.*, p. 133.

[991] *P.I.*, p. 178.

[992] *Essay*, p. 106.

non-existence or even God's indifference to us, a world of unrequited needs speaks eloquently of His loving concern for us. Everything exists for a beneficent purpose and there is nothing in created existence that is wasted or useless.[993] Neither is anything in the universe truly evil for all of creation performs some positive role in the benign master plan. The raw materials of nature, for example, are deliberately 'dispersed on the earth and often concealed at great depths below its surface.' The 'mixture of order' and 'apparent disorder in the distribution of these materials' is designed, not to frustrate us, but 'to encourage [our] hopes, and to protract [our] labours in the search of them.'[994] Similarly the irregular, and seemingly malign, distribution of natural resources throughout the globe leads, by necessity, to exchange, commerce, international trade and global mutual enablement.[995]

From the point of view of our moral and intellectual development, Peter Hanns Reill suggests that Ferguson conceived the 'material world as a system of 'signs and expressions' created by God' for the express purpose of stimulating our interpretation of them.[996] As Ferguson wrote:

> [W]e may consider... the material world as made, not for itself, but *for the mutual communication of minds*, and forming a system of *signs and expressions*, in which the infinite Author makes himself known to his intelligent creatures. It is a *magnificent but regular discourse*.[997]

Our efforts at science and history are, accordingly, the fulfilment of the Creator's desire that we investigate and disclose the laws of nature for ourselves. Furthermore, the reason why the earth was not presented to humankind complete (with 'every mountain' already 'cloathed' in 'full grown trees') is so that the species could observe and comprehend for itself the processes of nature unfolding and, armed with this knowledge, thereafter finish the task by its own hand.[998] The telic function of this process is two-fold: Firstly, we must discern these laws in order that we might live and profit by them; secondly, by this process, we are enabled, gradually, to perfect ourselves. The 'passion' to discover and enumerate the 'laws of nature' is 'busy in every breast; and the ordinary race of men in every nation and in every age, are greatly advanced in the gratification of it.'[999]

The earth is really a 'vast semiotic field' encompassing our physical environment and the historical actions and artefacts of our species. It is the task of the sage to order and interpret these artefacts and signs. We have a mandate to 'decode the discourse of nature'[1000] which has been created, in part at least, to stimulate the intelligent curiosity of our species.

---

[993] 'Of Things That are or May Be', *Collection of Essays*, No. 27 (2), p. 237: 'That power whose work is universe and consummate order does nothing in vain'.

[994] *P.I.*, p.243.

[995] *P.I.*, pp. 246-7.

[996] P.H. Reill, 'Narration and Structure in Late Eighteenth Century Historical Thought', *History and Theory*, Vol. 25 (3), 1986, pp. 286-98, p. 286.

[997] *P.I.*, pp. 274-5. My emphasis. See also: 'Of Cause and Effect, Ends and Means, Order, Combination and Design', *Collection of Essays*, No. 13, p. 123.

[998] 'Distinction of Value and Its Source in Existence', *Collection of Essays*, No. 7, p. 84.

[999] *P.I.*, p. 278.

[1000] Reill, 'Narration and Structure', p. 286.

Ferguson's optimism about nature's brutality represents a deliberate break with the Augustinian view of our relationship to the material world. Augustine took a morbid view of nature, perceiving it as hostile, dangerous and punitive. Disasters, famines, diseases and floods are all attributed to Adam's sin.[1001] 'The accursed earth', he wrote, 'shall bring forth thorns and thistles for thee. Are you not ordained for sorrow and not for delights.'[1002] By contrast, Ferguson believed in a world created perfect, 'sublime' and 'beautiful'[1003] where even 'thorns and thistles' are benign.

> [W]hat appears a war of the elements is the peace of that world they compose: The winds are instruments of beneficence; rain and snow are the gifts of bounty; what seems to be irregular is the perfection of order; the rugged crag and broken hill give a sheltered recess to many inhabitants, and, in all their asperity, fit up the residence of animals, and adorn the prospect of man...the movement of parts in nature conspires to the preservation and well-being of the whole.[1004]

Ferguson perceived the natural environment with all its vicissitudes and dangers as a wonderful place, filled with challenges, mysteries, excitement and the promise of adventure. Having created a creature utterly in love with strife and action, 'God' takes care to accommodate 'him' appropriately.

> The difficulties and hardships of human life, are supposed to detract from the goodness of God; yet many of the pastimes men devise for themselves are fraught with difficulty and danger. The great inventor of the game of human life knew well how to accommodate the players. The chances are matter of complaint: But if these were removed, the game itself would no longer amuse the parties.[1005]

Ferguson's attitude to the environment embodies a theodicy that rejects the dichotomy promulgated by Augustine of a pre-Fall paradise on the one hand and a post-Fall dystopia on the other. Ferguson has a more integrated perception of the world as an eternally and fundamentally benign, if challenging and somewhat confusing place. The theodicy that gives rise to this view has its source in Stoicism. The universe is at once 'perfect' yet oftentimes 'harsh and unpleasing'.[1006]

All of nature, then, exists for humanity and for its *telos*, moral perfection. Ferguson works from the argument from design and retains, throughout his body of work all the terminology of the chain of being. Briefly, the doctrine of 'the chain of being' is based on the concept of plenitude; the design of the universe encompasses 'a complete scale of beings from the lowest to the highest', ranging vastly in type and species and ordered hierarchically according to the chain of dependence.[1007]

[1001] D.J. Herlihy, 'Attitudes Toward the Environment in Medieval Society' in Lester J. Bilsky (ed.), *Historical Ecology: Essays on Environment and Social Change*, New York: Kennikat Press, 1980, p. 103.

[1002] Saint Augustine, *Against Julian*, in *The Fathers of the Church, a New Translation*, Translated by Matthew A. Schumacher, New York: 1977, p. 21.

[1003] *P.II.*, p. 27.

[1004] *P.I.*, p. 19.

[1005] *Essay*, p. 45. This passage was added to the 1773 edition.

[1006] Marcus Aurelius, *Meditations*, 5. 8. pp. 81-2; 4. 44. p. 73.

[1007] Viner, *The Role of Providence*, p. 90. For the definitive exposition of the concept of the chain of being see Arthur O. Lovejoy's, *Great Chain of Being: A Study of the History of an Idea*, Cambridge, Mass: Harvard University Press, 1964.

Humanity is situated at the peak of this great chain of mutual subserviency. Ferguson's impassioned summation of the busy, monistic, perfection of the universe sets 'man' at the centre of activity:

> [T]he whole is alive and in action: The scene is perpetually changing; but in its changes exhibits an order more striking than could be made to arise from the mere position or description of any forms entirely at rest. *Man, with his intellectual powers, placed at the top of this terrestrial scale, like the keystone of the arch, completes the system.*[1008]

Many of Ferguson's most influential mentors had conceived the created world in almost identical terms. Aristotle arranged the species hierarchically with humanity at its zenith arguing that everything in nature exists, ultimately, to serve humanity.[1009] On this view, the sole purpose of the earth's flora is to provide for the needs of animals, who exist, in turn, to provide for human life.[1010] Stoicism is also highly anthropocentric and aristocratic. In *de Finibus* Cicero tells us that, for Chryssipus, 'the lower animals were created for the sake of man'[1011] while Marcus Aurelius made the same argument in the *Meditations*.[1012] Only humans have reason[1013] therefore no relation of justice holds between humans and animals. Animals are not rational therefore they may be used instrumentally.[1014] In fact, all of the material world exists to serve humanity. According to Cicero's Balbus:

> [W]e alone have the power of controlling the most violent of nature's offspring, the sea and the winds, thanks to the service of navigation...Likewise the entire command of the commodities produced on land is vested in mankind...the rivers and the lakes are ours...we give fertility to the soil by irrigating it, we confine the rivers and strengthen or divert their courses...by means of our hands we essay to create as it were a second world within the world of nature...all the things in this world which men employ have been created and provided for the sake of men.[1015]

There is also a Christian precedent here. God has placed all of nature under humanity's control to do with as it pleased, thereby promoting, in David Herlihy's words, 'a kind of ecological triumphalism, a sense that in their dealings with the material world, [people] need only consult their immediate self-interests.' In this conception, humanity bears no moral responsibility for the welfare of those living things under its control. Such lesser organisms exist only to serve it.[1016] Ferguson's

---

[1008] *P.I.*, p. 174, 'Characteristics of Human Nature', *Collection of Essays*, No. 32, p. 280.

[1009] Aristotle, *Politics*, I i. 1256b, p. 16. See also Owens, 'Teleology of Nature in Aristotle', p. 169.

[1010] Owens, '*Teleology of Nature in Aristotle*', p. 68.

[1011] Cicero, *de Finibus*. 3.67; Reesor, *The Political Theory of the Old and Middle Stoa*, p. 23.

[1012] Marcus Aurelius, *Meditations*, 5. 30. p. 88.

[1013] R. Sorabji, *Animal Minds and Human Morals*, Ithaca: Cornell University Press, 1993, p. 124.

[1014] Diogenes Laertius, *Lives of Eminent Philosophers*, Translated by R.D. Hicks, London: William Heinemann, 1958, 7. 129, p. 233; Cicero, *De Finibus*, 3. 67, pp. 287-9 and Epictetus, *Discourses*, 1. 6. 18-22, p. 45. See also Stanton, 'The Cosmopolitan Ideas of Epictetus and Marcus Aurelius', p. 185.

[1015] Cicero, *De Natura Deorum*, with an English translation by H. Rackham, London: William Heinemann Ltd, 1951, 2. 60, 152-4, pp. 269-71.

[1016] Herlihy, 'Attitudes Toward the Environment', p. 102. In the book of Genesis, we are told that God commissioned Adam to 'replenish the earth and subdue it: and have dominion over the fish of the sea, and very the fowl of the air, and over every living thing that moveth upon the earth' (The Holy Bible, Containing the Old and New Testament, Authorised King James Version, London: Collins Cleartype Press, 1952, Genesis I. 26. 28. p. 7. St Francis of Assisi is a notable exception to this type of Christian

conception of humanity's relationship to the material word is soaked in speciesism. '[A]ll is made for man',[1017] he declares, and everything in creation exists for humanity to consume, mould, master and even plunder at will.[1018] Humanity is God's 'favourite tenannt of the earth…Who can doubt that [he] was intended to be [its] husbandman and proprieter?'[1019]

Yet, Ferguson's model differs from those of its classical and Christian ancestors in one crucial respect: it is not static. Within this chain there is constant change, flux, adjustment and progression: In a sense, God has left his creation unfinished so that humanity becomes 'the collaborative finisher' who drains the marshes and domesticates the wilderness.[1020] And unlike earlier promulgators of the great chain of being doctrine, Ferguson does not conceive creation as a simultaneous event. Rather it is a continuous process.[1021] 'In this wonderful scene', he wrote, 'the power that works was originally creative, and is equally so in every successive period of time'.[1022]

---

triumphalism. In any case Glacken disputes the influence of early Christianity and especially the sentiments expressed in Genesis. Rather he sees exploitative attitudes to nature as a function of humanity's increasing power over nature via increasing technological progress. Glacken, *Traces on the Rhodian Shore*, p. 494.

[1017] 'Distinction of Value and its Source in Existence', *Collection of Essays,* No. 7, p. 73.

[1018] 'Of Things that Are or May Be' (Part 1), *Collection of Essays*, No. 27, p. 223. '[W]e must acknowledge the intention of nature to subject this globe to the dominion of man' 'A Little Boy', *Collection of Essays*, Appendix 1, p. 292.

[1019] 'Distinction of Value and Its Source in Existence', *Collection of Essays*, No. 7, pp. 84-5.

[1020] Simmons, *Changing the Face of the Earth*, p. 7. Matthew Hale, who wrote before both Ferguson and Montesquieu, had a particularly sophisticated take on this issue. He perceived the existence of humankind as 'a balancing force in the existence of other forms of life. He becomes an arbiter, checking the spread of the wild plants and the wild animals, encouraging the dispersion of the domesticated plants and animals'. Glacken, *Traces on the Rhodian Shore*, p. 494.

[1021] As first noticed by Lois Whitney. *Primitivism and the Idea of Progress*, p. 151.

[1022] *P.I.*, p. 175. '[C]reation itself is a continual supply of defects'. 'Of Things That Are or May Be', *Collection of Essays*, No. 27 (2), p. 240.

5. CONCLUDING REMARKS

Material circumstances play a key role in social change and development and go a long way to explaining the striking diversity of human cultures. However, it could not be said that these environmental variables are constitutive of Ferguson's evolutionism, nor even that they are among the decisive factors of change; rather, they are, one of a host of variables that make up the complex system created as the context and motor of human progress. But by far the most important role of the environment in Ferguson's scheme is the role it plays in his theodicy. Rather than negating the existence of a benign and loving God or giving proof of human sin, the material world, even at its harshest, is both a challenging playground and a vast semiotic puzzle designed to stimulate the scientific and moral progress of God's favourite creation.

CHAPTER 10

CORRUPTION AND PROBLEMS OF MODERNITY

Because of his tendency to focus on the vicissitudes and complexity of human existence, there is a particular stress on the disadvantages of the polished age in Ferguson's writings. This tendency suggests that he opposed progress. In fact, his position was more subtle and ambivalent than this.

Along with many other eighteenth century thinkers, the subject of the decline of civilisations and the concomitant onset of political corruption interested Ferguson enormously. But Ferguson's approach differed from many of those of the period in two important respects. Firstly, he voices his concerns within the context of a linear rather than cyclical or palingenetic historiography, accordingly his attitude to progress is, by and large, positive. Secondly, rather than moralising in ecclesiastical or strictly primitivistic tones, his diagnosis of the ills of modern life is extremely thoughtful, sophisticated and prescient, particularly where he investigates the effects of specialisation and the causes of the deterioration of social intimacy, friendship and social and moral capital. Political demobilisation and social breakdown become central issues in Ferguson's hands. His concerns foreshadow 'the problems of over-rationalisation, dehumanisation, atomisation, alienation and bureaucratisation' which have absorbed nineteenth and twentieth century thinkers[1023] and his affinity with Durkheim, Tönnies and Marx has often been noted.[1024] Ferguson thus appears to us, not only as a moralist, but as an early social scientist intent on understanding the dynamics and effects of social change.

1. GENERAL DISCUSSION

Ferguson believed that civic virtue was the cost of modernity and its loss via increased specialisation, over-extension and hedonism inevitably led to national ruin wherever the signs of moral decay were not detected early enough to be rectified. Imperialism and the division of labour lead to bureaucratisation, which strictly circumscribes popular engagement in civic affairs, while the new commercial ethic obliterates communal sentiments. The corrupted state excludes people from political life and makes citizens with neither the skills, nor the inclination, to participate.[1025] Specialisation causes individuals to become estranged from public affairs as it

---

[1023] Kettler, Social and Political Thought of Adam Ferguson, pp. 8-9.

[1024] See Hirschman, *Passions and Interests*, p.120; Lehmann, *Adam Ferguson*, pp. 154-5; Bryson, 'Some Eighteenth Century Conceptions of Society', p. 421 and Horne, 'Envy and Commercial Society', pp. 552-3.

[1025] *Essay*, p. 178.

effects a gradual dismemberment of the human personality. Meanwhile the private and public realms become ever more strictly separated. 'The members of a community may...be made to lose the sense of every connection...and have no common affairs to transact but those of trade...in which the national spirit...cannot be exerted'.[1026]

Ferguson's absorption with retrogression was not, of course, original to him. It was a concern for classical historians like Polybius, Thucydides and Tacitus as well as contemporaries like Edward Gibbon. Like Gibbon, Ferguson conceived progress as generated by a process which simultaneously undermined 'civilisation'.[1027] But as John Brewer points out, the *Essay* is 'the first extensive study of this paradox' and this is why Marx lauded Ferguson's achievement and inaccurately identified him as Smith's teacher.[1028] Duncan Forbes, in also detecting this paradox in Ferguson, suggests that the *Essay* signposts a 'crossroads' in the history of thought in its bridging of Machiavellian civic humanism with the nineteenth century focus on the theme of alienation.[1029]

Ferguson does indeed anticipate many of the concerns of nineteenth century sociology in disclosing the causal nature of such variables as the division of labour and over-extension, though, typically, he finds his inspiration in the civic humanist concerns of citizenship and virtue.[1030] This fact does little, however, to detract from the originality and importance of his exposition because he translates this inspiration into a groundbreaking approach, a kind of 'economic sociology' that yields insights both 'profound and important'.[1031]

2. BACKGROUND

During Ferguson's time Scotland experienced enormous upheavals in its social, political and economic life. Scotland became a commercial society during the second half of the eighteenth century[1032] and although capitalism was not yet the dominant economic mode of eighteenth-century Scotland[1033] Ferguson was witness

---

[1026] *Essay*, p. 208.

[1027] Pocock, 'Between Machiavelli and Hume', pp.153-69, p. 162.

[1028] Brewer, 'Adam Ferguson and the Theme of Exploitation', p. 465. According to Brewer, 'Ferguson's account of the decline of the Roman empire...influenced Gibbon's more famous study'. Adam Ferguson and the Division of Labour', p. 15. For Marx's reference to Ferguson see K. Marx, *Capital,* Progress Publishers, Moscow, 1977, 3 Vols, Vol. 1, pp. 334, 341-2; *The Poverty of Philosophy*, International Publishers, New York: 1969, p. 129-30. For further discussion on the Marx/Ferguson link see Lehmann, 'Review', p.169; Meek, 'The Scottish Contribution to Marxist Sociology'; R. Bendix, 'Mandate to Rule, An Introduction', *Social Forces*, Vol. 55 (2), 1976, pp. 252-3; E. Garnsey, 'The Rediscovery of the Division of Labour', *Theory and Society*, Vol. 10, 1981, pp. 337-58, p. 341; Hamowy, 'Adam Smith, Adam Ferguson and the Division of Labour' and Ballestrem, 'Sources of the Materialist Conception of History', pp. 3-9.

[1029] Forbes, 'Introduction' to *Essay*, p. xxxi.

[1030] Brewer, 'Adam Ferguson and the Theme of Exploitation', p. 473.

[1031] Gellner, 'Adam Ferguson and the Surprising Robustness of Civil Society', p. 119.

[1032] Strasser, *The Normative Structure of Sociology*, p. 53.

[1033] Camic, *Experience and Enlightenment*, p. 95.

to its advent and was well acquainted with its encroaching effects in both Britain and abroad.[1034] He witnessed the drastic changes to the agricultural economy of the highlands, and the effects this wrought on the social life of the villages. [1035] Ferguson was present at the birth of the following industrial changes: The mechanisation and specialisation of labour (after 1745 machine industry was introduced into the lowlands);[1036] enormous increases in productive output; the advent of the large scale workshop; the geographical concentration of manufacture; the growth of cities and an accompanying explosion in population growth;[1037] the division of the manufacturing population into either owners/employers of wage labour and workers and the transformation of Britain from a largely rural to a mainly urban society.[1038] Though 'industrial revolution' is too grand a term for the changes Ferguson witnessed, 'pre-industrial' or 'proto-industrial' certainly describe the conditions of mid-eighteenth century Scotland. Ferguson was acutely aware of the manner in which labour processes and their accompanying social relations had changed. Because labourers were increasingly less likely to own their own means of production, they were forced by necessity to sell their labour to those who did.[1039]

Increasing centralisation of government and its institutions was another of Ferguson's concerns. Apart from the more general expansion and proliferation of imperial bureaucracy throughout the globe, two major historical events in Scotland doubtless intensified this interest. Firstly, the 1707 Act of Union meant the loss of the Scottish Assembly and therefore the exacerbation of government at a distance. Secondly, Scotland's decline as a military power was accompanied by increasing centralisation and professionalisation of military might in London.

2.1   The Decline of Nations

It was a common seventeenth-century view that the world was in its senility[1040] and the idea of degeneration was still very popular in the eighteenth century.[1041] But concern with the theme of retrogression is centuries old. A tension between faith in scientific progress and fears of moral decrepitude may be found in the writings of many ancient writers, among them Plato, Seneca, Lucretius and Posidonius.[1042]

[1034] For example, after travelling through Manchester and Birmingham he reported how impressed he was by the level of industrial development. Letter to John Douglas July 21, 1781, *Correspondence*, No. 198, II, pp. 267-8.

[1035] Strasser, *The Normative Structure of Sociology*, p. 53.

[1036] Brewer, 'Adam Ferguson and the Division of Labour', p. 24.

[1037] 'Population growth in Scotland's five main cities between 1755 and 1175 was three times the national average'. Brewer, 'Adam Ferguson and the Division of Labour', p. 25.

[1038] These changes became fully realised by the nineteenth century. Joseph Mahon, 'Engels and the Question about Cities', *History of European Ideas*, Vol. 3 (1), 1982, pp. 43-77, pp. 43-4.

[1039] Brewer, 'Adam Ferguson and the Division of Labour', pp. 24-5; See also C.P. Kindleberger, 'The Historical Background: Adam Smith and the Industrial Revolution', in T. Wilson and A. Skinner (eds), The Market and the *State*, Oxford University Press, 1976, p. 24.

[1040] Passmore, *The Perfectibility of Man*, p. 198.

[1041] Whitney, *Primitivism and the Idea of Progress*, p. 43.

[1042] E. R. Dodds, *The Ancient Concept of Progress*, Oxford: Clarendon Press, 1985, pp. 25-30.

Ferguson agrees with Montesquieu and Rousseau that moral corruption is often the attendant of greatness and that political decline is more likely in prosperous empires.[1043] He endorses Montesquieu's suggestion in *Consideration of the Causes of the Greatness of the Romans and Their Decline* (1734) that the decline of the Roman republic was traceable to the moral corruption engendered by the decline of Stoicism and the popularity of Epicureanism. According to this argument, Epicureanism in the late republic represented hedonism and the priority of private interest over the public good.[1044] As Richard Sher has noted, for Ferguson 'Epicureanism was associated with Julius Caesar, Stoicism with [his] beloved Cato. Ferguson implied that Caesar's will to political power was directly linked to his Epicurean will to political pleasure'. The triumph of Epicureanism over Stoicism culminated, in Ferguson's mind, in the destruction of the republics of virtue presided over by Cato and Marcus and the establishment of despotism made possible by the moral degeneration of Roman citizens.[1045] He indicates that his Roman *History* should be viewed as a moral lesson for all affluent nations, especially Britain,[1046] which was the most commercially advanced state and the first to industrialise. The widespread optimism about progress to which these developments gave rise is evident in Ferguson's writings yet this optimism is undercut by a deep curiosity about their potentially adverse effects.

Peter Burke has noticed a correlation in the history of ideas between our expectation and actual experience of progress. Conversely, when progress is slowing, expectations are lowered and writers begin to focus on the theme of corruption. Accordingly in the last centuries of the Roman empire we find Polybius, Cicero and Tacitus focusing on corruption.[1047] Yet Britain was expanding rapidly in Ferguson's time and did not seem to be on the verge of any kind of economic collapse. Rather, the general concern seemed to be with the dissipation of virtue, one of the most urgent problems of political philosophy in the eighteenth century.[1048] Gibbon's *Decline and Fall of the Roman Empire* was just one instance of the British preoccupation with the subject of national corruption represented in academic treatises and in the press and popular writing of the time.[1049]

[1043] Though Ferguson does admit that corruption can also take place in nations neither prosperous nor advanced. *Essay*, p. 229.

[1044] *History*, pp. 169-70.

[1045] Sher, *Church and University*, p. 201; *P.I.*, p. 238.

[1046] Rome is 'a signal example of the vicissitudes to which prosperous nations are exposed...To know it well is to know mankind'. *History,* pp. 1-2.

[1047] Peter Burke, 'Tradition and Experience: The Idea of Decline from Bruni to Gibbon', *Daedelus*, Vol. 105, Summer, 1976, pp. 137-52, p. 145. Dodds makes the same observation. *Ancient Concept of Progress*, p. 25.

[1048] Pocock, *Machiavellian Moment*, p. 462.

[1049] Jean Willke, *Historical Thought of Adam Ferguson,* p. 170. According to Addison Ward: 'The special relevance of Roman history for England arose from the observation that both countries had "mixed" government, composed of monarchical, aristocratic, and popular elements, whose balance assured a maximum both of stability and personal liberty'. 'Tory View of Roman History', p. 418.

It has been suggested that Smith also exhibits a 'profound pessimism'[1050] about the commercial age but Smith's reservations were minor compared to Ferguson's. The latter's concern for the malignant potential of commercialisation persisted throughout his life and, more than any of his Scottish contemporaries, he was conscious of the public dangers posed by the emergence of 'commercial spirit', namely the degeneration of society into a 'tyranny.' His avowed purpose in writing the *Essay* was 'to describe that remissness of spirit...that state of national debility, which is likely to end in political slavery'.[1051] Ferguson expounds the causes of these effects at great length in the *Essay*, the *History*, the *Institutes*, the *Principles* and in his assorted essays and pamphlets. The new prosperity of the polished age brought comfort and 'convenience' but it could also bring social ruin. History is replete with cases of states that have experienced 'a kind of spontaneous return to obscurity and weakness.' Little wonder that people commonly assume that 'the progress of societies to what we call national greatness, is not more natural than their return to weakness and obscurity is necessary and unavoidable'. The application to nations of '[t]he images of youth and of old age' seems entirely reasonable.[1052]

3. CORRUPTION

Ferguson honours the ancient Polybian project of attempting to isolate the variables leading up to imperial atrophy. The latter referred to two possible sources of decay from natural causes: the 'external', which has no 'fixed principle', and the 'internal' which is self produced and occurs according to a predictable and 'regular sequence'. Polybius describes the typical pattern of the prosperous and secure 'Commonwealth' which, if it enjoys 'supremacy and uncontested sovereignty' for a long enough period, will inevitably end up with a dissolute citizenry.[1053] Ferguson identifies the latter endogenous type of decay as his focus of concern in declaring that 'no nation ever suffered internal decay but from the vice of its members.'[1054]

Ferguson adopts Polybius' usage of the term corruption, as did Machiavelli and most eighteenth century thinkers.[1055] For Machiavelli 'corruzione' represented any form of deterioration in the quality of government and it could affect people, not

---

[1050] Robert L. Heilbroner, 'The Paradox of Progress: Decline and Decay in the *Wealth of Nations*' *Journal of the History of Ideas*, Vol. 34 (2) 1973, pp. 243-262, p. 243. By contrast, Pocock suggests that Smith did not share Ferguson's gloom about the commercial age. Pocock, 'Between Machiavelli and Hume', p. 162.

[1051] *Essay*, p. 247.

[1052] *Essay*, pp. 197-8.

[1053] Polybius, *Rise of the Roman Empire*, 6.57. p. 350.

[1054] *Essay*, p. 264. '[N]ational spirit is frequently transient, not on account of any incurable distemper in the nature of mankind, but on account of their voluntary neglects and corruptions'. *Essay*, p. 212. See also *History*, pp. 305-6.

[1055] The term also started to become synonymous with bribery during this period and eventually this latter, exclusively monetary, meaning replaced the Machiavellian meaning. Hirschman, *Passions and Interests*, p. 40.

only individually, but *en masse* in pervasive attitudinal and behavioural trends.[1056] Ferguson tells us that 'nations cease to be eminent' when the citizen's active nature is deprived of 'objects which served to excite [his] spirit.' A healthy state is predicated upon, and chiefly characterised by, vigorous public interest and popular participation in municipal affairs. Dissipation sets in the moment this spirit wanes.[1057] It is not enough for government to be competent or even to secure satisfactorily material prosperity; it must also seek actively to enlist the participation of citizens in public affairs.[1058] History teaches us that nations with high levels of political apathy are extremely susceptible to the designs of despots. Ferguson's greatest fear is of any condition that might give rise to or necessitate the arbitrary rule of 'military government'. This fear was a longstanding one and is constantly reiterated in all his published works and private correspondence.[1059]

Ferguson relates corruption to changes in conditions that tend to debase the 'civil' and 'political virtues'[1060] namely, specialisation, over-extension and hedonism. His aetiology of modern corruption is linked to his views on the causes of the decline of Republican Rome, all of which could be traced, in turn, to the triumph of Epicureanism over Stoicism. Epicureanism taught people prodigality, described a Godless world governed by chance, reduced morality to hedonism and taught that 'all good was private'. Devotion to the tenets of Epicureanism resulted in prodigality and ruination.[1061] Conversely the cures for the ills of modern times lay in the teachings of Stoicism.[1062] Ferguson's elaboration of the source and nature of this debasement testifies to a moralistic yet sophisticated mind grappling with immense social change.

Loss of virtue is fatal because, unlike Smith or Mandeville, Ferguson does not judge the prosperity of societies by such quantitative indicators as wealth, military might or population levels,[1063] but by the Stoic index of the moral and civic disposition of its citizenry.[1064] A key subtext here might be the perceived unpatriotism and venality of those who voted for the Act of Union. The popular

---

[1056] S. M. Shumer, 'Machiavelli; Republican Politics and Its Corruption', *Political Theory*, Vol. 7 (1), 1979, pp. 5-34, p. 9.

[1057] *Essay*, p. 200.

[1058] *P.II.*, p. 509.

[1059] See, for example, letter to William Pulteney, 1 December, 1769, *Correspondence*, No. 57, I, p. 88.

[1060] *Essay*, p. 260.

[1061] *History*, pp. 169-70 Ferguson explains elsewhere that, although these beliefs were not truly representative of Epicureanism, the vulgar, hedonistic understanding of Epicureanism was generally adopted. *Institutes*, pp. 138-40.

[1062] *History*, p. 170.

[1063] Population size was commonly used as a measure of national wealth in the eighteenth century. Ann Firth, 'Moral Supervision and Autonomous Social Order: Wages and Consumption in Eighteenth Century Economic Thought', *History of the Human Sciences*, Vol. 15 (1), pp. 39-57, p. 44. Smith asserted that 'the most decisive mark of the prosperity of any country is the increase in the number of inhabitants'. *WN*. I. Viii. 23. pp. 87-8.

[1064] *Essay*, p. 62. Rousseau took a similar line, arguing that 'it is better to count on the vigour which comes of good government than on the resources a great territory furnishes'. But it should also be noted that Rousseau thought that the 'surest sign' of a well-governed state was population growth. *Social Contract*, p. 221.

view in Scotland was that the Union had been caused by 'the corruption of the Scottish leadership' who had been bribed with financial and other rewards (for example, peerages) for voting in its favour.[1065] But it is likely that he subscribed to the more benign view that Scotland's leadership were already reconciled to the Union or, at worst, had been forced by the English (who threatened, among other things, to 'ban the importation to England of the main articles of Scottish trade')[1066] to put the economic well being of Scots before that of independence.[1067]

In any case, Ferguson sees a healthy state as chiefly characterised by vigorous public interest and involvement. The capacity of constitutions to encourage political and military participation (and therefore civic virtue) is the true index of sound government.[1068] Though Smith regretfully acknowledges the loss of civic virtue with the advent of commercialism,[1069] on balance he seems to believe that material prosperity has moral and ontological priority. Virtue and citizenship, though desirable, must be sacrificed for the sake of progress and wealth. Ferguson is more ambivalent:

> Wealth, commerce, extent of territory, and the knowledge of arts, are, when properly employed, the means of preservation, and the foundations of power. If they fail in part, the nation is weakened; if they were entirely withheld, the race would perish: their tendency is to maintain numbers of men, but not to constitute happiness...but...are of little significance, when only employed to maintain a timid, dejected and servile people.[1070]

The primary distinction between Smith and Ferguson on the question of corruption is that Smith's views are ultimately those of an early liberal and classical political economist[1071] whereas Ferguson, while cautiously embracing both of these perspectives, is reluctant to abandon the civic humanist diagnostic tradition.

4. PROBLEMS OF SOCIAL COHESION AND SCALE: 'ANOMIE', IMPERIALISM AND BUREAUCRATISATION

One of the primary causes of imperial atrophy is the growth of small-scale communities into impersonal, unwieldy, cities and empires. In fact, Ferguson reckons that, of all the routes to despotism, over-extension is the surest.[1072] This

---

[1065] For a discussion of the validity of this belief see Shaw, *The Political History of Eighteenth Century Scotland*, pp. 1-17.

[1066] Shaw, *The Political History of Eighteenth Century Scotland*, p. 1.

[1067] The issue seems to have been an extremely complicated one for Ferguson because we know that his political sympathies were anti-Jacobite and there is no evidence that he pushed for Scottish independence. It is possible, though, that his emotional attitude to the Union differed from his political position which seems to have been fairly complacent, if not positive.

[1068] *P.II.*, p. 509.

[1069] *WN.* V. i. f. 50, p. 782.

[1070] *Essay*, p. 60.

[1071] Though only in a precursory sense. Liberalism and laissez-faire did not become fully conflated until the nineteenth century. Zaret, 'From Political Philosophy to Social Theory', p. 159.

[1072] *Essay*, p. 257. Montesquieu and Gibbon both linked the decline of empires to over extension. Burke, 'The Idea of Decline from Bruni to Gibbon', p. 146. Hume also disapproved of 'extensive

could occur as a result of deliberate acts of militaristic imperialism or more naturally as a result of economic growth which, in turn, stimulates population levels and leads to the development of cities. Both processes would lead to over-bureaucratisation, over-centralisation, social disorientation and conditions we now think of as 'anomic'. When these conditions coincide with market society based on contracts and the profit-motive the destructive potential is exacerbated still further. This combination of factors, Ferguson warns, is a prelude to tyranny and, ultimately, a complete social and economic breakdown. Civilisation is defined, not just in terms of cultural, technical or economic development but also in terms of its sense of community. Yet this is precisely what is lost when polished nations tip into decline.[1073]

While Ferguson's exposition of the effects of over-extension certainly anticipates some of the concerns of nineteenth century sociology it should be noted that Ferguson's published inspiration comes from the Stoic absorption with the solidary principles of *sympathia* and social intimacy which he then applies to 'contemporary' conditions in order to create a more modern effect. Troubled by the emergence of the individuated society, he reflects nostalgically on the golden age of the small tribal community where the 'friendly intercourses of men, even in their rudest condition is affectionate and happy'.[1074] At times he (perhaps inadvertently) waxes primitivistic as he eulogises the intimate societies of Thucydides' ancient Athens, the Germany of Tacitus' reports and contemporary 'anthropological' accounts of life in 'savage' societies. In all of them, citizens enjoy relationships based on spontaneous affection rather than duty or expectation of reward.[1075] Compared to the communal spirit of savage and barbarous ages there reigns in polished, market society a spirit of individualism, competition and legalism where social relationships are defined and constrained by contract and the pursuit of profit. Ferguson confronts Smith's relative optimism about progress with a lament on the psychological and social costs exacted by the modern market economy. Foreshadowing Marx on the effects of commercialisation on 'social essence' he suggests that in polished nations 'man is sometimes found a detached and solitary being' who 'has found an object which sets him in competition with his fellow creatures, and he deals with them as he does with his cattle and his soil, for the sake of the profits they bring.'[1076]

Ferguson mourns the passing of village life as he expresses deep misgivings about the inexorable development towards large-scale social organisations. The advent of cities introduces an unprecedented set of social and moral problems. Ferguson lists 'People' before 'Wealth and Revenue' as the premier 'National resource'. But he provides the important qualification that mere size of the population does not reflect its value. Rather, the value of the key national resource is

---

conquests', asserting that aggressive expansionism 'must be the ruin of every free government'. Hume, 'Idea of a Perfect Commonwealth', *Essays*, p. 529. Smith seems to have had a similar attitude. Dalphy I. Fagerstrom, 'Scottish Opinion and the American Revolution', *The William and Mary Quarterly*, Vol. 11 (2), 1954, pp. 252-75, p. 259.

[1073] Forbes, 'Adam Ferguson and the Idea of Community', p. 43.

[1074] *Essay*, p. 104.

[1075] *Essay*, pp. 84-94. Contemporary sources included accounts of life among the indigenous peoples of North America by Lafitau, Charlevoix and Colden.

[1076] *Essay*, p. 24. See also *P.II.*, pp. 376-7.

computed qualitatively as being proportionate to a people's sense of 'union and character.' Regrettably, there are times when a populace becomes 'disunited and corrupted and incapable of public affections' in direct 'consequence of their numbers', especially when these numbers congregate in close proximity.[1077] Like Aristotle, Ferguson personally believed that it was in the small to moderate-scale city state that people stood the best chance of living the 'good life', that is, as civic animals.[1078] Those least affected by commercialism 'and the most to be trusted with its internal Peace' are people who remain on the land.[1079] Concerns about the effects of cities on the moral and physical health of people was a popular theme of the nineteenth century, particularly in the writings of Frederick Engels, but Ferguson was among the few eighteenth century minds to take up the theme.[1080]

But it is military imperialism that is the fastest and most destructive route to over-extension and it was by this means that Rome 'put the finishing hand' to its own 'internal corruption'.[1081] According to Ferguson it is in the nature of the prosperous nation to augment its wealth by the perpetual enlargement of territory. This argument was pioneered by Thucydides who attributed the desire for conquest to the vice of *hubris*, a characteristic exclusive to wealthy states and which drives them to expand in excess of need and beyond reason. *Hubris* results from overconfidence gained through past successes and this is why successful (that is, large and prosperous) nations are more likely to tip into decline.[1082]

The worst effect of imperialistically induced over-extension is loss of political vigour and integrity. Ferguson notes that in proportion as nations become larger and increase their territories, people become more and more alienated, both physically and psychologically, from the affairs of government. In addition, government itself becomes ever more centralised, bureaucratised, and therefore less 'democratic'. China is identified as the most conspicuous exemplar of the pathological imperial bureaucracy. Here the arts of government are refined to the highest degree in order to satisfy those 'vulgar minds' for whom national 'felicity and greatness' is synonymous with the ferocious march towards specialisation, compartmentalisation, professionalisation, atomisation, differentiation, routinisation, depersonalisation and the rationalisation of governance and authority: Note that this process is associated, not with increasing democratisation and liberalisation, but with increasingly despotic forms of discipline and policing.

> They have done what we are very apt to admire; they have brought national affairs to the level of the meanest capacity; they have broke them into parts, and thrown them into separate departments; they have clothed every proceeding with splendid ceremonies,

---

[1077] *Institutes*, pp. 243-4.

[1078] Dodds, *The Ancient Concept of Progress*, p. 17.

[1079] *Reflections*, p. 19. Even so, Ferguson also accepted the naturalness of progress and held that the good life was still possible in large-scale societies provided that virtue was consciously cultivated. To be discussed further.

[1080] Mahon, 'Engels and the Question about Cities', passim.

[1081] *Essay*, p. 262.

[1082] Jacqueline De Romilly, *Thucydides and Athenian Imperialism*, Translated by Philis Thody, New York: Arno Press, 1979, pp. 322-4. See *Essay*. p. 142, where Ferguson cites Thucydides as an authority on the subject of foreign conquests.

and majestical forms; and where the reverence of forms cannot repress disorder, a rigorous and severe police, armed with every species of corporal punishment, is applied to the purpose...Every department of state is made the object of a separate profession, and every candidate for office must have passed through a regular education; and, as in the gradations of the university, must have obtained by his proficiency, or his standing, the degree to which he aspires. The tribunals of state, of war, and of the revenue, as well as of literature, are conducted by graduates in their different studies: but while learning is the great road to preferment, it terminates in being able to read, and to write; and the great object of government consists in raising, and in consuming the fruits of the earth. With all these resources, and this learned preparation, which is made to turn these resources to use, the state is in reality weak; has repeatedly given the example which we seek to explain; and among the doctors of war or of policy, among the millions who are set apart for the military profession, can find none of its members who are fit to stand forth in the dangers of their country.[1083]

History has shown that 'human nature' prospers and excels in moderately sized states whereas in 'in states overgrown, has generally declined and degenerated.'[1084] The community is the nursery for virtue and is usually more effective in this role where it remains 'independent' and 'of a small extent.'[1085] A nation's territory must be small enough to admit universal participation and thereby foster communal sentiments. But when people inhabit a 'large and extensive territory, they are disunited and lose sight of their community.' Government falls to a few who 'withhold from the many every subject of public zeal or political occupation.' The great mass of people inevitably lapse into 'a state of languor and obscurity', the political efficacy of citizens dissipates and the people begin to suffer 'themselves to be governed at discretion.'[1086] Where people play no part in the affairs of state there can be no civic virtue. Where there is no civic virtue and no sense of subjective political efficacy, despots are likely to ascend, unfettered by the usual constraints of public scrutiny and accountability. Over-extension and over-bureaucratisation lead to disintegration of the polity and of the invisible threads that bind a community together. The healthy agitations and co-operations of a robust constitution gradually fall into abeyance. Paradoxically, over-extension narrows rather than expands the 'compass' of 'national affairs'. The process of government becomes ever more distant and oppressive as 'the majority' come 'to consider themselves the subjects of a sovereignty, not as the members of a political body'. Now the numbers who 'are consulted in legislation, or in other matters of government' become fewer and fewer. Ferguson accords with Montesquieu's belief that despotism is unavoidable in large empires because the unwieldy scale of empires necessitates centralised government, while promptness of resolutions and ruthless expediency are necessary in order to compensate for the problems of distance.[1087] The costs of over-extension are the loss

---

[1083] *Essay*, pp. 214-15.

[1084] *Institutes*, pp. 243-4.

[1085] *Essay*, p. 60. Rousseau made the same argument, giving reasons almost identical to those cited by Ferguson. Rousseau, *Social Contract*, pp. 219-20.

[1086] *Institutes*, p. 243.

[1087] *Essay*, pp. 256-7. Montesquieu, *Laws*, 1. 8. 19, p. 126.

of civic virtue, social intimacy, 'national' cohesion, external and internal political efficacy in subjects[1088] and representativeness and moderation in government.[1089]

Like Thucydides, Ferguson is convinced that, despite its obvious economic benefits, 'conquest' is ultimately 'no advantage to those who make it, any more than to those over whom it is made.' It is foolish 'to felicitate a nation on the measure of its opulence' or 'the extent of its territory' particularly when these things are conceived as ends in themselves. Not only does luxury by itself 'give scope to evil passions' but where it is obtained unjustly, the evil is doubly compounded. Wealth secured by conquest represents a 'symptom of misery rather than of happiness' since it cannot fail to be 'productive of prodigality, licentiousness and brutal sensuality.' This had been the sorry fate of Rome, the 'centre to which the wealth of nations was collected, and at which it was consumed in gross sensuality, or in cruel and idle ostentation of power.'[1090]

There is no outright proscription on imperialism in Ferguson however he does stipulate that it is only truly defensible in the pursuit of national safety or the exercise of the other-regarding passions. Vanity, self-aggrandisement and a desire for wealth and living space are not sufficient motives and can never justify the misery which it inevitably produces.[1091] Unfortunately self-defence is rarely the motive for expansionism. It generally stems from 'ambition', used in this instance in its earlier, pejorative sense as hubristic desire for fortune.[1092] Ferguson apparently believes that there is a causal relationship between archetypal or natural social forms and the means by which these types are held together. 'Families are united by affection; companies by the desire of society [and] nations by the desire of security'. But 'empires' are united 'by force.'[1093] Ferguson seems to be suggesting that all except the latter are natural units because underpinned by endogenous drives. Empires are unnatural because they are driven by an artificial 'need' for greater territory and wealth.[1094]

From a moral point of view, Ferguson also objects to imperialism on the grounds that it necessarily involves an unjust restriction of freedom. Conquered nations are

---

[1088] Political efficacy is a modern term that refers to a 'person's belief that political and social change can be effected or retarded and that [her/]his efforts, alone or in concert with others can produce desired behaviour on the part of political authorities'. K. Prewitt, 'Political Efficacy', *International Encyclopedia of the Social Sciences*, Vol. 12, London: MacMillan, 1968, p. 225.

[1089] In Rousseau's list of the disadvantages of imperialism, he argues that these demobilisation effects are actually intentional rather than incidental by-products of over-extension. He thought that the real motive for conquest was not 'to aggrandise the Nation' but rather to 'increase the authority of rulers at home' and divert the minds of citizens from home affairs. Rousseau, *A Discourse on Political Economy*, in *Social Contract and Discourses*, p. 157.

[1090] *P.II.*, pp. 500-1. Ferguson's critique of imperialism does not conflict with his views on the positive effects of war, as might be thought, because his arguments on the latter topic generally apply to communities intent on self-defence. Violence against neighbours is only defensible in the context of necessity.

[1091] *P.II.*, p. 501.

[1092] *P.I.*, p. 34.

[1093] *Institutes*, p. 22. See also *P.I.*, p. 34.

[1094] Because population levels are spontaneously regulated by the size and fertility of a given territory, any perceived need for more living space must be misplaced.

always subdued by force and, as Thucydides had pointed out much earlier, such force, being military, is always tyrannical. Ferguson makes one of his occasional forays into the realm of international relations by insisting that the freedom of every individual depends upon an even balance of powers between nations; even citizens of nations who enjoy considerable liberties suffer a kind of *de facto* enslavement when they subjugate other nations. 'From the history of mankind, to conquer, or to be conquered, has appeared, in effect, the same'.[1095] There are, therefore, high security costs in enlarging territory by force because when one nation enslaves another, the aggressor paradoxically secures its own enslavement in terms of the enormous costs of constantly guarding acquired territory and conquered subjects.[1096]

Imperialism has a number of other disadvantages. To begin with, it invariably leads to bloodshed. Reporting a provincial uprising in which twenty thousand were killed, Ferguson notes with approval attempts on the part of the indigenous population to 'to rid their country forever' of their 'imperious and insatiable guests', who had perversely 'branded every act of resistance to their unjust usurpation with the name of defection and rebellion.'[1097] Imperialism is always attended with injustice and inconvenience. The distractions of colonies leads to the neglect of domestic concerns; provinces are subject to pillaging on the part of soldiers and exorbitant taxes on the part of governing states, while imperial governors are apt to inspire dread in their subjects.[1098]

Ferguson's list of imperialistically induced afflictions is almost identical to that compiled by Thucydides in his critique of Athenian imperialism and, like the latter, he was convinced that rule by force would eventually precipitate the collapse of states exercising it.[1099] Imperialism is seen to impugn the operations of spontaneous order; the naturally evolved 'spirit' of a given nation — reflected in its idiosyncratic institutions and customs — is subordinated to imposed and therefore artificial laws and mores. Following Montesquieu, Ferguson suggests that it is unwise to expect to unite disparate peoples under centralised legal and political arrangements that completely disregard cultural differences and the organic, evolved character of human social life.[1100] Thus, growth via military expansion is always disastrous. Empires collapse because they are always ruined by the despots who ordinarily govern   them.[1101] At this point Ferguson makes a rare exception to his prohibition on

---

[1095] *Essay*, p. 257. '[F]ree nations, under the shew of acquiring dominion, suffer themselves, in the end, to be yoked with the slaves they had conquered'. *Essay*, p. 62.

[1096] In a similar vein Rousseau had written that it is a certainty 'that no peoples are so oppressed and wretched as conquering nations'. *A Discourse on Political Economy*, in *Social Contract and Discourses*, p. 157.

[1097] *History*, p. 217.

[1098] *History*, pp. 70, 77-80, 98, 309, 350, 360, 391, 405.

[1099] De Romilly, *Thucydides and Athenian Imperialism*, pp. 315-19. Like Ferguson, Thucydides also lists rule by force, hatred of rulers, neglect of domestic concerns, and unprofitability as negatives of imperialism.

[1100] *P.I.,* pp. 34-5.

[1101] *Essay*, pp. 261-4.

revolutionary activity of any kind; 'revolution' is now not only unavoidable but 'necessary' in order to 'preserve [the society] in its former progressive state'.[1102]

5. THE DIVISION OF LABOUR

Ferguson's exposition of the nature, development and effects of specialisation is noteworthy partly because it has afforded him, in hindsight, some minor claim to fame. It is commonly suggested that his work represents the first sustained critique of capitalism and market society based on the detection of alienation effects and a theory of class exploitation. Indeed, Peter Gay once wrote that 'Ferguson's pages on the division of labour are a minor triumph of eighteenth century sociology'.[1103]

Ferguson was less interested than Smith in the economic effects of specialisation, focusing instead on its social ramifications. In this regard the *Essay* breaks new ground and probably constitutes the first fully developed sociological account of the effects of specialisation.[1104] As William Lehmann notes, Ferguson's treatment of specialisation 'makes a distinct advance...in a way that definitely anticipates, if it does not influence in order, St. Simon, Comte, Spencer and Durkheim'.[1105] Marx also quoted Ferguson approvingly, indicating that he had been inspired by the latter's treatment of the de-humanising effects of the division of labour.[1106]

Ferguson was particularly struck by the fact that, paradoxically, the division of labour was both the cause and product of progress yet operated, at the same time, as a key source of retrogression, especially in its effect on statecraft, martial and political disposition and defence capability.[1107] He notes, not without enthusiasm, the tremendous advantages attributable to specialisation: an increasing accumulation of wealth, a soaring population and an infinitely expanding refinement in artistic skills, as we have seen. But in general, he seems to hold to the view that modern commercial society, while affording many advantages, is yet the scene of what modern authors now label 'alienation', the primary cause of which is the social and work-function division of labour.

5.1   Alienation? Exploitation?

Ferguson's outline of the de-humanising consequences of specialisation on workers seems to foreshadow Marx's discourse on the same subject to the extent that it hints at the effects of fragmentation, product alienation and alienation from species

---

[1102] *History*, p. 5. Curiously, though, when confronted with concrete examples like those of America and Ireland, Ferguson's declamations are abandoned for the sake of what appears to be political expediency. See Chapter 12 for a more complete discussion of this point.

[1103] Gay, *The Enlightenment,* Vol. II, pp. 342-3. See also Brewer 'Adam Ferguson and the Division of Labour', passim.

[1104] A. Swingewood, *A Short History of Sociological Thought*, London: Macmillan, 1984, p. 23.

[1105] Lehmann, *Adam Ferguson*, p. 187.

[1106] Marx, *The Poverty of Philosophy*, pp. 129-30; *Capital,* I, pp. 334, 341-2.

[1107] *Essay*, pp. 206-7.

being.[1108] At times, the affinity with Marx is remarkable with the development of ideas at times almost as fully realised.[1109] In fact it is Ferguson's treatment which partly inspired Marx's ferocious polemic on the same subject.[1110] The affinity with Marx and Ferguson should not, however, be over-emphasised for reasons that will be given presently.

Though Smith also outlined the pernicious consequences of advanced specialisation in the *Wealth of Nations*.[1111] Ferguson supplies more detail about its social effects and is more reserved about its benefits. Whereas Smith saw specialisation as generating a kind of organic solidarity[1112] for Ferguson it has the opposite effect. He describes the emergence of a division of labour between 'manual and mental labour' whereby those employed in manual labour come to be debased by it. The specialised worker becomes oblivious to any concerns outside her/his own narrow work sphere as labour becomes mindless and mechanical. Specialisation 'contract[s] and...limit[s] the views of the mind' making workers unfit for public duties.[1113] Soon, those involved in factory labour become mindless automatons, mere cogs in a vast machine.

> Many mechanical arts...require no capacity; they succeed best under a total suppression of sentiment and reason....Manufactures...prosper most where the mind is least consulted, and where the workshop may...be considered as an engine, the parts of which are men.[1114]

5.2   Social Effects

Ernest Gellner has noted that Ferguson is far less worried than Marx about the effect of specialisation on the 'soul than about what it may do to society.'[1115] Certainly, Ferguson displays great originality in his exploration of the idea that the separation of tasks leads to social disorientation or conditions sociologists have described as anomic, alienated or, more recently, as undermined by low levels of social and moral capital. Humans are naturally (and exclusively) co-operative beings, able to 'unite their labours for some common purpose, and distribute the burdens of the

---

[1108] As noticed by Kettler. *Social and Political Thought of Adam Ferguson*, pp. 8-9.

[1109] See, for example, Of the Separation of Departments', *Collection of Essays*, No. 15, passim.; Hamowy, 'Progress and Commerce', p. 87.

[1110] Marx credits Ferguson with the idea of worker alienation and suggests that Smith took the idea from Ferguson. But he was unaware that Smith discussed the topic in his Glasgow Lectures before the *Essay* was published. However it is possible 'that Ferguson suggested the theme in the first place'. Forbes, Introduction to *Essay*, p. xxxi. The subject is a vexed one and Smith and Ferguson are thought to have become embroiled in a priority controversy over it. For further details see: See Amoh, 'Adam Ferguson and the Division of Labour'; Hamowy, 'Division of Labour'; H. Mizuta, 'Two Adams in the Scottish Enlightenment', *Studies on Voltaire and the Eighteenth Century*, Vol. 191, 1981, pp. 812-19; Dickey, 'Historicising the Adam Smith Problem', p. 591; Kettler, *Social and Political Thought of Adam Ferguson*, p. 74.

[1111] See Smith, *WN.* V.i, passim.

[1112] Smith, *LJ (A)* vi. 46-49, pp. 348-49; *WN*. I.ii.1-3, pp. 25-7.

[1113] *Essay*, pp. 174-5, 206-7.

[1114] *Essay*, p. 174.

[1115] Gellner, *Conditions of Liberty*, p. 80.

community according to some rule of instinct or reason.'[1116] Specialised work destroys this capacity. While seeming 'to promise' national wealth and 'improvement of skill', in reality, specialisation erodes those most precious commodities, civic ardour, sociality and moral community. To use Ferguson's terms, the 'separation of professions...break[s] the bands of society'.[1117] The community loses its vigour, its sense of intimacy and unity as the division of labour becomes more sophisticated and ubiquitous. Specialisation encourages political apathy and suppresses peoples' natural liveliness and 'ingenuity'. Attention is gradually diverted from public concerns as people are drawn into the private, individuated realm of commerce and manufacturing. Work specialisation alienates people 'from the common scene of occupation, on which the sentiments of the heart, and the mind, are most happily employed' with the effect that eventually 'society is made to consist of parts, of which none is animated with the spirit of society itself.' The most pernicious form of specialisation is the professionalisation of martial functions.[1118] Inevitably, political and military demobilisation leads to a loss of virtue and a lapse into a generalised civic incompetence; when these circumstances combine with the anomie-inducing effects of over-extension and the enervation brought on by idleness and luxury national strength is imperilled. Simple or 'barbarous' nations have never laboured under such difficulties for in them '[t]he public is a knot of friends,' bound by a sense of common danger.[1119] In such communities, each citizen assumes a portion of responsibility for the defence of common territory and this gives rise to the vital bonds which define and preserve community. But in polished society '[c]ommercial spirit' comes to displace vital civic spirit. Martial valour wanes as 'an admiration, and desire of riches' tends to bring with it 'an aversion to danger'.[1120]

Ferguson's remarks, though clearly anticipatory, should not be interpreted as basically proto-Marxist, as some scholars have suggested. Ferguson registers the drawbacks of specialisation but never recommends its devolvement and unlike Marx (probably exaggerating his own affinity with Ferguson)[1121] he regards specialisation as a perfectly natural development originating in our natural diversity and in our inventive, progressive faculties.

Ferguson readily acknowledges that economic exploitation of workers aggravates imbalances in wealth and he agrees with Smith that rank distinctions and class inequalities are reinforced by specialisation.[1122] He also shows great sympathy for the unfortunate labouring 'classes'.[1123] For example, laws intended to protect them may actually serve to preserve property inequalities.[1124] The conditions of their

---

[1116] *Institutes*, p. 22.

[1117] *Essay*, pp. 206-7.

[1118] *Essay*, p. 207.

[1119] *Essay*, p.208.

[1120] *Essay*, p.231.

[1121] See Marx, *Capital*, I., p. 334.

[1122] *Essay*, p. 178.

[1123] As first noticed by John Brewer. Brewer, 'The Scottish Enlightenment', pp. 15-23 who draws our attention to the above examples.

[1124] *Essay*, p. 151.

work is less than ideal and the work itself tends to be uninteresting and mind-numbing. Ferguson notes that 'the genius of the master…is cultivated, while that of the inferior workman lies waste.'[1125] He also acknowledges that, in, commercial states, 'the exaltation of the few' tends to 'depress the many'[1126] and that some of its 'occupations' are even 'more debasing than slavery'.[1127] But far from launching an attack on class exploitation, Ferguson is quite supportive of the system of rank distinctions. Class distinctions are located in natural inequalities which are unavoidable, therefore Ferguson rebukes that 'absurdity of pretension to equal influence and consideration after the characters of men have ceased to be similar.'[1128] Subordination is not only necessary to society and the attainment of the 'ends of government' but is immanent in the 'order established by nature.' People 'are fitted to different stations' therefore 'they suffer no injustice on the side of their natural rights' when 'classed' accordingly.[1129] Thus Ferguson's critical exposition of specialisation contains no programmatic calls for change. Like Smith he thought that the problems of specialisation could be solved within existing social and political arrangements.[1130] While his diagnosis of the pitfalls of commercialisation has clear Marxian implications the normative implications, for Ferguson at least, are quite different. Unlike Marx, he regards economic exploitation as an inevitable feature of commercial states[1131] and notes the unpleasant facts of commercial life with regret but with no sustained sense of revolutionary outrage or condemnation. The division of labour has drawbacks but it also has benefits. As Ferguson muses philosophically, 'the lot of man is never free of inconvenience, so the inconvenience he suffers is never deprived of all compensation'.[1132] Further, his concern lies more with the damage to *virtue* wrought by specialisation than with any alienation effects. Moreover, his chief worry here is with the effect of specialisation upon civic virtue in elites and 'statesmen' rather than on workers.

5.3   Decline of Military

What early proto-Marxist readings of Ferguson may have overlooked is that Ferguson describes the division of labour as a total process permeating all strata of

---

[1125] *Essay*, p. 175.

[1126] *Essay*, p. 177.

[1127] 'Of the Separation of Departments', *Collection of Essays*, No. 15, p. 142.

[1128] *Essay*, p. 179.

[1129] *Essay*, pp. 63-4. Yet Ferguson shows signs of real ambivalence here. Some occupations are so debasing that Ferguson is moved to comment that 'the less there is of this sort, the better…subordination however valuable is too dearly bought by the debasement of any order or class of the people'. 'Of the Separation of Departments' , *Collection of Essays*, No. 15, pp. 142-3.

[1130] To quote Norbert Waszek. 'Division of Labour', p. 56.

[1131] *Essay*, p. 177. Ferguson notes that: 'Property, in the common course of human affairs, is unequally divided: we are therefore obliged to suffer the wealthy to squander, that the poor may subsist; we are obliged to tolerate certain orders of men, who are above the necessity of labour, in order that, in their condition, there may be an object of ambition, and a rank to which the busy aspire'. *Essay*, p. 225. The only regime under which equality of wealth is appropriate is a democratic one: 'in such only it has been admitted with any degree of effect'. *Essay*, p. 151.

[1132] *P.I.*, p. 251.

society. And, unlike Marx, Ferguson thought that it was the ruling classes, the statesmen and military leaders, who bore the worst of specialisation effects and that it was at this level that the most disabling social consequence took place.[1133]

Specialisation and professionalisation in martial functions held great significance, not only for Ferguson, but for Scottish society in general. Historically, Scottish identity and social structure had been closely bound up in its claims to military prowess. According to John Robertson, this identity was the product of a number of distinctive historical circumstances and events. The introduction in the twelfth and thirteenth centuries of the traditional system of feudal 'knight service' overlaid the more longstanding system of military organisation known as the 'Scottish service'. Under this system the earls raised armies from among the 'lower' ranks. But as feudalism declined, the Scots insured against a deterioration of martial vigour and social intimacy by adopting a system of 'voluntary bands of "manrent" between lords and their followers — bands which themselves were usually based on the still more enduring ties of kinship'. Though martial social structure was common in Europe, Scotland was distinctive in combining this social structure with a strong martial ethnic and cultural identity. This distinctiveness was dealt a blow in 1663 when the Scottish Estates voted a Militia Act 'in which they acknowledged his Majesty's royal prerogative and undoubted right of the sole power of the raising, arming and commanding of his subjects'.[1134] The final blow came while Ferguson was away serving with the Black Watch regiment in Flanders. At home, the Battle of Culloden (1746) saw the highland clans decisively eliminated as a military force.[1135] As John Robertson observes, the effect on Scottish Highland society and Scottish national identity in general was disastrous:

> When confronted finally with English professional soldiers at Culloden in 1746, the Highland army disintegrated. Outright repression, disarming legislation and the abolition of hereditary jurisdictions then completed the destruction of their society and cause so efficiently that within eleven years the Highlanders too could safely be absorbed, complete with the newly invented kilt, into the British army.[1136]

Though Ferguson seems to have been politically resigned to all of these developments his attitude to their moral and cultural effects was less complacent.[1137] No Scots militia meant greater reliance upon professional standing armies, a trend Ferguson vehemently opposed. He adopted and expanded upon the observation of Polybius that the union of Rome's military and civil orders was its chief strength.[1138]

[1133] Ibn Kaldhoun (of whose work Ferguson seems to have been unaware) had also argued much earlier that the delegation of security to specialists leads to a politically and militarily weakened state. Gellner, 'Adam Ferguson and the Surprising Robustness of Civil Society', p. 121. Rousseau's observations on the same topic are also closely reiterated. Rousseau, 'Discourse on the Moral Effects of the Arts and Sciences', in *Social Contract and Discourses*, p. 20.

[1134] Robertson, *The Scottish Enlightenment and the Militia Issue*, pp. 1-5.

[1135] Smith, *The Political Philosophy of Adam Ferguson*, pp. 19, 11.

[1136] Robertson, *The Scottish Enlightenment and the Militia Issue,* p. 7.

[1137] Whereas he vigorously campaigned for a Scottish Militia Ferguson was more complacent about the 'shift of politics to London'. Smith, *The Political Philosophy of Adam Ferguson*, pp. 19-20.

[1138] Willke, *The Historical Thought of Adam Ferguson*, p. 148. The theme of the standing army as an instrument of corruption is also present in the writings of Shaftesbury, another of Ferguson's sources.

For Ferguson, the most dangerous separation in functions is that which occurs between soldier and statesman; roles that are otherwise 'naturally' conjoined. Ferguson conceives this split as creating a kind of schism in the human psyche. To separate 'the arts of policy and war, is an attempt to dismember the human character'.[1139] Moreover, a statesman 'ignorant of war' is about as useful to the defence of a state as a 'mariner' who is 'unacquainted with variable winds and storms'.[1140]

The militia issue had been a longstanding one in Scottish political discourse (most notably in the activities of Andrew Fletcher). Ferguson developed his own views on the subject most fully in the *Essay* and in two of his unpublished essays ('Of the Statesman and Warriour' and 'Of the Separation of Departments, Professions and Tasks Resulting from the Progress of Arts in Society'). In them he focuses on the civic humanist themes of public virtue and the importance of civic personality and virtue. Because the militia question was particularly controversial during the latter half of the eighteenth century Ferguson's two pro-militia pamphlets were published anonymously.[1141] *Reflections Previous to the Establishment of a Militia* (1756) and *The History of the Proceedings in the Case of Margaret, Commonly Called Peg, only Lawful Sister to John Bull, Esq.* (1761) argued for the right of Scotland to have its own citizen militia. They were written in anticipation of and in response to Scotland's pointed exclusion from the William Pitt sponsored militia bill of 1757 and the failure of the Scottish Militia Bill (1760) and against the background of the threat of invasion by France.[1142] Like the Scottish Militia Bill, the Pitt sponsored bill reflected British fears of a further Jacobite uprising.[1143] Both of Ferguson's pamphlets excited considerable attention and in 1762 he was a founder member of 'The Poker Club' which led the campaign for the establishment of a Scots militia.[1144] Other members included John Home and Alexander Carlyle.[1145]

Security was not Ferguson's only concern. Dependence on professional armies coupled with the growth of market culture resulted in a generalised decline in virtue. In his *Reflections* Ferguson argued that Scotland had become 'a Nation of Manufacturers, [in] which each is confined to a particular branch and sunk into the Habits and Peculiarities of his Trade.' On the one hand, the positive effect of this development is that '[w]e furnish good Work' but, on the other, there is the negative

---

F.. J. McLynn, 'The Ideology of Jacobitism — Part II', *History of European Ideas*, Vol. 6 (2), 1985, pp. 173-88, p. 179.

[1139] *Essay*, p. 218. Forbes, 'Adam Ferguson and the Idea of Community', p. 45.

[1140] 'Of the Separation of Departments', *Collection of Essays*, No. 15, p. 148.

[1141] Sher, 'Problem of National Defense', pp. 258-65

[1142] Fagg, *Biographical Introduction*, p. xxxiv.

[1143] Hamowy, *Social and Political Philosophy of Adam Ferguson*, p. 198.

[1144] Sher, 'Problem of National Defense', p. 259. See also Ferguson, *Biographical Sketch or Memoir of Lieutenant-Colonel Patrick Ferguson Originally Intended for the British Encyclopedia*, Edinburgh: Printed by John Moir, 1816, p.10.

[1145] The latter also produced a widely read pro-militia pamphlet. It was entitled: *The Question Relating to a Scots Militia Considered* (1760) and was edited by Ferguson and William Robertson. Sher, *Church and University*, p. 225.

tendency to 'educate men, gross, sordid, void of sentiments and Manners, who may be pillaged, insulted, and trod upon by the enemies of their country'.[1146] The spirit of nations is 'considerably impaired' where the civil and military character has become separated.[1147] To Ferguson's mind standing armies were little better than deracinated mercenaries whose loyalties were always in question. 'The most celebrated warriors', he says, 'were also citizens',[1148] and Themistocles, Aristides and Pericles are identified as paragons of the synthesised civic personality about which Ferguson is so nostalgic. Ferguson lavishly idealised the warrior-statesman of classical reports and expressed his views on the subject with great vigour. His support for James Macpherson's *Ossian* also reflects his admiration for the vital martial virtues which attached to pre-commercial subjects. At times this admiration borders on a primitivism which Ferguson would undoubtedly have wished to avoid given his other important commitments to modernity and material and moral progress.

Adam Smith also expressed regret at the dismemberment of human character brought about by specialisation but seems to have been more concerned with the division of labour's effect on intelligence than on martial or political virtues.[1149] Smith and Ferguson seem to have disagreed greatly on the question of militias; indeed Richard Sher has argued that Ferguson's views developed in direct response to Smith's.[1150] Though Ferguson probably overrated their differences[1151] nevertheless Smith's views on national defence differ from Ferguson's because the former 'has no dilemma of wealth and strength'.[1152] According to Smith professional armies

---

[1146] Ferguson, *Reflections*, p. 12.

[1147] *History*, pp. 183, 348, 399; *Reflections*, passim.

[1148] *Essay*, p. 149.

[1149] Phillipson, in Hont and Ignatieff (eds.), *Wealth and Virtue,* p.181. The textual evidence certainly supports this view. See Smith *WN*. V.i.f-g. p. 788.

[1150] Sher, 'Problem of National Defense', p. 267 and passim.

[1151] Smith's views on this topic were more complex than Ferguson's perception because in later passages of Book V of the *Wealth of Nations* Smith qualifies his position thus: 'That in the progress of improvement the practice of military exercises, unless government takes proper pains to support it, goes gradually to decay, and together with it, the martial spirit of the great body of the people, the example of modern Europe sufficiently demonstrates. But the security of every society must always depend, more or less, on the martial spirit of the great body of people. In the present times, indeed, that martial spirit alone, and unsupported by a well-disciplined standing army, would not perhaps, be sufficient for the defence and security of any society. But where every citizen had the spirit of a soldier, a smaller standing army would surely be requisite. That spirit besides, would necessarily diminish very much the dangers to liberty, whether real or imaginary, which are commonly apprehended from a standing army. As it would very much facilitate the operations of that standing army against a foreign invader, so it would obstruct them as much if unfortunately they should ever be directed against the constitution of the state'. *WN*. V. i. f. 59, pp. 786-7. Furthermore, in his response to Alexander Carlyle's attack on his views Smith wrote to Andreas Holt: 'When he wrote this book, he had not read mine to the end. He fancies that because I insist that a Militia is in all cases inferior to a well-regulated and well-disciplined standing Army, I disapprove of Militias altogether. With regard to that subject, he and I happened to be precisely of the same opinion'. Adam Smith, *The Correspondence of Adam Smith*, Mossner, E.C., and Ross, I.S., (eds), Oxford: Oxford University Press, 1987, Letter 208, October 26 1780, p. 251. Nevertheless, Smith insistence on the technical superiority of standing armies was a genuine point of disagreement with Ferguson. For a more detailed discussion on the relationship of the two Adams here see Sher, 'Problem of National Defense', pp. 240-268.

[1152] Mizuta, 'Two Adams in the Scottish Enlightenment', p. 815.

were more capable and efficient, and better protectors of liberty than militias[1153] and after he outlined these views in the *Wealth of Nations* Ferguson wrote him the following letter. In it he pointed out that, although he supported many of Smith's opinions, he drew the line at those relating to standing armies:

> You have provoked, it is true, the church, the universities, and the merchants, against all of whom I am willing to take your part; but you have likewise provoked the militia, and there I must be against you. The gentlemen and peasants of this country do not need the authority of philosophers to make them supine and negligent of every resource they might have in themselves.[1154]

Although a professional standing army was acceptable in times of peace this did not mean that the rest of the able population 'should forego the use of arms'.[1155] Ferguson regarded the modern professional soldier as defective because morally, technically and mentally fragmented. It is all very well for the skills and manners of people to be improved in the course of specialisation but when that same specialisation leads to a corrupt state the price cannot be worth paying. The average 'trader' may find that while 'his' manners are greatly enhanced by modernity 'he' suffers the loss of the all-important martial virtues. The trade-off is a zero sum game because the merchant made rich by specialisation 'has every virtue, except the force to defend his acquisitions'. The 'wealth or virtue' trade-off is a complicated one for Ferguson because without true virtue, wealth cannot be sustained and yet virtue is generally the cost of material wealth. Note also that the newly acquired virtues to which Ferguson refers are merely the cool, secondary, virtues of enterprise, punctuality and commercial probity, whereas the virtues sacrificed in attaining them are the cardinal civic virtues, hardly a profitable exchange from his point of view.[1156]

Though Ferguson's views on the subject of militias would have been informed by his years in the Black Watch regiment[1157] the influence of classical and neo-classical sources like Machiavelli and Polybius is also undoubted. Both endorsed citizen militias on the grounds that technical and tactical superiority could never compensate for lack of courage. Since citizen armies are always 'fighting for their country and their children, [they] can never weaken in the fury of their struggle.'[1158] Ferguson disparaged mercenaries for their unreliability and lack of energy. They are notoriously difficult to control, and it is impossible to maintain their goodwill. They

---

[1153] Smith *WN*. V.i.a.22-41, pp. 699-707. Smith did, however, concede with Ferguson that the standing armies of the Roman republic and Cromwell were pernicious but insisted that under ideal conditions, that is, where 'the sovereign is himself the general...a standing army can never be dangerous to liberty. On the contrary, in some cases it may be favourable to liberty'. *WN.*, Vi.a.41, pp. 706-7.

[1154] Adam Ferguson in a letter to Adam Smith, April 18, 1776. *Correspondence of Adam Smith*, pp. 193-4.

[1155] *P.II.*, p. 492.

[1156] *Essay*, p. 138. See also *P.I.*, p. 302 and *Essay*, pp. 242-3.

[1157] Willke, *The Historical Thought of Adam Ferguson*, pp. 2-3.

[1158] Polybius, *Rise of the Roman Empire*, 6.52. p. 346. Identically, Machiavelli argued that 'the reason why mercenary troops are useless' is that 'they have no cause to stand firm when attacked, apart from the small pay which you give them'. Therefore the only way to keep the state intact is 'to arm oneself with one's own subjects'. Machiavelli, *Discourses*, I. 43. p. 218. See also Machiavellli, 'The Citizen Army', *The Art of War*, in *The Chief Works and Others*; Vol. II, Allan Gibert (ed.), Durham, North Carolina: Duke University Press, 1965, pp. 579-87.

are more prone to disloyalty, insubordination and mutiny and are hazardous to the civic spirit of the general population because their venality is contagious. Apart from providing poor security from invaders, professional armies are a potential source of internal instability because they are more likely than citizen soldiers to usurp power or to promote aspiring tyrants.[1159] (Machiavelli made an almost identical litany of charges against mercenaries in *The Prince*).[1160] Militias have three key advantages over standing armies: they have a personal stake in the territory they defend; they will always be more numerous than the enemy and they are cheaper. Against the claim that standing armies exhibit greater levels of competence, Ferguson counters, somewhat optimistically, that in times of crisis, though 'inferior at first', militias are always highly motivated to promptly meet professional standards.[1161]

Ferguson speculates wistfully that it would have been impossible to convince an ancient Roman that the time would come when a 'refined and intelligent' nation like Great Britain...

> ...would make the art of war to consist in a few technical forms; that citizens and soldiers might come to be distinguished as much as women and men; that the citizen would become possessed of a property which he would not be able, or required, to defend; that the soldier would be appointed to keep for another what he would be taught to desire, and what he would be enabled to seize for himself; that, in short, one set of men were to have an interest in the preservation of civil establishments, without the power to defend them; that the other were to have this power, without either the inclination or the interest.[1162]

Ferguson thought that military service should be an avocation; a duty incumbent on all[1163] in order to protect the state from both internal and external threat. The loyalty of soldiers to an employer as opposed to a homeland makes it easier for them to become enemies of the commonwealth should that employer (usually a general) decide to advance 'his' own cause. An armed populace, meanwhile, is always prepared and able to secure its rights from the encroachments of aspiring tyrants whereas a populace accustomed to reliance upon professionals for their defence is ineffectual, timid and 'effeminate'.[1164] A people become 'disarmed in compliance' with the 'fatal refinement' of task specialisation have injudiciously 'rested their safety on the pleadings of reason and justice at the tribunal of ambition and force.'[1165] In the case of Britain, Ferguson probably has in mind the chastening lesson delivered by Cromwell who mobilised a professional army to successfully effect and sustain a revolution.[1166] Ferguson's suggested reforms on this issue were

---

[1159] *History*, pp. 28-32, 104, 127, 288, and *Reflections*, passim.

[1160] Machiavelli, *The Prince*, 12. pp. 77-9.

[1161] Adam Ferguson's unpublished moral philosophy lecture notes dated April 9, 1776, quoted in Sher, 'Problem of National Defense', p. 256.

[1162] *Essay*, pp. 218-19.

[1163] A view shared by Francis Hutcheson. Lawrence Delbert Cress, 'Radical Whiggery on the Role of the Military: Ideological Roots of the American Revolutionary Militia', *Journal of the History of Ideas*, Vol. 40 (1), 1979, pp. 43-60, p. 52.

[1164] *Essay*, pp. 213-20.

[1165] Essay, p. 256.

[1166] Lois Schwoer, *'No Standing Armies!'*, pp. 51-71.

his only significant departure from his otherwise firm commitment to the natural course of spontaneous order. In all other respects he was basically conservative.[1167]

6. FRIENDSHIP AND SOCIAL CAPITAL

Another source of corruption for Ferguson is the effect of commercial culture on personal and social relations. The new contract society can be alienating, isolating and affectively sterile. The contractual relationships of market society 'introduce the spirit of traffic into the commerce of affection.' Associations in the polished age have become so debased that 'the duties of friendship are exacted by rule.' Under the 'growing sensibility to interest' and the reigning ethic of the market, we 'consider kindness itself as a task.'[1168] The 'bands' of friendship in commercial society appear to us of a 'feeble texture, when compared to the resolute ardour with which [precommercial] man adheres to his friend, or to his tribe.' The subject of barbarous ages 'clings' to his friends with 'ardent affection' regardless but especially so in their 'season of peril'. Those living in the 'simplest condition' do not associate in order to maximise advantage, rather the 'ardours of friendship...kindle a flame in the human breast, which the considerations of personal interest or safety cannot suppress.' Neither do pre-commercial agents feign the indiscriminate friendship of polite society for they 'have not learned to affect what they do not actually feel'.[1169] Compare these observations to those made by Weber a century and a half later:

> Where the market is allowed to follow its own autonomous tendencies, its participants do not look toward the persons of each other but only toward the commodity; there are no obligations of brotherliness or reverence, and none of those spontaneous human relations that are sustained by personal unions. They all would just obstruct the free development of the bare market relationships, and its specific interests serve, in their turn, to weaken the sentiments on which these obstructions rest. Market behaviour is influenced by rational, purposive pursuit of interests.[1170]

Or to Ferguson's contemporary, Rousseau:

> Politeness requires this thing; decorum that; ceremony has its forms and fashion its laws, and these we must always follow, never the promptings of our own nature. We no longer dare seem what we really are, but lie under a perpetual restraint; in the meantime the herd of men, which we call society, all act under the same circumstances exactly alike, unless very particular and powerful motives prevent them. Thus we never know with whom we have to deal; and even to know our friends we must wait for some critical and pressing occasion; that is, till it is too late; for it is on those very occasions that such knowledge is of use to us. What a train of vices must attend this uncertainty! Sincere friendship, real esteem, and perfect confidence are banished from among men. Jealousy, suspicion, fear, coldness, reserve, hate, and fraud lie constantly concealed

---

[1167] See Chapter 12 fior further discussion.

[1168] *Essay*, pp. 86-8.

[1169] *Essay*, pp. 22-3.

[1170] Max Weber, *Economy and Society: An Outline of Interpretive Sociology*, Berkeley: Berkeley University Press 1978, p. 636.

under that uniform and deceitful veil of politeness; that boasted candour and urbanity, for which we are indebted to the enlightened spirit of this age.[1171]

In contrast to Ferguson's perception Smith and Hume both saw commerce, not as an alienating phenomenon, but as creating superior forms of sociability by enhancing personal relations and mutual dependencies.[1172] Both reject the simple social forms admired by Ferguson in favour of large scale, non-particularistic communities regulated by impartial justice. Dismissing Ferguson's fond portrait of an intimate pre-commercial 'knot of friends' united by beneficence and common interest, Hume regards barbarity as a dreary state of 'solitude' in which each is compelled to live with their fellows in a 'distant manner'. The barren affective climate of pre-commercial life pales in comparison to the vivacity and sociability of commercial society where people 'flock into cities [and] love to receive and communicate knowledge'.[1173] Commercial life gives rise to a new type of civil society characterised by candour, openness, friendliness, and a proliferation of clubs and societies, all of which reflect the breakdown of aristocratic privilege and other exclusivistic social categories. Meanwhile, Smith thought that commercial society was best held together by sympathy and the principles of justice and utility rather than by the primary virtue of beneficence.[1174] Ferguson finds this claim untenable because it ignores the 'fact' that the 'bands of society' are actually stronger in communities where material conditions are difficult and hostile[1175] (though it will not have escaped the attentive reader's notice that this 'fact' actually supports, rather than contradicts, the utilitarian position).

7. HEDONISM: COMMERCE, WEALTH AND LUXURY

A key source of corruption is the displacement of traditional values and concerns with the new commercial 'spirit' or mentality, with its emphasis on productivity and profitability and its perverse elevation of individual prosperity to a kind of cool virtue. Ferguson disagreed with Smith and Hume that progress and the strength of the state were synonymous and appeared to harbour great reservations about the future of modern economies. Smith was particularly optimistic and sought to demonstrate that modern economies differed from those of classical reports because they were capable of exponential progress. There was to be no inevitable cycle of 'luxury, corruption, and decline' but a continual advance in prosperity for all.[1176]

The *History*, the *Essay* and the *Principles* are a sustained attack on Epicureanism[1177] and in them Ferguson pursues the Christian/Stoic theme of

---

[1171] Rousseau, 'A Discourse on the Moral Effects of the Arts and Sciences', in *Social Contract and Discourses*, pp. 6-7.

[1172] Silver, 'Friendship in Commercial Society', pp. 1480-81.

[1173] Hume, 'Of Refinement in the Arts', *Essays*, pp. 270-271.

[1174] *TMS*. II. ii. 3. 2. p. 86.

[1175] *Essay*, pp. 23-4.

[1176] Istvan Hont and Michael Ignatieff, 'Needs and Justice in the *Wealth of Nations*: An Introductory Essay', in Hont and Ignatieff, (eds.), *Wealth and Virtue*, p. 6.

[1177] Kettler, 'History and Theory in Ferguson's *Essay*', p. 452.

corruption by stressing the pitfalls of prosperity and the 'prodigality, licentiousness and brutal sensuality'[1178] which riches engender. Even though Ferguson's attempt to address the problem of luxury results in a qualified defence of it, he cannot disguise a deep ascetic streak when he associates luxury with the perversion of communal values and encouragement of individualism and selfishness. Ferguson's Stoic prejudices are doubtless responsible for this. The Stoics linked luxury with decline;[1179] Seneca inveighed against the pursuit of gratifications beyond our natural needs[1180] suggesting that 'avarice and luxury split human beings up and got them to abandon partnership for plunder'[1181] while Epictetus admonished readers of the *Enchiridion* that needs must be constrained by the demands of the body and that the concerns of the body are subordinate to those of the mind.[1182] (Ferguson agrees; the failure of citizens of the late Roman republic to observe this dictum resulted in its ruin.)[1183] Seneca regarded the increasing 'bestialisation' of morals as a sign of impending palingenesis[1184] while Polybius and all his imitators, particularly Machiavelli, make explicit that unending lust for power and gratification engender moral corruption.[1185] Meanwhile, Ferguson's more immediate inspiration, Montesquieu, (also a disciple of Stoicism) declared that 'a soul corrupted by luxury has many other desires; soon it becomes the enemy of the laws that hamper it'.[1186] The belief that prosperity and intemperate living dissipated moral character was prevalent as early as the fifth century BC. There was also the concomitant belief that virtue could be recovered via a return to primitive conditions.[1187] Ferguson personally scorned luxury, stating that ornament and equipage was 'of no value at all'[1188] and he recommended the imposition of a tax on luxury goods.[1189] He admits that the term 'luxury is somewhat ambiguous' but concludes that it may be of two types; either it is indulgence in bodily appetites beyond need or it is the indulgence of 'vanity, in what relates to the decorations of rank'.[1190] Both types are capable of corrupting.

Though Ferguson rejects primitivism in principle, he inadvertently betrays a primitivist bent in harking back to a putative golden age, the existence of which he infers from ancient history and contemporary reports of the New World. For

---

[1178] Bernstein, 'Adam Ferguson and the Idea of Progress', p. 113; *P.II.*, p. 501.

[1179] Reesor, *The Political Theory of the Old and Middle Stoa*, p. 16.

[1180] Seneca, *Letters From a Stoic*, Selected and Translated with an Introduction by Robin Campbell, London: Penguin, 1969, Letter 114. 10, p. 216.

[1181] Seneca, *Letters From a Stoic*, Letter 90, 37, p. 173.

[1182] Epictetus, *Enchiridion*, 39, pp. 37-8.

[1183] *History*, pp. 464-9, 169-70.

[1184] Roche, *Rousseau: Stoic and Romantic*, p. 10.

[1185] Springborg, *Western Republicanism*, p. 63.

[1186] Montesquieu, *Laws*, 1. 7. 2, p. 98.

[1187] Reesor, *The Political Theory of the Old and Middle Stoa*, p. 16.

[1188] *Institutes*, p. 247.

[1189] But for reasons related to equity and 'justice' rather than asceticism: Whereas taxes on the consumption of 'ornament' and 'costly accommodation' are acceptable, taxes on 'the necessaries of life, are a tax on the poor' and this is wrong. *Institutes*, pp. 256-8.

[1190] *P.I.*, p. 243; *History*, p. 109.

example, he notes with approval how the 'American tribe[s]' have fortuitously evaded 'the poison which is administered by our traders of Europe'.[1191] By contrast, populations of the polished age must cope with the displacement over time of the solid, traditional and sociable norms in favour of moralities which fail to censure, and implicitly reward personal ambition, consumerism and acquisitiveness. Because market society nurtures the self-regarding passions and provides poor encouragement for the development of the civic and other-regarding passions citizens soon succumb to avidity and hedonism. When people neglect the public, despotism is sure to follow.

By contrast, Hume and Smith both celebrated the positive, 'softening' effects of commerce. Hume, in particular, regarded Ferguson's fears as exaggerated. Remonstrating against pessimists 'who declaim against present times, and magnify the virtue of remote ancestors', he declared that all the good things in life are linked causally and are, moreover, peculiar to modernity. He also believed that '[t]he liberties of England, so far from decaying since the improvements in the arts, have never flourished so much as during that period.'[1192]

Both Smith and Hume cite the proliferation of luxury goods as a key cause of the welcome demise of feudalism and the new 'age of freedom and civilisation'.[1193] With the development of exchange and manufactures it became possible for the feudal barons to acquire luxury commodities whereas under a purely feudal system wealth could only be deployed in the maintenance of retainers for the purposes of military security. The availability of luxuries allowed the wealth of the barons to be dispersed in other ways and for the labour power of the now independent serfs to be employed productively. Gradually and without intending it, the barons destroyed their own power base. This most important 'revolution' led, in turn, to the growth of a new class of burghers (the 'merchants and artificers') whose material and moral influence brought about greater liberty and a more even distribution of power.[1194] Once the great mass of tenants had attained their independence, feudal proprietors 'were no longer capable of interrupting the regular execution of justice'.[1195] For Smith and Hume, then, the proliferation of luxury goods is basically innocent and a major cause of national prosperity and positive social change. Smith did not think that increased prosperity and consumption led to corruption but argued instead for the communal benefits of self-interest and division of labour via a trickle down effect.[1196] He also believed that commerce had a tendency to enhance social cohesion and to provide conditions for greater freedom, security, and better government.

It may seem surprising that John Sekora has argued that Ferguson attempted 'to remove the concept of luxury altogether from the arena of politics'[1197] by demonstrating its naturalness. Despite the abundance of ascetic and moralistic

---

[1191] *Essay*, p. 80.

[1192] Hume, 'Of Refinement in the Arts'; *Essays*, pp. 278, 270-2, 276-7.

[1193] Hume, *History*, Vol. II. Ch. 23, p. 522.

[1194] Smith, *WN*. III.iv.5, pp. 412-14; III. iv. 11-18, pp. 419-22.

[1195] Christopher Berry, *The Idea of Luxury*, Cambridge: Cambridge University Press, 1994, pp. 157-8.

[1196] Smith, *WN*, I.i.10-11, pp. 22-4.

[1197] Sekora, *Luxury*, p. 104.

rhetoric in Ferguson, this is basically correct. Ferguson took part in the reformulation of questions of luxury by linking luxury to benign and ordained progress, thereby stripping it of any moral dimension. But his ultimate commitments here are obscured by an abiding ambivalence. On an initial reading he seems to be saying that luxury is pernicious and that the 'practice of commercial arts' and pursuit of 'private advantage' causes agents to become increasingly 'effeminate, mercenary, and sensual'.[1198] But on closer inspection it is also clear that, from an economic point of view, '[d]ecadence has...a very real place in Ferguson's scheme of evolution'.[1199] He concedes that luxury is a function of natural progress and admits that our naturally insatiable needs have utility because they generate progress and prosperity. The universal human predilection for fripperies resulting from unchecked desire is unavoidable: The 'list of articles' which attract our 'attention' is not restricted to those of 'subsistence or safety'. Our 'views extend to decoration and ornament, as well as to use and convenience' and all these wants are deemed 'original'.[1200]

It must be remembered that Ferguson is extremely conflicted about the increased prosperity of the modern age; on the one hand he fears its dissipating effects yet, on the other, it represents progress, which is, after all, natural and brings with it many positive effects.[1201] His views can be understood in the context of contemporary developments in economic thinking on the question of luxury. Prior to the eighteenth century luxury had been condemned by 'oeconomists' as both morally and economically destructive, but by the beginning of the eighteenth century, despite dissent in some quarters (for example Rousseau and Henry Home, Lord Kames)[1202] it became an increasingly acceptable view that 'the domestic consumption of luxury items by the rich created employment...stimulated the circulation of money and commodities' and indirectly encouraged population growth.[1203] Smith, Hume, Josiah Tucker and James Steuart all subscribed to this latter view and Ferguson seems to have been strongly influenced by it. He even agreed with Mandeville who had controversially pioneered the argument that the distinction between a luxury and a necessity was socially constructed, or in Ferguson's terms, 'vague and relative'.[1204] His views on luxury were not, therefore, identical to those of his Stoic predecessors

---

[1198] *Essay*, p. 237.

[1199] Lehmann, *Adam Ferguson*, p. 148.

[1200] *History*, p. 109.

[1201] Sekora, *Luxury*, p. 104.

[1202] Rousseau wrote: '[W]ithout insisting on the necessity of sumptuary laws, can it be denied that rectitude of morals is essential to the duration of empires, and that luxury is diametrically opposed to such rectitude?'. 'A Discourse on the Moral Effects of the Arts and Sciences', in *The Social Contract and Discourses*, p. 17. An important difference, though, is that Ferguson did not endorse Rousseau's view that the 'dissolution of morals' was a '*necessary* consequence of luxury'. Ibid., p. 19. My emphasis. Kames was particularly preoccupied with the theme of the pernicious effect of luxury, declaring it to be 'the ruin of every state where it prevailed'. Cited in Scheffer, 'Idea of Decline', p. 168.

[1203] Nevertheless, some economists remained committed to the view that, because luxury was pernicious, a sumptuary law should be introduced. Thomas Alcock was one such advocate. Firth, 'Moral Supervision and Social Order', pp. 45, 48. See also, John E. Crowley, 'The Sensibility of Comfort', *The American Historical Review*, Vol. 104 (3) 1999, pp. 749-782.

[1204] *Essay*, pp. 231-2. See also *P.I.*, p. 248.

who regarded it as both unnatural and vicious.[1205] He does not (at least ultimately) conceive luxury as contrary to nature; neither is it synonymous with vice. Luxury only becomes a vice, as seemed to be the case with polished nations, when it is 'unsupported by personal elevation and virtue'.[1206] The 'imagination' of the undisciplined epicure is so 'debauched' that s/he loses all sense of what it is to lead a meaningful or natural life.[1207] Even in the indulgence of their frivolous pursuits they may be seen to 'exhibit a state of agitation'. They are bored without even being aware of it: in the midst of their pleasures they are actually experiencing a form of 'suffering and pain' because their civically active natures are not employed in 'manly occupation[s]' natural to our species. Though superficially possessed of all that a person could wish for, the idle rich are really destitute, 'wretched' and 'corrupt'; life, for them, Ferguson concludes with somewhat misplaced sympathy, is 'listless... unprofitable' and meaningless. They have chosen the Epicurean way and denied the key lesson of Stoicism that happiness consists in living according to our active, other-regarding urges. But where people take proper care about the cultivation of the civic virtues, the problems of consumption are containable. It is possible to enjoy luxury so long as the pleasures of the body remain subordinate to those of the mind and heart.[1208] For Ferguson it is mental, not physical, dissipation that is most to be feared for '[e]ven delicate living, and good accommodation, are not found to enervate the body.'[1209]

Once again, Ferguson attempts to steer a course between antique and modern traditions by arguing that it is only the *abuse* of wealth that leads to national decay. The tension between his civic-humanist and commercial-humanist tendencies is resolved by the claim that wealth is itself innocent, especially when obtained by hard work and the exercise of virtue, but its improper acquisition and use precipitates corruption.[1210] The source of evil, is located, not in progress itself, but in the failure of people to regulate their insatiable desires. According to Ferguson, this is closer to the Stoic position than is commonly thought. 'They preferred pleasure to pain and the constituents of prosperity to those of adversity: but they maintained that good and evil consisted not in the presence or absence of either, but in the proper habit and disposition of the mind relating to them'.[1211]

Human needs are naturally infinite, reflecting our lively, progressive natures and unlimited creativity[1212] but their pursuit should be externally directed to the community and to such higher, nobler objects as knowledge and virtue, rather than inwardly to private pleasures.[1213] After we have secured the relatively 'easily supplied...wants of nature' our desires persist but, so long these 'appetites' are

---

[1205] 'Luxury has turned her back on nature'. Seneca, *Letters from a Stoic*, Letter 90, 19. p. 168.

[1206] *Essay*, p. 241.

[1207] *P.II.*, p. 342.

[1208] *Essay*, pp. 248-51.

[1209] *Essay*, p. 216.

[1210] *Institutes*, p. 146. Hiroshi Mizuta makes this same point in 'Two Adams in the Scottish Enlightenment'.

[1211] *Institutes*, p. 138.

[1212] *P.I.*, p. 244.

[1213] *P.II.*, p. 341.

'uncorrupted', all will be well. Ferguson conceives this balance as 'fully consistent with the higher and better pursuits of human life'. The 'voluptuary' mistakes the proper objects of insatiable need because 'he' pursues 'his' animal needs beyond the natural 'force of his appetite' and contrary to the 'solicitations of sense'.[1214] There must be a clear distinction made between positive, dynamic insatiability and corrupted greed; between desires which perfect and those which merely bloat and vitiate. Ferguson thus distances himself from many of his classical sources on the question of material progress. With proper care it was indeed possible to distinguish — and therefore hopefully quarantine — 'technological and material development from the moral and psychological realms'.[1215]

Though Ferguson seems a little confused here (possibly as a result of Stoic inconsistency on the same subject but also, undoubtedly, because he is genuinely conflicted) his ultimate interest in canvassing the effects of luxury is not to moralise on consumption so much as to critique the loss of values experienced by commercial society and to caution against the likely consequences. The *Essay* conveys the most important lesson of history and moral philosophy: that wealth is not the key determinant of national happiness. Since luxury is not in itself a vice, and comfortable accommodations by themselves do not drain strength, we must look out for the presence of social and political arrangements which allow the mercenary tendencies of commercial agents to flourish. As noted, these conditions are the division of labour (in particular the use of standing armies) over-extension and a neglect of the civic virtues. Citizens who pursue material reward alone and 'bestow their attention on trifles', who have specialised their labour to the extent that they find themselves unable to fulfil their civic duties, are most susceptible to the encroachment of despotism. As Ferguson tells us: 'He whose office is to govern a supine or abject people, cannot, for a moment, cease to extend his powers.'[1216] People must guard jealously their civic virtue, their political efficacy and their readiness to defend their political 'rights'. Where a nation's inhabitants suffer from 'the disadvantages of a feeble spirit' their 'national constitution' must be imperilled and the state's 'political welfare' tenuous.[1217]

7.1   Perverted Authority Values and the Degeneration of Statesmen

Part of the danger of commercial society is that values have become so distorted that, not only is statecraft a forgotten art, but the people themselves have lost all sense of appropriate authority values; they have lost their ability to discriminate between good and bad leaders. Polished nations experience a shift in values where rank merit is calculated, not in terms of 'higher' criteria such as wisdom or chivalry, but by the vulgar index of wealth. Ferguson nowhere rejects rank distinctions out of hand; in fact he conceives them as socially useful, even invaluable. His objection was that rank distinctions based on wealth alone tend to create fertile conditions for

---

[1214] *P.II.*, p. 342.

[1215] To use Fania Oz-Salzberger's words. *Translating the Enlightenment*, p. 113.

[1216] *Essay*, p. 253.

[1217] *Essay,* p. 245.

the ascendance of despots since they psychologically predispose citizens to slavish relations.[1218] The superficial criterion of wealth is an inadequate indication of fitness for public service. 'Mere wealth', Ferguson opines, 'has no natural connection with merit' contrary to the 'odious presumption' of the 'purse-proud.'[1219] Public dangers follow where 'the disparities of rank and fortune which are necessary to the pursuit or enjoyment of luxury, introduce false grounds of precedency and estimation'.[1220] The 'reputation of courage, courtly manners, and a certain elevation of mind', is replaced by a reverence for 'equipage and mere decoration' and the desire to 'feed a personal vanity, or to indulge a sickly and effeminate fancy.' Fripperies and 'pageant' constitute 'our estimate of what is excellent.' We begin to 'pay our court to [our master's] station, and look up with an envious, servile or dejected mind, to what is, in itself, scarcely fit to amuse children'.[1221]

Ferguson's target here might well be Smith. Although the latter also ridiculed 'the frivolous accomplishments' of the 'man of fashion' while lauding the 'solid and masculine virtues of a warrior, a statesman, a philosopher or a legislator'[1222] he does endorse the 'slavish' relations that Ferguson finds so objectionable. According to Smith, because of the vulgarity of 'the great mob of mankind', social distinctions are more securely founded on 'the plain and palpable difference of birth and fortune, than upon the invisible and often uncertain difference of wisdom and virtue'.[1223] Ferguson disagrees: the hero of the commercial age is a dubious, indeed dangerous, role model for 'he' will undoubtedly infect 'all orders of men, with equal venality, servility and cowardice'.[1224]

The sources for Ferguson's views here all seem to have been classical or neo-classical. Seneca made an almost identical case for the contagious effect of hedonism in Letter VII.[1225] In the *Republic* Plato envisages the collapse of his ideal state in terms which foreshadow Ferguson's; mistakes made in the eugenics programme would lead to the instatement of unworthy leaders.[1226] Polybius argued that the debauchery of the sons of statesmen 'transformed an aristocracy into an oligarchy'[1227] while Chryssipus attacked the whole conception of noble birth, underlining the conceit of the nobles and arguing that the rank of a person's parents was irrelevant.[1228] Machiavelli discoursed on the degeneracy of the heirs of hereditary princes,[1229] while Montesquieu feared that the degeneration of aristocracy

---

[1218] *Essay*, p. 240.

[1219] *P.I.*, p. 245.

[1220] *Essay*, p. 237.

[1221] *Essay*, pp. 238-9.

[1222] *TMS.* I.iii.3. 6., p. 63.

[1223] *TMS.* VI. ii. 1.20-1, pp. 225-6.

[1224] *Essay*, p. 241.

[1225] Seneca, *Letters from a Stoic*, Letter 7, 10. p. 43.

[1226] Passmore, *The Perfectibility of Man*, p. 195.

[1227] Polybius, *Rise of the Roman Empire*, 6. 8. p. 308. See also Springborg, *Western Republicanism*, p. 66 for further discussion.

[1228] Reesor, *Political Theory of the Old and Middle Stoa*, p. 23.

[1229] Machiavelli, *Discourses*, 1. 2. p. 107.

would introduce 'a spirit of nonchalance, laziness, and abandon, which will make a state with neither force nor spring.'[1230]

But Ferguson's position is slightly different from those he emulates. It is not only the dissipation of the ancient nobles he seems to fear but the undiscipline of the nouveau riche, a new breed of elites, oblivious to the obligations imposed by the traditional codes of chivalry and noblesse oblige.[1231] Approving the maxim of Tacitus that 'the admiration of riches leads to despotical government'[1232] Ferguson censures the bacchanalian pursuits of the newly rich with unbridled wrath. Those '[n]ursed in luxury' would undoubtedly lack 'courage in the field', the real testing ground of virtue.[1233] Any respect held for them would have to be, not only misguided, but dangerous because it introduces 'a species of monarchical subordination, without that sense of high birth and hereditary honours which render the boundaries of rank fixed and determinate, and which teach men to act in their stations with force and propriety.' Mindless 'respect towards mere wealth' casts 'a shade on the lustre of personal qualities, or family distinction.'[1234]

Increased prosperity brings an ever-widening wealth gap and the community becomes polarised; at one extreme, a class of prodigal rich, at the other a class of 'supine', alienated poor infected with the servility of those who rule them and kept at arm's length from public life by specialisation and centralised rule.[1235] Once people have become corrupted, despotism is only a step away for '[t]he rules of despotism are made for the government of corrupted men'.[1236] 'Servility' is extremely dangerous to the integrity of a mixed monarchy which, Ferguson argues, is the only constitution that actually benefits from conflict, agitation, faction and dissension. An opinionated, critical and vocal public secures the virtue of leaders but once a population has become apathetic and corrupted, the tendency for a constitutional monarchy to degenerate into despotism becomes likely. 'Sensuality is a disorder of the mind'[1237] which suppresses or perverts our natural urges, particularly those with civic functions. People, naturally factious and adversarial, become docile and apathetic under the influence of sensuality. The healthy conflict that characterises a robust constitution dissipates where the 'cravings of luxury silence even the voice of party and faction'.[1238]

All of the above conditions conspire to make an easy path for ambitious tyrants to achieve their aims. The apathetic stupor induced by luxury, the politically demobilising effects of specialisation, and the disorienting and alienating conditions generated by over-extension, all create conditions that subvert and eventually

---

[1230] Montesquieu, *Laws*,1.8. 5, pp. 115-16.

[1231] *P.I.*, p. 245.

[1232] *Essay,* p. 248.

[1233] *History*, pp. 277-8, 294.

[1234] *Essay*, p. 223.

[1235] Here the discussion becomes a little confusing. Ferguson seems to be condemning the system of rank distinctions whereas at other times he suggests that it is both natural and beneficial.

[1236] *Essay,* p. 228.

[1237] Yet Ferguson is careful to explain that the pursuit of pleasure is natural but only if it is indulged in occasionally and temporarily. *P.II.*, pp. 386.

[1238] *Essay*, p. 248.

destroy the polity, terminating in one inevitable outcome: tyranny, defined as either military or autocratic rule by force. Corruption is thus the result of both political and moral degeneration. Those who fail to live according to nature and to actively exercise the other-regarding passions will meet with the same fate as the citizens of ancient Rome. Though progress might be inevitable and, in many respects beneficial, it pays to remember that '[t]he boasted refinements...of the polished age, are not divested of danger.'[1239]

8. CONCLUDING REMARKS

Ferguson's account of progress and corruption is noteworthy because he synthesises traditional aetiologies of retrogression with causes novel to a commercialising age, thereby signalling the first tremors of a paradigm shift in the study of social life. The impressions of actual modern conditions are combined with a classical perspective to produce an original outlook on modernity.

Ferguson's treatment of corruption shows him attempting to steer a course between Stoic austerity and a more modern embrace of progress. There are moments where his navigation falters, causing him to seem inconsistent and even confused. Specifically, while he denies the moral dimension of luxury and decrees social and technical progress to be inevitable and positive, he frequently assumes an, apparently unconscious, primitivistic asceticism. Similarly, his policy on militias jars against his general view of progress and seems arbitrary. Nevertheless, the discussion is replete with many prescient, sometimes brilliant insights, some of which anticipated and influenced nineteenth and twentieth century sociology. He provided the first penetrating analysis of the social effects of commercial expansion, bureaucratisation and specialisation and although there is no fully developed critique of 'capitalism' inside his analysis, there are clear intimations of an embryonic (albeit purely descriptive rather than normative) theory of alienation and anomie effects. Ferguson also provides one of the earliest accounts of the negative impact of consumerism on friendship and political life and the importance of social capital and political efficacy in the maintenance of strong polities.

[1239] *Essay,* p. 219.

CHAPTER 11

PROGRESS AND DECLINE

Ferguson's Ambivalence

Throughout his body of work Ferguson is trying to show us that society has progressed naturally and predictably from a 'rude' to a 'polished' state in accordance with the species' naturally progressive tendencies. And yet, despite his insistence that progress is immanent in the divine plan,[1240] and that the commercial stage is a 'natural' step in this process, Ferguson harbours great reservations about progress, particularly with respect to developments in the 'polished' or commercial stage. He seems to be saying that the commercial age brings with it the likelihood of national ruin and that if Britain continues on its present path, it is bound to meet with the same fate as Rome, namely to degenerate and decline, potentially resulting in complete social, economic and political breakdown. Ferguson's ominous critique of progress seems at odds with the optimism and theodicy of the whole idea of spontaneous order. Even as he lauds progress he seems also to fear it and this creates a deep ambiguity, even a rupture, within his system.

Ferguson's fear of corruption and interest in diagnosing and remedying the ills of the commercial age was not a peripheral concern incidental to a generally progressive history, but consumed a good deal of his attention. How does this apparent pessimism fit with an interpretation of Fergusonian order as self-regulating, progressivist and even perfectibilist? The following discussion seeks to reconcile this conundrum'[1241] in terms of Fergusonian theology.

1. POSSIBLE EXPLANATIONS

There are a number of explanations which could account for the tension in Ferguson's historiography. It could be argued, for example, that Ferguson was either inconsistent, ambivalent or that his views changed over time. Alternatively, one could pursue an interpretational line by reading his history as eschatological, cyclical or palingenetic.

The first suggestion that Ferguson was simply inconsistent has been the quite understandable conclusion of more than one scholar.[1242] Though Ferguson is

---

[1240] Effected by divinely endued drives. *Essay*, p. 14; *P.I.*, pp. 190, 313.

[1241] Robert Heilbroner has argued for a similar dualism in Adam Smith's work. The present discussion owes much to his analysis. Heilbroner, 'The Paradox of Progress', pp. 243-62.

[1242] Kettler, for example, identifies Ferguson's inconsistency as a function of 'conflicting commitments'. *The Social and Political Thought of Adam Ferguson* p. 293. See also Camic, *Experience and Enlightenment*, p. 54.

definitely ambivalent, especially when compared to Smith or Hume, it seems unlikely that any professional philosopher would remain so *consistently* inconsistent to the extent that such an explanation demands. Since Ferguson's reservations about progress were far from incidental it seems unlikely that he neglected to think their implications through more carefully. Nor does it seem likely that he would have submitted for publication work this poorly developed, especially over such a protracted lifetime of scholarship.

Another suggestion is that Ferguson's views changed over time, that the intense interest in retrogression displayed in the *Essay* faded as he matured.[1243] Although it could be said that Ferguson pursued the subject with less vigour in his later works his absorption with the theme of corruption stayed with him right up to and including his last and most optimistically perfectibilist work, the *Principles*. This title contains numerous references to the theme of retrogression including some trenchant criticisms about prodigality and imperialism.[1244] The closing paragraphs underline Ferguson's enduring commitment to the theme of retrogression; in them he focuses on what he has decided is the key lesson of history and philosophy; that proper care of the 'human mind' will determine whether a nation progresses or declines.[1245] Ferguson's reduced emphasis on corruption in the *Principles* is more likely to be attributable to the fact that his subject matter had shifted from history to the more general topic of moral philosophy. This explanation is borne out by the fact that the much earlier *Institutes*, upon which the *Principles* is based, also contains fewer references to the theme of decline than either the *Essay* or the *History* even though it was published just two years after the *Essay* and a full fourteen years prior to the publication of the *History*. In other words, the varying intensity of Ferguson's concern with corruption cannot be explained chronologically but is more likely related to differences in scope and focus between his various publications.

Another possibility is that Ferguson thought the world was in its senility, or that he was anticipating a final judgement day heralding the destruction of the earth.[1246] This seems reasonable enough given that some of Ferguson's most influential predecessors did push this type of fatalistic line. Notwithstanding the traditional Christian teaching of a final judgement day, there is also a pessimistic strain in Isaac Newton's thought. Newton believed that the world 'unwound' or tended towards dissolution and could only be reconstituted with the Providential introduction of comets.[1247] Rousseau, meanwhile, conceived history in typically primitivist terms as continually declining.[1248] It would not have been unusual, therefore, for Ferguson to take such a line; in addition, the decline of benevolence decried with such urgency

---

[1243] Whitney, *Primitivism and the Idea of Progress*, p. 153.

[1244] See, for example, *P.I.*, pp. 34-5, 238, 313-14; *P.II*, pp. 295, 487, 501.

[1245] *P.II.*, p. 512.

[1246] See Istvan Hont, 'The 'Rich Country, Poor Country' Debate in Scottish Classical Political Economy', in Hont and Ignatieff (eds.), p. 296. Hont also argues that Ferguson saw commercial growth as unending.

[1247] D. Kubrin, 'Newton and the Cyclical Cosmos: Providence and the Mechanical Philosophy', *Journal of the History of Ideas*, Vol. 28 (3), 1967, pp. 325-46, p. 342.

[1248] Leigh, 'Rousseau and the Scottish Enlightenment', p. 3.

by Ferguson was precisely the argument employed by eighteenth century primitivists to confirm the theory of degeneration.[1249]

Richard Sher has argued that Ferguson's preoccupation with corruption is really a variation on the traditional Calvinist and Scottish Presbyterian sermonising device of a jeremiad whereby national calamities are conceived as punishments by God for immorality and sinfulness. This interpretation is, initially, quite a persuasive one. Like Ferguson, the preacher of impending doom posits luxury, apathy, selfishness and atheism as its precursors, with the resulting catastrophe subsequently redeeming the people in the eyes of God.[1250] Yet, while Ferguson's discourse on corruption is infused with the sermonising spirit of the jeremiad, his rejection of the concept of sin and his Deistic conception of God as a distant, non-interventionist First Cause, strictly precludes this option. Neither can his interest in corruption be linked to the kind of primitivistic leanings so often attributed to Rousseau because he explicitly rejects primitivism. Despite some residual nostalgia, Ferguson, ultimately, mourns no lost paradise. The 'polished' or commercial stage is, after all, natural and, moreover, divinely ordained. Ferguson rejects eschatology outright, subscribing unequivocally to an open-ended view of history.[1251] Even though he outlines only three stages of history he never suggests that the polished age is the final or end point of history. His much publicised aversion to conjecture would prevent him from making any predictions about a possible fourth stage.[1252] Human progress is an asymptotic process and, though subject to interruption, there is no reason to suppose that retrogression is an inevitable effect of modernity.[1253] Rome was, after all, a pre-modern state. What it had failed to do was secure the virtue of its citizens. The 'duration' of our social and political institutions, Ferguson insists, 'is not fixed to any limited period'. In other words, the life spans of civilisations are not finite or determined but are contingent on internal political condition. Ferguson's fear is not of modernity itself, but of any of its aspects that might threaten public virtue, and these, in Britain's case, happened to have been brought on by industrialisation, commercialism and imperialism. Retrogression threatens all prosperous, successful nations, not just the polished ones. Ferguson did not, therefore, believe that

---

[1249] Whitney, *Primitivism and the Idea of Progress*, p. 22. A number of scholars have concluded that progress, for Ferguson, was not necessarily inevitable. Duncan Forbes, for example, suggests that Ferguson's history 'certainly does not belong to the history of the idea of progress'. Forbes, Introduction to *Essay* p. xiv. See also Lehmann, *Adam Ferguson*, pp. 148-9 and Hopfl, 'From Savage to Scotsman', p. 37.

[1250] Sher, *Church and University*, pp. 43, 198-201.

[1251] *P.I.*, pp. 313-16, 47, 184-5, 190-1; *Essay*, pp. 12-14. Other scholars have also given Ferguson's history a perfectibilist/progressivist reading. Willke suggests that Ferguson's conception of nature 'would not permit him to accept a necessary cycle of advance and decline. Nature's plan is one of improvement and prosperity'. For Willke, the progress/decline tension is resolved by the explanation that Ferguson's references to corruption are 'related to the life of national or political units' whereas his discussion of progress is generalised to 'mankind at large'. Willke, *Historical Thought of Adam Ferguson*, pp. 172, 112. Bernstein argues that, despite the 'intermissions in national exertions' he records, Ferguson believed in the 'long-range inevitability' of human progress. Bernstein, 'Ferguson and Progress', p. 115. According to Mossner, Ferguson's insistence on the inevitability of progress was Hume's major objection to the *Essay*. Mossner, *Life of David Hume*, p. 543.

[1252] *P.I.*, p. 316.

[1253] *P.I.*, p. 194.

civilisation was winding down. But can it be said that he held to a cyclical or *ana*cyclical view of history? The latter might perhaps seem the more viable option since it accommodates some progress.

It has, indeed, been argued that Ferguson subscribes to a cyclical view of history.[1254] This seems superficially plausible given that he had ample precedent for a cyclical historiography. Some of his most important influences (Plato, Aristotle, the Stoics, Machiavelli and Montesquieu) held to cyclical or palingenetic views of history. Machiavelli, for example, insisted that the 'inevitability of corruption' was 'the one great observable fact in human affairs'[1255] while the doctrine of palingenesis (the periodic destruction and re-creation of the world) is fundamental to Stoic theory.[1256] Cicero maintained that the world would be destroyed by fire[1257] and Seneca attributed one of causes of the decline of the Roman Empire to the malevolence of the natural order which lets nothing stay at the peak of its development: 'Nothing', he wrote, 'is durable, whether for an individual or for a society'.[1258]

But this interpretation also fails to withstand close scrutiny. Ferguson states his aversion to the cyclical view unequivocally in both the *Principles* and the *Essay*. The device of dividing history up into categories and periods (which Ferguson himself employs) is, he admits, problematic, for this type of thinking can mislead us to an endist conception of human history: '[I]n no period is the subject stationary'.[1259] Indeed, as if to correct any false impression that Ferguson might himself have conveyed by his use of the 'childhood, manhood, old age' analogy to describe the three stages of our development, he explains that, although the 'image indeed is apposite', it is 'obvious, that the case of nations, and that of individuals, are very different'. While the 'human frame has a general course...and a limited duration', society, 'whose constituent members are renewed in every generation' enjoys *'perpetuated youth, and accumulating advantages'*.[1260]

Ferguson conceived progress as linear and asymptotic, a process of 'continual increments of knowledge and thought' and 'continual accessions' of skills, habits, arts, powers and moral 'discernment'. Granted, human history is subject to 'vicissitude' and 'interruption' but it is always able to get itself back onto a progressive track.[1261] Societies are not like individual people; they do not have finite life-spans but are continually renewed and borne along by fresh generations: '[W]e

---

[1254] For example, William Lehmann asserts: 'In fact Ferguson holds quite definitely to a cyclical view of history'. *Adam Ferguson*, p. 149.

[1255] Mullen, 'Republics for Expansion', p. 324.

[1256] Marcus Aurelius referred to 'the great cyclic renewals of creation'.*Meditations*, 11.1, p. 165. See also, Epictetus, *Discourses*, 2. 1. 17-24, p. 219; 3. 8. 2-7, p. 89.

[1257] Cicero, *De Republica*, 6. 21, p. 277.

[1258] Seneca, *Letters from a Stoic*, Selected and Translated with an Introduction by Robin Campbell, London: Penguin, 1969, Letter 91, p. 179. Marcus also wrote: 'All parts of the Whole...must in time decay'. Marcus Aurelius, *Meditations*, 10. 7. p. 153.

[1259] *P.I.*, p. 192.

[1260] *Essay*, p. 199. My emphasis. Humanity is 'susceptible of indefinite advancement'. *P.I.*, p. 183. To 'advance... is the state of nature relative to' humanity. *P.I.*, p. 199.

[1261] *P.I.*, pp. 190-2.

cannot expect to find imbecilities connected with mere age and length of days'.[1262] Apart from the textual evidence there are also other arguments against a cyclical or palingenetic interpretation of Fergusonian corruption. To begin with, his aetiology of corruption expounds causes which are entirely unprecedented, some of which have positive, progressive dimensions or are by-products of an ultimately progressive process. These are the division of labour, the growth of cities, the increased wealth and luxury of nations, the introduction of commercial values and reduced levels of conflict and war. Ferguson never recommends any devolvement or social revisionism in these directions.[1263] The ubiquitous Roman analogy can be misleading. It stands as a generalised model of a prosperous empire but its usefulness as an analogy has limitations and there is no reason to assume that Ferguson definitely expected the British empire to take the same path. Rome stands as a lesson, not a forecast.

Furthermore, Ferguson's history is Providentially teleological. History has a purpose and, despite his presentation of it in the form of a stadial thesis, Ferguson rejects Aristotle's static sequence of development that is based on a doctrine of immutable forms. On this latter view development is merely the realisation of limited, determined potential with no leeway for genuine progress. Ferguson's God would never condemn 'His' favourite creation to a meaningless cycle of growth and degeneration. Rather, God has destined us for moral perfection and a continual accession of attainments that can only be striven for in the context of a linear history.

Another argument against this kind of interpretation is that the cyclical (and *ana*cyclical) view of history is related to the law of nature Machiavelli adopted from Polybius that single types of polities are unstable and therefore doomed to 'degenerate'.[1264] Unlike the Roman Republic (in which 'all the powers of the Roman Senate had been transferred to popular assemblies' thereby bringing 'the Liberty of Rome' to 'an end.')[1265] the Britain Ferguson wrote about was a more balanced, mixed monarchy, therefore any pessimism would have been checked by this fact. Ferguson frequently advertised his opinion that a mixed monarchy was the constitutional form best suited to British conditions[1266] therefore the fate of Britain and Rome need not be identical.

In any case neither the cyclical nor *ana*cyclical interpretation throws any light on the decline/progress paradox. The more promising *ana*cyclical view (promising because it seems to accommodate some progress) is not applicable to Ferguson's history because it is still dependent on an invariable cycle of constitutions which the existence of a mixed monarchy (in Britain's case) obviated. And anyway, the whole

---

[1262] *Essay*, p. 199.

[1263] Except in the case of soldiering. 'Separation of the Departments', *Collection of Essays*, No. 15, pp. 150-1.

[1264] Stewart Crehan, 'The Roman Analogy', *Literature and History*, Vol. 6 (1), pp. 19-42, p. 23. For Machiavelli's views on the superiority of mixed forms of government see *Discourses*, 1. 2, p. 109.

[1265] *Remarks*, p. 14.

[1266] *Remarks*, pp. 15-16; *Institutes*, p. 273. Ferguson believed that a sound constitutional framework is marked by its complexity, and by its broad distribution and clear separation of powers. For more detail see Chapter 12.

idea of cycles is anathema to Ferguson. They make no sense in a universe created by a benign Deity intent on our development. 'God' created us in order to preserve us along with all of our accomplishments. Recognising the perils of presuming to apprehend the Creator's mind, Ferguson ventures to suggest that we may infer this purpose from the evidence of observable tendencies. Only life forms which possess souls are destined to progress indefinitely and although humans possess identical natures, this should not lead us to a view of these natures as static or invariable: The 'uniformity' of human nature belies our adaptable, dynamic and progressive tendencies.[1267]

The pronounced ambivalences in Ferguson have led one scholar to conclude (possibly in exasperation) that Ferguson held no thesis of history at all, that his historiography was neither cyclical, inevitably progressive, nor inevitably retrogressive.[1268] But it is hard to doubt that Ferguson's historiography is basically progressivist. Certainly, he admitted that some societies did not progress due to environmental disadvantages or an unwillingness on the part of a populace to exert its active energies[1269] but, on the whole, he thought that progress was inevitable because it was universally and biologically inherent. The 'law of estimation or progression' is an 'ultimate fact in the nature of man'.[1270] In other words it is self-evidently and incontrovertibly true. Further, the Creator has ensured that '(t)he system of nature is secured from decay'.[1271] The telic dimension of Ferguson's historical sociology confirms the inevitability of progress while allowing for the unavoidable interruptions: 'Man is *made* for ...the attainments of reason. If, by any conjuncture, he is deprived of these advantages, he will sooner or later find his way to them'.[1272]

The misleading thing about Ferguson's history is that even as he keeps the argument from design, a teleological framework and the chain of being doctrine, it still embodies a highly developed theory of progress. The other misleading aspect is that Ferguson's aetiology of corruption is influenced profoundly by ancient authors of cyclical, *ana*cyclical or palingenetic histories. In addition, Ferguson himself does little to avert confusion; indeed, the sense of ambivalence he visits on his reader almost seems intentional.

In any case, Ferguson's history is neither eschatological, cyclical, nor *ana*yclical. Neither is it arbitrary but rather, open-ended, purposeful and inevitable. How, then, can the retrogression theme be accommodated within an otherwise optimistic scheme? The remainder of the discussion reveals a textual resolution to the Ferguson paradox via an examination of his approach to the problem of theodicy. The key construct in this solution is the Christian/Ciceronian principle of free will which causes people to err unwittingly. *Error*, not evil, is the cause of retrogression[1273] and

---

[1267] *P.I.*, pp. 321-4.
[1268] McDowell, 'Commerce, Virtue and Politics', p. 541.
[1269] *P.I.*, pp. 194-5.
[1270] *Institutes*, p. 90.
[1271] *Institutes*, p. 126.
[1272] *P.I.*, p. 199. My emphasis.
[1273] As Ferguson states explicitly in the *Essay*, p. 212.

since error is always amenable to correction Ferguson is able to demonstrate the contingent nature of retrogression and even its constructive role in the divine master plan. By this reasoning he is able to balance his recognition of the pathologies of modernity while simultaneously maintaining an optimistic commitment to the laws of spontaneous order.

2. THE PROBLEM OF THEODICY: PERFECTIBILISM, FREE WILL AND SELF-CREATION

As a self-confessed 'theist' who believed in a world created perfect, 'sublime' and 'beautiful', Ferguson is confronted with the problem of explaining the relationship between progress and the problem of theodicy, that is, the nature and existence of evil (in this case, the social evils attendant on modernity).[1274] If humankind is progressive does that mean we are imperfect, tainted with the burden of original sin? Moreover, if we *are* imperfect, what is our relationship to the perfect goodness of God? Ferguson addresses the same puzzle which first absorbed the Stoics: 'If man is a particle of God, why is he not automatically perfect?'[1275]

Ferguson responds by showing how apparent evil (in this case corruption) is an inevitable result of our capacity for free will. Though unpleasant, evil has many positive effects particularly as it hones the moral faculties. Corruption is therefore conceived as an unavoidable consequence of our perfectibility, a natural by-product of our desire to develop, grow, and effect our ultimate union with the mind of the Creator.[1276] In other words, any misfortune resulting from human independence is always compensated by its long-term benefits because a certain degree of evil is unavoidable in the pursuit of moral goodness.[1277] Ferguson reformulates the problem of theodicy by replacing the idea of original sin with that of original *ignorance* and by taking on board the Socratic (later Stoic) doctrine that vice is synonymous with ignorance and that our progress through the stages of history represents a perpetual quest to shed this ignorance.[1278] Ferguson was not alone among the moderns in resorting to this type of solution. Under the influence of Francis Hutcheson, moral cognitivism was commonplace among the moderate literati of the Scottish enlightenment.[1279] But what makes Ferguson's approach so interesting is that, of all the Scots, he seems to be the least optimistic about modern life; he did not seem to share in the widespread optimism about progress that prevailed in the Enlightenment

---

[1274] *P.I.*, p. 173; *P.II.*, p. 27.

[1275] Passmore, *The Perfectibility of Man*, p. 55. For Ferguson's most exhaustive treatment of this question see, 'Of the Things That Are or May Be', *Collection of Essays*, No. 27, passim.

[1276] *P.II.* p. 412; *P.I.* pp. 283-4. This idea was particularly favoured by Epictetus. Stanton, 'The Cosmopolitan Ideas of Epictetus and Marcus Aurelius', p. 194.

[1277] *P.I.*, p. 183.

[1278] *P.I.*, p. 175. Thus, Ferguson contradicts Rousseau's claim that learning is antithetical to virtue. Rousseau, 'Discourse on the Moral Effects of the Arts and Sciences', *Social Contract and Discourses*, pp. 10-14.

[1279] K. Haakonssen, 'Natural Law and Moral Realism: The Scottish Synthesis', *Studies in the Philosophy of the Scottish Enlightenment*, M. A. Stewart (ed.), Oxford: Clarendon Press, 1990, p. 62.

period. Because the problem of theodicy looms so large in Ferguson's mind his body of work embodies a particularly energetic and elaborately worked out response to it. His moral cognitivism is extremely well developed because the problem to which it is applied is such a prominent feature of his corpus; accordingly it plays a crucial role in unifying his system of thought.

The 'ignorance thesis' enables Ferguson to deal with the difficult question of the need for improvement in the absence of original sin. Ferguson recognises that the presence of free will often results in vice but he holds optimistically to a faith in the spontaneous order of the universe. The learning process never fails to reveal the triumph of good over vice. The 'experience of evil' resulting from free will offers a powerful lesson in our moral education for its effects guide us toward 'rectitude and truth'. Humanity is an 'order of being who must choose for himself and is in essence a self-forming power'.[1280] Ferguson's theodicy closely resembles that of Marcus Aurelius who allowed for a universe simultaneously 'perfect' yet sometimes 'harsh' and 'unpalatable'.[1281] Existence is beset with many dangers and obstructions that have been deliberately set in place by God in order to stimulate our growth as moral agents.[1282] Original ignorance must be overcome; and in the process we discover that good may come out of vice and that adversity can be a positive social force.

Humans *do* possess free will. Although we are 'destined to grow in perfection...without end' Ferguson denounces indignantly any conception of human beings as programmed automatons playing out a meaningless, deterministic, charade. The 'good' of our species consists in 'advancement, and its evil decline'.[1283] But if decline is our 'evil' what function does it serve in a Universe created perfectly benign and where nothing is useless?

Ferguson's conception of progress is closely bound up in his moral perfectibilism. As the species develops in skills and accomplishments through time, so it also intuitively strives for union with the mind of the Creator. The only certain route to becoming a moral agent, Ferguson explains, is through self-discovery and self-creation. This occurs, not in religious isolation or introspective contemplation, but in the practice of our daily lives and in our interactions with other members of society. We learn from each other through trial and error and in the everyday process of securing our 'accommodations'. Essential to this process is the assumption that, as individuals, we exercise a fair degree of independence. On balance, Ferguson believes that any evil resulting from human independence will be offset by the advantages gained by the progress it affords us in our moral education. Ultimately more good comes of free will than bad. People evolve morally through experiencing the disagreeable effects of poor choices.[1284] Ferguson couches his arguments concerning human choice and volition in teleological terms, that is, the Creator has fashioned people for progress through the free exercise of their faculties.[1285]

[1280] 'Of Things that are or May Be', *Collection of Essays*, No. 27 (2) pp. 240-1.

[1281] Marcus Aurelius, *Meditations*, 5. 7. pp. 80-1.

[1282] 'Of Things that are or May Be', *Collection of Essays*, No. 27, Parts 1 and 2 *passim*;. *P.II.*, p. 511.

[1283] *P.I.*, p. 191.

[1284] *P.I.*, p. 183.

[1285] *P.I.*, p. 202.

Progress is defined as a process of self-education based on a desire, not to atone for sin, but to shed our natural defects and ignorance. This notion of leaving behind our original ignorance through progress is highly reminiscent of the Stoic idea of the emerging sapient. Epictetus suggests that we work our way towards union with the mind of God through a process of acquiring knowledge.[1286] For Ferguson, our salvation from the ills of modernity is secured, paradoxically, not by a return to some atavistic or imaginary golden age but through *more* progress; that is, progress in knowledge which enhances moral awareness.[1287] Individuals are assisted in making their choices if they strive to become acquainted with the laws of progression that govern human nature. Indeed, Ferguson goes as far as to suggest that 'God' is deliberately obscure about these matters in order to stimulate our curiosity about them. Agents must learn the distinction between good and evil and acknowledge that the law of human 'advancement', when subject to abuse, leads to 'degradation and ruin'.[1288] Choice brings with it the risk of failure and this is what makes it truly educative. We exercise volition within certain constraints (those of our environment and the irresistible imperatives of our primordial nature) which nevertheless afford ample scope for error. 'A design may be perceptible', Ferguson remarks, 'but if directed by folly or malice is an object of disgust or of reprobation'.[1289] The laws of nature are fixed; they simply await discovery.[1290] Ferguson reasons, somewhat awkwardly, that the very fact of our having been endowed with rational faculties confirms their constancy.[1291] The shape or form of human history is determined in the long view but in the short view, in its rate and content, it is largely the result of human volition. The transcendent order is immutable and invariable yet we are, at the same time, fated to act voluntarily within it.[1292] The full extent of our influence is, however, impossible to discern.[1293]

Thus, some of the answers to the problem of theodicy (the existence of evil, or in this case, corruption) are to be found in Ferguson's theory of progress; a theory founded on arguments about free will. Our species' worldly accomplishments are part of (perhaps even by-products of) our intuitive quest for union with the mind of God. Because Fergusonian perfectibilism is means- rather than ends-oriented, it is inconceivable without the assumption of free will.

3. SOCIAL STRUCTURE VERSUS INDIVIDUAL AGENCY

What then, is the precise relationship between the transcendent order and human agency? In other words, how does Ferguson's insistence on free will fit with his

---

[1286] *P.I.*, pp. 312-13.

[1287] Willke, *The Historical Thought of Adam Ferguson*, p. 182.

[1288] *P.I.*, p. 202. See also *P.II.*, p. 54.

[1289] *P.II.*, pp. 27-8.

[1290] *P.II.*, p. 54.

[1291] *P.I.*, p. 179.

[1292] 'The powers that operate cannot be controuled by his will; but the laws, according to which they proceed, may be known, and measures taken to influence the result of their operations'. *P.II.*, p. 54.

[1293] 'Of the Separation of the Departments', *Collection of Essays*, No. 15, p. 144.

belief in irresistible and unalterable social laws? Ferguson's answer is a subtle variation on the longstanding theological debate about free will. Human progress is linear and open-ended but not purposeless; uniform in form though not in content. The three developmental stages (savage, barbarous and polished) encountered thus far were never avoidable though variations and errors naturally occur and this is attributable to the operations of free will in concert with obvious variations in nature (topographical and climatic diversity). Despite the prevalence of vice (error) Ferguson's optimism remains intact due to his insistence that 'contingence itself is a perfection in (God's) works'.[1294] Progress is transcendentally teleological in the sense that the super-trajectory of the species is determined by God and fulfilled through human agency. Ferguson's history is really a type of salvation history, though with two important qualifications: the first is that we are not redeeming ourselves from sin, but from an insufficiency of knowledge about ourselves and the role we play in God's master plan. The second is that we secure our own redemption. God's efficacious grace is supplanted by efficacious self-education.[1295] Providence provides an immutable framework (the three stage schema and whatever is to come after it) and then endows the species with the raw materials of will, choice, judgement and the progressive instinct of 'ambition', all of which enable and impel it to effect a lineal and infinite progress.

There is a striking tension between the Creator's will and human independence in Ferguson's writings and this is largely a function of his simultaneous commitment to a Christian/Ciceronian conception of agency[1296] and a Stoic tendency towards resignation. David Kettler has described the tension in Ferguson between free will, on the one hand, and the transcendent order, on the other, as 'discordant', suggesting that the latter's views on their relationship are incompatible.[1297] This charge seems justified but it may underestimate the subtlety of Ferguson's vision which can be summed up as follows: Human beings are the principal bearers of history; they exercise considerable independence in the process, yet they are also engaged in fulfilling the Creator's telic blueprint. Ferguson urged each agent to act as God's 'willing instrument in what depends on his own will; and...a conscious instrument at the disposal of Providence in matters which are out of his power' yet insisted ultimately that humans are 'voluntary agents'.[1298] He summarises his position in the following passage:

> In one sense the career of fortune is independent of human power. For no *single* man or number of men plan and execute it or are in no [sic] condition to stop or execute its course. *And yet the whole is the result of human nature and the actions of men.* What is the individual to do afloat upon this torrent? To commit himself to its direction without any Effort! No, for if every individual were to do so there would be no action. The torrent is formed by united impulses of such efforts as his own. And the direction is taken from the prevailing dispositions of men not from any external or fatal necessity.

[1294] *P.I.,* p. 154.

[1295] Willke, *The Historical Thought of Adam Ferguson,* passim.

[1296] Cicero argues that since we are fragments of divine intelligence, of a first cause capable of moving itself, so we are also capable of self-movement. Cicero, *De Republica,* 6. 24-26, pp. 279-83.

[1297] Kettler, 'Constitution in Permanence', p. 221.

[1298] *P.I.,* pp. 130-1, 313; *Institutes,* p. 11.

And every individual is to consider himself as a constituent part of the moving power, not merely as a matter to be moved or disposed of by another. *It would be absurd to acquiesce in any defect because defects are real.* Or to decline any advantage because those that we choose may not be obtained. Human affairs are mixed and it is the object of man to *hasten* and *increase* the good, to *retard* and *diminish* the evil. It is not even in the Power of man to refrain from acting this Part to the amount of his conception. He pleads fate sometimes to excuse his not doing what he is otherwise averse to attempt.[1299]

Ferguson directs his reader to take a conceptual step backwards so as to appreciate that it is the species through time, not the individual agent, who generates history. He then directs her to take a further step back in order to see that human actions merely represent efficient causes; final causes being the exclusive province of the Creator.[1300] We are a self-created species capable of discerning appropriate action by studying the *logos* of the universe, knowledge of which is reflected in God's works.[1301] We are capable of inferring our destiny, albeit imperfectly, from the tendency of our own progress; consequently we can exercise a high degree of independence in pursuing it. The ends are prescribed and fixed, but the means employed in attaining them are left entirely to individual judgement.[1302] We also exercise considerable latitude in determining our own time frame. The three-stage sequence seems to be fixed, since it is immanent in a human nature which is invariable, but each society will proceed at a different *rate* of advancement given the diversity of physical environments, the variability of culture and the operations of volition. Moreover, human development may not be strictly linear but may regress or even veer tangentially for a period as a result of bad choices. Ferguson seems to be well aware of the tensions here. Since progression is instinctive, he concedes in passing, we should naturally expect to find a 'continual advancement' of the species. However, we cannot fail to perceive that 'human affairs are subject to vicissitudes and the human species is observed to decline in some periods, no less than to advance in others'.[1303]

We cannot manipulate the laws of nature (since they are fixed) but we can certainly familiarise ourselves with them in order to maximise our advantage, minimise any disadvantages and properly submit ourselves to the will of the

---

[1299] Ferguson's unpublished lecture notes cited in Kettler, 'Constitution in Permanence', p. 218. Yet Ferguson clearly struggled with defining and understanding this relationship. According to Kettler: 'In his notes for 1779-1780, Ferguson arrives in December at a series of lectures designed above all to refute the notion that constitutions arise from some social contract or comprehensive legislative will, without at the same time making them appear as natural products unaffected by choice and action. A change in the text of the introductory lecture signals the difficulties. He first wrote that man "is led and determined in every case by peculiar circumstances" but then crossed that out and substituted: "There are circumstances in every case that aid and that limit his choice and impede or facilitate his attainments" '. Kettler, ibid, p. 217.

[1300] *P.I.*, p. 53.

[1301] 'Distinction of Value and its Source in Existence', *Collection of Essays*, No. 7, p. 73.

[1302] *P.I.*, p. 54.

[1303] *P.I.*, pp. 313-14.

Creator.[1304] This aspect of Ferguson's thought is difficult to reconcile with his belief in spontaneous order as dependent upon human blindness of higher ends. In fact, this is one of the main tensions in his system of thought and one which seems difficult to reconcile.

Different obstacles are encountered and different choices made in the vast range of human experience. Poor choices can lead to disastrous detours in the human developmental journey but the results are ultimately the same on the level of form. The species passes from its 'infancy' (savagery) through to 'manhood' (barbarity) and into the wisdom of its old age (polished civilisation). There are natural stages in the development of the species yet they are obtained by diverse means. Certain psychogenetic variables, representing the seeds of our *telos* or destiny, remain constant whereas circumstantial variations and human agency result in eccentricities, variety and sometimes temporary disasters. This explains why Ferguson can be simultaneously pessimistic about progress and still wax teleological. Our approach to perfection is achieved dialectally via our capacity to err and to learn from our mistakes. This capacity to err, as teleologically conceived, is one of the most compelling aspects of Fergusonian perfectibilism. It will now receive some closer attention.

4. IGNORANCE AND ERROR

Error born of ignorance is the cause of corruption. Yet the whole notion of our capacity to err is built into Fergusonian perfectibilism. Error is teleologically conceived. We are *destined* to err, to benefit by the disagreeable effects of our mistakes and thereby advance intellectually, practically, and morally.[1305] This is how Ferguson's teleology differs from the Aristotelian; it is genuinely progressive because our misdemeanours actually alter the course of events.[1306]

According to the Stoic view, imperfection flows from the failure of people to see things as they really are, while Socrates conceived vice as a function of ignorance. This is exactly how Ferguson approached the problem of evil; good and evil are not binary opposites. Evil is either the misidentification of phenomena that are really indirectly positive[1307] or the title we give to pernicious events that result from poor judgement. The causes of national and constitutional corruptions are directly traceable to errors in judgement. Hedonism, for example, comes from mistaking the proper objects of attention, imperialism is an error of *hubris* and so on. Ferguson thus resists a dualistic solution to the problem of evil by appealing to a monistic solution which denies the existence of evil out of hand. Apparent evil is really just

---

[1304] *P.I.*, p. 54. See also *P.I.* p. 108 and 'Of the Things That Are or May *Be*', *Collection of Essays*, No. 27, passim; 'Of Cause and Effect, Ends and Means, Order, Combination and Design' *Collection of Essays*, No. 13, passim.

[1305] 'Of Good and Evil, Perfection and Defect', *Collection of Essays*, No. 23, passim.

[1306] Aristotle does hold, though, that there is inherent in matter a 'certain degree' of imperfection therefore things can go wrong even in nature. Aristotle, *Ethics*, Appendix F. p. 358.

[1307] For example, 'Cold and heat must be felt by animals, that each may shun his own destruction'. Even 'pain is necessary, and a blessing to the whole'. *P.I.*, p. 338.

an absence of good, a state of imperfection. God deliberately endowed people with defects in order to stimulate their progress: 'A being that is destined to acquire perfection must originate in defect' and the errors to which our defective natures inevitably give rise are perfectly natural.[1308] Ferguson's recasting of the problem of theodicy in terms of original ignorance allows him to dispose of any troubling questions about the necessity for improvement in the absence of original sin. Error is a natural result of our perpetual quest to leave behind a dearth of self-knowledge.[1309]

Ferguson is able to retain his Stoically inspired belief that we are godlike particles[1310] by asserting that there is godlike *potential* in each person. He accords with the Stoic view of defining happiness as a (civically) virtuous state of mind[1311] and of identifying our ultimate goal as union with the mind of God.[1312] Agents pursuing their moral perfection are in a permanent state of *emergent* godliness. The knowledge each moral agent seeks is self-knowledge that will allow 'him' to live according to God's laws and avoid future error.[1313] 'Man' is distinguished by his destination to know 'himself'[1314] and 'knowledge is the sap which nature has supplied to nourish the growing mind'.[1315] The whole planet is a galvanising school for virtue and a 'nurser(y) for the great world of intelligent beings'.[1316]

History is, therefore, the gradual liberation of people from ignorance, a dialectical process which is liable to exact heavy costs. Although our insatiable ambition to shed our original ignorance is the unconscious cause of all the evil and corruption in the world, this same desire has produced order, progress and civilisation. Our capacity for spontaneous order contains, necessarily and simultaneously, the capacity for entropy. This explains why the progress/decline themes consistently shadow each other in Ferguson's writings.

5. PERFECTION AS PROCESS

Ferguson conceives our moral progress as a process rather than an absolute goal; it is the *effort* of things to achieve their goals that is the source of world order. Since only God is perfect, humanity strives to draw ever closer to God, who, outside and transcending the world, is the distal and final cause of all motion. The process of advancement is no less important to the development of the moral personality than

---

[1308] *P.I.*, p. 181.

[1309] *P.I.*, p. 185; See also 'Of Cause and Effect, Ends and Means, Order, Combination and Design', *Collection of Essays,* No. 13 passim and *P.I.*, p. 175.

[1310] See, for example, 'Of Things that are or May Be', *Collection of Essays*, No. 27 (2) p. 235.

[1311] *P.II.*, p. 412, *P.I.*, pp. 313, 179. Ferguson shared this conception in common with other Moderates. Sher, *Church and University*, p. 211.

[1312] *P.I.*, p. 329; 'The Different Aspects of Moral Science', *Collection of Essays*, No. 29, p. 257.

[1313] *P.I.*, p. 181. Jean Willke adopts a similar line in *The Historical Thought of Adam Ferguson*, pp. 60-1.

[1314] *P.I.*, pp. 3-5.

[1315] *P.I.*, p. 175.

[1316] *P.II.*, p. 325. See also 'Of Cause and Effect, Ends and Means, Order, Combination and Design', *Collection of Essays,* No. 13.

its actual attainment[1317] and acts become important ends in themselves.[1318] This conception of perfection as an ongoing, means- focused process is necessitated by Ferguson's recognition of the practical unattainability of perfection; since only the Creator is perfect Ferguson responds by identifying our improvement as mere 'progress'.[1319] We do not achieve perfection in some remote afterlife but may attain some measure of it here in our daily lives where each individual contributes to the ongoing perfection of the species through time. Moral perfection, while being a worthy goal, is unrealisable. We can, however, express virtue practically and socially in the exercise of beneficence which Ferguson describes romantically as one of the 'godlike principles'.[1320] This is as much as we can hope for in one lifetime. Our moral and practical progress depends on the degree of ardour with which we exercise our virtues and faculties.[1321] Since the highest virtues are civic, Ferguson emphasises that participation in community life is particularly efficacious and he agrees with Cicero that civic virtue flows from knowledge of duties and station.[1322] Ferguson follows the Stoic example in conceiving moral perfection on two levels; the first is practical and civic virtue which we can exercise on a day to day basis; the second is moral perfection expressed in our perpetual quest for union with the mind of the Creator. The two kinds of virtue intersect when we exercise the other-regarding passions and fulfil our civic obligations, thereby exhibiting the signs of our potentially God-like nature and our willingness to accord with the desires of Providence.[1323] Ferguson is unique among his immediate contemporaries in linking the 'moral perfection of individuals with the common good'[1324] though there is a precedent in Cicero as well as Hutcheson.[1325]

When we exercise the other-regarding passions and fulfil our civic obligations we represent a fragment or mirror of our potentially God-like nature. We love each other as God loves us and thereby accord with His will; we are in harmony with our essential nature.[1326] Since God is so distant from us, it makes more sense for us to concentrate our efforts on the practice of virtue here on earth via a discernment and observance of the *logos* of the universe. Yet, even when we exercise civic virtue individually we are also contributing to our long-term, collective moral perfection. It

---

[1317] *P.I.*, p. 184.

[1318] *P.I.*, p. 250. See also 'Of the Things That Are or May Be', *Collection of Essays*, No. 27 (1 and 2), *passim.*

[1319] *P.II.*, p. 403.

[1320] *P.II.*, pp. 32-4.

[1321] *P.I.*, p. 193.

[1322] Cicero, *Selected Works*, Robert Baldick, C.A. Jones and Betty Radice, eds., Great Britain: Penguin, 1971, Ch. 4, 'A Practical Code of Behaviour', passim and Commentary, p. 158; Sher, *Church and University*, p. 201.

[1323] *P.II.*, p. 61; *P.I.*, pp. 313, 318.

[1324] Willke, *The Historical Thought of Adam Ferguson*, p. 138.

[1325] Cicero made the connection between private virtue and the internal regulation of the individual soul, on the one hand, and civic action and service, on the other. We see the same conception pre-figured in Hutcheson's thinking whereby civil society 'is essentially an institution for the moral development of mankind... [it] exists not just to maximise happiness, but to inculcate the benevolent or beatific motivation of the citizenry'. Haakonssen, 'Natural Law and Moral Realism', p. 77.

[1326] *Institutes,* pp. 224-5.

is the Creator's wish that we direct our virtuous efforts to the here and now, an interpretation Ferguson finds evidence for in God's apparently deliberate ambiguity about a future state. This uncertainty about our 'immortality' or otherwise serves the 'final cause' of drawing our attention to the more pressing concerns and immediate duties of the present.[1327] After all, '[t]he immediate uses of moral law are choice, practice and conduct'.[1328] People seek their highest perfection in discovering their niche in society and pursuing communal or civic values; a person is excellent 'in the degree to which he loves his fellow creatures; he is defective, in the degree to which he hates or is indifferent to their welfare'.[1329]

To be precise, then, Ferguson expounds a teleology without an attainable *telos*. The *telos*, human moral perfection, is unrealisable, but is conceived as an ongoing process of 'diminishing' imperfection; the progress of the species traces a curve which never finds a point of repose. Our 'capacity for advancement is nowhere exhausted'.[1330] Ferguson employs a geometrical analogy to demonstrate his point that the perfective process is asymptotic:

> What is created can never equal its creator...the least defect is the greatest perfection. A defect which is always diminishing, or in a regular course of supply, we may suppose to be the perfection of created nature...In its continual approach to the infinite perfection of what is eternal, it may be compared to that curve, described by geometers, as in continual approach to a straight line, which it can never reach.[1331]

In order to ensure that our quest for improvement in all our pursuits is both challenging and unending, the Creator has deliberately 'baffled our project; and placed nowhere within our reach this visionary blessing of absolute ease'.[1332] 'Intelligence' knows 'no specific place' and our destination 'is yet hid from our sight'.[1333] Ferguson conceives our moral perfection as a *continuous* event, a 'boundless course',[1334] a 'baffled project', an infinite 'curve' and a perplexing 'labyrinth', rather than a precise goal. Once again, this is a typically Stoic idea, which Epictetus, for example, sets out in his *Discourses*.[1335] Seneca also noted that 'nature does not give a man virtue: the process of becoming a good man is an art'.[1336] Ferguson quotes Cato in Cicero's *De Finibus* for the statement that 'action' and process are far more important than 'the end or purpose to which the action was directed'.[1337]

[1327] *P.I.*, p. 318.

[1328] *Institutes*, p.6.

[1329] *P.II.*, p. 41.

[1330] *P.I.*, p. 316.

[1331] *P.I.*, pp. 184-5. See also *P.I.,* pp. 298, 302 and 'Of Things that Are or May Be', *Collection of Essays*, No. 27, (2) pp. 240-3 and 'The Different Aspects of Moral Science', No. 29, *Collection of Essays*, p. 257.

[1332] *Essay*, p. 205.

[1333] *P.I.*, pp. 315-16; See also *P.I.*, pp. 330-1.

[1334] *P.II.,* p. 324.

[1335] Epictetus, *Discourses*, 1. 4. 1-27, pp. 27-35.

[1336] Seneca, *Letters,* Letter 90, 43. p. 176.

[1337] *P.II.*, p. 327.

5.1   The Perfective Ideal

The strictly teleological concept of perfection, defined in terms of attaining some
remote end is supplanted in Ferguson by a more attainable goal in which a
harmonious and balanced moral character is the ideal. The familiar idea of a
'rounded character' seems to have been what he had in mind. Marcus Aurelius
described the perfected soul by means of a geometrical metaphor; it assumes a
'perfectly rounded form'[1338] and will be good in every department of virtue. We may
begin to approach this ideal in the present, in the course of daily life, not in some
remote future state or distant point in the evolution of humanity.[1339] A capacity to
develop and exercise communal values, civic goodness and the practical, other-
regarding virtues, are all manifestations of this development.

Some are likely to make more progress than others. While everyone is
potentially capable of discerning natural laws only a small number realise this
potential. In every age, there are those few who, manifesting a kind of quasi-divine
understanding, are deemed fit to receive and communicate to others, 'the indications
of supreme intelligence and goodness' that 'operate in the great system of the
world'. Such a person might resemble Socrates, Epictetus, or Newton, all lavishly
eulogised by Ferguson as 'sublime' in their understanding.[1340] An 'imitation and
resemblance to the supreme God' is likewise attributed to Marcus Aurelius singled
out as a paragon of 'godlike eminence' possessing all the best practical and moral
virtues.[1341] Ferguson has taken the not unprecedented step of making his ideal
'concrete as a person'. Human perfection consists in the imitation of such exemplary
personalities. The Stoics, for example, idealised Socrates[1342] whereas Jesus
represented perfection for the Christians.[1343] Ferguson's modern ideal is not
Christlike but a rather more human exemplar; his contemporary (and relation)[1344] the
chemist and physician Dr. Joseph Black. Always sociable and ever 'engaged in the
details of his public station', 'his manner unaffected and plain...he never had
anything about him for ostentation'.[1345] He appeared at all times calm, even in death.
Abstemious in his diet and accommodations he, 'lived within the means of his
station'; 'wise' and sober. Joseph Black personified the public-minded sage
exhibiting all the Stoic virtues of wisdom, sobriety and frugality and competently
performing those duties confluent with his assigned station with Stoic calm. He had
lived a life, Ferguson notes with unreserved approbation, 'which had passed in the

---

[1338] Marcus Aurelius, *Meditations* 11.12, p. 170. To perfect oneself, says Marcus quoting Empedocles,
is to become a 'totally rounded orb, in its rotundity joying'. *Meditations*, 12. 3, p. 180.

[1339] Passmore, *Perfectibility of Man*, pp. 56, 153.

[1340] *P.I.*, p. 312-13. Ferguson also admired Homer. Sher, *Church and University*, p. 108.

[1341] *P.I.*, pp. 331-2. See also *P.I.*, p. 336.

[1342] As did Ferguson himself. *P.I.*, p. 4.

[1343] Passmore, *Perfectibility of Man*, p. 22.

[1344] Black was Ferguson's second cousin and also the uncle of his wife, Katherine Ferguson. Fagg,
Biographical Introduction, p. xcvii.

[1345] Adam Ferguson, 'Minutes of the Life and Character of Joseph Black MD, Addressed to the Royal
Society of Edinburgh', *Royal Society of Edinburgh Transactions*, Scotland, Vol. V, Part iii, 1801, pp.
101-17, hereafter cited as 'Joseph Black'.

most correct application of reason and good sense to all the objects of pursuit which Providence had prescribed in his lot'.[1346] Black, a scientist, had devoted his life to the archetypal project of sagehood; endeavouring to evince the divine purpose while serving others in the process.[1347]

Despite the solubility of the decline/progress problem, a further problem is generated by the solution. It is this: Because Ferguson's model is not static, we should, presumably, be getting better and better at civic virtue. For, if virtue is knowledge, why has not virtue accumulated with progress? Yet he refers to the growth of knowledge but also to a concomitant increase of vice. Further, if virtue is happiness[1348] what is the point of all the tertiary, *material* benefits of progress without the primary *moral* benefits?[1349] There are two ways in which Ferguson might have resolved this difficulty. The first is that he might have made a clearer distinction between two different types of knowledge; one pertaining to social progress and one to individual moral progress. Ferguson does not adopt this strategy. The second solution would have been to follow Smith in giving moral priority to the growth of knowledge and wisdom over the growth of classical virtue in the commercial age.[1350] It would have been far easier for him to demonstrate a growth of knowledge than to insist on the inevitability of moral progress in the face of all his own evidence for increasing vice. But Ferguson does not adopt this line either. The knowledge to which Smith refers is of a technical and wealth-generating nature, and would, therefore, be regarded by Ferguson as, not only inferior to true wisdom, but a potential cause of degeneration.

Ferguson's solution to the 'paradox of progress and decline' is therefore flawed or at least incomplete. His perhaps overly ambitious project of attempting to synthesise a classical perspective with modern political economy and actual conditions yields a somewhat awkward result. Yet he *does* make clear that things will ultimately improve even if he doesn't provide complete explanations as to how this will happen. The universe as an immense, self-righting unit with its own inbuilt laws of equilibrium. The relationship of these laws to his response to the problem of theodicy will now be canvassed.

6. THE SELF-RIGHTING UNIVERSE

Though Ferguson seems ambiguous on the subject of the natural history of falling and fallen states, he seems to be saying that the universe we inhabit is an, ultimately,

---

[1346] 'Joseph Black', pp. 112-117.

[1347] 'Joseph Black', p. 109.

[1348] '[V]irtue is happiness'. 'The Different Aspects of Moral Science', *Collection of Essays*, No. 24, p. 256. '[T]he Creator in laying a scheme of progression for man towards the perfection of his intellectual being has at the same time projected his happiness as the end of Creation'. 'Of Perfection and Happiness', *Collection of Essays*, No. 1, p. 2.

[1349] Thanks to David Millar and Geoffrey Smith for drawing my attention to the difficulty with Ferguson's approach here.

[1350] As Nicholas Philippson has argued with respect to Smith. 'Adam Smith as Civic Moralist', in Hont and Ignatieff, (eds.), p. 181; Smith, *WN*, V. i., pp. 788-96.

self-righting one. It was created for our benefit as 'God's' favourite creatures and the Creator has foreseen 'that absolute evil... cannot befall the universe: for whatever be the contingent effects of freedom, it is ever susceptible of remedy and it is ever good that intelligent beings should be free'.[1351] Periods of decline are not necessarily permanent states of affairs nor are they stages in eternally recurring cycles but are better understood as 'temporary intermissions'. In the ordinary course of life our progress as a species will tend to be punctuated by interruptions and temporary setbacks but the ultimate effect seems to be a natural, progressive order.[1352] Any inconvenience must be understood as a necessary event in the dialectical progress of our moral and practical evolution. Paradoxically, the more errors we commit, the further we are drawn along the inexorable path of perfection. Only through exhausting all the possible incorrect choices can we truly earn our virtue.[1353] It is manifestly our species' 'state of nature' to progress without 'any necessary limit', however that progress is disrupted wherever citizens fail to cultivate the civic virtues. Each of our natural, normally positive drives holds the potential to harm us because they are always alloyed with freedom of choice without which real progress would be impossible. In the normal course of things, natural ambition and insatiable need bring progress and moral development but, when directed towards unworthy objects, the same drives lead to *hubris*, selfishness and vitiating hedonism. Yet without these original tendencies there would be no order and no progress at all. This is why Ferguson fails to censure such seemingly pernicious developments as the division of labour, the love of 'trifling' conveniences and even luxury since they are products of our natural urges and therefore productive of spontaneous order and progress.

Ferguson seems to believe that the human universe contains its own self-correcting mechanisms. The ills of the bloated, over-extended state have within them their own antidotes. This is reminiscent of Thucydides' view that aggressive empires always contain the seeds of their own destruction. Rule by force, which is a necessary feature of empires, invariably leads to revolt. Tyrants inevitably meet their end at the hands of their own subjects. Because despotism is induced by apathy, over-extension and dissipation it cannot survive; it is a dead and unnatural constitution with no potential for growth[1354] and an inability to withstand change and accommodate progress. Since constitutions are simultaneously nurseries of, and objects for, the honing of civic virtue, they must be supple, organic, alive and responsive. Ideally, constitutions are social products; the single, scheming architect of tyranny neglects the fundamental law of history; that institutions are the natural and gradual result of the efforts of countless free agents.

[1351] *P.I.*, p. 155.

[1352] '[T]he capacity of his progress is indefinite, the steps which we observe him make are but part of the scheme of a nature which is destined to endure for ever'. 'Of Things that Are or May Be' (Part 1), *Collection of Essays*, No. 27, p. 229; *P.I.*, pp. 310-11.

[1353] *P.I.*, p. 298.

[1354] *Essay*, pp. 262-3.

Ferguson reflects at length on the injustice and evil of those 'tyrants' who govern 'at discretion' referring to the perpetual 'war that subsists, in despotic governments, between the oppressor and the oppressed'.[1355] Commerce eventually falters under conditions of political and economic slavery for 'the hopes of gain and the secure possession of property must perish under the precarious tenure of slavery and under the apprehension of danger arising from the reputation of wealth'. National poverty and misery follow and the community inevitably collapses under the insupportable weight of adversity. The driving engine of commerce, self-interest, (which is contingent on the prospect of being able to enjoy the fruits of one's labour) falters, and with it prosperity.[1356] Despotism drags citizens into a wretched state of poverty, isolation, and insecurity, subjecting them to the 'horrors of fear [and] despair', and stripping them of any capacity to defend themselves or even to form social ties. Subjects become unruly, crime escalates and 'devastation and ruin appear on every side'. Eventually the oppression of subjects becomes so great as to be rendered a paradoxical kind of freedom. A populace with no rights and no property to defend has nothing to lose and subjects with nothing to lose are always dangerous.[1357] At this point citizens 'quit their habitations' and turn to a nomadic life of crime. The extremity of the situation warrants, in turn, the extreme reaction of a full-blown revolution. Ferguson inveighed against the whole notion of revolution using the evolutionist dimension of spontaneous order as his rationale. In the case of tyranny, however, he makes a rare exception because, apart from the misery it causes, tyranny impugns the progressivist dimension of spontaneous order.[1358]

But Ferguson neglects to stipulate how, precisely, this process of reconstitution is supposed to come about. In fact, the whole discussion lacks clarity. How exactly will nations rise up from their ruins and get themselves back onto a progressive track, especially once people have lost their capacity for solidary action and united defence? From the discussion, the re-establishment process seems to involve some kind of devolvement in social scale and level of sophistication. But the detail Ferguson provides is too sketchy to permit any clear scenario to emerge. Even if this were Ferguson's intention (i.e. devolvement), it would represent a contradiction of such other important views as his rejection of primitivism and his belief that the cure for the ills of modernity lies in *more* progress, rather than in a return to a more basic mode of existence such as is hinted at here. In any event, the only clue he provides is a passage in the *Essay* where it is suggested that once citizens have quit the villages and towns they will reform into smaller social units elsewhere and begin to re-establish their sense of community and eventually their civic virtue: '*When human nature appears in the utmost state of corruption, it has actually begun to reform*'.[1359] Ferguson seems to expect a kind of spontaneous restoration of civil society, implying that history testifies to his claims of self-righting polities. Jean Willke has

---

[1355] *P.II.*, p. 503.

[1356] '[N]ational poverty...and the suppression of commerce are the means by which despotism comes to accomplish its own destruction'. *Essay*, p. 263.

[1357] *Essay*, pp. 262-3.

[1358] *History*, p. 5. See also *P.II.*, pp. 292, 497.

[1359] *Essay*, p. 264. My emphasis.

detected the weakness of his analysis here: '[T]he further he departs from historical examples the more incomplete his discussion...he offers no concrete illustration of his theory of national re-emergence from despotism'.[1360] Further, Ferguson neglects to explain the failure of the Roman empire to recover and return to its former greatness, thus undermining his postulate of a self-righting universe.[1361]

In any case, this latter picture is a worst-case scenario. The point is that he insists all along that our natural urges (under the auspices of a transcendent scheme) cannot fail to realise our progressive destiny. Existence has a purpose and no matter what befalls us in the course of our dramatic and arduous developmental process, that purpose must, and will, be realised. Periods of great tumult inevitably subside but such events are not without a positive side for they afford citizens a valuable learning experience:

> [I]n the case of states that are fortunate in their domestic policy, even madness itself may, in the pursuit of violent convulsions, subside into wisdom; and a people return to their ordinary mood, cured of their follies and wiser by experience; or, with talents improved, in conducting the very scenes which frenzy had opened, they may then appear best qualified to pursue with success the object of nations. Like the ancient republics, immediately after some alarming sedition, or like the kingdom of Great Britain, at the close of its civil wars, they retain the spirit of activity, which was recently awakened, and are equally vigorous in every pursuit, whether of policy, learning or arts.
>
> From having appeared on the brink of ruin, they pass to the greatest prosperity.[1362]

7. CONCLUDING REMARKS

The tension between the apparently competing themes of progress and decline in Ferguson does appear to be reconcilable but only after some determined textual effort and in spite of some gaps in logic. Notwithstanding his apparent pessimism, Ferguson seems convinced that while there is always the danger of retrogression it is not inevitable in prosperous states and is rarely, if ever, a permanent state of affairs when it does occur. This is confirmed in the final remarks of the *Essay* where he winds up his discourse on despotism on an optimistic note, declaring that activism, not fatalism is the only way of managing the threat of corruption.[1363] So long as there

---

[1360] Willke, *The Historical Thought of Adam Ferguson*, p. 190.

[1361] Though in the passage below he seems to be limiting his claims of self-righting polities to cases of less violent and disruptive civil unrest such as Britain had already survived.

[1362] *Essay*, p. 202.

[1363] *Essay*, p. 264.

are citizens guarding and cultivating their civic virtues, and so long as there are constitutions that encourage and admit popular participation, polished states can forestall any incipient descent into decline. As Ernest Gellner notes, Ferguson's 'warnings have more the tone of an uneasy disquiet, rather than a confident prediction of disaster'.[1364]

[1364] Gellner, 'Adam Ferguson and the Surprising Robustness of Civil Society', p. 121.

CHAPTER 12

FERGUSON'S CONSERVATISM

We have seen that the decline of civilisations and the concomitant onset of political corruption is an extremely important theme in Ferguson's social and political science. We have also seen that his assessment of modernity is so critical that he has sometimes been mistaken for an early Marxian. Yet there is an almost complete lack of recommended reforms to address the problem of how to prevent corruption. Ferguson never suggests that Britain should return its colonies to their 'rightful' owners, makes no global recommendations to reverse the push towards increasing specialisation and there are no calls for controls on luxury. Even more conspicuously, despite his stress on the importance of popular participation in public affairs there are no calls for a broadening of the franchise or for any other significant institutional changes that might address the problems of apathy, civic demobilisation and political corruption.

His relative silence here seems to be completely out of step with the general tone of his writing; indeed, it has led to charges of inconsistency, fecklessness and irresponsibility on his part. For example, David Kettler has interpreted Ferguson's conservatism as a kind of wilful neglect of his duty as a moralist; namely, to challenge an unjust political order. He writes that Ferguson was 'completely unable or largely unable to challenge the prevailing distribution of power' and that 'in his capacity as ally and supporter of the status quo, he could rest content with applying a rationalising gloss over the problems of his time'.[1365] William Lehmann also notes that there is 'no revolutionary activism' in Ferguson and, like Kettler, perceives Ferguson's lack of suggested reforms as symptomatic of either some kind of philosophical disability or a moral unwillingness to follow his analysis through to its logical conclusion. 'Why', he asks rhetorically, 'was Ferguson unable or unwilling to [demand]...more than merely a moral appeal to right the more flagrant wrongs incident to the existing system?'[1366] This chapter seeks to clarify Ferguson's position, explain his omission and defend him, in part at least, against his critics by aligning his conservatism with key aspects of his social thought, namely his prior commitments to spontaneous order and Christian-Stoicism.

Some explanations for Ferguson's apparent willingness to gloss over what was, effectively, the problematic centrepiece of his corpus will be given presently but for the moment it may be worthwhile to note that Ferguson was not completely neglectful of his 'responsibilities' here. In fact does in fact suggest a few constitutional and social reforms to address the problems that apparently absorbed him so much. Granted, his presentation of these was extremely vague and disjointed

---

[1365] Kettler, *Adam Ferguson*, pp. 179, 211.
[1366] Lehmann, 'Review', p. 170.

and they have to be culled out by the reader, nevertheless, the pattern that does finally emerge is in the classic mould of civic humanism. Ferguson tells us that in order to avoid the inevitable consequences of the destructive trends he quite presciently identifies governors must devise the appropriate political arrangements by which inactive and apathetic citizens will be distracted from their narrow, self-regarding concerns and redirect their attention to the public sphere and more solidary forms of activity.[1367] He therefore recommends greater levels of popular participation in public life, the introduction of a citizen militia, the insertion of a civics education programme into the existing school curriculum and the maintenance of constitutionally limited government.

1. REMEDIES

1.1 Activism and Pluralism

It has been noted that Ferguson held to the view that civic moral character (and therefore political freedom) is preserved by an active, informed and highly factious citizenry. Institutions that 'engage the minds of citizens in public duties...tend to preserve and cultivate virtue'. Conversely, corrupt institutions 'tend to beget tyranny and insolence in the sovereign, servility and vileness in the subject...and to fill every heart with jealousy or dejection'.[1368] Where a citizenry is vigilant, degeneration may be sidestepped altogether, therefore the best way to avoid impending political slavery is to enhance civic competence, awareness and capacity. Mass participation also guards against the fatal weakness of simple or total forms of rule: '[T]he error that results from the freedom of one person is best corrected by the wisdom that results from the concurring freedom of many'.[1369] The relationship between civic temper and the political order is intimately symbiotic; civic virtue will lead to the just political order and the pursuit of the just political order will, in turn, preserve and enhance civic virtue. The edifice of a just political order represents both the matrix *for* and object *of* creative civic exertions. The main goal of these efforts is 'to guard against the abuses of power, and procure to individuals equal security in their respective stations'.[1370] In fact, Ferguson notes that it would be naïve to expect people to exercise civic virtue merely for its own sake or even as a means to cultivate their 'genius'. Instead, they must be shown that their virtue is likely to yield some 'external advantage' such as 'public safety', security of 'personal freedom' or even security of 'private property'.[1371]

The presence of appropriate 'political establishments', however sound, cannot compensate for the fact that the integrity of a constitution lies ultimately in the hands

---

[1367] McDowell, 'Adam Ferguson's Constitutionalism', pp. 546-7.
[1368] *Institutes*, pp. 293-4.
[1369] *P.II.*, p. 510.
[1370] *P.I.*, p. 263.
[1371] *Essay*, pp. 132-3.

of the public and in its 'firm and resolute spirit'.[1372] Political quiescence is indicative of corruption whereas civic activity and even party faction fighting is both beneficial and virtuous. For this reason John Robertson suggests that Ferguson favoured the institutionalisation of 'a permanent party system' as a means of entrenching factional conflict within the political culture.[1373]

The ideal political order is one that is characterised by the protection of such civil and political rights as right of political 'redress', right of 'resistance' and 'freedom of speech as well as thought'. Ferguson judges their existence as symptomatic of both 'just' and 'vigorous government'.[1374] But typically, he fails to stipulate just how extensive these rights should be or how they would be achieved and protected. Neither does he cast any light on the appropriate forms or fora for political activism, though it should be noted that in Scotland's case Ferguson's imagination would have been severely restricted by the fact that, due to the Act of Union (1707) the Scottish Parliament and Privy Council had been abolished and Scotland had thereby lost its key political institutions. It is possible that, given the lack of concrete institutions available to Scots, Ferguson's idea of citizenship was social and cultural, rather than directly political. If this is true, he might have felt that he had already gone some way towards achieving this goal in his efforts to reinvent Scottish national identity. It is also possible that he conceived the new civil society as being enacted within informal rather than formal political fora.

1.2   Militia Scheme

While Ferguson is a perfectibilist committed to progress he is also a kind of nostalgic moralist alarmed at the damage done to the moral personality by that same, presumably natural, progress. His practical solution to the wealth/virtue problem lay in recommending the institution of a citizen militia believing this to be the best chance of restoring civic virtue while in no way impairing productivity. Ferguson, in company with the majority of the Scottish Moderate literati, supported militias in general, but was particularly keen for Scotland's right to raise them and made a special, though discreet, point of underlining this fact when writing in support of them generally.[1375] This concern stemmed partly from the fact that martial

---

[1372] *Essay*, p. 251.

[1373] John Robertson, *The Scottish Enlightenment and the Militia Issue*, p. 205. John Stuart Shaw has interpreted the particularly fierce faction fighting of English and pre-Union Scottish politics as partly a function of the '*absence* of formal party organisations'. John Stuart Shaw, *The Political History of Eighteenth Century Scotland*, Basingstoke: MacMillan, 1999, pp. 18-19. My emphasis.

[1374] *P.II.*, pp. 510-11. See also *Essay*, pp. 209-10. This attitude seems to have been partly a function of his views on spontaneous order. Ferguson notes: 'As uniformity...in a particular way of thinking, proceeds from communication, and is preserved by habit, it were absurd to employ any other method, to obtain or preserve unanimity. The use of force in particular, to dictate opinion, is preposterous and ineffectual'. *P.I.*, p. 219. Ferguson also cautions against the popular but misplaced belief that the 'silence' of the people denotes consent. *Essay*, p. 260.

[1375] As Sher notes, 'the *Reflections* is notable for its delicate handling of the Scottish question, Without ever mentioning Scotland by name, Ferguson contended that denying the militia to one allegedly factious part of Great Britain would have the effect of increasing disaffection and hostility in that area'. Sher, *Church and University*, p. 221.

valour was central to Scottish identity but it also stemmed from (well-founded) fears that the Scots would be excluded from Pitt's impending militia bill. Although Scotland's right to its own militia was made 'legally impossible' as a consequence of the Jacobite rebellion in 1745,[1376] Ferguson held out hopes that Scotland would some day be permitted to raise its own militia. In fact, militias were probably his best and only institutional hope for reinvigorating Scottish civic virtue, not only because the likelihood of Scotland's recovering its political institutions seemed remote, but because he accepted the Act of Union as generally beneficial to Scotland.[1377] Ferguson's motivation was also practical: The threat of a French invasion[1378] made local defence an urgent theme in Scottish public discourse.[1379] There was also the issue of 'hurt national pride' due to the fact that Pitt's 1757 Militia Act granted England and Wales the right to raise militias, but pointedly excluded Scotland. The defeat of the Scottish Militia Bill of 1760 was a further and compounding source of wounded Scottish dignity. The Jacobite rebellion of 1745-6 was undoubtedly the cause of London's wariness, nevertheless, Ferguson and other militia agitators, being avowedly anti-Jacobite, regarded Scottish exclusion as unjust.[1380] Along with other members of the Select Society (where the issue was frequently debated) Ferguson campaigned vigorously for a Scots militia. Both Ferguson and his friend, Alexander Carlyle, wrote pamphlets on the topic.[1381]

The beacon of the citizen militia model was the Swiss system which Ferguson praised enthusiastically. '[T]he only People in Europe who are regularly Armed', he wrote, are also 'the most Industrious and the most Peaceable Citizens.'[1382] The Swiss example demonstrated that, contrary to the claims of sceptics, an armed citizenry did not threaten either productivity or internal security. Ferguson is thus committed, simultaneously, to wealth and virtue, apparently believing that it is possible, after all, to accommodate the two primary goals of a state: security and prosperity. According to Ferguson, soldiering should be singled out and exempted from the normal course of task specialisation. Deploring the separation of political, civil and military 'departments' which render practitioners mere 'tradesmen', he recommends instead a 'union of departments' to avoid the 'ruinous ignorance' which always leads to corruption.[1383] But his resolve seems weak here. Significantly, he stresses that the military should be dominated by the upper classes, in order to prevent rebellion against the established social order. Because people of high rank are 'best

---

[1376] Oz-Salzberger, 'Introduction' to *Essay*, p. xii.

[1377] Smith, *The Political Philosophy of Adam Ferguson*, pp. 19-20.

[1378] '[I]n the summer and autumn of 1759'. Sher, *Church and University*, p. 222.

[1379] Oz-Salzberger, 'Introduction' to *Essay*, p. xii.

[1380] Broadie, *The Scottish Enlightenment*, p. 91. And yet the reaction in Scotland was mild considering the insult. Alexander Carlyle was particularly dismayed by this attitude and regarded Scottish acceptance of the defeat as 'servil[e]'. Sher, *Church and University*, p. 221.

[1381] Ferguson's was entitled: *Reflections Previous to the Establishment of a Militia* (1756) while Carlyle wrote *The Question Relating to a Scots Militia Considered* (1760).

[1382] Letter to William Eden (later Baron Auckland) January 2, 1780, *Correspondence,* No. 170, I, p. 228. See also Sher, 'Adam Ferguson, Adam Smith, and the Problem of National Defence', pp. 240-68.

[1383] 'Separation of Departments', *Collection of Essays*, No. 15, pp. 141-51.

educated' they tend to 'have the greatest interest in [the state's] preservation.'[1384] Ferguson conveys the impression throughout his corpus that, ideally, it is preferable that the entire population of able men are 'familiar with arms' but in these lecture notes he makes the important qualification that this ideal is impossible in a modern, large scale, differentiated nation like Britain where citizens were not 'nearly upon a footing of equality' that would otherwise prevent rebellion and threats to the existing order.[1385] The next best thing, then, is the limitation of arms to persons of 'a certain condition' (the words 'to exclude the rabble' were crossed out by Ferguson).[1386] On a practical note, though some of Ferguson's Scottish contemporaries argued for militia schemes that called for compulsory conscription, Ferguson's seems to have been based on voluntary participation. In preparation for his scheme, he called for legislation freeing up the use of arms, such as the Game Laws, and the right for free-holders to arm one man.[1387]

In any case, its seems that on this count, at least, Ferguson's classical prejudices win out over his otherwise unerring belief that specialisation is a natural process. The dismemberment of the moral personality defies nature yet this very dismemberment is also a product of a natural, spontaneously generated process. Ferguson's solution to resolving his entrapment in a contradiction of his own making is to arbitrarily draw the line at the martial arts while approving all other forms of specialisation, especially the 'industrial' and commercial. So, while the division of labour is a generally positive development there is one arena of life that must be carefully quarantined from its effects: the art of war. To deprive a people of military valour is to deprive them of their essential humanity,[1388] their 'dignity and strength,'[1389] their enjoyment of the highest virtues, and a degree of national security which would otherwise equal that of 'invincible' Rome.[1390]

1.3   Educational Programme

Another solution is found in Ferguson's suggestion that governments could justifiably insert some kind of remedial educational programme into the existing school curriculum. Acutely aware of this intrusion into the system of 'natural liberty' (as Smith referred to it) Ferguson invokes an argument identical to that used by Smith in the *Wealth of Nations,* namely, that although education is a strictly private concern we may 'except' from 'this general rule...every case in which defence or publick safety is at stake'. Ferguson recommends that a...

> ...committee of Parliament or other publick authority might no doubt with great advantage be interposed to report from Age to Age what regulations might be required

---

[1384] Unpublished lecture notes of April 9th, 1776, quoted in Sher, 'National Defense', p. 253.

[1385] Quoted in Sher, 'National Defense', p. 252.

[1386] Letter to William Eden, January 2, 1780, *Correspondence,* No. 170, I, p. 228.

[1387] Hamowy, 'Progress and Commerce', p. 85.

[1388] 'Separation of Departments', *Collection of Essays,* No. 15, pp. 142-3.

[1389] *Reflections,* London, 1756, p. 13.

[1390] *Reflections,* p. 36.

in publick schools to prepare the rising generations for that part which necessity might
impose on every individual for the safety of his country.

Ferguson implies that this might be some kind of citizenship training with an
emphasis on martial skills, for the passage which immediately follows stresses that a
person 'who cannot defend himself is not a Man and he who cannot take part in the
defence of his country is not a Citizen'.[1391]

1.4   Mixed Monarchy

Apart from this, and the limited militia scheme, there are no positive
recommendations for institutional or constitutional reforms to accommodate the high
levels of civic engagement Ferguson seems to be demanding. And there are certainly
no remedial suggestions for the problem of elite rule and mass exclusion. In his early
work he seems much more amenable to the idea of a wider franchise. For example, it
is suggested in the *Institutes* that so long as the 'inferior class' is not 'greatly
debased or corrupted' they 'may have a share' (but not an 'active' one) 'in the
government' either by exercising veto power over the 'determinations of the
aristocracy' or by being enabled to choose 'those who are to act for them'.[1392] But in
his later writings, there is little enthusiasm for the idea of popular suffrage, let alone
for the alluded-to veto mechanism.

Ferguson's preferred constitution is generally the existing one[1393] (except, of
course, in the case of despotism or any other form of total rule) since, to his mind, it
has evolved naturally via the various processes of spontaneous order. In Britain's
case, this led him to recommend the retention of its existing constitutional
monarchy. Despite his theoretical and personal 'predilection' for 'small',
independent states[1394] Ferguson distrusts, *in practice*, 'popular or republican'
governments in any setting other than a small and intimate tribal community. For
more developed or extensive societies, they were little more than 'mob rule' and
therefore practically inferior to his preferred model, the 'mixed monarchy'.[1395]

[1391] Ferguson, 'Separation of Departments' *Collection of Essays,* No. 15, p. 150. Rousseau had taken
an almost identical line when he argued that, in order to limit 'that personal interest' which 'enfeeble[s]'
the state and guard against the 'evils' resulting from 'the indifference of the citizens to the fate of the
Republic', any 'careful and well-intentioned government' will be 'vigilant incessantly to maintain or
restore patriotism and morality among the people' via a system of publicly funded civics education.
Rousseau, 'A Discourse on Political Economy', *Social Contract and Discourses,* p. 150. Ferguson also
agreed with Rousseau that the ideal political community is one in which every citizen enjoys a degree of
independence and yet is also 'very dependent on the city' whose strength, in turn, is the only sure way to
'secure the liberty of its members'. Rousseau, *Social Contract,* p. 227.

[1392] *Institutes,* pp. 272-3.

[1393] *P.II.,* pp. 496-8.

[1394] Letter to William Eden, January 2, 1780, *Correspondence,* No. 170, I, p. 230.

[1395] Contrary to Alan Smith's claims that 'Ferguson explicitly disapproved of mixed monarchy of the
British type', preferring instead 'a certain sort of pure monarchy'. *The Political Philosophy of Adam
Ferguson,* pp. 18-19. See, for example, Ferguson, *Remarks,* p. 13; *History,* p. 407; *Essay,* p. 252. It was
also Montesquieu's preference. *Laws,* 2. 11.6. p. 157. For Ferguson's disapproval of republican
movements (by which he meant suffragists) see Letter to John Mcpherson, January 10, 1780,
Correspondence, No. 171, I, p. 233.

Popular rule is a threat to liberty, says Ferguson. After all, '[w]hen all the powers of the Roman Senate were transferred to the popular assemblies, the Liberty of Rome came to an end.'[1396] Clearly 'the power of the people is not the good of the people.'[1397] Ferguson applauds attempts in Rome 'to prevent, as much as possible...ill-informed assemblies of people from deliberating on matters of state'.[1398] He cautions that '[w]hen power is transferred to the populace it is exercised with malice and poor judgement' noting that popular assemblies are generally tumultuous, 'capricious', 'disorderly'[1399] and informed by 'superstition' rather than 'reason'. When a constitution is 'overcharged by the numbers that part[ake] of its sovereignty' it becomes 'overwhelmed' and destroyed. Consequently, attempts to engage the masses ('citizens of least consideration') in public decisions are, at the very least, 'presumptuous'.[1400] Commercial nations with a well-developed system of rank distinctions, even where of 'a small extent' are 'best fitted to aristocratical government or to mixed republic'.[1401] In some, very rare, cases, hereditary monarchies may be appropriate, but only among a populace whose social order is underpinned by such a rigid class structure that distinctions are maintained exclusively from a sense of 'vanity and...personal importance'. 'Such a people' are so lacking in virtue that they 'are not fit to govern themselves'. Their willingness to defer to the authority of rank and rank alone means that only an hereditary monarch will enjoy legitimacy. But these arrangements are far from ideal because even the monarch in such a regime will lack virtue and can only be relied upon to attend 'to the public safety and ...order' out of a concern 'for the preservation of his own person and dignities.'[1402]

Of course, mixed or constitutional (but *not* hereditary) monarchies are not entirely antithetical to the civic tradition (especially the version of civic humanism that the Scots both worked within and carved out for themselves) which is not, as is commonly thought, reducible to constitutional republicanism. They can be accommodated within the tradition so long as they represent regularly constituted government[1403] which is precisely what Ferguson had in mind. Mixed monarchies are endorsed because they are at least one way of preventing degeneration. Such had been Machiavelli's view when he restated in the *Discourses* the Polybian argument that single types of polities were instable and doomed to collapse.[1404] Ferguson thus endorses a kind of neo-Polybian model with its system of checks and balances, and

---

[1396] *Remarks*, p. 14. Ferguson's emphasis.

[1397] *Remarks* p. 52. See also *History*, p. 407.

[1398] *History*, p. 309.

[1399] *History*, pp. 116, 119-20.

[1400] *History*, pp. 108-22.

[1401] *Institutes,* p. 273.

[1402] *Institutes*, p. 274-5.

[1403] Robertson, 'The Scottish Enlightenment at the Limits of the Civic Tradition', in Hont, and Ignatieff, (eds), pp. 139-40. Robertson provides a subtle and detailed treatment of the distinctiveness of the Scottish variant of the civic tradition, especially of their attitude to what regularly constituted government consisted in.

[1404] Machiavelli, *Discourses*, 1. 2, p. 109.

division of powers.[1405] 'It is well known', he opines, 'that constitutions framed for the preservation of liberty, must consist of many parts; and that senates, popular assemblies, courts of justice, magistrates of different orders, must combine to balance each other, while they exercise, sustain, or check the executive power'.[1406] The British system was just such a constitution. Any attempt to introduce a pure or unitary constitutional form could result in either tyranny or anarchy.[1407] Conversely, one of the 'beauties' of the mixed constitution is that 'it can withstand many evils without being overthrown'.[1408] This is because in 'governments properly mixed' a 'counterpoise' is found 'in which the public freedom and the public order are made to consist.'[1409]

2. DISCUSSION

We have seen that, despite his sustained and intensive critique of mechanisation, political elitism, bureaucratic centralisation and the mercenary spirit of commercialism, there is little or no spirit of revolution or dramatic reform in Ferguson. Notwithstanding his persistent rhetorical enthusiasm for mass political mobilisation, the absence of calls for such reforms as universal suffrage (or even a modest broadening of the franchise), mass representative institutions, a universal militia scheme or a devolvement in specialisation functions seems at odds with his seemingly enlightened critique of British social arrangements. Accordingly, Kettler and Lehmann both seem justified in their condemnation of Ferguson's conservatism and his apparent willingness to pay only lip service to the ideal of mass political engagement.

Ferguson was consistently averse to radical innovation of any kind. He never recommended the devolvement of any of the institutions or developments he identified as destructive agents of civil society because, ultimately, he was a defender of commerce and the status quo. Though he led the campaign to secure a Scottish militia, Ferguson rallied to the government side in defence of the Union. In addition, Christopher Wyvill was rebuffed when he tried to enlist Ferguson's support for the Parliamentary Reform movement which sought a broadening of the franchise.[1410] And whereas Ferguson ordinarily condemned imperialism and asserted the right of all nations to self-determination, in the case of the American revolt he vigorously defended Britain's right of imperial rule. Indeed, in 1778 he acted as

---

[1405] *Essay*, p. 123-4; See also Crehan, 'The Roman Analogy', p. 20.

[1406] *Essay*, p. 252; *P.II.*, p. 498.

[1407] *Essay*, p. 124-5.

[1408] Letter from Adam Ferguson to the Reverend Christopher Wyvill, December 2, 1782, *Correspondence*, II, No. 215, p. 292.

[1409] *Essay,* p. 158. '[N]ations' intent on 'acting wisely in pursuit of public order and freedom' will avoid any 'simple' constitutional forms. Republics are unsuitable for any society characterised by rank inequalities while reserving 'the enactment, as well as the execution of the law to any single power' is rarely, if ever 'safe'. Instead, the 'fortunate' will 'adopt some mixed' form. *P.II.*, p. 497.

[1410] Kettler, *Social and Political Thought of Adam Ferguson*, pp. 86-8; Fagg, *Biographical Introduction*, lxi-ii. For a copy of Wyvill's letter see, Letter to Adam Ferguson, November 14, 1782, *Correspondence*, No. 212, II, p. 289.

secretary to the Carlisle Commission, sent to Philadelphia to effect conciliation[1411] and was likely involved in the authorship of the 'Manifesto and Proclamation to the Members of Congress', October 3 1778. The 'Manifesto', issued by Ferguson and the other reconciliation commissioners (George Johnston, Sir Henry Clinton and William Eden) towards the end of their failed mission, was addressed to Congress, the state legislatures and 'all the inhabitants of the state'. It denounced the 'rebels' and threatened them with total war if they failed to capitulate.[1412] Ferguson wrote in private letters that the Americans deserved a 'sound drubbing', complaining that their resistance to being forced into 'submission' was a troublesome drain on British resources. He declared, with self-confessed 'contempt', that he was 'partial enough to Great Britain to wish them in the bottom of the Sea'[1413] and even devised a military plan to subdue them. He lays out this plan in an unpublished essay entitled 'Memorial Respecting the Measures to be Pursued on the Present Immediate Prospect of a Final Separation of the American Colonys (sic) From Great Britain'. Along with the 'Manifesto' it reveals how prejudiced was his attitude and how badly he judged the hopelessness of the American situation in his stubborn insistence that Britain should not 'relax her operations, give way to any claim of her enemys nor abandon a single possession in America'.[1414]

Ferguson's opposition to American independence is explored in detail in a pamphlet commissioned by the British government and published anonymously.[1415] It was entitled *Remarks on a Pamphlet Lately Published by Dr Price*.[1416] Richard Price had published in 1776 a pamphlet defending the American point of view (*Observations on the Nature of Civil Liberty, The Principles of Government, and the Justice and Policy of the War with America*).[1417] In Ferguson's rejoinder to Price he defends the status quo against what he regards as the Americans' ill-considered attempts at democracy and social equality which he was convinced would 'plung[e]

[1411] Following General Burgoyne's surrender to the Americans at Saratoga in October 1777, the Commission was instructed to 'offer everything short of independence if the colonies would remain loyal'. Fagg, *Biographical Introduction*, pp. xlviii, li. Ferguson was thwarted by the refusal of a passport to the capital. Lehmann, *Adam Ferguson*, p. 19.

[1412] As reported by Benson J. Lossing. *The Pictorial Field Book of the Revolution*, in 2 Vols, New York: Harper and Brothers Publishers, 1859, Vol. II. p. 144. The 'Manifesto' was '[p]robably wholly or chiefly the work of Ferguson'. Oz-Salzberger, *Translating the Enlightenment*, p. 320. It should be noted that the manifesto did not bear his signature; only those of Clinton, Carlisle and Eden appeared. Lossing, *Field Book of the Revolution*, p. 144. See also a letter by Ferguson entitled: 'To the President and other Members of Congress', Appendix G, *Correspondence*, II, pp. 552-4. It was sent to Congress prior to the issuing of the 'Manifesto' and was more conciliatory in tone, most likely because it was written before the Americans had made it clear that they were not prepared to negotiate.

[1413] Letter to John Macpherson, October 27, 1777, *Correspondence*, No. 100, I, p. 156.

[1414] 'Memorial Respecting the Measures to be Pursued on the Present Immediate Prospect of a Final Separation of the American Colonys From Great Britain', Appendix III, *Collection of Essays*, p. 306.

[1415] Fagg, *Adam Ferguson: Scottish Cato*, pp. 142-5.

[1416] The full title was *Remarks on a Pamphlet Lately Published by Dr Price, Intitled Observations on the Nature of Civil Liberty, The Principles of Government, and the Justice and Policy of the War with America*, etc. *In a Letter From a Gentleman in the Country to a Member of Parliament.*

[1417] 'The work...provoked an outpouring of pamphlets on both sides of the issue'. Fagg, *Biographical Introduction*, p. l.

[them] at once into military government'.[1418] The American problem could be solved easily, not by succession but by granting the colony representation in parliament.[1419] The pamphlet served the government's interests perfectly, reportedly prompting a 'pleased' response.[1420]

Ferguson defended his position by asserting, somewhat slyly, that 'Great Britain and its dependencies was not really 'an Empire but a kingdom'. As members of the 'same state' they had obligations to one another, obligations that the Americans now sought to avoid.[1421] Quite probably he believed this to be reasonable considering that Britain was at war with an originally British population of settlers rather than with an indigenous one. Further, within his own milieu, he was hardly isolated in his support for Britain against the American colonists for it was a view common among the Moderate literati.[1422] For example, William Robertson opposed the Americans and so did Lord Kames, at least in some respects. By the same token, others equally close to Ferguson had alternative views. Hume roundly condemned Britain's colonial policy and his attitude to the American revolutionaries is neatly expressed in a letter he wrote to Sir Gilbert Elliot: 'Let us…lay aside all Anger; shake hands, and part Friends'.[1423] Partly in the name of free trade, Smith took the view that Britain should either renounce its sovereignty over the colonies or else institute a 'new imperial arrangement, in which the colonies assumed the burdens of defence and civil administration'.[1424] John Millar also supported the Americans (as well as the French revolutionaries).[1425]

Ferguson adopted a conservative (though far less harsh line compared to his position on America) on the subject of Irish independence. He acknowledged that the grievances of the Irish should be taken seriously and hoped a solution could be found in order to 'obtain some Equitable Measures for the improvement of their Condition and Propertys'.[1426] But he baulked at the idea of granting independence. Admitting that although his 'predilection' was 'in favour of Small States and Separate Legislatures' he stipulated that he 'would carry this no farther with respect to the States I love than is consistent with their Safety'. Ferguson believed that '[e]ventual Union' with Ireland was essential to ensure, not only internal prosperity, but security against Britain's 'Rivals in Europe'.[1427]

[1418] Due to the fact that America was too extensive to support a democracy. *Remarks*, pp. 23-4.

[1419] *Remarks,* pp. 10-11.

[1420] Fagg, *Biographical Introduction*, p. i.

[1421] *Remarks*, pp. 19-22, 57-8

[1422] Fagg, *Biographical Introduction*, p. xlvii.

[1423] Dated July 22, 1768. *Letters of David Hume*, II. pp. 184-5.

[1424] 'Separation from the colonies, with free trade secured through a commercial treaty, seems to have been the most satisfactory solution in Smith's opinion, but since no nation could be expected to relinquish dominion voluntarily, the best that could be hoped for was imperial reform'. Dalphy I. Fagerstrom, 'Scottish Opinion and the American Revolution', *The William and Mary Quarterly*, Vol. 11 (2), 1954, pp. 252-275, p. 259.

[1425] Meek, 'The Scottish Contribution to Marxist Sociology' p. 46.

[1426] Letter to John Macpherson, December 18, 1779, *Correspondence*, No. 169, I. p. 223.

[1427] Letter to William Eden, January 2, 1780, *Correspondence*, No. 170, I. pp. 230-1. The 'rivals' in question were French ones. As Andrew Stuart later wrote to Ferguson: 'I congratulate you upon the good accounts we have lately had from Ireland, and the appearance of the Rebellion there being in a fair way of

3. EXPLANATIONS

Discrepant — even politically servile — as it at first appears, in fact Ferguson's conservatism can be traced easily to his prior theological and sociological commitments. The most important of these is the spontaneous order arrangement.

It has been noted that Ferguson emphasised the polygenesis of our key institutions and the absence of any long-term human design in their development. To expose them to the caprices of intemperate reformers would be nothing short of a disastrous. The Americans, and their supporters, he suggested gloomily, 'may not *know what they are doing.*' History has taught us 'that there is no time of more danger than those times of... enthusiastic expectation, in which mankind are bent on great and hazardous change.'[1428] In the *Principles* Ferguson poses the rhetorical question: 'To what government we should (sic) have recourse, or under what roof should we lodge?' In reply he declares emphatically, 'The present!'[1429] Our greatest achievements do not arise overnight; the incrementalism of developments is precisely what fits them to human needs. Our wisdom and competence grow with and through our institutions which are simultaneously the products *of*, and matrixes *for* the natural order. Revolutions bring rapid institutional changes with which we are ill-equipped to cope because we have not evolved with them; 'sudden innovations of any sort, precipitate men into situations in which they are not qualified to act.'[1430] Each age must be permitted to make its own contribution to the species' development and, since all innovations are time-bound, 'no age can with advantage Legislate unalterably for the Ages that follow.'[1431]

Ferguson's support for the existing order and his reluctance to play the role of the 'Great Legislator' was not, therefore, purely strategic or based on weakness of resolve (though there were undoubtedly elements of both involved) but on a genuine commitment to an order he conceived as already scientifically perfect and, moreover, divinely ordained. His investigations as a moral philosopher and historian revealed to him a complex pattern of seemingly irrefutable evidence confirming the existence of a social system which was *designed* to be self-ordering, self-adjusting and self-perpetuating, a system which could only be disrupted by meddlers with rationalistic delusions of grandeur. Ferguson tells us that it is not only the 'will of providence' that wherever there is society 'there should be government also' but further, that it is also willed by providence that 'man...accommodate himself to its forms' not the other way round. After all, 'there is greater danger from change than from any trivial inconvenience attending the actual order to things', namely the 'difficulty' of predicting 'all the consequences' and 'effects'. The radical reformer is like an insane 'architect' who presents 'his plan' to the commissioning client long

---

being crushed before the arrival of their French friends'. Letter to Adam Ferguson, June 4, 1798, No. 340, *Correspondence*, pp. 435-6.

[1428] *Remarks*, pp. 23-4, 59. Ferguson's emphasis.

[1429] *P.II.*, pp. 496.

[1430] *Institutes*, p. 274.

[1431] 'Separation of Departments', *Collection of Essays*, No. 15, p. 150.

'after the house is built'.[1432] Ferguson sought to avoid revisionism in any of the causes of corruption he identified because they were the products of our otherwise positive and progressive spontaneous order drives. While conceding that in most cases 'the present government may have its defects, as the walls or roof of the building in which we lodge may be insufficient', he admonishes revolutionaries to '[b]eware you take not away so much of the supports at once as that the roof may fall in.'[1433]

But Ferguson is not absolute in his conservatism, admitting that there are instances where, under conditions of abuse and tyranny, the people have a right to 'reclaim' their sovereignty.[1434] He was prepared to advocate change and even revolution but only if it could be shown that the existing regime was a state of political slavery that suppressed civic virtue.[1435] Ferguson finds himself on the same problematic ground as Burke in attempting (not altogether successfully) to reconcile the Whig principle of freedom with Tory notions of order.[1436] Despotism may sometimes inspire a kind of revolutionary madness, resulting in justifiable tumults:

> When the multitude, whose interests so much it is to have settled government, tear down the power by which themselves are protected, we must suppose that they are either seized by madness, or that by wrongs they are driven to despair.[1437]

And yet this was the most extreme scenario. Ferguson's endorsement of Francis Hutcheson's earlier defence of the right to resistance[1438] contains the important qualification that the present order, however seemingly intolerable, is almost always preferable to 'innovation', which, no matter how minor, brings on unforeseen changes which may be not be welcome. Innovation should only be a 'last remedy'.[1439]

It has been suggested that the significance of this last remark is that it was written during the French revolution and published by Ferguson during the great anti-Jacobin hysteria in Britain.[1440] But Ferguson's position here had been established long before this period, though it did harden over time. He saw no reason why British subjects living in 'America' had any more right to 'withdraw their allegiance' than subjects residing in 'Hounslow Heath or on Finchley-Common'.[1441] In addition, aside from his objection to revolution, the whole idea of American democracy alarmed Ferguson who strongly believed that large-scale republics were

---

[1432] P.II., pp. 496-8.

[1433] P.II., pp. 497. Ferguson's emphasis.

[1434] P.II., p.292; P.II., p. 234-5.

[1435] Kettler, Adam Ferguson, p. 217.

[1436] It should be noted that this would have been less problematic for an eighteenth century mind since party labels were then 'notoriously ambiguous'. Ward, 'The Tory View of Roman History', p. 413.)

[1437] P.II., p. 291.

[1438] Waszek, Man's Social Nature, p. 56.

[1439] P.II., p. 497.

[1440] Kettler, Adam Ferguson, p. 299. Though Ferguson eventually opposed the revolution he was however, impressed by the 'vigour and fervor' of the French'. Cited in Fagg, Biographical Introduction, lxxxii.

[1441] Remarks, p. 35.

unstable.[1442] Finally, there is an economic aspect to Ferguson's objections. Britain could not afford to forego its considerable investment in settling, 'nursing' and 'protecting' America[1443] and should not be expected to do so without a fight. [1444]

Nevertheless, Ferguson's position on the Irish situation is less readily reconciled within this framework for surely the *English* had been the radical innovators when they imposed rule on the Irish? Ferguson never deals with this problem satisfactorily and neither does he explain why Ireland is not a straightforward case of hubristic imperialism and tyranny. Further, despite all his efforts to avoid an ethnocentric anthropology, neither does he account for the fact that America was already populated at the time of British settlement and could hardly be deemed a vacant territory to be disputed over by its divided imperialistic settlers. Ferguson's disappointed critics are certainly on surer ground in this regard.

Aside from the spontaneous order constraint, Ferguson also wrote from the perspective of Whig-Presbyterian conservatism which conceived its role, philosophically, as one of justifying 'support for the existing institutional order' and of equating this support with civic virtue. Though the Moderates were liberal on questions of religious and intellectual freedom they were generally conservative on social and political issues.[1445] Equally, one could see Ferguson's position as a typically Stoic one; resignation to the established order is equated with wisdom and a dedication to the universal good.

> *I am in the station which God has assigned me*, says Epictetus. With this reflection, a man may be happy in every station; without it he cannot be happy in any. Is not the appointment of God sufficient to outweigh every other consideration? This rendered the condition of a slave agreeable to Epictetus, and that of a monarch to Antoninus. This consideration renders any situation agreeable to a rational nature, which delights not in partial interests, but in universal good.[1446]

Accordingly, Ferguson considered as unsociable any disturbance to the social fabric. '(W)e are ill members of society, or unwilling instruments in the hand of God' when 'we do our utmost to counteract our nature, to quit our station, and to undo ourselves.'[1447] Ferguson's conservatism was thus bolstered by the twin supports of a philosophical commitment to spontaneously generated order and to his Christian/Stoic beliefs. Such a reading fits with the view that Ferguson's conservatism was of the theological utilitarian variety.

[1442] *Remarks*, pp. 9-10, 23.

[1443] *Remarks*, pp. 28-30.

[1444] Yet, he was to write as late as 1798 that 'men are Such Idiots as to Think that conquests is prosperity and for themselves would sett no limits to either. We complain that the French would be a Conquering and the great Nation by Land: but our publick Scribblers at least are as Offensive in their turn by Sea. Is not rule Britania ov[e]r the Waves as bad as ça ira?'. Letter to Sir John Macpherson, May 14, 1978, *Correspondence*, No. 339, p. 433.

[1445] Sher, *Church and University*, pp. 180, 189, 262.

[1446] *Institutes*, pp. 158-9. This comment should not be interpreted as an endorsement of slavery which Ferguson condemned. Sher, *Church and University*, p. 180. One of the constituents of happiness is a willingness to submit 'to the will of God, in whatever he has assigned for our lot'. *P.II.*, p. 61. Although it does seem to contradict Ferguson's activism his position is best understood thus: people should accommodate themselves to any evolved constitution and serve it actively.

[1447] *Institutes*, p. 158.

Although he lavishly praised the Spartan approach to the avoidance of corruption (which was to avoid luxury altogether) Ferguson also rules out austerity as a solution to the ills of the modern commercial state. Such a remedy would have required him to renounce the commercial arts and market society itself,[1448] something which his abstract commitment to the laws of spontaneous order and concrete concern for the prosperity of Britain (and especially Scotland) could not permit.

Luxury, Ferguson suggests, is unavoidable because we are progressive animals constantly accruing advances in accommodations and comforts. We could 'propose to stop the advancement of arts at any stage of their progress', however, we would 'still incur the censure of luxury from those who have not advanced so far'.[1449] This is because 'the *necessary of life* is a vague and a relative term. It is one thing in the opinion of the savage; another in that of the polished citizen.'[1450] There is to be no return to some imagined halcyon age of primitive virtue. The excoriation of luxury in the debates of Ferguson's time are dismissed as a moralistic evasion of the real issue; the heralding of imminent corruption due to natural advances in conveniences is nothing more than the hackneyed catch-cry of the 'casuist.' Progress is inevitable and the conveniences it affords are morally indifferent.[1451] Those who apprehend virtue and the promise of future immortality in a life of denial should be made to recognise that it 'is not by any means necessary, that men should forego the happiness of their present state, in order to obtain that of a future one.'[1452] Ferguson and other Moderates of the Scottish Presbyterian Church generally eschewed asceticism and were, as Jane Fagg notes, 'liberal men enjoying Sunday night supper parties, play-going, card playing and dancing'.[1453] Ferguson argued publicly in defence of stage-plays and admonished their critics for railing 'against objects of a harmless or indifferent nature' when they should be reserving their 'opposition' for 'real vices and corruptions.'[1454]

There are other sound reasons for the toleration of luxury. Were private property and the methods of commercialism to be abolished, acquisitiveness, the driving force of commerce, would be undermined and polished society — not to mention progress itself — would falter. The conspicuous consumption of the wealthy inspires the labours of the poor, secure in the knowledge that they may some day enjoy the fruits of their labours in the manner of their 'social superiors'. The vital engine of commercialism, self-interest, is thus secured.[1455] Furthermore, since the insatiability of human needs is a key galvaniser of progress, any attempt to adopt a Stoic limitation-of-needs type strategy would be inadvisable, if not disastrous. The pursuit of the commercial arts is not only a natural expression of innate ambition but 'constitute(s) a material part, in the exercise of those faculties in which human

---

[1448] 'The policy of Sparta arose from a principle directly opposed to the maxims of trade, and went to restrain and suspend the commercial arts in all their effects'. *P.I.*, p. 252.

[1449] *Essay*, p. 232.

[1450] *Essay*, pp. 137-8. Ferguson's emphasis. See also *P.I.*, pp. 247-8.

[1451] *Essay*, pp. 232-4.

[1452] *P.I.*, p. 185.

[1453] Fagg, *Adam Ferguson: Scottish Cato*, p. 33.

[1454] Adam Ferguson, *The Morality of Stage Plays Seriously Considered*, Edinburgh, 1767, pp. 1-2.

[1455] *Essay*, p. 225. See also *P.II.*, p. 371.

nature is destined to improve'. Specifically, it has been shown that commerce develops 'prudence' and other cool virtues such as enterprise, frugality, sobriety and negative justice. It is our destiny as creative beings to invent, to specialise and refine our talents, and to pursue the commercial arts. The attainment of wealth normally requires discipline and the exercise of the above-mentioned virtues. The wealth itself and the self-restraint requisite to its proper use are thus acquired simultaneously. Our pursuit of wealth felicitously and spontaneously generates the governing mechanism for its proper use once attained: The 'very progress' that affords wealth also provides 'a taste of enjoyment and decency of manners'.[1456] Luxury can even be of positive benefit to nations with a mixed or monarchical constitution and a highly developed class system.[1457] '[B]esides the encouragement to arts and commerce' it provides, the 'lustre' it bestows on 'hereditary or constitutional dignities', gives vital support to the established social order.[1458] Luxury also indirectly generates social cohesion, providing 'a method by which different ranks are rendered mutually dependent and mutually useful.' We must therefore 'suffer the fruits' of commercial arts and labour 'to be enjoyed'.[1459]

Luxury only becomes a problem under two conditions: the first is when it is pursued at the expense of a proper attention to civic life; the second is where the wealth used to acquire luxury is obtained by depredation, rather than by the industry that would otherwise regulate its consumption:

> [S]uppose this end [wealth] to be obtained at once, and without any effort; suppose the savage to become suddenly rich, to be lodged in a palace, and furnished with all the accommodations or means of enjoyment, which an ample estate or revenue can bestow; he would either have no permanent relish for such possessions, or, not knowing how to use or enjoy them, would exhibit effects of gross and ungovernable passion, and a brutality of nature, from which, amidst the wants and hardships of his own situation, he is in great measure restrained.

This is why the luxury acquired through imperialism is so pernicious for it is 'unattended with...the virtues of industry, sobriety and frugality, which nature has prescribed as the means of attainment.'[1460] Accordingly, Ferguson enjoins his reader to disregard the puritanical complaints of moralists and recognise that luxury is the innocent and inevitable result of a positive process of development, the creative by-product of work.[1461] In addition, the wise will perceive that character is not necessarily associated with outward appearances: 'We must look for the characters of men in the qualities of the mind, not in the species of their food, or in the mode of their apparel.'[1462] Luxury and corruption need not be synonymous once a proper sense of priorities is adopted; the moralist's fixation on concerns of the body should

---

[1456] *P.I.*, pp. 253-5.

[1457] Note, though, that luxury is deemed to be detrimental to societies characterised by universal equality. *Essay*, p. 241.

[1458] *Essay*, p. 235.

[1459] *Essay*, pp. 232-4.

[1460] *P.I.*, pp. 254-5.

[1461] *P.II.*, p. 326-7.

[1462] *Essay*, p. 234.

be substituted for a more constructive focus on the education of the mind.[1463] In sum, so long as luxury is not 'preferred' to 'duty', 'friends...country or...mankind'[1464] polished nations should be able to enjoy, simultaneously, wealth, security and power, on the one hand, and virtue on the other.

4. CONCLUDING REMARKS

Though Ferguson was profoundly concerned about existing trends he did not appear to believe that the system needed a major overhaul. It seems that a little judicious tinkering was more what he had in mind. Like Burke, he thought that a few minor reforms were sometimes permissible in order to prevent a degenerative trend which might in all likelihood otherwise lead to complete revolution or 'innovation'.[1465]

Ferguson's reluctance to countenance reforms in a number of likely areas is partly traceable to the fact that his conservative tendencies seem to have hardened just as the opportunities for reform presented themselves, specifically, in the later stages of his life. At the same time, any reader of Ferguson will quite sensibly be puzzled by his failure to suggest any institutional mechanisms for generating the new civic realm he seems so anxious to promulgate. There is little to inspire optimism beyond his relatively modest calls for a selective citizen militia scheme, a single allusion to a civics education programme, the protection (by undisclosed means) of such liberties as free speech, right of 'resistance' and right of protest and the maintenance of the existing constitution. The most glaring omission, perhaps, is his abandonment of the principle of political equality which, confusingly, he both defends and repudiates in turn. His attitude to Ireland and America is also hard to align with the rest of his thought (notwithstanding his unusually positive attitude to war and conflict in general) as is his seemingly arbitrary attitude to martial specialisation. Given his commitment to progress and free will and his belief that humans are the bearers of history, one wonders how the principle of change is to be accommodated within his politics. He seems to be closing off the possibility for human institutions to evolve, allowing little scope for human agency. It is one thing

---

[1463] 'The use of morality on this subject, is not to limit men to any particular species of lodging, diet or cloaths, but to prevent their considering these conveniencies as the principal objects of human life'. *Essay*, p. 234.

[1464] *Essay*, pp. 232-4.

[1465] On this basis Burke made a lexical distinction between the terms 'reform' and 'innovation'. He wrote: 'It was then not my love, but my hatred to innovation, that produced my Plan of Reform. Without troubling myself with the exactness of the logical diagram, I considered them as things substantially opposite. It was to prevent that evil, that I proposed the measures'. Edmund Burke, 'A Letter to a Noble Lord', *Further Reflections on the Revolution in France*, Daniel E. Ritchie (ed.), Indiana: Liberty Press, 1992, p. 292. Even Rousseau, a far more trenchant critic of modernity, did not advocate radical solutions such as a return to primitive conditions but resorted to the cultivation of virtue as the best guard against corruption. 'Discourse on the Origin of Inequality', *Social Contract and Discourses*, pp. 125-6.

to insist that progress should proceed insensibly and by degrees but quite another to apparently resist all change, rationalistic or otherwise.[1466]

The lack of concrete solutions to address the problems which Ferguson made his life's work are partly symptomatic of a paralysed philosophical position. As a moralist with both sociological sensibilities and a social conscience, he was alarmed at the state of commercialising Britain, but as a perfectibilist anti-contractarian committed to defending the laws of spontaneous generation, he could encourage neither radical reform nor a return to primitive conditions.

Ferguson seemed to believe that the warning he was delivering to the British public, and especially its statesmen, would be incentive enough to bring about the appropriate modifications. This was his particular contribution to the social problems of his day; the textual warning was itself a civic act. Referring to himself in a letter to Christopher Wyvill as 'a Sincere friend of the Constitution' he reflected that since he was 'so little able to serve it in practice' he was at least enabled 'to pay it all due respect in [his] Speculations.'[1467] Notwithstanding the awkward corner into which he had painted himself, Ferguson's conservatism, while at times disappointing, should not be interpreted purely as a sign of irresponsibility or insincerity but also as a logical function of his attachment to a mature set of philosophical and moral precepts, namely his dual commitment to Stoic-Presbyterianism, and perhaps more importantly, the spontaneous order arrangement.

[1466] Even though, *in principle*, he admits that some degree of rationalistic reform is often necessary. The 'form of society...may be rude or defective and require the exercise of reason to remove its inconveniencies, or to obtain the advantages of which it is susceptible'. *P.I.,* p. 263.

[1467] Letter from Adam Ferguson to the Reverend C. Wyvill, December 2, 1782, *Correspondence*, No. 215, II, p. 292. For further discussion see Ian R. Christie, *Willkes Wyvill and Reform*, London: Macmillan and Co. Ltd, 1962.

CHAPTER 13

CONCLUSION

Ferguson's Achievement

Like all centuries, the eighteenth was characterised by its own set of conflicts. There were collisions between a number of opposing worlds including the religious with the profane; the classical with the modern and the hedonistic with the moralistic. More specifically, social and political writers waged disputes over the competing values of progress and the need for order; duty versus political and economic expediency; wealth and virtue; belief and reason; religion and science, as well as the respective roles of reason and passion in understanding social life.

Ferguson engaged in all of these conflicts and he did so in a dialect that combined two competing languages of eighteenth century Scottish discourse: civic humanism and commercial or liberal humanism. The fact that he spoke both of these languages fluently and simultaneously sometimes resulted in awkwardness. But there are other times when the effect is original and striking.

Ferguson was a moral philosopher who employed — and helped shape — the developing methodologies of social science in order to combat his atheistic, hedonistic and revolutionary adversaries and to persuade an increasingly sophisticated, enlightenment readership that 'God', teleology and arguments from design were still relevant to the scientific study of society. He wanted to *prove* scientifically, rather than assert as a matter of belief, that the world, even in its most banal and discordant aspects, is the result of design and beneficent purpose. He saw himself as a latter day Stoic sage whose mission it is to disclose, empirically, the uniform laws governing human nature in order to submit them as moral guidelines for living. Therefore, whenever we detect a sociological flavour in Ferguson's work, we need to be mindful of the moral agenda that is being played out as well as the theological context within which this agenda is framed. But these facts need not disqualify Ferguson's insights as original and anticipatory mainly because of his heavy reliance on efficient or secondary causes for explaining social processes and equilibrium.

Ferguson's methodological approach builds on and advances the early social science of Montesquieu, bringing us a step closer to modern social science as it is now understood. Although his project was still bound up in the methodologies of the distinctively eighteenth-century disciplines of pneumatics, moral philosophy and politics, Ferguson's interest in anthropology and his perception of universal, underlying structure and function allowed him to speak in terms of social laws. Coupled with his acute sensitively to the effects of social change, this capacity made him a kind of early historical sociologist.

Ferguson is not *the* 'Father of sociology' but he is certainly one of its many parents and there is certainly a wealth of original insights in his work. His development of the idea of spontaneous order laid important groundwork for the commencement of social science proper and subsequently influenced an important strand of liberal theory and political economy. His appreciation of social change is as profound as it is comprehensive and he provided the first penetrating analysis of the social effects of economic expansion, bureaucratisation, over-extension and specialisation. Ferguson also gives us a groundbreaking account of the negative impact of consumerism on political life in which is stressed the importance of social capital and political efficacy to the maintenance of strong polities. His observations on the social function of habit and the role of the physical environment exhibit great prescience, as do his observations on the positive effects of conflict. Finally, his anti-rationalist and anti-contractarian sociology of emotion is important; by treating our 'passions', 'sentiments', 'desires and aversions' as independent variables he gives us a proper theory of social development that represents a significant break with traditional historiographies.

Though his influences are mainly religious and antique, the innovative perspective Ferguson introduces constitutes a foreshadowing of many of the concerns of the much later social sciences. The sociological impression is effected by the application of an antique diagnostic tradition to the novel conundrums of market society. Ferguson's concern with '*anomie*', for example, is really a contemporary adaptation of the Stoic interest in community and social intimacy; his critique of market ethics and contractualism, again, is a reformulation of Stoic concerns with the mechanisms of solidary association and the virtues of *humanitas* and '*sympatheia*'; his comments on the positive effects of conflict are revitalised and expanded observations of Tacitus, Thucydides and Machiavelli; his absorption with corruption is originally Aristotelian, Stoic and Polybian; over extension, Thucydidean; and luxury and civic participation, Stoic. Ferguson's unique contribution lay in his ability to give classical insights a 'sociological twist'[1468] thereby bridging the gap between modern and antique traditions. His work has value partly because it demonstrates that nineteenth and twentieth century sociology reformulated antique concerns with the organic unity of society.

Ferguson offered his readership a timely reminder of the pitfalls of progress and the importance of safeguarding civil society from its ill effects. The temperate rhythms of cool friendship, amicable strangership and political calm acclaimed by progress triumphalists do bring benefits but they also invite apathy, political torpor and the possibility of tyranny. Ferguson also has social scientific objections to the increasing rationalisation and institutionalisation of social and political arrangements. Increased central planning, bureaucratisation and rational constructivism might not bring about the order and prosperity anticipated by those Enlightenment thinkers who put all their faith in reason. In fact, they were equally liable to have the opposite effect.

[1468] To borrow John Brewer's words. Brewer, 'Adam Ferguson and the Theme of Exploitation', p. 473.

Ferguson's philosophy is a form of theodicy, a sustained attempt to defend his deep faith in a benevolent deity and a universe devoid of evil. Against claims that the world is in its senility due to the growth of vice, and consistent with his positive stress on the benefits of adversity, Ferguson suggests that corruption is merely the result of error, conceived, in the long view, as highly efficacious in our moral development. We are not like other animals whose instincts always direct them reliably, but possess consciousness and ambition, foresight, judgment and will which we alloy with our non-cognitive drives in the execution of any given act. Our peculiar freedom to choose has a regrettable by-product; we sometimes behave self-destructively, something other species never do. Other 'animals' never exceed the demands of the body, they always obey the herd instinct and they never exceed their personal territory beyond reasonable need. But because we are 'special animals', destined for progress and divine union, and therefore equipped with the requisite faculties for this privileged destination, things sometimes go awry.

Yet our actions are never truly evil; the corruption of the commercial age is simply the misdirected result of appetites that serve otherwise positive functions. Our natural ambition, belligerence and self-preservation normally lead us to progress and moral perfection, but when misapplied, result in the pursuit of such improper objects of attention as unnecessary territory, wealth for its own sake, hedonism and leisured pursuits. Ferguson was eager to remind his reader that there is more to life than self-interest, individual preference, conspicuous consumption, commodious accommodations, leisure and political calm. But since he also accepts progress as inevitable and natural, he directs his energies to minimising the negative impact of its corollaries by seeking a balance between community and commerce, wealth and virtue, civic duty and private liberty. It has been suggested here that the solutions he proposes are both institutional and cultural, yet Ferguson pays far more attention to outlining the *causes* than he does to indicating any remedies. These are only hinted at, and usually in the most vague of terms. This is curious and out of proportion to Ferguson's persistently advertised anxiety about the problem of corruption. Perhaps he considered the protracted warning embodied in a lifetime of scholarship to be a sufficient remedy in itself.

Further, it is not at all clear that Ferguson ever settles in his own mind the problem of balancing wealth with virtue. Indeed, ambivalence about economic progress is one of the most consistent threads running through his *oeuvre* and even the most patient reader will find Ferguson's attempts at reconciliation indecisive. For example, he clearly regards commerce as quite a sordid business and yet devotes considerable space to extolling its positive social and economic effects. At one point he describes 'the wealth...aggrandisement and power of nations' as a common effect of 'virtue' and 'the loss of these advantages' as a consequence of vice' yet for the most part he makes the reverse argument.[1469] He vehemently condemns imperialism yet supports Britain's treatment of America, Ireland and even Scotland. There is considerable criticism of the devastating effects of the division of labour, yet no recommendation to reverse it, except militarily. He discourses at length on the vitiating effects of luxury then decides that it is probably harmless after all, provided

---

[1469] *Essay*, p. 196; Sher, 'From Troglodytes to Americans', pp. 394-5.

its pursuit and consumption are properly regulated. And he never seems to find a definitive position on the relationship between interest and beneficence. Further, despite all the nostalgia and apparent regret it is also clear that Ferguson thinks much is gained through progress. There is an expansion of freedom and legal rights,[1470] a diffusion of wealth and economic independence, more and better security, and less brutality, 'religious superstition', cruelty and malice.[1471]

Ferguson's divided loyalties — his classical and atavistic prejudices, on the one hand, and his embrace of progress as an effect of the Providentially inspired laws of spontaneous order, on the other — cause him many problems. He demands a lot of his reader and a good deal of effort is required in order to properly untangle the various threads of his system. Nevertheless, many of his ambivalences are either reconciled or reconcilable. For example, beneath the ascetic rhetoric, his final position on luxury is discernable; the tension between conflict and Stoicism is also resolvable and so is much of his apparent political quietism. At other times, the reconciliation gives rise to further tensions; for example, the solution to 'the paradox of progress and decline' answers a lot of questions but it also compromises Ferguson's anti-rationalist commitments. In addition, he fails to show that history really *has* been a process of gradual improvements in the moral realm; in fact he seems to be demonstrating the opposite by dwelling on the growth of vice and the affective superiority of pre-commercial civilisations.

Ferguson's achievement lies partly in his acuity as an observer of the effects of modernity and market ethics on social life and his preparedness to deal with the constraints of *actual* economic and social conditions. His treatment of corruption represents a sustained effort to balance Stoic values with a modern acceptance of progress; to blend a classical republican sensibility with the conditions and constraints of rapid commercialisation. Ferguson pledges his commitment to the idea of spontaneous order by accepting all drives, even self-interest, as natural while simultaneously holding to the core canons of civic humanism, hence the claim that he is a liberal-Stoic, wary of progress and yet mindful of its benefits.

It has been mentioned that Ferguson was a disorderly, sometimes exasperating scholar. This is partly related to the tension between his romantic idealism and pragmatic realism but it also has a lot to do with his appreciation of the complexity of the human condition and his belief that it is not only reason, but the unseen, unplanned, sub-rational and visceral forces, that keep the human universe in motion. Ferguson's profound appreciation of this fact, and his ability to make social science of it, was a major accomplishment.

[1470] *Essay*, p. 247.
[1471] *P.I.*, p. 305.

BIBLIOGRAPHY

1. PRIMARY SOURCES

Ferguson, Adam. *A Sermon Preached in the Ersh Language to His Majesty's Highland Regiment of Foot, Commanded by Lord John Murray, at their Cantonment at Camberwell on the 18ᵗʰ Day of December. Being appointed as a Solemn Fast,* 1745, London: A. Millar, 1746.

—*Reflections Previous to the Establishment of a Militia,* London: R and J. Dodsley, 1756.

—*The Morality of Stage Plays Seriously Considered,* Edinburgh: n.p., 1757.

—*The History of the Proceedings in the Case of Margaret, Commonly Called Peg, Only Lawful Sister of John Bull, Esq.,* Edited and with an Introduction and Notes by D. R. Raynor, Cambridge: Cambridge University Press, [1761] 1982.

—*Analysis of Pneumatics and Moral Philosophy,* For the Use of Students in the College of Edinburgh, Edinburgh, A. Kincaid and J. Bell, 1766.

—*An Essay on the History of Civil Society,* Edited and with an Introduction by Fania Oz-Salzberger, Cambridge: Cambridge University Press, [1767] 1996.

—*Institutes of Moral Philosophy,* New York: Garland Publishing Company, [1769] 1978.

—*Remarks on a Pamphlet lately Published by Dr. Price, intitled 'Observations on the Nature of Civil Liberty...', in a Letter from a Gentleman in the Country to a Member of Parliament,* London: T.Cadell, 1776

—*The History of the Progress and Termination of the Roman Republic,* London: Jones and Company, [1783] 1834.

—*Principles of Moral and Political Science: Being Chiefly a Retrospect of Lectures Delivered in the College of Edinburgh, in Two Volumes,* Edinburgh: Printed for A. Strahan and T. Cadell. London; and W. Creech, Edinburgh, 1792.

—'Minutes of the Life and Character of Joseph Black, M.D, Addressed to the Royal Society of Edinburgh', *Royal Society of Edinburgh Transactions,* Vol. 5 (3), 1801, pp. 101-117.

—*Biographical Sketch or Memoir of Lieutenant-Colonel Patrick Ferguson, Originally Intended for the British Encyclopedia,* Edinburgh: Printed for J. Moir, 1816.

—*The Correspondence of Adam Ferguson,* Edited by V. Merolle with an Introduction by J.B. Fagg, in Three Volumes, London: William Pickering, 1995.

—*Collection of Essays,* Edited and with an Introduction by Yasuo Amoh, Kyoto: Rinsen Book Co., 1996.

—'Memorial Respecting the Measures to be Pursued on the Present Immediate
Prospect of a Final Separation of the American Colonys From Great Britain', in
Ferguson, *Collection of Essays*, Appendix III.[1472]

2. SOURCES KNOWN OR LIKELY TO HAVE BEEN CONSULTED BY
FERGUSON[1473]

Abulgaze, Bahadur Chan. *Genealogical History of the Tartars*, Translated into
English from the French, with Additions, in 2 Vols.1730.

Alison, Archibald. *Essays on the Nature and Principles of Taste*, Edinburgh: Bell
and Bradfute, 1790.

Appianus of Alexandria. The History of Appian of Alexandria, London: Printed for
John Amery, at the Peacock against S. Dunstan's Church in Fleet-street, 1692.

Arbuthnot, John. *Miscellaneous Works* (including *The History of John Bull*),
London, in 2 Vols, 1770.

Aristotelis. *Opera Omnia quae Exstant*, Graece et Latine,1629.

Bacon, Francis. *The Works of Francis Bacon ... In Four Volumes. With Several
Additional Pieces*, London: Printed for A. Millar, 1740.

Baxter, Andrew. *An Enquiry into the Nature of the Human Soul; Wherein the
Immateriality of the Soul is Evinced from the Principles of Reason and
Philosophy*, London: Printed by James Bettenham, for the Author, 1733.

Beccaria, Cesare. *An Essay on Crimes and Punishments*. Translated from the Italian.
With a Commentary, Attributed to Mons. de Voltaire, Translated from the French,
London: Printed for J. Almon, 1767.

Berkeley, George. *A Treatise of the Principles of Human Knowledge*, London: 1710.

Blackstone, William. *Commentaries on the Laws of England*, Oxford: Clarendon
Press, 1765.

Blair, Hugh. *Lectures on Rhetoric and Belles Lettres.* London: Printed for W.
Strahan; T. Cadell and W. Creech, in Edinburgh, in 2 Vols, 1783.

Buffon, Georges Louis Leclerc, Comte de. *Buffon's Natural History,* London: C.
and G. Kearsley, 1792.

Burke, Edmund. *A Philosophical Enquiry into the Origin of our Ideas of the Sublime
and Beautiful*, London: J. Dodsley, 1782.

—*Observations on the Late State of the Nation,* London: J. Dodsley, 1769.

[1472] A recently discovered essay almost certainly written by Ferguson. Amoh, Introduction to
Collection of Essays, p. xvi.

[1473] Aside from standard references to sources such as: Homer, Virgil, Shakespeare and The Holy
Bible.
There is no known record of the contents of Ferguson's library. This list has been compiled by referring
to works directly cited by Ferguson or likely to have been available to him. Exact editions are not known
though the likely edition is determined, where possible, by date and availability and by cross-referencing
with editions owned by either Hume or Smith. Full publishing details are provided where available. For
further details on the contents of the Smith and Hume libraries see: David Fate Norton and Mary J.
Norton, *The David Hume Library*, Edinburgh: Edinburgh Biographical Society, 1996 and Hiroshi Mizuta,
Adam Smith's Library: A Catalogue, Edited and with an Introduction and Notes by Hiroshi Mizuta,
Oxford University Press: New York, 2000. For editions used by the author, see below, Section III.

—*Speech of Edmund Burke, esq. on American Taxation*, April 19, 1774. London: J. Dodsley, 1775.

—*Speech of Edmund Burke, esq. On Moving his Resolutions for Conciliation with the Colonies, March 22, 1775,* London: J. Dodsley, 1775.

—*Thoughts on the Cause of the Present Discontents,* London: J. Dodsley, 1770.

—*A letter from Edmund Burke, esq; One of the Representatives in Parliament for the city of Bristol, to John Farr and John Harris, esqrs. Sheriffs of that City, on the Affairs of America.* London: J. Dodsley, 1777.

Butler, Joseph. *The Analogy of Religion, Natural and Revealed, to the Constitution and Course of Nature,* London: 1736.

—*Fifteen Sermons Preached at the Rolls Chapel,* London: 1726.

Burnett, James (Lord Monboddo). *Antient Metaphysics: or, the Science of Universals,* Edinburgh: J. Balfour and Co. Edinburgh, 1779 and London: T. Cadell, 1784.

Carceri, Giovanni Francesco Gemelli. *A Voyage Around the World, 1699-1700,* English transl, London: 1704.

Chardin, J. *The Travels of Sir John Chardin into Persia and the East-Indies, Through the Black Sea, and the Country of Colchis,*[1474] London: Christopher Bateman, 1691.

Ciceronis M. Tullii. (Cicero) Opera, *cum delectu commentariorum.* Edebat Josephus Olivetus . Tomus Primus [-nonus] Editio Tertia, Emendatiossima. Genevae: apud Fratres Cramer, 1758.

—De *Officiis ad Marcum Filium Libri Tres.* Glasguae: Excudebant Rob. et And. Foulis, 1757.

Clarke, Samuel. 'Discourse Concerning the Unchangeable Obligations of Natural Religion', *The Boyle Lectures of 1705,* London: 1706.

—*A Discourse Concerning the Being and Attributes of God,* London: 1716.

Colden, Cadwallader, *The History of the Five Indian Nations of Canada, which are Dependent on the Province of New-York in America,* London: T. Osborne, 1747.

Charlevoix, Pierre, *Journal of a Voyage to North-America, Undertaken by Order of the French King,*[1475] Translated from the French of P. de Charlevóix, London: Printed for R. and J. Dodsley, .1761.

Cooper, Anthony Ashley, (Lord Shaftesbury) *Characteristics of Men, Manners, Opinions, Times,* Edited and with an Introduction and Notes by John.M.Robertson, in 2 Vols, London: Grant Richards, 1723.

—*An Enquiry Concerning Virtue, or Merit,* London:1699.

D'Arvieux, The Chevalier, *Travels in Arabia the Desert,* London: 1718.

Dalrymple, J. *An Essay Towards a General History of Feudal Property in Great Britain,* Edinburgh: 1757.

[1474] *'[C]ontaining the author's voyage from Paris to Ispahan: to which is added, The coronation of this present King of Persia, Solyman the III.'.*

[1475] *'Containing the geographical description and natural history of that country, particularly Canada; together with an account of the customs, characters, religion, manners and traditions of the original inhabitants in a series of letters to the Duchess of Lesdiguières.'*

—*Memoirs of Great Britain and Ireland from the Dissolution of the last Parliament of Charles the Second, till the Capture of the French and Spanish Fleets at Vigo*, 3 Vols, Edinburgh: 1771-88.

Dampier, William. *A New Voyage Round the World, A Collection of Voyages*,[1476] London: James and John Knapton, 1729.

Davila, Enrico Caterino. *The History of the Civil Wars of France*, Translated into English by W. Aylesbury, London: 1647, and by Charles Cotterel, London: 1666.

De Retz, Jean François Paul de Gondi, Cardinal. *Memoirs of the Cardinal de Retz*, Nancy: 1717 and Edinburgh: 1731.

Diogenes Laertius. *De Vitis, Dogmatibus et Apophthegmatibus Clarorum Philosophorum Libri X. Graece et Latin*, Amstelaedam: apud Henricum Wetstenium, 1692.

Dion Cassius Cocceianus. *Historiae Romanae quae Supersunt*, Hamburg: Christiani Heroldi, 1750.

Epictetus. *Enchiridion*, et Cebetis Tabula, Graece et Latine. Prioribus editionibus Emendatiora & auctiora, Amstelodami: apud Joannem Ravensteinum, 1670.

—*His Morals, with Simplicius His Comment. With the Life of Epictetus, from Monsieur Boileau*, in 8. Vols, London: Printed by W.B. for Richard Sare, 1721.

Frederick the Great. *Memoirs of Brandenberg*, English Translation, 1752.

Florus, Lucius Annaeus. *The History of the Romans*, Done into English; Corrected, Amended, and with Annotations illustrated by M. Causabon, D.D. London: Printed by R.B. for Daniel Pakeman, 1658.

Gibbon, Edward. *The History of the Decline and Fall of the Roman Empire*, in 6 Vols, London: 1776-88.

Gray, Thomas. *The Poetical Works of Thomas Gray*, London: William Pickering, 1836.

Grotius, Hugo. *De Jure Belli ac Pacis*, Amsterdam: 1667.

Halley, E. 'An Estimate of the Degrees of Mortality of Mankind',[1477] *Philosophical Transactions*, Vol. 17, 1693, pp. 596-610.

Harris, James. *Hermes: or, a Philosophical inquiry Concerning Language and Universal Grammar*, London: Printed by H. Woodfall, for J. Nourse and P. Vaillant, 1751.

—*An Essay Upon Money and Coins*, Parts I and II, London: 1757-8.

Hartley, David. *Observations on Man, His Frame, His Duty and His Expectations*, London: 1749.

Hawkesworth, John. *An Account of the Voyages Undertaken by the Order of His Present Majesty, For Making Discoveries in the Southern Hemisphere, and Successively Performed by Commodore Byron, Captain Wallis, Captain Carteret,*

[1476] '*Containing I. Captain William Dampier's voyages round the world II. The voyages of Lionel Wafer ... III. A voyage round the world: containing an account of Capt. Dampier's expedition into the South Seas ... By W. Funnell ... IV. Capt. Cowley's voyage round the globe. V. Capt. Sharp's journey over the Isthmus of Darien ... VI. Capt. Wood's voyage ... VII. Mr. Robert's adventures and sufferings amongst the corsairs of the Levant'.*

[1477] '*[D]rawn from curious tables of the births and funerals at the city of Breslau, with an attempt to ascertain the price of annuities on lives'.*

and Captain Cook, in the Dolphin, the Swallow, and the Endeavour,[1478] London: W. Strahan and T. Cadell, 1773.

Helvetius, Claude Adrian. *De L'Esprit*, Paris: 1758.

Herbert, Edward. *The Life of Lord Herbert of Cherbury*, Written by Himself and Continued to his Death. London: Horace Walpole, 1764.

Hobbes, Thomas. *Elementa Pilosophica de Cive*, Amsterodami: apud Danielem Elzevirium, 1669.

—*Leviathan, or the Matter, Forme, & Power of a Commonwealth Ecclesiasticall and Civill.* London: Andrew Crooke, 1651.

Home, Henry (Lord Kames). *Essays on the Principles of Morality and Natural Religion*, Edinburgh: 1751.

—*Essays Upon Several Subjects Concerning British Antiquities*, Edinburgh: 1747.

—*Essays Upon Several Subjects in Law*, Edinburgh: 1732.

—*Historical Law Tracts*, Edinburgh, 1758.

—*Principles of Equity*, Edinburgh, 1760.

Home, Rev. John, *Douglas: A Tragedy*, London: 1780.

Hume, David. *A Treatise of Human Nature*, in 2. Vols, London: 1738.

—*An Enquiry Concerning Human Understanding*, Edinburgh: 1748.

—*An Enquiry Concerning the Principles of Morals*, Edinburgh: 1751.

—*The Natural History of Religion*, Edinburgh: 1757.

—*The History of England, from the Invasion of Julius Caesar to the Revolution in 1688*, in 6 Vols, London: 1770.

Hutcheson, Francis. *An Essay on the Nature and Conduct of the' Passions and Affections. With Illustrations on the Moral Sense*, London: 1728.

—*An Inquiry into the Original of our Ideas of Beauty and Virtue*, London: 1725.

—*An Enquiry Concerning Moral Good and Evil*, London: 1726.

—*A System of Moral Philosophy, in Three Books*, in 2 Vols, Glasgow and London: R. Foulis et al., 1755.

Johnson, Samuel. *Dictionary of the English Language*, London: Printed by W. Strahan, for J. and P. Knapton 1755.

Jones, Sir William. *A Grammar of the Persian Language*, London: 1771.

—*Dissertations and Miscellaneous Pieces Relating to the History and Antiquities, the Arts, Sciences, and Literature of Asia* (co-authored by W. Chambers, W.Hastings, Gen. Carnac, H. Vansittart, C. Wilkins, J. Rawlins, J. Shore, J.Williams, Arch. Keir Col. Pearse, Lieut. Col. Polier and others, London: Printed for G. Nicol, J. Walter, and J. Sewell, 1792.

Kolbe, Pieter. *The Present State of the Cape of Good Hope,* London: 1731.

Lafitau, Joseph-Francois. *Moeurs des Sauvages Ameriquains, Comparees aux Moeurs des Premiers Temps,* Paris: 1724.

Law, William. *Remarks Upon a Late Book, Entitled the Fable of the Bees*, London: 1724.

Leibnitz, M. De. *Essais de Theodicèe sur la Bonte di Dieu, la Libertè de L'Homme, et L'Origine du Mal*, Amsterdam: 1720.

[1478] *'Drawn up from the journals which were kept by the several commanders and from the papers of Joseph Banks, Esq. by John Hawkesworth'.*

Livy. *The Roman Historie Written by T. Livius of Padua*, Translated out of Latine into English, by Philemon Holland, London: Printed by W. Hunt, for George Sawbridge at the Bible on Ludgate Hill, 1659.

Locke, John. *An Essay Concerning Human Understanding*, London: 1694.

—*Two Treatises of Government*, London: 1690.

Long, A.A. 'Freedom and Determinism in the Stoic Theory of Human Action', in A. A. Long, (ed.), *Problems in Stoicism*, London: The Althone Press, 1971.

Lowthorp, John. *Philosophical Transactions and Collections to the End of the Year 1700,* Abridged and Dispos'd under General Heads by John Lowthorp and F.R.S. in 2 Vols, London: 1705.

Machiavelli, Niccolo. *Machivael's Discourses Upon the First Decade of T. Livius, Translated out of the Italian. To which is added his Prince.* With some marginal animadversions noting and taxing his errors by E.D., London: Printed for G. Bedell, and T. Collins, 1663.

—*The Florentine Historie*, London: Printed by T. Creede for W. Ponsonby, 1595.

—*Works of the Famous Nicolas Machiavel, Citizen and Secretary of Florence*, London: Printed for John Starkey, 1675.

MacPherson, James. *Fragments of Ancient Poetry Collected in the Highlands of Scotland*. Edinburgh:1760

—*Fingal, An Ancient Epic Poem in Six Books, Together with Several other Poems Composed by Ossian*, London: 1762.

MacPherson, James. *Temora, An Ancient Epic Poem in Eight Books Composed by Ossian*, London: 1763.

Mandeville, B., *The Fable of the Bees or Private Vices, Publick Benefits, With an Essay on Charity and Charity Schools*, London: 1723.

Marcus Aurelius, T*he Meditations of the Emperor Marcus Aurelius Antoninus. A new translation from the Greek original; with a life, notes, etc.,* by R. Graves Bath, Printed by R. Cruttwell, for G. G. J. and J. Robinson, London, 1792.[1479]

Marsden, William. *The History of Sumatra,*[1480] London: Printed for the author by J. McCreery and sold by Longman, Hurst, Rees, Ormeand Brown, 1811.

Maupertuis, Pierre-Louis Moreau. *Essai de Philosophe Morale,* Berlin: 1749.

Metelief, Cornelius. *An Historicall and True Discourse, of a Voyage Made ... into the East Indies*. London: William Barrett, 1608.

Millar, John. *The Origin of the Distinction of Ranks*, Edinburgh: 1771.

Milton, John. *Paradise Lost*, London: 1732.

Montesquieu, Charles-Louis. *Lettres Persanes*, in 2 Vols, Cologne: 1730.

—*De L'Esprit des Loix*, in 2 Vols, Geneve: 1750.

[1479] Ferguson cites this, the Robert Graves translation, first published in 1792 though he probably used an earlier and different translation for work published before 1792, possibly Hutcheson's translation (*Meditations of M. Aurelius Antoninus,* 1742) or *Antoninus the Roman Emperour, his Meditations Concerning Himselfe*, Translated out of the Originall Greeke; with Notes by Meric Casaubon, London: Printed by M. Flesher, for Richard Mynne, 1635.

[1480] *'[C]ontaining an account of the government, laws, customs and manners of the native inhabitants, with a description of the natural productions, and a relation of the ancient political state of that island, 3rd ed., with corrections, additions, and plates'.*

—*Les Considerations sur les causes de la grandeur et de la Decadence des Romains*, Amsterdam: 1734.

Newton, Isaac. *Opticks: or, a Treatise of the Reflections, Refractions, Inflections and Colours of Light*, London: Printed for William and John Innys,1721.

—*Philosophiae Naturalis Principia Mathematica*. Editio tertia aucta & emendata. Londini: apud Guil. & Joh. Innys, 1726.

—*A Treatise of the Method of Fluxions and Infinite Series, with its Application to the Geometry of Curved Lines*, London: Printed for T. Woodman and J. Millan, 1737.

Orosius, Paulus. *The Seven Books of History Against the Pagans*, (edition unknown).

Plato. *Platonis Omnia Opera*, Basileae: apud Henrichum Petri, 1556.

Plinius Caecilius Secundus Gaius. (Pliny). *Secundi Opera quae Supersunt Omnia*. Glasguae: Robertus et Andreas Foulis,1751.

Polybius. *Polibii Lycortae F. Meglapolitani* (*History of Rome*), Amsterdam: 1670.

Pope, Alexander. *The Works of Alexander Pope esq.* London: Printed for J. and P. Knapton, H. Lintot, J. and R. Tonson, and S. Draper, 1751.

Price, Richard. *Observations on the Nature of Civil Liberty*, London: T. Cadell, 1776.

—*Additional Observations on the Nature and Value of Civil Liberty, and the War with America*, London: Printed for T. Cadell, 1777.

—*An Essay on the Population of England*, London: T. Cadell, 1780.

—*Observations on the Importance of the American Revolution, and the Means of Making it a Benefit to the World*, London: T.Cadell, 1784.

—*A Discourse on the Love of our Country*: Delivered on Nov. 4, 1789, London: T. Cadell, 1790.

Priestley, Joseph. *An Essay on the First Principles of Government; and on the Nature of Political Civil, and Religious Liberty*, London, 1768.

Pufendorf, Samuel. *The Whole Duty of Man According to the Law of Nature*, London: Printed by Benj. Motte for Charles Harper and John Jones, 1698.

Quintilian. *M. Fabii Quintiliani de Institutione Oratoria Libri* XII. Parisiis: Ex officina Antonii Augerelli,1533.

Ramsay, David. *The History of the American Revolution*, Philadelphia: Printed and Sold by R. Aitken, 1789.

Reid Thomas. *An Inquiry into the Human Mind on the Principles of Common Sense*, Edinburgh:1764.

Robertson, William. *History of Scotland*, in 2 Vols, Peter Hill, Edinburgh: 1759.

—*The Situation of the World at the Time of Christ's Appearance*, Edinburgh: 1759.

Rousseau, Jean-Jacques, *Ouvres Diverses*, in 2 Vols, Amsterdam: 1762.

Rubruquis, William De, *Travels into Tartary and China*, 1253. English translation, 1747 (edition unknown).

Sallust. *The Workes of Caius Crispus Salustius Contayning the Conspiracie of Cateline The Warre of Iugurth. V. Bookes of Historicall Fragments. II Orations to Cæsar for the Institution of a Commonwealth and One against Cicero*, London : Elizabeth Allde, 1629.

Seneca, Lucius Annaeus. *Epistulae morales ad Lucillium*. London: Printed for Charles Brome,1685.

—*Seneca his Tenne Tragedies*, translated into Englysh, Imprinted at London: Thomas Marsh, 1581.

Shakespeare, William. *The Works of, Collected and Corrected by Alexander Pope*, London: 1723-5, Vols. 1-6.

Smith, Adam. *An Inquiry into the Nature and Causes of the Wealth of Nations*, London: A. Strahan; and T. Cadell, 1776.

—*The Theory of Moral Sentiments,* Edinburgh: J.Bell, 1759.

Strahlenberg, Philip Johan Tabbert von. *An Historical-Geographical Description of the North and Eastern Part of Europe and Asia*, London: W. Innis and R. Manby, 1736.

Stuart, Gilbert. *An Historical Dissertation Concerning the Antiquity of the English Constitution*, London and Edinburgh, 1768.

—*A View of Society in Europe*, Edinburgh: Bell and Murray, 1778.

Suetonius Tranquillus. *The Historie of Twelve Cæsars, Emperours of Rome*, newly translated into English, by Philêmon Holland, London: Matthew Lownes, 1606.

Swift, Jonathon. *Travels into Several Remote Nations of the World*, London: Benjamin Motte, 1726.

Tacitus C. *Cornelii Taciti Opera quae Supersunt.* Ex editione Jacobi Gronovii fideliter expressa, 4 Vols, Glasguae: Rob. et And. Foulis, 1753.

Thucydides. *Eight Bookes of the Peloponnesian Warre,*[1481] London: Imprinted for Laurence Sadler, 1648.

Velleius Paterculus, C. *Ex historiae Romanae Voluminibus Duobus.* Cum integris scholiis, notis, variis lectionibus, et animadversionibus doctorum Curante Petro Burmanno, Leyden: Samuel Luchtmans, 1719.

Voltaire, François–Marie Arouet Francheville. *Le Siecle de Louis Fourteenth*, in 2 Vols, Edinburgh: 1752.

Wallace, Robert. *Dissertation on the Numbers of Mankind in Ancient and Modern Times*, Edinburgh: Printed for G. Hamilton and J. Balfour, 1753.

Woollaston, William. *The Religion of Nature Delineated*, London: 1724.

3. BIOGRAPHICAL ACCOUNTS OF FERGUSON[1482]

Fagg, J. B. *Biographical Introduction* in Ferguson, Adam, *The Correspondence of Adam Ferguson*, in 3 Vols, Edited by V. Merolle, London: William Pickering, 1995.

Fagg, J. B. *Adam Ferguson: Scottish Cato*, Unpublished Doctoral Dissertation, University of North Carolina at Chapel Hill, 1968.

Kettler, David. 'Adam Ferguson: Biography', Chapter III, in Kettler, D. *The Social and Political Thought of Adam Ferguson*, Indiana: Ohio State University Press, 1965.

[1481] *'Written by Thucydides the sonne of Olorus. Interpreted with faith and diligence immediately out of the Greeke by Thomas Hobbes the author of the booke De cive secretary to ye late Earle of Deuonshire'.*

[1482] See Fagg, 'Biographical Introduction', pp. cxix-x for further sources.

Raphael, D.D., Raynor, D.R., Ross, I.S. '"This Very Awkward Affair": An Entanglement of Scottish Professors with English Lords', *Studies on Voltaire and the Eighteenth Century*, Vol. 278, 1990, pp. 419-63.

Small, J. 'Biographical Sketch of Adam Ferguson', *Edinburgh Review*, Vol.75 (255), 1897, pp. 48-85.

Willke, J. *The Historical Thought of Adam Ferguson*, Unpublished Doctoral Dissertation, Washington D.C: The Catholic University of America, 1962.

4. SOURCES USED BY THE AUTHOR

A Biographical Dictionary of Eminent Scotsmen, Vol.II, Edinburgh: Blackie and Son, 1864.

Abel, T. *The Foundations of Sociological Theory*, New York: Random House, 1970.

Adams, W.P. 'Republicanism in Political Rhetoric Before 1776', *Political Science Quarterly*, Vol. 85, 1970, pp. 397-421.

Allan, D. *Virtue, Learning and the Scottish Enlightenment*, Edinburgh: Edinburgh University Press, 1993.

Anderson, M. S. *Europe in the Eighteenth Century*, London: Longman, 1961.

Anonymous. 'Review of 'Adam Ferguson'', *Edinburgh Review*, Vol. 125, 1867, pp. 48-85.

Anspach, R. 'The Implications of The Theory of Moral Sentiments for Adam Smith's Economic Thought', *History of Political Economy*, Vol. 4, 1972.

Arnold, R. 'Hayek and Institutional Evolution', *The Journal of Libertarian Studies*, Vol. 4 (4), 1980, pp.341-51.

Aristotle. *Ethics*. Translated by J.A.K. Thomson, London: Penguin, 1976.

Aristotle. *Politics: The Athenian Constitution*, Edited and with an Introduction by John Warrington, London: Heron Books, 1959.

Arnold, E.V. *Roman Stoicism*, New York: The Humanities Press, 1958.

Atkinson, A. *Principles of Political Ecology*, London: Belhaven Press, 1991.

Bacon, F. *Novum Organum*, Edited and with an Introduction by Thomas Fowler, Oxford: Clarendon Press, 1878.

Ballestrem, K.G. 'Sources of the Materialist Conception of History in the History of Ideas', *Studies in Soviet Thought*, Vol. 26, (1), 1983, pp. 3-9.

Balme, D. M. 'Greek Science and Mechanism: Aristotle on Nature and Chance', *Classical Quarterly*, Vol. 33, 1939, pp. 198-224.

Barbalet, J. M. *Emotion, Social Theory and Social Structure*, Cambridge: Cambridge University Press, 1998.

Barber, B. 'An Essay on the History of Civil Society', *Contemporary Sociology*, Vol.9 (2), 1980, pp. 258-59.

Barker, E. *The Politics of Aristotle*, Oxford: Oxford University Press, 1961.

Barnes, H. 'Sociology before Comte: A Summary of Doctrines and an Introduction to the Literature', *American Journal of Sociology*, Vol. 23, July, 1917, pp. 174-247.

Barry, N. 'The Tradition of Spontaneous Order', *Literature of Liberty*, Vol. 5 (2), 1982, pp. 7-58.

Baxter, B. 'The Self, Morality and the Nation-State', *Ethics and International Relations*, in A. Ellis, (Ed.), Manchester: Manchester University Press, 1986.

Becker, C.L. *The Heavenly City of the Eighteenth Century Philosophers*, New Haven: Yale University Press, 1932.

Beiderwell, B. 'Scott's *Redgauntlet* as a Romance of Power', *Studies in Romanticism*, Vol.28 (1), 1989, pp. 273-89.

Belcher, G.L. 'Commonwealth Ideas in the Political Thought of the Defenders of the Eighteenth Century English Constitution', *Eighteenth Century Life*, Vol 3 (2), 1976, pp. 63-9.

Bendix, R. 'The Mandate to Rule: An Introduction', *Social Forces*, Vol. 55 (2), 1976, pp. 242-56.

—'Tradition and Modernity Reconsidered', *Comparative Studies in History and Society*, Vol. 9, 1967, pp. 293-348.

— 'The Intellectual's Dilemma in the Modern World', *Society*, Vol. 25, 1987, pp. 65-71.

Benton, T. 'How Many Sociologies?', *Sociological Review*, Vol. 26, 1978, pp. 217-36.

Bernal, M. *Black Athena,* London: Free Association Books, 1987.

Bernstein, J.A. 'Adam Ferguson and the Idea of Progress', *Studies in Burke and His Time*, 19 (2), 1978, pp. 99-118.

Bernstein, J.A. 'Shaftsbury's Identification of the Good with the Beautiful', *Eighteenth Century Studies*, Vol. 10, 1976-77, pp. 304-25.

Berry, C. J. 'Nations and Norms', *The Review of Politics*, Vol. 43, 1981, pp.74-87.

—'Review-The Nature of Wealth and the Origins of Virtue: Recent Essays on the Scottish Enlightenment', *History of European Ideas*, Vol. 7 (1), 1986, pp. 85-99.

—'Adam Smith and the Virtues of Commerce', *Nomos*, Vol. 34, 1992, pp. 69-88.

—*The Idea of Luxury*, Cambridge: Cambridge University Press, 1994.

—*Social Theory of the Scottish Enlightenment*, Edinburgh: Edinburgh University Press, 1997.

—'Sociality and Socialisation' in Alexander Broadie (ed.), *The Scottish Enlightenment*, Cambridge: Cambridge University Press, 2003.

Bierstedt, R. 'Sociological Thought in the Eighteenth Century', in T. Bottomore and R. Nisbet, (eds.), *A History of Sociological Analysis*, London: Heinemann, 1979.

Bisset, R. 'Adam Ferguson', *Public Characters of 1799-1800*, London: 1799.

Bitterman, H.J. 'Smith's Empiricism and the Law of Nature', *Journal of Political Economy*, Vol. 48 (5), 1940, pp. 487-520.

Bock, K.E. 'The Comparative Method of Anthropology', *Comparative Studies in Society and History*, Vol. 8, 1965-6, pp. 269-80.

Bognor, A. 'The Structure of Social Processes: A Commentary on the Sociology of Elias Norbert', *Sociology*, Vol. 20 (3), 1986, pp. 387-411.

Bottomore T.B. and Nisbet, R, (eds.). *A History of Sociological Analysis*, London: Heinemann, 1979.

Bottomore, T.B. *The Founding Fathers of Social Science*, London: Penguin, 1979.

—'The Ideas of the Founding Fathers', *European Journal of Sociology*, Vol.1 (1), 1960, pp. 33-49.

Bowlby, J. *Attachment and Loss*, Vol. I, London: Hogarth Press, 1969.

Bowles, P. 'John Millar, The Four Stages Theory and Women's Position in Society', *History of Political Economy*, Vol. 16, 1984, pp. 619-38.

—'The Origin of Property and the Development of Scottish Historical Science', *Journal of the History of Ideas*, Vol. 46 (2), 1985, pp. 197-209.

Boyd, R. 'Reappraising the Scottish Moralists and Civil Society', *Polity*, Vol. 33 (3), 2000, pp. 101-25.

Branson, B. 'James Madison and the Scottish Enlightenment', *Journal of the History of Ideas*, Vol. 40 (2), 1979, pp. 235-50.

Bresky, D. 'Schiller's Debt to Montesquieu and Adam Ferguson', *Comparative Literature*, Vol. 13 (3), 1961, pp. 239-53.

Brewer, J. D. 'Conjectural History, Sociology and Social Change in Eighteenth Century Scotland: Adam Ferguson and the Division of Labour', in *The Making of Scotland: Nation, Culture and Social Change*, Edited by D. McCrone, S. Kendrick and P. Straw, Edinburgh: Edinburgh University Press, 1989.

—'Adam Ferguson and the Theme of Exploitation', *The British Journal of Sociology*, Vol. 37, 1986, pp. 461-78.

Brissenden, R.F. 'Authority, Guilt and Anxiety in *The Theory of Moral Sentiments*', *Texas Studies in Literature and Language*, Vol. 11, 1969, pp. 945-62.

Broadie, A. *The Scottish Enlightenment*, Edinburgh: Birlinn Ltd., 2001.

Brown, R. *The Nature of Social Laws : Machiavelli to Mill*, Cambridge: Cambridge University Press, 1984.

Brown, Terence. (ed.), *Celticism*, Amsterdam: Rodopi, 1996.

Bryson, G. 'Some Eighteenth Century Conceptions of Society', *The Sociological Review*, Vol. 31, 1939, pp. 401-21.

Bryson, G. *Man and Society: The Scottish Inquiry of the Eighteenth Century*, Princeton: Princeton University Press, 1945.

Bryson, G. 'Sociology Considered as Moral Philosophy', *Sociological Review*, Vol. 24 (1), 1932, pp. 26-36.

Buchdahl, G. *The Image of Newton and Locke in the Age of Reason*, London: Sheed and Ward, 1961.

Burke, Edmund. *A Vindication of Natural Society*, Edited and with an Introduction by Frank N. Pagano, Indianapolis: Liberty Classics, 1982.

—*Further Reflections on the Revolution in France*, Edited by Daniel E. Ritchie, Indiana: Liberty Press, 1992.

Burke, P. 'Tradition and Experience: The Idea of Decline from Bruni to Gibbon', *Daedelus* Vol. 105, Summer, 1976, pp. 137-51.

Butts. R.E. *The Methodological Heritage of Newton*, Oxford: Basil Blackwell, Oxford, 1970.

Camic, C. *Experience and Enlightenment; Socialisation for Cultural Change in Eighteenth Century Scotland*, Chicago: University of Chicago Press, 1983.

—'Experience and Ideas: Education for Universalism in Eighteenth Century Scotland', *Comparative Studies in Society and History*, Vol. 25, Jan.1983, pp. 50-82.

—'The Matter of Habit', *American Journal of Sociology*, Vol. 91 (5), March, 1986, pp. 1039-87.

Campbell, R.H. and Skinner, A.S. (eds.), *The Origins and Nature of the Scottish Enlightenment*, Edinburgh: John Donald Publishers Ltd, 1982.

Carlyle, A. *Autobiography of Dr Alexander Carlyle of Inveresk, 1722-1805*, John Hill (ed.), Edinburgh and London, 1910.

Casini, P. 'Newton: The Classical Scholia', *History of Science*, Vol. 22, 1984, pp. 1-23.

Castiglione, L. Introductory Preface to New Edition of Adam Ferguson's *Principles of Moral and Political Science*, New York: AMS Press, 1973.

—'Mandeville Moralised', *Anna della Fondazione Luigi Einaudi Torino*, Vol. 17, 1983, pp. 239-90.

Chaplin, J.E. 'Slavery and the Principle of Humanity: A Modern Idea in the Early Lower South', *Journal of Social History*, Vol. 24 (1), 1990, pp. 299-315.

Chappell, V.C. (ed.), *Hume*, New York: Anchor Books, 1966.

Chiasson, E.J. 'Bernard Mandeville: A Reappraisal', *Philological Quarterly*, Vol. 49, 1970, pp. 489-519.

Chitnis, A. *The Scottish Enlightenment*, London: Croom Helm Ltd., 1976.

Christie, I.R. *Willkes, Wyvill and Reform*, London: Macmillan and Co. Ltd, 1962.

Cicero, *Selected Works*, Robert Baldick, C.A. Jones and Betty Radice, (eds.), London: Penguin, 1971.

Cicero. *De Finibus Bonorum et Malorum*, with an English Translation by H. Rackham, London: William Heinemann Ltd., 1961.

—*De Natura Deorum*, With an English translation by H. Rackham, London: William Heinemann Ltd, 1951.

—*De Officius*, With an English Translation by Walter Miller, London: Harvard University Press, 1990.

—*De Republica; De Legibus* With an English Translation by Clinton Walker Keyes, London: William Heinmann Ltd. 1988.

Clark, Henry, C. 'Conversation and Moderate Virtue in Adam Smith's *Theory of Moral Sentiments*', *Review of Politics*, Vol. 54, 1992, pp. 185-210.

Clarke, S.R.L. 'The City of the Wise', *Apeiron*, Vol. 20 (1), 1987, pp. 63-80.

Collini, S.D. Winch and J. Burrow, *That Noble Science of Politics*, Cambridge: Cambridge University Press, 1983.

Collins Dictionary of Philosophy, G.Vesey and P.Foulkes, (eds), London: Collins, 1990.

Conway, S. 'Bentham Versus Pitt: Jeremy Bentham and British Foreign Policy 1789', *The Historical Journal*, Vol. 30 (4), 1987, pp. 791-809.

Coplestone, F.A., *History of Philosophy V: Hobbes to Hume*, London: Burns Oates and Washbourne Ltd., 1959.

Corrigan, B. 'Dichotomy as Contradiction: On Society as Constraint and Construction. Remarks on the Doctrine of the Two Sociologies', *Sociological Review*, Vol. 23, 1975, pp. 211-43.

Coser, L. 'Social Conflict and the Theory of Social Change', *British Journal of Sociology*, Vol. 8, 1957, pp. 197-206.

—*Continuities in the Study of Social Conflict*, New York: The Free Press, 1970.

—*The Functions of Social Conflict*, London: Routledge and Kegan Paul, 1956.

Costain, K. 'The Community of Man: Galt and Eighteenth Century Scottish Realism', *Scottish Literary Journal*, Vol. 8 (1), 1981, pp. 10-29.

Crehan, S. 'The Roman Analogy', *Literature and History*, Vol.6 (1), 1980, pp. 19-42.

Cress, L.D. 'Radical Whiggery on the Role of the Military: Ideological Roots of the American Revolutionary Militia', *Journal of the History of Ideas*, Vol. 40 (1), 1979, pp. 43-60.

Crocker, L.G. 'Interpreting the Enlightenment: A Political Approach', *Journal of the History of Ideas*, Vol. 45 (2), 1985, pp. 211-30.

—*The Age of Enlightenment*, London: MacMillan, 1969.

Cronk, Lee. 'Spontaneous Order Analysis and Anthropology', *Cultural Dynamics*, Vol. 1 (3), 1988, pp. 282-308.

Cropsey, J. *Polity and Economy: An Interpretation of the Principles of Adam Smith*, The Hague: Martinus Nijhoff, 1957.

Crowley, John, E. 'The Sensibility of Comfort', *The American Historical Review*, Vol. 104 (3), 1999, pp. 749-82.

Curtis, R. 'Institutional Individualism and the Emergence of Scientific Rationality', *Studies in History and Philosophy of Science*, Vol. 20, 1989, pp. 77-113.

Davie, G.E. 'Berkeley's Impact on Scottish Philosophers', *Philosophy*, Vol. 40, 1965, pp. 222-34.

Davis, J.B. 'Smith's Cunning of Reason', *International Journal of Social Economics*, Vol. 16 (6), 1989, pp. 50-68.

De Romillly, J. *Thucydides and Athenian Imperialism*, Translated by Philis Thody, New York: Arno Press, 1979.

Dickey, L. 'Historicizing the "Adam Smith Problem": Conceptual, Historiographic, and Textual Issues', *The Journal of Modern History*, Vol. 58, 1986, pp. 579-609.

Dickey, L. *Hegel: Religion, Economics and the Politics of Spirit 1770-1807*, Cambridge: Cambridge University Press, 1987.

Dictionary of National Biography, Leslie Stephen and Sidney Lee (eds.), Vol. VI, 1917, London: Oxford University Press.

Diggins, J.P. 'The Misuses of Gramsci', *The Journal of American History*, Vol. 75 (1), 1988, pp. 141-45.

Dio Cassius. *Roman History*, With an English Translation by Ernest Cary, Cambridge, Mass: Harvard University Press, 1960-68.

Diogenes, Laertius. *Lives of Eminent Philosophers*, Translated by R.D. Hicks, London: William Heinemann, 1958.

Dodds, E.R. *The Ancient Concept of Progress*, Oxford: Clarendon Press, 1985.

Downie, R.S. 'An Essay on the History of Civil Society', Edited by Duncan Forbes: A Book Review', *Philosophy*, Vol. 42, 1967, pp. 382-3.

Driesch, H. *The History and Theory of Vitalism*, London: Macmillan, 1914.

Dumont, L. *From Mandeville to Marx*, Chicago: University of Chicago Press, 1977.

Durkheim, E. *Montesquieu and Rousseau*, Ann Arbor: University of Michigan Press, 1960.

Dwyer, J. 'The Melancholy Savage' in Howard Gaskill (ed.), *Ossian Revisited*, Edinburgh: Edinburgh University Press 1991.

Dwyer, J. and Sher, R.B (eds.). *Sociability and Society in Eighteenth Century Scotland*, Edinburgh: The Mercat Press, 1993.

Dybikowski, J. 'Civil Liberty', *American Philosophical Quarterly*, Vol. 18, 1981, pp. 339-46.

Edel, A. *Aristotle and His Philosophy*, London: Croom Helm, 1982.

Elias, N. and Dunning, E. *Quest for Excitement: Sport and Leisure in the Civilising Process,* Oxford: Blackwell, 1986.

Emerson, R. 'Peter Gay and the Heavenly City', *Journal of the History of Ideas*, Vol. 28, (3) 1967, pp. 383-402.

—'Conjectural History and Scottish Philosophers', *Historical Papers*, Vol. 63. 1984, pp. 63-90

Epictetus. *Enchiridion*, Translated by George Long, New York: Prometheus Books, 1991.

Epictetus. *The Discourses as Reported by Arrian, the Manual and Fragments*, With an English Translation by W.A. Oldfather in Two Volumes, London: Harvard University Press, 1989.

Eriksson, B. 'The First Formulation of Sociology: A Discursive Innovation of the Eighteenth Century', *European Journal of Sociology*, Vol. 34(1), 1993 pp.251-76.

Fagerstrom, D.I. 'Scottish Opinion and the American Revolution', *The William and Mary Quarterly*, Vol. 11 (2), 1954, pp. 252-75.

Fagg, J.B. *Adam Ferguson, Scottish Cato*, Unpublished Doctoral Dissertation: University of North Carolina at Chapel Hill, 1968.

—*Biographical Introduction* in Ferguson, Adam, *The Correspondence of Adam Ferguson*, in 3 Vols, Edited by V. Merolle, London: William Pickering, 1995.

Farr, James. 'Political Science and the Enlightenment of Enthusiasm', *American Political Science Review*, Vol. 82, March 1988, pp. 51-69.

Fearnley-Sander, M. 'Philosophical History and the Scottish Reformation: William Robertson and the Knoxian Tradition', *The Historical Journal*, Vol. 33 (2), 1990, pp.323-38.

Ferguson, Adam. *The Unpublished Essays of Adam Ferguson*, in 3 Volumes Edited and Published Privately by Winifred Philip: Argull, 1986.

Ferrarotti, F. 'Civil Society and State Structures in Creative Tension', *State, Culture and Society,* Vol.1, Fall, 1984, pp. 3-25.

Firth, A. 'Moral Supervision and Autonomous Social Order: Wages and Consumption in Eighteenth Century Economic Thought', *History of the Human Sciences*, Vol. 15 (1), pp. 39-57.

Fitzgibbons, A. *Adam Smith's System of Liberty, Wealth and Virtue: The Moral and Political Foundations of the Wealth of Nations*, Oxford: Clarendon Press, 1995.

Fletcher, F.T. *Montesquieu and English Politics 1750-1800*, London: Edwards Arnold and Company, 1939.

Flew, A. 'Three Questions About Justice in Hume's Treatise', *The Philosophical Review*, Vol. 26 (102),1976, pp. 1-13.

—'Social Science: Making Visible the Invisible Hands', *The Journal of Libertarian Studies*, Vol. 8 (2), 1987, pp. 197-211

Flynn, P. 'Scottish Philosophers, Scotch Reviewers, and the Science of Mind', *The Dalhousie Review*, Vol. 68, 1988, pp. 259-83.

—'Scotland and Sin: Moral Philosophy and Scottish Culture in the Eighteenth and Early Nineteenth Centuries', *The Dalhousie Review*, Vol. 4 (1), 1984, pp. 50-73.

Foley, M. and Edwards, R. 'The Paradox of Civil Society', *Journal of Democracy*, Vol. 7 (3), 1996, pp. 38-52.

Forbes, D. 'Scientific Whiggism: Adam Smith and John Millar', *Cambridge Journal*, Vol. 6, 1954, pp. 643-70.

—'Adam Ferguson and the Idea of Community' in *Edinburgh in the Age of Reason*, Douglas Young et al. (eds), Edinburgh: Edinburgh University Press, 1967.

—'Introduction' to Ferguson, Adam, *An Essay on the History of Civil Society*, Edited and With an Introduction by Duncan Forbes, Edinburgh: Edinburgh University Press, 1967.

—*Adam Ferguson and the Idea of Community*, Paisley, Scotland: Gleniffer, Press, 1979.

Force, J.E. 'Hume and the Relation of Science to Religion Among Certain Members of the Royal Society', *Journal of the History of Ideas*, Vol. 45 (4), pp. 517-36.

Fox, C, Porter, R, and Wokler, R. *Inventing Human Science: Eighteenth Century Domains*, Berkeley: University of California Press, 1995.

Francesconi, D. 'William Robertson on Historical Causation and Unintended Consequences', *Cromohs*, Vol. 4, 1999, pp. 1-18.

Frankena, W. 'Hutcheson's Moral Sense Theory', *Journal of the History of Ideas*, Vol. 16 (3), 1955, pp. 356-75.

Fuchs, O. *The Psychology of Habit According to William Ockham*, St. Bonaventure, N.Y.: The Franciscan Institute, 1952.

Furet, Francois. Civilisation and Barbarism in Gibbon's History, *Daedelus*, Vol. 105, 1976, pp. 209-16.

Garnsey, E. 'The Rediscovery of the Division of Labour', *Theory and Society*, Vol. 10, 1981, pp. 337-58.

Gascoigne, J. 'From Bentley to the Victorians: The Rise and Fall of Newtonian Natural Theology', *Science in Context*, Vol. 2 (2), 1988, pp. 219-56.

Gaskill, Howard, (ed.). *Ossian Revisited*, Edinburgh: Edinburgh University Press 1991.

Gaukroger, S, (ed.). *The Uses of Antiquity*, Amsterdam: Kluwer Academic Publishers, 1991.

Gay, P. *The Enlightenment: An Interpretation*, in 2 Vols, London: Weidenfield and Nicholson, 1970.

—(ed.). *The Enlightenment: A Comprehensive Anthology*, New York: Simon and Schuster, 1973.

Gellner, E. 'Adam Ferguson and the Surprising Robustness of Civil Society', in *Liberalism in Modern Times: Essays in Honour of Jose G. Merquior,* Edited by Ernest Gellner and Cesar Cansino, London: CEU Press, 1996.

—'Adam Ferguson', in *Conditions of Liberty: Civil Society and Its Rivals*, London: Penguin Books, 1994.

Gibbons, L. 'Ossian, Celticism and Colonialism' in Terence Brown (ed.), *Celticism*, Amsterdam: Rodopi, 1996.

Giddens, Anthony. *Sociology: A Brief but Critical Introduction*, 2nd ed., London: MacMillan Education, 1986.

Gill, Christopher. 'Personhood and Personality: The Four Person*ae* Theory in Cicero, *De Officiis* I', *Oxford Studies in Ancient Philosophy*, Vol. 6, 1988, pp. 169-200.

Glacken, C.J. *Traces on the Rhodian Shore*, Berkeley: University of California Press, 1967, pp. 562-8.

Gluckman, Max. *Custom and Conflict in Africa,* Oxford: Blackwell, 1955.

Goetsch, P. 'Linguistic Colonisation and Primitivism. The Discovery of Native Languages and Oral Traditions in Eighteenth Century Travel Books and Novels', *Anglia*, Vol. 106, (3-4), 1988, pp. 338-57.

Goldman, L. *The Philosophy of the Enlightenment*, London: Routledge and Kegan Paul, 1973.

Goldsmith, M. 'Regulating Anew the Moral and Political Sentiments of Mankind: Mandeville and the Scottish Enlightenment', *Journal of the History of Ideas*, Vol. 49 (4), 1988, pp. 587-606.

—*Private Vices, Public Benefits*, Cambridge: Cambridge University Press, 1985.

Gould, E.H. 'To Strengthen the King's Hands: Dynastic Legitimacy, Militia Reform and Ideas of National Unity in England 1745-1760', *The Historical, Journal*, Vol. 34 (2), 1991, pp. 329-48.

Grave, S.A. *The Scottish Philosophy of Common Sense*, Oxford: Clarendon Press, 1960.

Gray, E. 'The Population Terror Might be Just Around the Corner', *History of European Ideas*, Vol 4 (2), 1983, pp. 237-41.

Gray, John. 'F.A. Hayek on Liberty and Tradition', *Journal of Libertarian Studies,* Vol. 4 (2), Spring 1980, pp. 119-137.

Griffin, M. *Seneca, A Philosopher in Politics,* Oxford: Clarendon Press, 1976.

Grobman, N.R. 'Thomas Blackwell's Commentary on the Oral Nature of Epic', *Western Folklore*, Vol. 26 (1), Jan., 1967, pp. 186-198.

—'Adam Ferguson's Influence on Folklore Research: the Analysis of Methodology and the Oral Epic', *Southern Folklore Quarterly*, Vol. 38, 1974, pp. 11-22.

—'David Hume and the Earliest Scientific Methodology for Collecting Balladry', *Western Folklore*, Vol. 34, 1975, pp. 16-51.

Groenwegan, P.D. 'Adam Smith and the Division of Labour: A Bicentenary Estimate', *Australian Economic Papers*, Vol. 16 (29), 1977, pp. 161-74.

Grotius, Hugo, *Prolegomena*, to *The Life and Works of Hugo Grotius*, W.S.M. Knight, London : Sweet & Maxwell Ltd., 1925, 1869.

Gunn, J.A.W. 'Interest Will Not Lie: A Seventeenth Century Political Maxim', *Journal of the History of Ideas*, Vol. 29 (4), 1968, pp. 551-64.

—*Politics and the Public Interest in the Seventeenth Century*, London: The Chaucer Press, 1969.

—'Influence, Parties and the Constitution: Changing Attitudes, 1783-1832', *The Historical Journal*, Vol. 17 (2), 1974, pp. 301-28.

Haakonssen, K. 'Natural Law and Moral Realism: The Scottish Synthesis', *Studies in the Philosophy of the Scottish Enlightenment*, M.A. Stewart (ed.), Oxford: Clarendon Press, 1990.

Hale, Sir Matthew. *The Primitive Origination of Mankind*, London: Printed by W. Godbid for W. Showsbery, 1677.

Hamowy, R. 'Adam Smith, Adam Ferguson and the Division of Labour', *Economica*, Vol. 35 (139), August, 1968, pp. 244-59.

—*The Social and Political Philosophy of Adam Ferguson*, Unpublished Ph.D. Dissertation: University of Chicago, 1969.

—'Progress and Commerce in Anglo-American Thought: The Social Philosophy of Adam Ferguson', *Interpretation*, Vol. 14, Jan. 1986, pp. 61-87.

—*The Scottish Enlightenment and the Theory of Spontaneous Order*, Southern Illinois: University Press, 1987.

Hampson, N. *The Enlightenment*, London: Penguin, 1982.

Harpham, E.J. 'Liberalism, Civic Humanism and the Case of Adam Smith', *American Political Science Review*, Vol. 78, 1984, pp. 764-44.

Haugan, K.L. 'Ossian and the Invention of Textual History', *Journal of the History of Ideas*, Vol. 58 (2), 1998, pp. 309-27.

Hayek, F.A. 'Dr. Bernard Mandeville ', *The Proceedings of the British Academy*, Vol. 52, 1966, pp. 125-141.

—'The Results of Human Actions But Not of Human Design', *Studies in Philosophy, Politics and Economics*, London: Routledge and Kegan Paul, 1967.

—'Kinds of Rationalism', in Hayek, F.A. *Studies in Philosophy, Politics, and Economics*, London: Routledge & Kegan Paul, 1967.

—'Adam Smith (1723-1790): His Message in Today's Language', in *The Trend of Economic Thinking*, London: Routledge, 1991.

Heidegger, M. *The Question Concerning Technology and Other Essays*, Translated and with an Introduction by William Lovitt, New York: Garland Publishing Inc., 1977.

Heilbroner, R.L. 'The Paradox of Progress: Decline and Decay in the Wealth of Nations', *Journal of the History of Ideas*, Vol. 34 (2), 1973, pp. 243-62.

Hellenbrand, H. 'Not to Destroy But to Fulfil: Jefferson, Indians and Republican Dispensation', *Seventeenth Century Studies*, Vol. 18 (4), 1985, pp. 522-48.

Herlihy, D. J. 'Attitudes Toward the Environment in Medieval Society' in *Historical Ecology: Essays on Environment and Social Change*', Edited by Lester J. Bilsky, New York: Kennikat Press, 1980.

Hill, L. 'Adam Ferguson and the Paradox of Progress and Decline', *History of Political Thought*, Vol. 18 (4), 1997, pp. 677-706.

—'Anticipations of Nineteenth and Twentieth Century Social Thought in the Work of Adam Ferguson', *European Journal of Sociology*, Vol. 37 (1), 1996, pp. 203-28.

—'Ferguson and Smith on 'Human Nature', 'Interest' and the Role of Beneficence in Market Society', Vol. 4 (1-2), 1996, *Journal of the History of Economic Ideas*, Adam Smith Special Edition, pp. 353-99.

—'The Liberal Psyche, *Homo Economicus* and Different Voices', *Journal of Applied Philosophy*, Vol. 13 (1), Spring, 1999, pp. 21-46.

—'The Two Republicae of the Roman Stoics', *Citizenship Studies*, Vol. 4 (1), 2000, pp. 65-79.

—'The First Wave of Feminism: Were the Stoics Feminists?', *History of Political Thought*, 22 (1) 2001, pp. 12-40.

—'The Hidden Theology of Adam Smith', *European Journal of the History of Economic Thought*, Vol. 8 (1), Spring 2001, pp. 1-29.

Hill, L. and McCarthy, P. 'Hume, Smith and Ferguson: Friendship in Commercial Society', in Preston King and Heather Devere, *The Challenge to Friendship in Modernity*, London: Frank Cass, 2000.

Hirschman, A.O. *The Passions and the Interests*, New Jersey: Princeton University Press, 1977.

Hobbes, T. *Leviathan*, Edited and with an Introduction by C.B. MacPherson, Middlesex: Penguin, 1981.

Hont, I, and Ignatieff, M, (eds.). *Wealth and Virtue: The Shaping of Political Economy in the Scottish Enlightenment*, Cambridge: Cambridge University Press, 1983.

Hont, I, and Ignatieff, M. 'Needs and Justice in the Wealth of Nations: An Introductory Essay', in Hont, I, and Ignatieff, M., (eds.), *Wealth and Virtue: The Shaping of Political Economy in the Scottish Enlightenment*, Cambridge: Cambridge University Press, 1983.

Hoogvelt, A.M. *The Sociology of Developing Societies*, London: The MacMillan Press, 1976.

Hope, V. *Philosophers of the Enlightenment*, Edinburgh: Edinburgh University Press, 1984.

Hopfl, H.M. 'From Savage to Scotsman: Conjectural History in the Scottish Enlightenment', *Journal of British Studies*, Vol. 17 (2), 1978, pp. 19-40.

Horne, T.A. 'Envy and Commercial Society: Mandeville and Smith on 'Private Vices, Public Benefits'', *Political Theory*, Vol. 8-9, November, 1981, pp. 551-569.

Horne, T.A. '"The Poor Have a Claim Founded in the Law of Nature": William Paley and the Rights of the Poor', *Journal of the History of Philosophy*, Vol. 23 (1), 1985, pp. 51-70.

Hoskin, M.A. 'Newton, Providence and the Universe of Stars', *Journal of the History of Astronomy*, Vol. 8, 1977, pp. 77-101.

Hothersall, D. *History of Psychology*: Philadelphia: Temple University Press, 1985.

Howe, D.W. 'Why the Scottish Enlightenment Was Useful to the Framers of the American Constitution', *Comparative Studies in Society and History*, Vol. 31, 1989, pp. 572-89.

Howe, D.W. 'The Political Psychology of the Federalist', *William and Mary Quarterly*, Vol. 44, July 1987, pp. 484-507.

Hume, David. *Essays Moral Political and Literary*, Edited by Eugene F. Miller, Indiana: Liberty Classics, 1987.

—*A Treatise of Human Nature*, Analytical Index by L.A. Selby-Bigge, Second Edition with Text Revised and Notes by P.H. Nidditch, Oxford: Oxford University Press, 1976.

—*Enquiries Concerning Human Understanding and Concerning the Principles of Morals*, Reprinted from the 1777 edition with Introduction and Analytical Index by L.A. Selby-Bigge and Text Revised and Notes by P.H. Nidditch, Oxford: Clarendon Press, 1992.

—*The History of England*, in Six Volumes, William B. Todd, (ed.), Indianapolis: Liberty Classics, 1983.

—*Dialogues Concerning Natural Religion*, Edited and with an Introduction by Martin Bell, London: Penguin, 1990.

—*Letters of David Hume*, in 2 volumes, J.Y.T. Greig, (ed.), Oxford: Clarendon Press, 1932.

Hunt, G. 'The Development of the Concept of Civil Society in Marx', *History of Political Thought*, Vol. 8 (2), 1983, pp. 263-75.

Issa, A. 'Ibn Khaldoun, Montesquieu and the Theory of Climate', *Studi de Sociologia* Vol. 30 (2), 1992, pp. 181-7.

Jack, M. 'Progress and Corruption in the Eighteenth Century: Mandeville's 'Private Vices, Public Benefits'', *Journal of the History of Ideas*, Vol. 37 (2), 1976, pp. 369-76.

James, William. *The Principles of Psychology*, in 3 Volumes, Cambridge MA: Harvard University Press, 1981.

Jary, D. and Jary, J. (eds.). *Collins Dictionary of Sociology*, Glasgow: Harper Collings, 1991.

Joad, C.E.M. *Guide to Philosophy*, London: Victor Gollancz, 1937.

Jogland, Herta Helena. *Ursprunge und Grundlagen der Sociologie bei Adam Ferguson*, Berlin: Dunker and Humbolt, 1959.

Kalyvas, A. and Katznelson, I. 'Adam Ferguson Returns: Liberalism Through a Glass Darkly', *Political Theory*, Vol. 26 (2), April 1998, pp. 173-97.

Kaye, F.B. 'The Influence of Bernard Mandeville', *Studies in Philology*, Vol. 19, Jan. 1922, pp. 83-108.

—'Mandeville on the Origin of Language', *Modern Language Notes*, Vol. 39 (1), 1924, pp. 136-42.

Keane, J. (ed.). *Civil Society and the State: New European Perspectives*, London: Verso, 1988.

—*Civil Society. Old Images, New Visions*, Stanford: Stanford University Press, 1988.

Kettler, David. *The Social and Political Thought of Adam Ferguson*, Indiana: Ohio State University Press, 1965.

—'The Political Vision of Adam Ferguson', *Studies in Burke and His Time*, Vol, 9 (1), No. 30, 1967, pp. 763-78.

—'History and Theory in Ferguson's *Essay* on the History of Civil Society: A Reconsideration', *Political Theory*, Vol. 5, 1977, pp. 437-60.

—'Ferguson's Principles; Constitution in Permanence', *Studies in Burke and His Time*, Vol. 19, 1978, pp. 208-22.

Kidd, Colin. 'Gaelic Antiquity and National Identity in Enlightenment Ireland and Scotland', *The English Historical Review*, Vol. 109 (434), November 1994, pp. 1197-214.

Kindleberger, C.P. 'The Historical Background: Adam Smith and the Industrial Revolution', in Wilson, T. and. Skinner A. (eds.), *The Market and the State*, Oxford University Press, 1976.

Krader, L. 'Social Evolution and Social Revolution', *Dialectical Anthropology*, Vol.1, 1976, pp. 109-20.

Kristol, I. 'Rationalism in Economics', *The Public Interest*, Special Issue, 1980, pp. 201-18.

Kubrin, D. 'Newton and the Cyclical Cosmos: Providence and the Mechanical Philosphy', *Journal of the History of Ideas*, Vol. 28 (3), 1967, pp. 325-46.

Kugler, Michael, 'Provincial Intellectuals: Identity, Patriotism, and Enlightened Peripheries', *The Eighteenth Century: Theory and Interpretation*, Vol. 37, 1996, pp. 156-73.

Kumar, K. 'Civil Society: An Inquiry into the Usefulness of an Historical Term', *The British Journal of Sociology*, Vol. 44 (3) September 1993, pp. 375-95.

Kurzweil, E. (ed.). *The Age of Structuralism: Levi Strauss to Foucault*, New York: Columbia University Press, 1980.

Lane, M. *Structuralism*, London: Jonathan Cape, 1970.

Lapointe, F. 'Origins and Evolution of the Term 'Psychology'', *American Psychologist*, Vol. 25, 1970, pp. 640-6.

Laurie, H. *The Scottish Philosophy in its National Development*, Glasgow: James Macklehose and Sons, 1902.

Lehmann, W.C. *Adam Ferguson and the Beginnings of Modern Sociology*, New York: Columbia University Press, 1930.

— *John Millar of Glasgow: 1733-1801*, London: Cambridge University Press, 1960.

— *Henry Home, Lord Kames, and the Scottish Enlightenment: A Study in National Character and in the History of Ideas*, The Hague: Martinuss Nijhoff, 1971.

— 'Comment on Louis Schneider; Tension in the Thought of John Millar', *Studies in Burke and His Time*, Vol. 13-14, 1971-72.

— 'Review of P. Salvucci's Adam Ferguson: Sociologica e Filosofia Politica', *History and Society*, Vol. 13 (2), 1974, pp. 163-81.

Leigh, R.A. 'Rousseau and the Scottish Enlightenment', *Contributions to Political Economy*, Vol. 5, 1986, pp. 1-21.

Lemay, J.A. Leo 'Notes on the Significance of the Comparative Method and the Stage Theory in Early American Literature and Culture', *American Antiquarian Society*, Vol. 88, October 1988, pp. 204-20.

Levine, N. 'The German Historical School and the Origins of Historical Materialism', *Journal of the History of Ideas*, Vol. 48 (3), 1987, pp. 431-51.

Locke, J. *Essay on the Laws of Nature*, 1676, W. Von Leyden, (ed.), Oxford: Clarendon Press, 1954.

Locke, John. *An Essay Concerning Human Understanding*, Edited and with a Forward by P.H Nidditch, Oxford: Clareondon Press,1979.

Lossing, B.J. *The Pictorial Field-Book of the Revolution*, in 2 Vols, New York, Harper & Brothers Publishers, 1859.

Lovejoy, A.O. 'The Parallel of Deism and Classicism', *Modern Philology*, Vol. 29, 1931-2, pp. 281-99.

Lovejoy, A.O. *Great Chain of Being: A Study of the History of an Idea*, Cambridge, Mass: Harvard University Press, 1964.

MacClancy, J. (ed.). *Sport, Identity and Ethnicity*, Oxford: Berg Publishers, 1996.

Macfie, A.L. 'The Scottish Tradition in Economic Thought', *Scottish Journal of Political Economy*, Vol. 2 (1), 1955, pp. 83-8.

— *The Individual in Society*, London: George Allen and Unwin Ltd., 1967.

—'The Invisible Hand of Jupiter', *Journal of the History of Ideas*, Vol. 32, (4), 1971, pp. 595-99.

Machiavelli, Niccolo. *The Chief Works and Others*; Edited by Translated by Allan Gibert, North Carolina: Duke University Press, Vols 1-2, 1965.

—*The Discourses*, Edited and with an Introduction by Bernard Crick, Suffolk: Penguin, 1998.

—*The Prince*, Translated and with an Introduction by George Bull, London: Penguin, 1981.

MacIntyre, A. *Whose Justice? Which Rationality?*, Indiana: University of Notre Dame Press, 1988.

Macrae, D. 'Adam Ferguson; Sociologist', *New Society*, Vol. 24, 1966, pp. 792-94.

—'Adam Ferguson' in T. Raison, (ed.), *The Founding Fathers of Social Science*, London: Penguin Books, 1969, pp. 27-35.

Mahon, J. 'Engels and the Question about Cities', *History of European Ideas*, 1982, Vol. 3 (1), pp. 43-77.

Malthus, T. *Three Essays on Population*, New York: Mentor Books, 1960.

Mandeville, B. *The Fable of the Bees or Private Vices, Publick Benefits*, Edited by F.B.Kaye, Oxford: Oxford University Press, 1924.

Marcus Aurelius. *Meditations*, Translated and with an Introduction by Maxwell Staniforth, London: Penguin, 1964.

Marshall, G, (ed.). *Oxford Dictionary of Sociology*, Oxford: Oxford University Press, 1998.

Marshall, P.J. 'Empire and Authority in the Later Eighteenth Century', *Journal of Imperial and Commonwealth History*, Vol. 15 (2), 1987, pp. 103-22.

Marx, K. *Capital*, Vol. I., Moscow: Progress Publishers, 1977.

—*The Poverty of Philosophy*, With and Introduction by Frederick Engels, International Publishers: New York, 1969.

Mason, S. 'Ferguson and Montesquieu: Tacit Reproaches?', *British Journal for Eighteenth Century Studies*, Vol. 2 (2) 1988, pp. 193-203.

McClurrie, H. *The Individual and the State*, London: Aldine Press, 1973.

McCosh, J. *The Scottish Philosophy*, New York: Robert Carter and Brothers, 1874.

McDonald, L. *Early Origins of the Social Sciences*, Montreal: McGill-Queen's University Press, 1993.

McDowell, G.L. 'Commerce, Virtue and Politics: Adam Ferguson's Constitutionalism', *Review of Politics*, Vol. 45 (4), 1983, pp. 36-52.

McGuire, J.E. 'Force, Active Principles and Newton's Invisible Realm', *Ambix*, Vol 15, 1968, pp.154-208.

McLachlan, H. *The Religious Opinions of Milton, Locke and Newton* Manchester: Manchester University Press, 1941.

McLynn, F.J. 'The Ideology of Jacobitism — Part II', *History of European Ideas*, Vol. 6 (2), 1985, pp.173-88.

Meek, R. *Economics and Ideology and other Essays*, London: Chapman and Hall Ltd., 1967.

—'Smith, Turgot and the 'Four Stages' Theory', *History of Political Economy*, Vol. 1, 1971, pp. 9-27.

—*Social Science and the Ignoble Savage*, Cambridge, Cambridge: University Press, 1976.

—'The Scottish Contribution to Marxist Sociology', *Economics Ideology and other Essays*, London: Chapman and Hall, 1967, pp. 34-45.

Merton, R.K. 'The Unintended Consequences of Purposive Social Action', *American Sociological Review*, Vol. 1, 1938, pp. 894-904.

Mill, John Stuart. *Collected Works of John Stuart Mill*, Edited by Robson, John. M. Mineka, Francis. Lindley, E. Dwight, N. Stillinger. J, and Robson. A. Toronto: University of Toronto Press, 1963.

Millar, John. *An Historical View of the English Government from the Settlement of the Saxons in Britain to the Accession of the House of Stuart*, in 4 Vols, Glasgow: 1787-1803.

Millar, W.W. 'Review of *Essay on the History of Civil Society, 1767*', *Sociology*, Vol. 1, 1967, pp. 201-05.

Minson, J. 'Men and Manners: Kantian Humanism, Rhetoric and the History of Ethics', *Economy and Society*, Vol. 18 (1), Feb.1989, pp. 191-220.

Mizuta, H. 'Towards a Definition of the Scottish Enlightenment', *Studies in Voltaire*, Vol. 154, 1976, pp. 1459-64.

—'The Two Adams in the Scottish Enlightenment', *Studies on Voltaire and the Eighteenth Century*, Vol. 191, 1981, pp . 812-19.

—*Adam Smith's Library: A Catalogue*, Edited and with an Introduction and Notes by Hiroshi Mizuta, Oxford University Press: New York, 2000.

Montesquieu, Charles-Louis. *Consideration of the Causes of the Greatness of the Romans and Their Decline*, New York: David Lowenthal, 1969.

—*Persian Letters*, Translated with an Introduction and Notes by C.J.Betts, London: Penguin, 1973.

—*The Spirit of the Laws*, Translated and Edited by A. M.Cohler B.C. Miller, H.M. Stone, Cambridge: Cambridge University Press, 1990.

Moore, J. 'Hume's Political Science and the Classical Republican Tradition', *Canadian Journal of Political Science*, Vol. 10, 1977, pp. 809-39.

—'Hutcheson's Theodicy: The Argument and the Contexts of *A System of Moral Philosophy*', in *The Scottish Enlightenment*, Paul Wood (ed.), Rochester: University of Rochester Press, 2000.

Moravia, S. 'The Enlightenment and the Sciences of Man', *History of Science*, Vol. 18, 1980, pp. 247-68.

Morgan, E.S. 'Slavery and Freedom: The American Paradox', *The Journal of American History*, Vol. 59, 1972, pp. 5-29.

Morrow, G.R. *The Ethical and Economic Theories of Adam Smith,* New York: Augustus M. Kelley, 1969.

Mossner, E. (ed) 'Of the Principle of Moral Estimation: A Discourse between David Hume, Robert Clerk, and Adam Smith: An Unpublished MS by Adam Ferguson.' *Journal of the History of Ideas*, Vol.21 (2), 1960, pp. 222-32.

—'Adam Ferguson's 'Dialogue on a Highland Jaunt' with Robert Adam, William Cleghorn, David Hume, and William Wilkie', *Restoration and Eighteenth-Century Literature: Essays in Honour of Alan Dugald McKillop*, Chicago: University of Chicago Press, 1963.

— *The Life of David Hume*: London: Thomas Nelson and Sons, 1954.

Mullen, W. 'Republics for Expansion: The School of Rome', *Arion*, Vol. 3, 1976, pp. 298-364.

Murphy, J.B. 'Nature, Custom and Stipulation in the Semiotic of John Poinset', *Semiotica*, Vol. 82 (1-2), 1990, pp. 33-68.

Myers, M. *The Soul of Modern Economic Man*, Chicago: University of Chicago Press, 1983.

Nazareth, J. M. 'Demography and Human Ecology', *Analise Social*, Vol. 28 (4-5), 1993, pp. 879-85.

Nederman, C.J. 'Nature, Sin and Origins of Society; The Ciceronian Tradition in Eighteenth Century Thought', *Journal of the History of Ideas*, Vol. 49 (1), 1988, pp. 3-26.

Nielson, T., 'The State, the Market and the Individual: Politics, Economics and the Idea of Man, in the works of Thomas Hobbes, Adam Smith and in Renaissance Humanism', *Acta Sociologica*, Vol. 29, (4) 1986, pp. 283-302.

Nisbet, R. *History of the Idea of Progress*, London: Heinemann, 1980.

Norton D.F. and Norton, M.J. *The David Hume Library*, Edinburgh: Edinburgh Biographical Society, 1996.

Noyen, P. 'Marcus Aurelius: The Greatest Practitioner of Stoicism', *Antiquite Classique*, Vol. 24, 1955, pp. 372-83.

Nussbaum, M. 'Kant and Stoic Cosmopolitanism', *Journal of Political Philosophy*, 1, 1997, pp. 1-25.

Owens, J. 'Teleology of Nature in Aristotle', *The Monist*, Vol. 52, 1968, pp. 158-73.

Oz-Salzberger, Fania. *Translating the Enlightenment: Scottish Civic Discourse in Eighteenth Century Germany*, Oxford: University Press, 1995.

—'Introduction' to Ferguson, Adam, *An Essay on the History of Civil Society*, Edited and with an Introduction by Fania Oz-Salzberger, Cambridge: Cambridge University Press, [1767] 1996.

Pack, Spencer. J. 'Theological (and Hence Economic) Implications of Adam Smith's 'Principles which Lead and Direct Philosophical Enquiries', *History of Political Economy*, Vol. 27 (2), 1995, pp. 289-307.

Pascal, R. 'Herder and the Scottish Historical School', *Publications of the English Goethe Society*, Vol. 14, 1938-9, pp. 23-49.

—'Property and Society: The Scottish Historical School of the Eighteenth Century', *Modern Quarterly*, Vol. 1, 1938, pp. 167-79.

Passmore, J. *Man's Responsibility for Nature*, (2nd Ed.) London: Gerald Duckworth and Co. Ltd., 1980.

Passmore, J. *The Perfectibility of Man*, London: Gerald Duckworth and Co. Ltd., 1979.

Patey, D.L. 'Art and Integrity: Concepts of Self in Alexander Pope and Edward Young', *Modern Philology*, Vol. 83 (4), 1986, pp. 364-378.

Petsoulas, Christina, *Hayek's Liberalism and its Origins, His Idea of Spontaneous Order and the Scottish Enlightenment*. New York: Routledge, 2001.

Philip, W. (ed.) *The Unpublished Essays of Adam Ferguson*, in Three Volumes, Edited and Published Privately, Argull: 1986.

Phillipson, N. 'Adam Smith as Civic Moralist', in Hont, I. and Ignatieff, M. (eds.). *Wealth and Virtue: The Shaping of Political Economy in the Scottish Enlightenment*, Cambridge: Cambridge University Press, 1983.

— 'The Scottish Enlightenment', in Porter, R. and Teich, M. (eds.), *The Enlightenment in National Context*, Cambridge: Cambridge University Press, 1981, pp. 19-40.

Phillipson, N. and Mitchison, R. *Scotland in the Age of Improvement*, Edinburgh: R and R Clarke Ltd., 1970.

Philp, M. 'English Republicanism in the 1790s', *The Journal of Political Philosophy*, Vol. 6 (30), 1998, pp. 235-62.

Pickens, D. 'Scottish Common sense Philosophy and Folkways', *Journal of Thought,* Vol. 22, 1987, pp. 39-44.

Pierce, J. 'The Scottish Common Sense School and Individual Psychology', *Journal of Individual Psychology*, Vol. 31, 1975, pp. 137-49.

Plato. *The Republic*, Translated by A.D. Lindsay, London: Everyman, 1995.

Plumb, J.H. *England in the Eighteenth Century*, Middlesex: Penguin, 1972.

Plutarch. *Fall of the Roman Republic: Six Lives*, Translated by Rex Warner, London: Penguin, 1958.

Pocock, J.G.A. 'Between Machiavelli and Hume: Gibbon as Civic Humanist and Philosophical Historian', *Daedelus*, Vol. 105, 1976, pp. 153-69.

— *The Machiavellian Moment*, Princeton: Princeton University Press, 1975.

— *Virtue, Commerce and History,* Cambridge: Cambridge University Press, 1985.

— *Barbarism and Religion,* Cambridge: Cambridge University Press, 1999.

Polanyi, Michael. *The Logic of Liberty: Reflections and Rejoinders*, London: Kegan Paul, 1951.

Polybius, *The Rise of the Roman Empire,* Translated by Ian Scott-Kilvert, Selected and with an Introduction by F.W. Walbank, London: Penguin, 1979.

Popkin, R. *Philosophy*, London: W.H. Allen and Company, 1969.

Prewitt, K. 'Political Efficacy', *International Encyclopedia of the Social Sciences*, Vol 12, London: MacMillan, 1968.

Purviance, S.M. 'Intersubjectivity and Sociable Relations in the Philosophy of Francis Hutcheson' in J. Dwyer, and R.B. Sher (eds.), *Sociability and Society in Eighteenth Century Scotland*, Edinburgh: The Mercat Press, 1993.

Radcliffe, E. 'Revolutionary Writing, Moral Philosophy, and Universal Benevolence in the Eighteenth Century', *Journal of the History of Ideas*, Vol. 54 (2), 1993, pp.221-40.

Rahe, P.A. 'The Primacy of Politics in Classical Greece', *American Historical Review*, Vol. 89 (2), 1984, pp. 65-93.

Raison, T. (ed.). *The Founding Fathers of Social Science,* London: Penguin Books, 1969.

Raphael, D.D. *Adam Smith*, Oxford: Oxford University Press, 1975.

Rapoport, D. 'The Corrupt State: The Case of Rome Reconsidered', *Political Studies*, Vol. 16 (3), 1968, pp. 411-32.

— 'Political Dimensions of Military Usurpation', *Political Science Quarterly*, Vol. 83 (4), 1968, pp. 551-72.

Rashid, S. 'Dugald Stewart, Baconian Methodology and Political Economy', *Journal of the History of Ideas*, Vol. 46 (2), 1985, pp. 245-57.

Rashid, S. 'Political Economy as Moral Philosophy; Dugald Stewart of Edinburgh', *Australian Economic Papers*, Vol. 48 (26), 1987, pp. 145-56.

— *The Myth of Adam Smith*, Cheltenham: Edward Elgar, 1998.

Redman, Deborah. A. 'Adam Smith and Isaac Newton', *Scottish Journal of Political Economy*, Vol. 40 (2), May 1993, pp. 210-20.

Reesor, M. E. *The Political Theory of the Old and Middle Stoa*, New York: J.J. Augustin, 1951.

Reill, Peter Hanns. 'Narration and Structure in Late Eighteenth Century Historical Thought', *History and Theory*, Vol. 25 (3), 1986, pp. 286-98.

Reisman, D.A. *Adam Smith's Sociological Economics*, London: Croom and Helm, 1976.

Reynolds L.T., and Reynolds, Janice. M. (eds.). *The Sociology of Sociology*, New York: McKay, 1970.

Rice, C.D. 'Archibald Dalzel, The Scottish Intelligentsia, and the Problem of Slavery', *The Scottish Historical Review*, Vol. 62, (174), Oct. 1983, pp. 121-36.

Richardson, A. and Bowden, J., (eds.). *A New Dictionary of Christian Theology*, London: S.C.M. Press Ltd, 1983.

Robbins, C. *The Eighteenth-Century Commonwealthmen*, Oxford: Oxford University Press, 1959.

Robertson, D.H. *Economic Commentaries*, London: Staples, 1956.

Robertson, J. 'Scottish Political Economy Beyond the Civic Tradition; Government and Economic Development in the *Wealth of Nations*', *History of Political Thought*, Vol. 4 (3), Winter 1983, pp. 451-82.

— 'The Scottish Enlightenment at the Limits of the Civic Tradition' in Hont, I, and Ignatieff, M., (eds.). *Wealth and Virtue: The Shaping of Political Economy in the Scottish Enlightenment*, Cambridge: Cambridge University Press, 1983.

— *The Scottish Enlightenment and the Militia Issue,* Edinburgh: John Donald, 1985.

— 'The Scottish Contribution to the Enlightenment', in *The Scottish Enlightenment, Essays in Reinterpretation*, Edited by Paul Wood, Rochester: University of Rochester Press, 2000.

Robin, L. *Greek Thought and the Origins of the Scientific Spirit*, New York: Russell and Russell, 1967.

Robinson, D.N. *Aristotle's Psychology*, New York: Columbia University Press, 1989.

Roche, K.F. *Rousseau: Stoic and Romantic*, London: Methuen, 1974.

Rosenberg, N. 'Adam Smith and the Stock of Moral Capital', *History of Political Economy*, Vol. 22 (1), 1990, pp. 1-17.

— 'Adam Smith on the Division of Labour: Two Views or One', *Economica*, Vol. 33, Feb., 1965, pp. 127-39.

— 'Adam Smith, Consumer Tastes and Economic Growth', *Journal of Political Economy*, Vol. 76, 1968, pp. 361-74.

Ross, D. *Aristotle*, London: Methuen, 1960.

Rousseau, J. *The Social Contract and Discourses*, Translation and Introduction by G. D.H. Cole, London: Everyman's Library, 1973.

Runciman, W.G. 'On the Tendency of Human Societies to Form Varieties', *Proceedings of the British Academy*, Vol. 72, 1986, pp. 149-65.

Ryan, A. 'An *Essay* on the History of Civil Society', *New Society*, Vol. 3, 1966, pp. 63-4.

Sabine, G.H. *A History of Political Theory*, Third Edition, London: George Harrop and Co. Ltd., 1964.

Sailor, D.P. 'Newton's Debt to Cudworth', *Journal of the History of Ideas*, Vol. 49 (4), Oct-Dec., 1988, pp. 511-16.

Scheffer, John D. 'The Idea of Decline in Literature and the Fine Arts in Eighteenth-Century England', *Modern Philology*, Vol. 34 (2), 1936, pp. 155-78.

Schneider, L. *The Scottish Moralists on Human Nature and Society*, Chicago: University of Chicago Press, 1967.

—'Mandeville as a Forerunner of Modern Sociology', *Journal of the History of Behavioural Sciences*, Vol. 6, 1979, pp. 219-30.

—'Tension in the Thought of John Millar' in *The Grammar of Social Relations: The Major Essays of Louis Schneider*, Edited by Jay Weinstein with an Epistolary Forward by R.K. Merton, New Brunswick: Transaction Books, 1984.

Schofield, T.M. 'Conservative Political Thought in Britain in Response to the French Revolution', *The Historical Journal*, Vol. 29 (3), 1986, pp. 601-22.

Schreyer, R. 'The Origin of Language: A Scientific Approach to the Study of Man', *Topoi*, Vol. 4, 1985, pp. 181-86.

Schultz, D.P. *A History of Modern Psychology*, New York: Academic Press, 1969.

Schumacher, Matthew A. (trans.), *Fathers of the Church: Saint Augustine Against Julian, a New Translation,* Catholic University of America Press: 2003.

Schwoerer, L. *'No Standing Armies!': The Anti-Army Ideology in Seventeenth Century England*, Baltimore: John Hopkins University Press, 1974.

Scott, P.H. *The Boasted Refinements: The Consequences of the Union of 1707*, Edinburgh: The Saltire Society, 1999.

Scruton, R. *A Dictionary of Political Thought*, London: Pan, 1982.

Seeman, M. 'On the Meaning of Alienation', *American Sociological Review*, Vol. 24, 1959, pp. 783-91.

Seigal, J.E. 'Civic Humanism or Ciceronian Rhetoric? The Culture of Petrach and Bruni', *Past and Present*, No. 34, July, 1966, p. 3-48.

Sekora, J. *Luxury*, London: Johns Hopkins University Press, 1977.

Selby-Bigge, L.A. (ed.). *British Moralists*, in 2 Vols. New York: Dover Publications, 1897.

Selwyn, P. 'Johnson's Hebrides: Thoughts on a Dying Social Order', *Development and Change* Vol. 10, 1979.

Seneca, *Moral and Political Essays*, with an English Translation by John W. Basore, Cambridge Mass: Harvard University Press, 1965.

—*Letters From a Stoic*, Selected and Translated with an Introduction by Robin Campbell, London: Penguin, 1969.

—*Moral Essays*, with an English Translation by J.W. Basore, London: William Heinemann Ltd, 1970.

Shaw, John Stuart. *The Political History of Eighteenth Century Scotland*, Basingstoke: MacMillan, 1999.

Sheehan B.W. 'Paradise and the Noble Savage in Jeffersonian Thought, *William and Mary Quarterly*, Vol. 26, 1969, pp. 327-59.

Sher, R.B. *Church and University in the Scottish Enlightenment*, New Jersey: Princeton University Press, 1985.

—'Adam Ferguson, Adam Smith, and the Problem of National Defense', *Journal of Modern History*, Vol. 61, (2), 1989, pp. 240-68.

—'Professors of Virtue: The Social History of the Edinburgh Moral Philosophy Chair in the Eighteenth Century', in M.A. Stewart (ed.), *Studies in the Philosophy of the Scottish Enlightenment,* Oxford: Clarendon Press, 1990.

—'From Troglodytes to Americans: Montesquieu and the Scottish Enlightenment on Liberty, Virtue, and Commerce', in *Republicanism, Liberty and Commercial Society* 1649-1776, David Wootton, (ed.), Stanford: Stanford University Press, 1994, pp. 368-402.

Shils, Edward. 'The Virtue of Civil Society', *Government and Opposition*, Vol. 26 (1), Winter, 1991, pp. 3-20.

Shott, S. 'The Development of Sociological Theory in America; A Sociology of Knowledge Interpretation' in Larry T. Reynolds and Janice M. Reynolds, (eds.). *The Sociology of Sociology,* New York: McKay, 1970.

Shott, S. 'Society, Self and Mind in Moral Philosophy', *Journal of the History of Behavioural Sciences*, Vol. 12, 1976, pp. 39-46.

Shumer, S.M. 'Machiavelli; Republican Politics and Its Corruption', *Political Theory*, Vol. 7 (1), 1979, pp. 5-34.

Siebert, D.T. *The Moral Animus of David Hume*, Newark: University of Delaware Press, 1990.

Silver, A. 'Friendship and Trust as Moral Ideals: An Historical Approach', *European Journal of Sociology*, Vol. 30, 1989, pp. 274-9.

—'Friendship in Commercial Society: Eighteenth-Century Social Theory and Modern Sociology', *American Journal of Sociology*, Vol. 95 (6), 1990, pp. 1474-1504.

Simmel, Georg. *Conflict* tr. by K.H. Wolff and *The Web of Group-Affiliations*, tr. by R. Bendix; with a foreword by E.C. Hughes, New York: Free Press 1966.

Simmons, Sir Matthew. *Changing the Face of the Earth*, Oxford: Basil Blackwell 1989.

Simpson, D. 'Joseph Schumpeter and the Austrian School of Economics', *Journal of Economic Studies*, Vol. 10 (4), 1983, pp. 15-28.

Skinner, A. *A System of Social Science: Papers Relating to Adam Smith*, Oxford: Clarendon Press, 1979.

Skinner, A. 'A Scottish Contribution to Marxist Sociology', Bradly, I. and Howard, M. (eds.). *Classical and Marxian Political Economy: Essays in Honour of Ronald L.Meek*, New York: St Martin's Press: 1982.

Skinner, A. 'Adam Ferguson: The History of Civil Society', *Political Studies*, Vol. 15, 1967, pp. 219-21.

Skinner, A. 'Economics and History-The Scottish Enlightenment', *The Scottish Journal of Political Economy*, Vol. 12, 1965, pp. 1-22.

—'Natural History in the Age of Adam Smith', *Political Studies*, Vol. 15, 1967, pp. 33-48.

Skinner, Q. *Machiavelli*, Oxford: Oxford University Press, 1981.

Small, Albion. *Origins of Sociology*, New York: Russell & Russell, 1967.

Smith, A. *The Theory of Moral Sentiments*, D.D. Raphael and A.L. MacFie, (eds.), Oxford: Clarendon Press, 1976.

—*An Inquiry Into the Nature and Causes of the Wealth of Nations*, R.H. Campbell, and A.S. Skinner, (eds.), Oxford: Clarendon Press, 1979.

—*Lectures on Jurisprudence*, R.L. Meek, D.D. Raphael and L.G. Stein (eds.), Oxford: Oxford University Press, 1978.

—*Essays on Philosophical Subjects*, I.S. Ross, (ed.), Oxford: Clarendon Press, 1980.

—*Lectures on Rhetoric and Belles Lettres,* Edited by J.C.Bryce, Oxford: Oxford University Press, 1983.

—*The Correspondence of Adam Smith*, Mossner, E.C., and Ross, I.S., (eds.), Oxford: Oxford University Press, 1987.

Smith, A.D. 'Nationalism and Classical Social Theory', *The British Journal of Sociology*, Vol. 3 (4), 1983, pp. 19-38.

Smith, A.G. *The Political Philosophy of Adam Ferguson Considered as a Response to Rousseau: Political Development and Progressive Development*, Unpublished Doctoral Thesis: Yale University, 1980.

Smout, T.C. *A History of the Scottish People, 1560-1830*, Suffolk: Collins/Fontana, 1972.

Sorabji, R. *Animal Minds and Human Morals*, Ithaca: Cornell University Press, 1993.

Spicer, E.E. *Aristotle's Conception of the Soul*, London: University of London Press, 1934.

Springborg, P. 'The Contractual State: Reflections on Orientalism and Despotism', *History of Political Thought*, Vol. 8 (3), 1987, pp. 395-433.

—*The Problem of Human Needs,* London: George, Allen and Unwin, 1991.

—*Western Republicanism and the Oriental Prince,* Oxford: Polity Press, 1991.

Spurr, J. 'Rational Religion in Restoration England', *Journal of the History of Ideas*, Vol., 49 (4), 1988, pp. 563-85.

Stafford, F. *The Sublime Savage: A Study of James Macherson and the Poems of Ossian*, Edinburgh: Edinburgh University Press, 1988.

Staniforth, Maxwell. 'Introduction' to Marcus Aurelius, *Meditations*, Translated and with an Introduction by Maxwell Staniforth, London: Penguin, 1964.

Stanton, G.R. 'The Cosmopolitan Ideas of Epictetus and Marcus Aurelius' *Phronesis: A Journal for Ancient Philosophy*, Vol. 8 (1), 1968, pp. 183-95.

—'Marcus Aurelius, Emperor and Philosopher', *Historia*, Vol. 93, 1969, pp. 570-87.

Steele, David Ramsay. 'Hayek's Theory of Cultural Group Selection', *The Journal of Libertarian Studies* Vol. 8 (2), Summer, 1987, pp. 171-95.

Stephen, L. *History of English Thought in the Eighteenth Century*, London, Smith, Elder and Co., 1902.

Stephen, L. and Lee, S. (eds.). *Dictionary of National Biography*, Vol. 6, London: Oxford University Press, 1917.

Stewart, Dugald, 'Account of the Life and writings of Adam Smith, LL D', I.S.Ross, (ed.), in Adam Smith *Essays on Philosophical Subjects*, W.P.D.Wightman and J.C.Bryce (eds.), Oxford: Oxford University Press, 1980.

Stewart, M.A. 'Religion and Rational Theology', in Alexander Broadie (ed.), *The Scottish Enlightenment*, Cambridge: Cambridge University Press, 2003.

— 'The Origins of the Scottish Greek Chairs', in *Owls to Athens: Essays on Classical Subjects*, E.M. Craik (ed.), Oxford: Clarendon Press, 1990.

—'The Stoic Legacy in the Early Scottish Enlightenment' in Margaret J. Osler (ed.). *Atoms, Pneuma and Tranquillity*, Cambridge: Cambridge University Press, 1991.

Stewart-Robertson, J.C. 'Cicero Among the Shadows: Scottish Prelections of Virtue and Duty', *Rivista Critical Di Storia Della Filosofia*, Vol. 38, 1983, pp. 25-49.

—'The Rhythms of Gratitude: Historical Developments and Philosophical Concerns', *Australasian Journal of Philosophy*, Vol. 68 (2), June, 1990 pp. 189-205.

Strasser, H. *The Normative Structure of Sociology: Conservative and Emancipatory Themes in Social Thought*, London: Routledge and Kegan Paul, 1976.

Sumner, W.G. *Folkways: A Study of the Sociological Importance of Usages, Manners, Customs, Mores and Morals*, Boston: Ginn, 1906.

Suttie, I. *The Origins of Love and Hate,* London: Kegan Paul, 1935.

Swingewood, A. 'Origins of Sociology: The Case of the Scottish Enlightenment', *The British Journal of Sociology,* Vol. 21, 1970, pp. 164-80.

—*A Short History of Sociological Thought*, London: Macmillan, 1984.

Tacitus. *The Agricola and the Germania*, Translated and with an Introduction by H. Mattingly, London: Penguin, 1970.

Tacitus. *The Annals of Imperial Rome*, Translated and with an Introduction by Michael Grant, London: Penguin, 1989.

Teggert, Frederick J. *Theory of History,* New Haven, Conn.: Yale University Press, 1925.

The Fontana Dictionary of Modern Thought, A. Bullock, O. Stallybrass and S. Trombley, (eds.), London: Fontana, 1989.

The Holy Bible, Containing the Old and New Testament, Authorised King James Version, London: Collins Cleartype Press, 1952.

Thoits, Peggy A. 'The Sociology of Emotions', *Annual Review of Sociology*, Vol. 15, 1989, pp. 317-32.

Thomson, Herbert, F. 'Adam Smith's Philosophy of Science', *Quarterly Journal of Economics*, Vol. 79, (2) 1965, pp. 212-23.

Thucydides. *History of the Peloponnesian War*, Translated by Rex Warner with an Introduction and Notes by M.I. Finley, London: Penguin, 1972.

Tomaselli, S. 'The Enlightenment Debate on Women', *History Workshop Journal: A Journal of Socialist and Feminist Historians*, Vol. 20, 1985, pp. 100-14.

Townsend, D. 'From Shaftsbury to Kant. The Development of the Concept of Aesthetic Experience', *Journal of the History of Ideas*, Vol. 48 (20), 1987, pp. 287-305.

Turner, F.M. 'British Politics and the Demise of the Roman Republic:1700-1939', *The Historical Journal*, Vol. 29 (3), 1986, pp. 577-59.

Ullmann-Margalit, E. 'Invisible Hand Explanations', *Synthese*, Vol. 39 (2), 1978, pp. 263-91.

Valauri, J.T. 'Social Order and the Limits of Law', *Duke Law Journal*, Vol. 3, 1981, pp. 607-18.

Van Den Bergh, P.L. 'Dialectic and Functionalism: Towards a Theoretical Synthesis', *Sociological Theory*, W.L. Wallace (ed.), Chicago: Aldine Publishing Company, 1969.

Van Krieken, R. *Norbert Elias,* London: Routledge, 1997.

Varty, J. 'Civil or Commercial? Adam Ferguson's Concept of Civil Society', *Democratisation* Vol. 4, 1997, pp. 29-48.

Veitch, J. 'Philosophy in the Scottish Universities', *Mind*, Vol. 2, 1877, pp. 74-91 and 207-34.

Vernon, Richard. 'Unintended Consequences', *Political Theory*, Vol. 7 (1), 1979, pp. 57-73.

Vidal, F. 'Psychology in the Eighteenth Century: A View from Encylopaedias', *History of the Human Sciences*, Vol. 6 (1), 1993, pp. 89-119.

Viner, J. *The Long View and the Short: Studies in Economic Theory and Policy,* Chicago: The Free Press, 1958.

Viner, J. *The Role of Providence in the Social Order,* Philadelphia: American Philosophical Society, 1972.

Wallech, S. 'The Elements of Social Status in Hume's Treatise', *Journal of the History of Ideas*, Vol. 45 (2), 1984, pp. 207-18.

Ward, Addison. 'The Tory View of Roman History', *Studies in English Literature, 1500-1900*, Vol. 4 (3), 1964, pp. 413-56.

Warner, James H. 'The Reaction in Eighteenth-Century England to Rousseau's Two Discourses', *Publications of the Modern Language Association of America*, Vol. 48 (2), June, 1933, pp. 471-87.

Waszek, N. 'The Division of Labour from the Scottish Enlightenment to Hegel', *The Owl of Minerva: Quarterly Journal of the Hegel Society of America*, Vol.15 (1), 1983, pp. 51-75.

—'Two Concepts of Morality: The Distinction of Adam Smith's Ethics and its Stoic Origin', *Journal of the History of Ideas,* Vol. 45 (4), 1984, pp. 591-606.

—*Man's Social Nature: A Topic of the Scottish Enlightenment in its Historical Setting*, Frankfurt: Peter Lang, 1986.

—*The Scottish Enlightenment and Hegel's Account of 'Civil Society'*, Boston: M. Nijhoff, 1988.

Waterman, A.M.C. 'Economics as Theology: Adam Smith's *Wealth of Nations*', *Southern Economic Journal*, Vol. 68 (4), 2002, pp. 907-21.

Watson, R. *The Great Psychologists From Aristotle to Freud,* Philadelphia: J.B. Lippincott Company, 1968.

Weber, Max. *Economy and Society: An Outline of Interpretive Sociology*, Berkeley: Berkeley University Press, 1978.

Wertheimer, M. *A Brief History of Psychology*, New York: Holt, Rhinehart and Winston, 1970.

West, E.G. 'Adam Smith's Two Views on the Division of Labour', *Economica*, Vol. 31, Feb. 1964, pp. 23-32.

—'The Political Economy of Alienation: Karl Marx and Adam Smith', *Oxford Economic Papers*, Vol. 21, 1969, pp. 1-23

—*Adam Smith and Modern Economics*, Aldershot: Edward Elgar, 1990.

Whitney, L. *Primitivism and the Idea of Progress*, Baltimore: The Johns Hopkins Press, 1934.

Willke, J. *The Historical Thought of Adam Ferguson*, Unpublished Doctoral Dissertation, Washington D.C: The Catholic University of America, 1962.

Wills, G. *Inventing America*, New York: Doubleday, 1978.

Wilsher, J.C. 'Power Follows Property–Social and Economic Interpretations in British Historical Writing in the Eighteenth and Early Nineteenth Centuries', *Journal of Social History*, Vol. 16 (3), 1983, pp. 7-26.

Wilson, E.K. 'What is This Sociology We Profess?', *Journal of Research and Development in Education*, Vol. 9 (1), 1975, pp. 3-12.

—'Comments from a Servant of the Scattered Family', *Contemporary Sociology*, Vol. 8 (6),1979, pp. 804-08.

Wimstatt, W.G. 'Teleology and the Logical Structure of Function Statements', *Studies in History and Philosophy of Science*, Vol. 3 (1), 1972, pp.1-80.

Winch, D. *Adam Smith's Politics*, Cambridge: Cambridge University Press, 1978.

Womack, Peter. *Improvement and Romance: Constructing the Myth of the Highlands*, Basingstoke: Macmillan 1989.

Wood, P.B. 'The Natural History of Man in the Scottish Enlightenment', *History of Science,* Vol. 28 (1), No.79, 1990, pp. 89-123.

Wright, J.P. 'Materialism and the life Soul in Eighteenth Century Scottish Physiology', in *The Scottish Enlightenment*, Paul Wood (ed.), Rochester: University of Rochester Press, 2000.

Xenakis, I. *Epictetus Philosopher-Therapist*, Martinus Nijhoff: the Hague, 1969.

Xenos, N. 'Classical Political Economy: The Apolitical Discourse of Civil Society', *Humanities in Society*, Vol. 3 (3), 1980, pp. 229-41.

Young, J.D. 'Mandeville: A Populariser of Hobbes', *Modern Language Notes*, Vol. 74 (1) 1958, pp.10-13.

Zaret, D. 'From Political Philosophy to Social Theory', *Journal of the History of the Behavioural Sciences*, Vol. 17, 1981, pp. 153-73.

5. SUGGESTED FURTHER READING ON THE TOPIC OF SPONTANEOUS ORDER

Adelstein, Richard. 'Language Orders', *Constitutional Political Economy* Vol. 7, Fall, 1996, pp. 221-38.

Berger, Peter and Luckmann, Thomas. *The Social Construction of Reality: A Treatise on the Sociology of Knowledge*, Garden City, NY: Doubleday, 1967.

Bromley, David W. 'Searching for Sustainability: The Poverty of Spontaneous Order', *Ecological Economics*, Vol. 24 (2-3), pp. 231-40.

Charny, D. 'Illusions of Spontaneous Order: "Norms" in Contractual Relationships', *University of Pennsylvania Law Review*, Vol. 144 (5), pp. 1841-58.

Cronk, Lee. *That Complex Whole: Culture and the Evolution of Human Behaviour,* Colorado: Westview Press, Boulder, 1999.

Di Zerega, Gus. 'Market Non-neutrality: Systemic Bias in Spontaneous Orders', *Critical Review,* Vol. 11 (1), 1997.

Diamond, Arthur. M. 'F.A. Hayek on Constructivism and Ethics', *The Journal of Libertarian Studies*, Vol. 4 (4), Fall 1980, pp. 353-65.

Dobuzinskis, Laurent. *The Self-Organizing Polity: An Epistemological Analysis of Political Life,* Boulder, Colorado: Westview Press, 1987.

—'The Complexities of Spontaneous Order', *Critical Review,* Vol 3 (2), 1989. pp. 241-66.

Dyke, C. *The Evolutionary Dynamics of Complex Systems: A Study in Biosocial Complexity*, New York: Oxford University Press, 1988.

Eisner, Wolfram. 'Adam Smith's Model of the Origin and Emergence of Institutions: The Modern Findings of the Classical Approach', *Journal of Economic Issues*, 23 (1), 1989, pp. 189-213.

Fehl, Ulrich. 'Spontaneous Order' in Peter J. Boettke (ed.), *The Elgar Companion to Austrian Economics*, Aldershot, UK: Elgar, 1994, pp. 197-205.

Fleetwood, S. 'Order Without Equilibrium: A Critical Realist Interpretation of Hayek's Notion of Spontaneous Order', *Cambridge Journal of Economics*, Vol 20 (6), pp. 729-47.

Foss, Nicolai Juul. 'Spontaneous Social Order: Economics and Schutzian Sociology', *American Journal of Economics and Sociology*. Vol 55 (1), January, 1996, pp. 73-86.

Gray, John. 'F.A.Hayek on Liberty and Tradition', *The Journal of Libertarian Studies*, Vol. 4 (2), Spring, 1980, pp. 119-137.

—*Hayek on Liberty,* Oxford: Basil Blackwell, 1985.

—*Liberalisms: Essays in Political Philosophy,* London: Routledge & Kegan Paul, 1989.

Haakonssen, K. *The Science of a Legislator: The National Jurisprudence of David Hume and Adam Smith*, Cambridge: Cambridge University Press, 1981.

Habermas, Jürgen. 'Towards a Theory of Universal Pragmatics', in Habermas, J. *Communication and the Evolution of Society,* Boston: Beacon Press, 1979.

Haller, Markus. 'Carl Menger's Theory of Invisible-Hand Explanations', *Social Science Information,* Vol. 39 (4), 2000, pp. 529-65.

Hayek, F.A. *The Road to Serfdom*. Chicago: University of Chicago Press, 1944.

—'The Use of Knowledge in Society', in Hayek, F. A. *Individualism and Economic Order*, Chicago: University of Chicago Press, 1948, pp. 77-91.

—*The Theory of Complex Phenomena*, New York: Simon and Schuster, 1967.

—'The Legal and Political Philosophy of David Hume', in Hayek, F.A. *Studies in Philosophy, Politics and Economics,* New York: Simon and Schuster, 1967, pp. 106-21.

—*Kinds of Order in Society*, Menlo Park, CA: Institute for Humane Studies, 1975.

—*The Mirage of Social Justice*, Chicago: University of Chicago Press, 1976.

—'Competition as a Discovery Procedure', in Hayek, F.A., *New Studies in Philosophy, Politics, Economics and the History of Ideas,* Chicago: University of Chicago Press, 1978, pp. 179-90.

—*The Political Order of a Free People,* Chicago: University of Chicago Press, 1979.

—*The Fatal Conceit*, W.W. Bartley (ed.), London: Routledge, 1989.

Horwitz, S. *Of Human Action But Not of Human Design*, Frank P. Piskor Lecture, Canton, NY: St Lawrence University, 1999.

—'From Smith to Menger to Hayek: Liberalism in the Spontaneous-Order Tradition', *The Independent Review,* Vol. 6, Summer, 2001, pp. 81-97.

Inayatullah, N. 'Theories of Spontaneous Disorder', *Review of International Political Economy*, Vol. 4 (2), pp. 319-48.

Keller, Rudi. 'Invisible Hand Theory and Language Evolution', *Lingua*, Vol. 77, 1989, pp.113-27.

Khalil, Elias L. 'Friedrich Hayek's Theory of Spontaneous Order: Two Problems', *Constitutional Political Economy*, Vol. 8 (4), 1997, pp. 301-17.

Kley, R. 'Hayek's Idea of a Spontaneous Social Order–A Critical Analysis', *Kölner Zeitschrift fur Sociologie und Sozialpsyclogie*, Vol. 44 (1), 1992, pp. 12-34.

—*Hayek's Social and Political Thought*, Oxford: Oxford University Press, 1994.

Lavoie, D. 'Democracy as Spontaneous Order', *Critical Review*, Spring, 1989, pp. 206-40.

—'Economic Chaos or Spontaneous Order- Implications for Political Economy of the New View of Science', *Cato Journal*, Vol. 8 (3), 1989, pp. 613-35.

—'Understanding Differently–Hermeneutics and the Spontaneous Order of Communicative Process', *History of Political Economy*, Vol. 22, 1990. pp. 359-77.

Lawrence, R. 'Hume's Theory of Social and Political Order', *South African Journal of Philosophy*, Vol. 4 (4), 1985, pp. 137-42.

Luhmann, N. *Social Systems,* Stanford: Stanford University Press, 1995.

Menger, K. *Investigations into the Method of the Social Sciences with Special Reference to Economics,* New York: New York University Press, 1985.

Merton, R.K. 'The Unintended Consequences of Purposive Social Action', *American Sociological Review*, Vol. 1, 1938, pp.894-904.

Moore, S.F. *Law as Process: An Anthropological Approach,* Boston: Routledge and Kegan Paul. 1978.

Nozick, R. *Anarchy, State and Utopia*, Oxford: Basil Blackwell, 1974.

Paul, Ellen Frankel. 'Liberalism, Unintended Orders and Evolutionism', *Political Studies*, 1988, Vol. 37, pp. 251-72.

Rappaport, Roy. *Ritual and Religion in the Making of Humanity*, Cambridge: Cambridge University Press, 1999.

Rosenberg, N. 'Mandeville and Laissez-Faire', *Journal of the History of Ideas*, Vol. 24 (2), 1963, pp. 183-96.

Rothschild, E. 'Adam Smith and the Invisible Hand', *American Economic Review*, Vol. 84 (2), pp. 319-22.

Rowland, B.M. *Ordered Liberty and the Constitutional Framework: The Political Thought of Frederick von Hayek*, New Haven: Greenwood Press, 1987.

Seidentop, L. 'Two Liberal Traditions', *The Idea of Freedom*, Alan Ryan, (ed.), Oxford: Oxford University Press, 1979. pp. 153-74.

Vanberg, V. 'Spontaneous Market Order and Social Rules', *Economics and Philosophy*, Vol. 2, 1986, pp. 75-100.

INDEX

ARCHIVES INTERNATIONALES D'HISTOIRE DES IDÉES

*

INTERNATIONAL ARCHIVES OF THE HISTORY OF IDEAS

1. E. Labrousse: *Pierre Bayle*. Tome I: *Du pays de foix à la cité d'Erasme*. 1963; 2nd printing 1984   ISBN 90-247-3136-4
    For Tome II *see below under Volume 6.*
2. P. Merlan: *Monopsychism, Mysticism, Metaconsciousness*. Problems of the Soul in the Neoaristotelian and Neoplatonic Tradition. 1963; 2nd printing 1969   ISBN 90-247-0178-3
3. H.G. van Leeuwen: *The Problem of Certainty in English Thought, 1630–1690*. With a Preface by R.H. Popkin. 1963; 2nd printing 1970   ISBN 90-247-0179-1
4. P.W. Janssen: *Les origines de la réforme des Carmes en France au 17ᵉ Siècle*. 1963; 2nd printing 1969   ISBN 90-247-0180-5
5. G. Sebba: *Bibliographia Cartesiana*. A Critical Guide to the Descartes Literature (1800–1960). 1964   ISBN 90-247-0181-3
6. E. Labrousse: *Pierre Bayle*. Tome II: *Heterodoxie et rigorisme*. 1964   ISBN 90-247-0182-1
7. K.W. Swart: *The Sense of Decadence in 19th-Century France*. 1964   ISBN 90-247-0183-X
8. W. Rex: *Essays on Pierre Bayle and Religious Controversy*. 1965   ISBN 90-247-0184-8
9. E. Heier: *L.H. Nicolay (1737–1820) and His Contemporaries*. Diderot, Rousseau, Voltaire, Gluck, Metastasio, Galiani, D'Escherny, Gessner, Bodmer, Lavater, Wieland, Frederick II, Falconet, W. Robertson, Paul I, Cagliostro, Gellert, Winckelmann, Poinsinet, Lloyd, Sanchez, Masson, and Others. 1965   ISBN 90-247-0185-6
10. H.M. Bracken: *The Early Reception of Berkeley's Immaterialism, 1710–1733*. [1958] Rev. ed. 1965   ISBN 90-247-0186-4
11. R.A. Watson: *The Downfall of Cartesianism, 1673–1712*. A Study of Epistemological Issues in Late 17th-Century Cartesianism. 1966   ISBN 90-247-0187-2
12. R. Descartes: *Regulæ ad Directionem Ingenii*. Texte critique établi par Giovanni Crapulli avec la version hollandaise du 17ᵉ siècle. 1966   ISBN 90-247-0188-0
13. J. Chapelain: *Soixante-dix-sept Lettres inédites à Nicolas Heinsius (1649–1658)*. Publiées d'après le manuscrit de Leyde avec une introduction et des notes par B. Bray. 1966
                            ISBN 90-247-0189-9
14. C. B. Brush: *Montaigne and Bayle*. Variations on the Theme of Skepticism. 1966
                            ISBN 90-247-0190-2
15. B. Neveu: *Un historien à l'Ecole de Port-Royal*. Sébastien le Nain de Tillemont (1637–1698). 1966   ISBN 90-247-0191-0
16. A. Faivre: *Kirchberger et l'Illuminisme du 18ᵉ siècle*. 1966   ISBN 90-247-0192-9
17. J.A. Clarke: *Huguenot Warrior*. The Life and Times of Henri de Rohan (1579–1638). 1966
                            ISBN 90-247-0193-7
18. S. Kinser: *The Works of Jacques-Auguste de Thou*. 1966   ISBN 90-247-0194-5
19. E.F. Hirsch: *Damião de Gois*. The Life and Thought of a Portuguese Humanist (1502–1574). 1967   ISBN 90-247-0195-3
20. P.J.S. Whitemore: *The Order of Minims in 17th-Century France*. 1967   ISBN 90-247-0196-1
21. H. Hillenaar: *Fénelon et les Jésuites*. 1967   ISBN 90-247-0197-X
22. W.N. Hargreaves-Mawdsley: *The English Della Cruscans and Their Time, 1783–1828*. 1967
                            ISBN 90-247-0198-8
23. C.B. Schmitt: *Gianfrancesco Pico della Mirandola (1469–1533) and his Critique of Aristotle*. 1967   ISBN 90-247-0199-6
24. H.B. White: *Peace among the Willows*. The Political Philosophy of Francis Bacon. 1968
                            ISBN 90-247-0200-3

ARCHIVES INTERNATIONALES D'HISTOIRE DES IDÉES
*
INTERNATIONAL ARCHIVES OF THE HISTORY OF IDEAS

25. L. Apt: *Louis-Philippe de Ségur.* An Intellectual in a Revolutionary Age. 1969
    ISBN 90-247-0201-1
26. E.H. Kadler: *Literary Figures in French Drama (1784–1834).* 1969 ISBN 90-247-0202-X
27. G. Postel: *Le Thrésor des prophéties de l'univers.* Manuscrit publié avec une introduction et des notes par F. Secret. 1969 ISBN 90-247-0203-8
28. E.G. Boscherini: *Lexicon Spinozanum.* 2 vols., 1970 Set ISBN 90-247-0205-4
29. C.A. Bolton: *Church Reform in 18th-Century Italy.* The Synod of Pistoia (1786). 1969
    ISBN 90-247-0208-9
30. D. Janicaud: *Une généalogie du spiritualisme français.* Aux sources du bergsonisme: [Félix] Ravaisson [1813–1900] et la métaphysique. 1969 ISBN 90-247-0209-7
31. J.-E. d'Angers: *L'Humanisme chrétien au 17ᵉ siècle.* St. François de Sales et Yves de Paris. 1970 ISBN 90-247-0210-0
32. H.B. White: *Copp'd Hills towards Heaven.* Shakespeare and the Classical Polity. 1970
    ISBN 90-247-0250-X
33. P.J. Olscamp: *The Moral Philosophy of George Berkeley.* 1970 ISBN 90-247-0303-4
34. C.G. Noreña: *Juan Luis Vives (1492–1540).* 1970 ISBN 90-247-5008-3
35. J. O'Higgens: *Anthony Collins (1676–1729), the Man and His World.* 1970
    ISBN 90-247-5007-5
36. F.T. Brechka: *Gerard van Swieten and His World (1700–1772).* 1970 ISBN 90-247-5009-1
37. M.H. Waddicor: *Montesquieu and the Pilosophy of Natural Law.* 1970 ISBN 90-247-5039-3
38. O.R. Bloch: *La Philosophie de Gassendi (1592–1655).* Nominalisme, matérialisme et métaphysique. 1971 ISBN 90-247-5035-0
39. J. Hoyles: *The Waning of the Renaissance (1640–1740).* Studies in the Thought and Poetry of Henry More, John Norris and Isaac Watts. 1971 ISBN 90-247-5077-6
    For Henry More, *see also below under Volume 122 and 127.*
40. H. Bots: *Correspondance de Jacques Dupuy et de Nicolas Heinsius (1646–1656).* 1971
    ISBN 90-247-5092-X
41. W.C. Lehmann: *Henry Home, Lord Kames, and the Scottish Enlightenment.* A Study in National Character and in the History of Ideas. 1971 ISBN 90-247-5018-0
42. C. Kramer: *Emmery de Lyere et Marnix de Sainte Aldegonde.* Un admirateur de Sébastien Franck et de Montaigne aux prises avec le champion des calvinistes néerlandais.[Avec le texte d'Emmery de Lyere:] *Antidote ou contrepoison contre les conseils sanguinaires et envinemez de Philippe de Marnix Sr. de Ste. Aldegonde.* 1971 ISBN 90-247-5136-5
43. P. Dibon: *Inventaire de la correspondance (1595–1650) d'André Rivet (1572–1651).* 1971
    ISBN 90-247-5112-8
44. K.A. Kottman: *Law and Apocalypse.* The Moral Thought of Luis de Leon (1527?–1591). 1972
    ISBN 90-247-1183-5
45. F.G. Nauen: *Revolution, Idealism and Human Freedom.* Schelling, Hölderlin and Hegel, and the Crisis of Early German Idealism. 1971 ISBN 90-247-5117-9
46. H. Jensen: *Motivation and the Moral Sense in Francis Hutcheson's* [1694–1746] *Ethical Theory.* 1971 ISBN 90-247-1187-8
47. A. Rosenberg: *[Simon] Tyssot de Patot and His Work (1655–1738).* 1972
    ISBN 90-247-1199-1
48. C. Walton: *De la recherche du bien.* A study of [Nicolas de] Malebranche's [1638–1715] Science of Ethics. 1972 ISBN 90-247-1205-X

ARCHIVES INTERNATIONALES D'HISTOIRE DES IDÉES

*

INTERNATIONAL ARCHIVES OF THE HISTORY OF IDEAS

49. P.J.S. Whitmore (ed.): *A 17th-Century Exposure of Superstition.* Select Text of Claude Pithoys (1587–1676). 1972   ISBN 90-247-1298-X

50. A. Sauvy: *Livres saisis à Paris entre 1678 et 1701.* D'après une étude préliminaire de Motoko Ninomiya. 1972   ISBN 90-247-1347-1

51. W.R. Redmond: *Bibliography of the Philosophy in the Iberian Colonies of America.* 1972
     ISBN 90-247-1190-8

52. C.B. Schmitt: *Cicero Scepticus.* A Study of the Influence of the *Academica* in the Renaissance. 1972   ISBN 90-247-1299-8

53. J. Hoyles: *The Edges of Augustanism.* The Aesthetics of Spirituality in Thomas Ken, John Byrom and William Law. 1972   ISBN 90-247-1317-X

54. J. Bruggeman and A.J. van de Ven (éds.): *Inventaire* des pièces d'Archives françaises se rapportant à l'Abbaye de Port-Royal des Champs et son cercle et à la Résistance contre la Bulle *Unigenitus* et à l'Appel. 1972   ISBN 90-247-5122-5

55. J.W. Montgomery: *Cross and Crucible.* Johann Valentin Andreae (1586–1654), Phoenix of the Theologians. Volume I: Andreae's Life, World-View, and Relations with Rosicrucianism and Alchemy; Volume II: The *Chymische Hochzeit* with Notes and Commentary. 1973
     Set ISBN 90-247-5054-7

56. O. Lutaud: *Des révolutions d'Angleterre à la Révolution française.* Le tyrannicide & *Killing No Murder* (Cromwell, *Athalie,* Bonaparte). 1973   ISBN 90-247-1509-1

57. F. Duchesneau: *L'Empirisme de Locke.* 1973   ISBN 90-247-1349-8

58. R. Simon (éd.): *Henry de Boulainviller* – Œuvres Philosophiques, Tome I. 1973
     ISBN 90-247-1332-3

     For Œuvres Philosophiques, Tome II *see below under Volume 70.*

59. E.E. Harris: *Salvation from Despair.* A Reappraisal of Spinoza's Philosophy. 1973
     ISBN 90-247-5158-6

60. J.-F. Battail: *L'Avocat philosophe Géraud de Cordemoy (1626–1684).* 1973
     ISBN 90-247-1542-3

61. T. Liu: *Discord in Zion.* The Puritan Divines and the Puritan Revolution (1640–1660). 1973
     ISBN 90-247-5156-X

62. A. Strugnell: *Diderot's Politics.* A Study of the Evolution of Diderot's Political Thought after the *Encyclopédie.* 1973   ISBN 90-247-1540-7

63. G. Defaux: *Pantagruel et les Sophistes.* Contribution à l'histoire de l'humanisme chrétien au 16ᵉ siècle. 1973   ISBN 90-247-1566-0

64. G. Planty-Bonjour: *Hegel et la pensée philosophique en Russie (1830–1917).* 1974
     ISBN 90-247-1576-8

65. R.J. Brook: *[George] Berkeley's Philosophy of Science.* 1973   ISBN 90-247-1555-5

66. T.E. Jessop: *A Bibliography of George Berkeley.* With: *Inventory of Berkeley's Manuscript Remains* by A.A. Luce. 2nd revised and enlarged ed. 1973   ISBN 90-247-1577-6

67. E.I. Perry: *From Theology to History.* French Religious Controversy and the Revocation of the Edict of Nantes. 1973   ISBN 90-247-1578-4

68. P. Dibbon, H. Bots et E. Bots-Estourgie: *Inventaire de la correspondance (1631–1671) de Johannes Fredericus Gronovius* [1611–1671]. 1974   ISBN 90-247-1600-4

69. A.B. Collins: *The Secular is Sacred.* Platonism and Thomism in Marsilio Ficino's *Platonic Theology.* 1974   ISBN 90-247-1588-1

ARCHIVES INTERNATIONALES D'HISTOIRE DES IDÉES
*
INTERNATIONAL ARCHIVES OF THE HISTORY OF IDEAS

70. R. Simon (éd.): *Henry de Boulainviller. Œuvres Philosophiques*, Tome II. 1975
ISBN 90-247-1633-0
For *Œuvres Philosophiques*, Tome I *see under Volume 58*.

71. J.A.G. Tans et H. Schmitz du Moulin: *Pasquier Quesnel devant la Congrégation de l'Index.*
Correspondance avec Francesco Barberini et mémoires sur la mise à l'Index de son édition des
Œuvres de Saint Léon, publiés avec introduction et annotations. 1974   ISBN 90-247-1661-6

72. J.W. Carven: *Napoleon and the Lazarists (1804–1809)*. 1974   ISBN 90-247-1667-5

73. G. Symcox: *The Crisis of French Sea Power (1688–1697)*. From the *Guerre d'Escadre* to the
Guerre de Course. 1974   ISBN 90-247-1645-4

74. R. MacGillivray: *Restoration Historians and the English Civil War.* 1974
ISBN 90-247-1678-0

75. A. Soman (ed.): *The Massacre of St. Bartholomew.* Reappraisals and Documents. 1974
ISBN 90-247-1652-7

76. R.E. Wanner: *Claude Fleury (1640–1723) as an Educational Historiographer and Thinker.*
With an Introduction by W.W. Brickman. 1975   ISBN 90-247-1684-5

77. R.T. Carroll: *The Common-Sense Philosophy of Religion of Bishop Edward Stillingfleet (1635–
1699)*. 1975   ISBN 90-247-1647-0

78. J. Macary: *Masque et lumières au 18ᵉ [siècle]*. André-François Deslandes, Citoyen et
philosophe (1689–1757). 1975   ISBN 90-247-1698-5

79. S.M. Mason: *Montesquieu's Idea of Justice*. 1975   ISBN 90-247-1670-5

80. D.J.H. van Elden: *Esprits fins et esprits géométriques dans les portraits de Saint-Simon.*
Contributions à l'étude du vocabulaire et du style. 1975   ISBN 90-247-1726-4

81. I. Primer (ed.): *Mandeville Studies.* New Explorations in the Art and Thought of Dr Bernard
Mandeville (1670–1733). 1975   ISBN 90-247-1686-1

82. C.G. Noreña: *Studies in Spanish Renaissance Thought*. 1975   ISBN 90-247-1727-2

83. G. Wilson: *A Medievalist in the 18th Century*. Le Grand d'Aussy and the Fabliaux ou Contes.
1975   ISBN 90-247-1782-5

84. J.-R. Armogathe: *Theologia Cartesiana*. L'explication physique de l'Eucharistie chez
Descartes et Dom Robert Desgabets. 1977   ISBN 90-247-1869-4

85. Bérault Stuart, Seigneur d'Aubigny: *Traité sur l'art de la guerre*. Introduction et édition par
Élie de Comminges. 1976   ISBN 90-247-1871-6

86. S.L. Kaplan: *Bread, Politics and Political Economy in the Reign of Louis XV.* 2 vols., 1976
Set ISBN 90-247-1873-2

87. M. Lienhard (ed.): *The Origins and Characteristics of Anabaptism / Les débuts et les car-
actéristiques de l'Anabaptisme.* With an Extensive Bibliography / Avec une bibliographie
détaillée. 1977   ISBN 90-247-1896-1

88. R. Descartes: *Règles utiles et claires pour la direction de l'esprit en la recherche de la vérité.*
Traduction selon le lexique cartésien, et annotation conceptuelle par J.-L. Marion. Avec des
notes mathématiques de P. Costabel. 1977   ISBN 90-247-1907-0

89. K. Hardesty: *The 'Supplément' to the 'Encyclopédie'*. [Diderot et d'Alembert]. 1977
ISBN 90-247-1965-8

90. H.B. White: *Antiquity Forgot.* Essays on Shakespeare, [Francis] Bacon, and Rembrandt. 1978
ISBN 90-247-1971-2

91. P.B.M. Blaas: *Continuity and Anachronism.* Parliamentary and Constitutional Development in
Whig Historiography and in the Anti-Whig Reaction between 1890 and 1930. 1978
ISBN 90-247-2063-X

ARCHIVES INTERNATIONALES D'HISTOIRE DES IDÉES
*
INTERNATIONAL ARCHIVES OF THE HISTORY OF IDEAS

92. S.L. Kaplan (ed.): *La Bagarre.* Ferdinando Galiani's (1728–1787) 'Lost' Parody. With an Introduction by the Editor. 1979   ISBN 90-247-2125-3

93. E. McNiven Hine: *A Critical Study of [Étienne Bonnot de] Condillac's [1714–1780] 'Traité des Systèmes'.* 1979   ISBN 90-247-2120-2

94. M.R.G. Spiller: *Concerning Natural Experimental Philosphy.* Meric Casaubon [1599–1671] and the Royal Society. 1980   ISBN 90-247-2414-7

95. F. Duchesneau: *La physiologie des Lumières.* Empirisme, modèles et théories. 1982
                    ISBN 90-247-2500-3

96. M. Heyd: *Between Orthodoxy and the Enlightenment.* Jean-Robert Chouet [1642–1731] and the Introduction of Cartesian Science in the Academy of Geneva. 1982
                    ISBN 90-247-2508-9

97. James O'Higgins: *Yves de Vallone* [1666/7–1705]: *The Making of an Esprit Fort.* 1982
                    ISBN 90-247-2520-8

98. M.L. Kuntz: *Guillaume Postel* [1510–1581]. Prophet of the Restitution of All Things. His Life and Thought. 1981   ISBN 90-247-2523-2

99. A. Rosenberg: *Nicolas Gueudeville and His Work (1652–172?).* 1982   ISBN 90-247-2533-X

100. S.L. Jaki: *Uneasy Genius: The Life and Work of Pierre Duhem* [1861-1916]. 1984
                    ISBN 90-247-2897-5; Pb (1987) 90-247-3532-7

101. Anne Conway [1631–1679]: *The Principles of the Most Ancient Modern Philosophy.* Edited and with an Introduction by P. Loptson. 1982   ISBN 90-247-2671-9

102. E.C. Patterson: *[Mrs.] Mary [Fairfax Greig] Sommerville* [1780–1872] *and the Cultivation of Science (1815–1840).* 1983   ISBN 90-247-2823-1

103. C.J. Berry: *Hume, Hegel and Human Nature.* 1982   ISBN 90-247-2682-4

104. C.J. Betts: *Early Deism in France.* From the so-called 'déistes' of Lyon (1564) to Voltaire's 'Lettres philosophiques' (1734). 1984   ISBN 90-247-2923-8

105. R. Gascoigne: *Religion, Rationality and Community.* Sacred and Secular in the Thought of Hegel and His Critics. 1985   ISBN 90-247-2992-0

106. S. Tweyman: *Scepticism and Belief in Hume's 'Dialogues Concerning Natural Religion'.* 1986
                    ISBN 90-247-3090-2

107. G. Cerny: *Theology, Politics and Letters at the Crossroads of European Civilization.* Jacques Basnage [1653–1723] and the Baylean Huguenot Refugees in the Dutch Republic. 1987
                    ISBN 90-247-3150-X

108. Spinoza's *Algebraic Calculation of the Rainbow* & *Calculation of Changes.* Edited and Translated from Dutch, with an Introduction, Explanatory Notes and an Appendix by M.J. Petry. 1985   ISBN 90-247-3149-6

109. R.G. McRae: *Philosophy and the Absolute.* The Modes of Hegel's Speculation. 1985
                    ISBN 90-247-3151-8

110. J.D. North and J.J. Roche (eds.): *The Light of Nature.* Essays in the History and Philosophy of Science presented to A.C. Crombie. 1985   ISBN 90-247-3165-8

111. C. Walton and P.J. Johnson (eds.): *[Thomas] Hobbes's 'Science of Natural Justice'.* 1987
                    ISBN 90-247-3226-3

112. B.W. Head: *Ideology and Social Science.* Destutt de Tracy and French Liberalism. 1985
                    ISBN 90-247-3228-X

113. A.Th. Peperzak: *Philosophy and Politics.* A Commentary on the Preface to Hegel's *Philosophy of Right.* 1987   ISBN Hb 90-247-3337-5; Pb ISBN 90-247-3338-3

ARCHIVES INTERNATIONALES D'HISTOIRE DES IDÉES
*
INTERNATIONAL ARCHIVES OF THE HISTORY OF IDEAS

114. S. Pines and Y. Yovel (eds.): *Maimonides* [1135-1204] *and Philosophy*. Papers Presented at the 6th Jerusalem Philosophical Encounter (May 1985). 1986   ISBN 90-247-3439-8

115. T.J. Saxby: *The Quest for the New Jerusalem, Jean de Labadie* [1610–1674] *and the Labadists (1610–1744)*. 1987   ISBN 90-247-3485-1

116. C.E. Harline: *Pamphlets, Printing, and Political Culture in the Early Dutch Republic*. 1987   ISBN 90-247-3511-4

117. R.A. Watson and J.E. Force (eds.): *The Sceptical Mode in Modern Philosophy*. Essays in Honor of Richard H. Popkin. 1988   ISBN 90-247-3584-X

118. R.T. Bienvenu and M. Feingold (eds.): *In the Presence of the Past*. Essays in Honor of Frank Manuel. 1991   ISBN 0-7923-1008-X

119. J. van den Berg and E.G.E. van der Wall (eds.): *Jewish-Christian Relations in the 17th Century*. Studies and Documents. 1988   ISBN 90-247-3617-X

120. N. Waszek: *The Scottish Enlightenment and Hegel's Account of 'Civil Society'*. 1988   ISBN 90-247-3596-3

121. J. Walker (ed.): *Thought and Faith in the Philosophy of Hegel*. 1991   ISBN 0-7923-1234-1

122. Henry More [1614–1687]: *The Immortality of the Soul*. Edited with Introduction and Notes by A. Jacob. 1987   ISBN 90-247-3512-2

123. P.B. Scheurer and G. Debrock (eds.): *Newton's Scientific and Philosophical Legacy*. 1988   ISBN 90-247-3723-0

124. D.R. Kelley and R.H. Popkin (eds.): *The Shapes of Knowledge from the Renaissance to the Enlightenment*. 1991   ISBN 0-7923-1259-7

125. R.M. Golden (ed.): *The Huguenot Connection*. The Edict of Nantes, Its Revocation, and Early French Migration to South Carolina. 1988   ISBN 90-247-3645-5

126. S. Lindroth: *Les chemins du savoir en Suède*. De la fondation de l'Université d'Upsal à Jacob Berzelius. Études et Portraits. Traduit du suédois, présenté et annoté par J.-F. Battail. Avec une introduction sur Sten Lindroth par G. Eriksson. 1988   ISBN 90-247-3579-3

127. S. Hutton (ed.): *Henry More (1614–1687)*. Tercentenary Studies. With a Biography and Bibliography by R. Crocker. 1989   ISBN 0-7923-0095-5

128. Y. Yovel (ed.): *Kant's Practical Philosophy Reconsidered*. Papers Presented at the 7th Jerusalem Philosophical Encounter (December 1986). 1989   ISBN 0-7923-0405-5

129. J.E. Force and R.H. Popkin: *Essays on the Context, Nature, and Influence of Isaac Newton's Theology*. 1990   ISBN 0-7923-0583-3

130. N. Capaldi and D.W. Livingston (eds.): *Liberty in Hume's 'History of England'*. 1990   ISBN 0-7923-0650-3

131. W. Brand: *Hume's Theory of Moral Judgment*. A Study in the Unity of *A Treatise of Human Nature*. 1992   ISBN 0-7923-1415-8

132. C.E. Harline (ed.): *The Rhyme and Reason of Politics in Early Modern Europe*. Collected Essays of Herbert H. Rowen. 1992   ISBN 0-7923-1527-8

133. N. Malebranche: *Treatise on Ethics* (1684). Translated and edited by C. Walton. 1993   ISBN 0-7923-1763-7

134. B.C. Southgate: *'Covetous of Truth'*. The Life and Work of Thomas White (1593–1676). 1993   ISBN 0-7923-1926-5

135. G. Santinello, C.W.T. Blackwell and Ph. Weller (eds.): *Models of the History of Philosophy*. Vol. 1: From its Origins in the Renaissance to the 'Historia Philosophica'. 1993   ISBN 0-7923-2200-2

136. M.J. Petry (ed.): *Hegel and Newtonianism*. 1993   ISBN 0-7923-2202-9

ARCHIVES INTERNATIONALES D'HISTOIRE DES IDÉES
*
INTERNATIONAL ARCHIVES OF THE HISTORY OF IDEAS

137. Otto von Guericke: *The New (so-called Magdeburg) Experiments* [Experimenta Nova, Amsterdam 1672]. Translated and edited by M.G. Foley Ames. 1994   ISBN 0-7923-2399-8

138. R.H. Popkin and G.M. Weiner (eds.): *Jewish Christians and Cristian Jews*. From the Renaissance to the Enlightenment. 1994   ISBN 0-7923-2452-8

139. J.E. Force and R.H. Popkin (eds.): *The Books of Nature and Scripture*. Recent Essays on Natural Philosophy, Theology, and Biblical Criticism in the Netherlands of Spinoza's Time and the British Isles of Newton's Time. 1994   ISBN 0-7923-2467-6

140. P. Rattansi and A. Clericuzio (eds.): *Alchemy and Chemistry in the 16th and 17th Centuries.* 1994   ISBN 0-7923-2573-7

141. S. Jayne: *Plato in Renaissance England*. 1995   ISBN 0-7923-3060-9

142. A.P. Coudert: *Leibniz and the Kabbalah*. 1995   ISBN 0-7923-3114-1

143. M.H. Hoffheimer: *Eduard Gans and the Hegelian Philosophy of Law*. 1995
    ISBN 0-7923-3114-1

144. J.R.M. Neto: *The Christianization of Pyrrhonism*. Scepticism and Faith in Pascal, Kierkegaard, and Shestov. 1995   ISBN 0-7923-3381-0

145. R.H. Popkin (ed.): *Scepticism in the History of Philosophy*. A Pan-American Dialogue. 1996
    ISBN 0-7923-3769-7

146. M. de Baar, M. Löwensteyn, M. Monteiro and A.A. Sneller (eds.): *Choosing the Better Part*. Anna Maria van Schurman (1607–1678). 1995   ISBN 0-7923-3799-9

147. M. Degenaar: *Molyneux's Problem*. Three Centuries of Discussion on the Perception of Forms. 1996   ISBN 0-7923-3934-7

148. S. Berti, F. Charles-Daubert and R.H. Popkin (eds.): *Heterodoxy, Spinozism, and Free Thought in Early-Eighteenth-Century Europe*. Studies on the *Traité des trois imposteurs*. 1996
    ISBN 0-7923-4192-9

149. G.K. Browning (ed.): *Hegel's* Phenomenology of Spirit: *A Reappraisal*. 1997
    ISBN 0-7923-4480-4

150. G.A.J. Rogers, J.M. Vienne and Y.C. Zarka (eds.): *The Cambridge Platonists in Philosophical Context*. Politics, Metaphysics and Religion. 1997   ISBN 0-7923-4530-4

151. R.L. Williams: *The Letters of Dominique Chaix, Botanist-Curé*. 1997   ISBN 0-7923-4615-7

152. R.H. Popkin, E. de Olaso and G. Tonelli (eds.): *Scepticism in the Enlightenment*. 1997
    ISBN 0-7923-4643-2

153. L. de la Forge. Translated and edited by D.M. Clarke: *Treatise on the Human Mind (1664)*. 1997   ISBN 0-7923-4778-1

154. S.P. Foster: *Melancholy Duty*. The Hume-Gibbon Attack on Christianity. 1997
    ISBN 0-7923-4785-4

155. J. van der Zande and R.H. Popkin (eds.): *The Skeptical Tradition Around 1800*. Skepticism in Philosophy, Science, and Society. 1997   ISBN 0-7923-4846-X

156. P. Ferretti: *A Russian Advocate of Peace: Vasilii Malinovskii (1765–1814)*. 1997
    ISBN 0-7923-4846-6

157. M. Goldish: *Judaism in the Theology of Sir Isaac Newton*. 1998   ISBN 0-7923-4996-2

158. A.P. Coudert, R.H. Popkin and G.M. Weiner (eds.): *Leibniz, Mysticism and Religion*. 1998
    ISBN 0-7923-5223-8

159. B. Fridén: *Rousseau's Economic Philosophy*. Beyond the Market of Innocents. 1998
    ISBN 0-7923-5270-X

160. C.F. Fowler O.P.: *Descartes on the Human Soul*. Philosophy and the Demands of Christian Doctrine. 1999   ISBN 0-7923-5473-7

ARCHIVES INTERNATIONALES D'HISTOIRE DES IDÉES
*
INTERNATIONAL ARCHIVES OF THE HISTORY OF IDEAS

161. J.E. Force and R.H. Popkin (eds.): *Newton and Religion*. Context, Nature and Influence. 1999
ISBN 0-7923-5744-2

162. J.V. Andreae: *Christianapolis*. Introduced and translated by E.H. Thompson. 1999
ISBN 0-7923-5745-0

163. A.P. Coudert, S. Hutton, R.H. Popkin and G.M. Weiner (eds.): *Judaeo-Christian Intellectual Culture in the Seventeenth Century*. A Celebration of the Library of Narcissus Marsh (1638–1713). 1999
ISBN 0-7923-5789-2

164. T. Verbeek (ed.): *Johannes Clauberg* and Cartesian Philosophy in the Seventeenth Century. 1999
ISBN 0-7923-5831-7

165. A. Fix: *Fallen Angels*. Balthasar Bekker, Spirit Belief, and Confessionalism in the Seventeenth Century Dutch Republic. 1999
ISBN 0-7923-5876-7

166. S. Brown (ed.): *The Young Leibniz and his Philosophy (1646–76)*. 2000
ISBN 0-7923-5997-6

167. R. Ward: *The Life of Henry More*. Parts 1 and 2. 2000
ISBN 0-7923-6097-4

168. Z. Janowski: *Cartesian Theodicy*. Descartes' Quest for Certitude. 2000
ISBN 0-7923-6127-X

169. J.D. Popkin and R.H. Popkin (eds.): *The Abbé Grégoire and his World*. 2000
ISBN 0-7923-6247-0

170. C.G. Caffentzis: *Exciting the Industry of Mankind. George Berkeley's Philosophy of Money*. 2000
ISBN 0-7923-6297-7

171. A. Clericuzio: *Elements, Principles and Corpuscles*. A Study of Atomisms and Chemistry in the Seventeenth Century. 2001
ISBN 0-7923-6782-0

172. H. Hotson: *Paradise Postponed*. Johann Heinrich Alsted and the Birth of Calvinist Millenarianism. 2001
ISBN 0-7923-6787-1

173. M. Goldish and R.H. Popkin (eds.): *Millenarianism and Messianism in Early Modern European Culture*. Volume I. Jewish Messianism in the Early Modern World. 2001
ISBN 0-7923-6850-9

174. K.A. Kottman (ed.): *Millenarianism and Messianism in Early Modern European Culture*. Volume II. Catholic Millenarianism: From Savonarola to the Abbé Grégoire. 2001
ISBN 0-7923-6849-5

175. J.E. Force and R.H. Popkin (eds.): *Millenarianism and Messianism in Early Modern European Culture*. Volume III. The Millenarian Turn: Millenarian Contexts of Science, Politics and Everyday Anglo-American Life in the Seventeenth and Eighteenth Centuries. 2001
ISBN 0-7923-6848-7

176. J.C. Laursen and R.H. Popkin (eds.): *Millenarianism and Messianism in Early Modern European Culture*. Volume IV. Continental Millenarians: Protestants, Catholics, Heretics. 2001
ISBN 0-7923-6847-9

177. C. von Linné: *Nemesis Divina*. (edited and translated with explanatory notes by M.J. Petry). 2001
ISBN 0-7923-6820-7

178. M.A. Badía Cabrera: *Hume's Reflection on Religion*. 2001
ISBN 0-7923-7024-4

179. R.L. Williams: *Botanophilia in Eighteenth-Century France*. The Spirit of the Enlightenment. 2001
ISBN 0-7923-6886-X

180. R. Crocker (ed.): *Religion, Reason and Nature in Early Modern Europe*. 2001
ISBN 1-4020-0047-2

ARCHIVES INTERNATIONALES D'HISTOIRE DES IDÉES
*
INTERNATIONAL ARCHIVES OF THE HISTORY OF IDEAS

181. E. Slowik: *Cartesian Spacetime*. Descartes' Physics and the Relational Theory of Space and Motion. 2001　　　　　　　　　　　　　　　　　ISBN 1-4020-0265-3
182. R.L. Williams: *French Botany in the Enlightenment*. The Ill-fated Voyages of *La Pérouse* and His Rescuers. 2003　　　　　　　　　　　　　　　ISBN 1-4020-1109-1
183. A. Leshem: *Newton on Mathematics and Spiritual Purity*. 2003　　　ISBN 1-4020-1151-2
184. G. Paganini (ed.): *The Return of Scepticism*. From Hobbes and Descartes to Bayle. 2003
　　　　　　　　　　　　　　　　　　　　　　　　　　ISBN 1-4020-1377-9
185. R. Crocker: *Henry More, 1614–1687*. A Biography of the Cambridge Platonist. 2003
　　　　　　　　　　　　　　　　　　　　　　　　　　ISBN 1-4020-1502-X
186. T.J. Hochstrasser and P. Schröder (eds.): *Early Modern Natural Law Theories*. Contexts and Strategies in the Early Enlightenment. 2003　　　　　ISBN 1-4020-1569-0
187. F. Tomasoni: *Modernity and the Final Aim of History*. The Debate over Judaism from Kant to the Young Hegelians. 2003　　　　　　　　　　　ISBN 1-4020-1594-1
188. J.E. Force and S. Hutton (eds.): *Newton and Newtonianism*. New Studies. 2004
　　　　　　　　　　　　　　　　　　　　　　　　　　ISBN 1-4020-1969-6
189. W. Schmidt-Biggemann: *Philosophia perennis*. Historical Outlines of Western Spirituality in Ancient, Medieval and Early Modern Thought. 2004　　ISBN 1-4020-3066-5
190. R. Faggionato: *A Rosicrucian Utopia in Eighteenth-Century Russia*. The Masonic Circle of N.I. Novikov. 2005　　　　　　　　　　　　　　　　ISBN 1-4020-3486-5
191. L. Hill: *The Passionate Society*. The Social, Political and Moral Thought of Adam Ferguson. 2005　　　　　　　　　　　　　　　　　　　ISBN 1-4020-3889-5
192. D. Offord: *Journeys to a Graveyard*. Perceptions of Europe in Classical Russian Travel Writing. 2005　　　　　　　　　　　　　　　　　　ISBN 1-4020-3908-5
193. S. Clucas (ed.): *John Dee: Interdisciplinary Studies in English Renaissance Thought*. 2006
　　　　　　　　　　　　　　　　　　　　　　　　　　ISBN 1-4020-4245-0
194. J.K. Jue: *Heaven Upon Earth*. Joseph Mede (1586-1638) and the Legacy of Millenarianism. 2006　　　　　　　　　　　　　　　　　　ISBN 1-4020-4292-2